UNCERTAIN FUTURES

UNCERTAIN FUTURES
Challenges for Decision-Makers

ROBERT U. AYRES

A WILEY-INTERSCIENCE PUBLICATION

JOHN WILEY & SONS

New York • Chichester • Brisbane • Toronto

Copyright © 1979 by John Wiley & Sons, Inc.

All rights reserved. Published simultaneously in Canada.

Reproduction or translation of any part of this work
beyond that permitted by Sections 107 or 108 of the
1976 United States Copyright Act without the permission
of the copyright owner is unlawful. Requests for
permission or further information should be addressed to
the Permissions Department, John Wiley & Sons, Inc.

Library of Congress Cataloging in Publication Data:

Ayres, Robert U
  Uncertain futures.

  "A Wiley-Interscience publication."
  Includes bibliographical references and index.
    1. Forecasting. 2. Economic forecasting. 3. Technological
forecasting. I. Title.
H61.4.A9   338.5'44   78-10252
ISBN 0-471-04250-1

Printed in the United States of America

10 9 8 7 6 5 4 3 2 1

PREFACE

Regrettably the discipline of forecasting is widely misunderstood, not only by the public but by many practitioners. The idea still lurks, both in our culture and in other cultures, that the future is preordained — *it exists,* though hidden from ordinary mortals. A forecaster is too often expected to *reveal.* Whether by mystical visions or by computer models, he is supposed to pierce the veil of time, disclosing what is to come — complete, as it were, like a play for which the script is written, the lines rehearsed, the scenery in place, and the action about to begin.

The concept overrates forecasters. It also undercuts and defeats the real purpose and value of systematic forecasting as an intellectual activity. If the future is fixed, what good is a forecast? The two obvious motives are simple curiosity — a kind of voyeurism — or a desire to cheat a little by peeking at the cards one has been dealt by life. What the peeker really hopes, one must suppose, is that he or she can personally gain, in some way, from such knowledge — as many characters in folklore have tried (and usually failed) to do. He imagines the future as fixed for everybody but himself! Of course, this is nonsense.

In my forecasting work, I think of the future as one might think of a play sketched in outline, with the characters and their initial relationships well defined, but the script as yet unwritten. (Indeed, the final script is *never* entirely written before the performance takes place.) The characters live out the play and create it as they go along. The real world is "ad lib" in important respects.

Balzac is alleged to have told the aspiring author George Sand that her plots were too "mechanical" — that she shaped her characters to the requirements of her plots. Balzac argued that the plot should be secondary — should flow *from the nature of the characters.* Thus a murder is performed only if the character of the murderer and victim and their relationships with other characters make the murder inevitable, and not because the plot "calls for" a murder. In effect, the plot is the last part of novel to emerge. This comment is as pertinent to real life — and to forecasting — as it is to fiction. The events of the future will happen because people, institutions, and nations are what they are and behave as their characters and circumstances dictate. Events do not happen at random. Nor can we reasonably appeal to teleology. Even if we accept an "ultimate" Prime Mover it is inconceivable that He behaves like a bad novelist, letting a predetermined plot dictate the action. On the contrary, action must follow from internal dynamics. This sounds at first like a restatement of the mechanical determinism I have taken pains to deny. But it is not, quite, because people have free will and are capable of change. In a good novel, as in life, characters can choose, grow, and develop. This is also true of institutions and nations.

Since the future is conceived as indeterminate to some degree, a forecaster deals with possibilities and probabilities, not certainties. Some forecasters, especially those of a visionary turn of mind, confuse possibilities with probabilities. Partly, this is because possibilities are relatively easy to establish. Anything not in conflict with known physical laws can be said to be possible, at least in the sense of "not impossible." It is possible that we may some day establish colonies on artificial satellites in space,[1] feed burgeoning populations with protein foods derived from algae or seaweed,[2] preserve human bodies indefinitely in cryogenic refrigerators for future revival,[3] or even learn to overcome the limitations of the human lifespan itself.[4] These things are all thought to be "not impossible" on the basis of known physical and biological laws. But are they *probable*? Are they likely to emerge from laboratory trials to make an impact on society at large? Could society itself tolerate them? These are much harder and more elusive questions. It is comparatively easy to portray a future studded with mind-boggling marvels thought to be scientifically possible. Appraising their probability and social impact is something else. Yet this step is essential if a forecast is to have any practical value beyond entertainment.

Arthur C. Clarke, in *Profiles of the Future,* stated frankly: "With a few exceptions, . . . I am limiting myself to a single aspect of the future —its technology, not the society that will be based on it. This is not such a limitation as it may seem; *for science will dominate the future even more than it dominates the present.*"[5] Perhaps it will, but there has been a tendency on the part of science-minded writers to assume that what *can* be done *will* be done, and there is a good deal of evidence from past experience that this not necessarily so. I discuss some of this evidence later.

A responsible forecaster cannot dodge the fact that neither technological nor any other kind of development occurs in isolation. Whatever occurs must be in the context of a society that is changing, and may be changing in a direction contrary to the anticipated development. Thus the forecaster is obliged to examine not only the technology but the trends in the culture – in society's political and social life, in its ideology, its institutions, its economy, its incentives, and its people's attitudes, beliefs, and customs. If he does not do this, his frame of reference is too narrow.

Take, as an example, grandiose proposals to irrigate the Sahara with desalted sea water.[6] No one to my knowledge has suggested how such a scheme would be financed or implemented in the light of the political instability, the rivalries and jealousies, and the fierce nationalism of the countries of the region (Egypt, Libya, Tunisia, Algeria, etc.). To bypass such questions and to say that the deserts will someday be irrigated merely because this is technically possible is sheer mental laziness. Obviously, some profound changes in *human* institutions would have to take place first. This is not to say that such changes in the international and social climate may not happen (they may, of course) but simply that a forecaster ought to make clear that his forecast is contingent on such changes. A major stumbling block for all such schemes as the irrigation of the Sahara is the lack of real incentive for rich nations to come to the aid of poor ones. Even rich Arab nations are slow to share their oil wealth with poor Arab nations, nor have communist countries displayed more eagerness to invest in this sort of project than capitalist ones. When will the lions lie down with the lambs?

Time after time, as we examine today's world, it turns out to be social, political, ideological, legal, economic, and religious issues that stand in the way of technological solutions to human problems. Most food experts admit that the world could feed adequately a considerably larger population than that of today. But the world is not adequately feeding even its present population. The Soviet Union, for example, is known to have significant potential for expansion of its agriculture. But to increase its agricultural efficiency it would probably have to create more effective incentives to farming than giant collective farms now provide. In other words, the USSR would have to modify its ideology and reform its bureaucracy. It would be naive to expect any country to do either of these things in a hurry, though they may happen gradually, by fits and starts, as the inadequacy of the present system becomes more glaring and costly.

India is an outstanding example of a country that has the potential to raise far more food than it does. Yet India cannot do so without profound changes in social structure, land ownership, government policy, and religious practices. To Hindus the cow is a sacred animal. Many beasts wander and forage at will, and the slaughtering of cows is forbidden by both religion and law. According to Harrison Brown,[7]

"There are perhaps 200 million cattle on the Indian subcontinent—by far the largest number in any region of comparable size in the world— and they probably consume about three times as many calories as are consumed by the human population. . . . In most Indian provinces useless and uneconomical stock, protected by religious conviction and by sentiment, forms the largest proportion of the cattle population. There is a colossal waste of food energy in India, and, in view of the religious restrictions, the waste can be remedied only by limitation and careful control of breeding, by more efficient use of grazing land, and eventually by mechanization of farms so that the proportion of work animals can be decreased." The simple fact is that India cannot solve her food problem without altering some age-old customs and beliefs.

Forecasts fall broadly into two types: *projections* and *predictions.* These are often confused. Predictions are statements or opinions about what *will* happen in the future. Since this is too much to ask except in limited circumstances, it is hardly surprising that most predictions are either disreputable or ambiguous. Palm readers, oracles, and astrologers typically hedge their statements and muddy their language to where the results are approximately equivalent to the cryptic statements printed on slips of paper found in Chinese fortune cookies. Serious predictions in the realm of social, political, and economic affairs are usually short-term; they deal with a few years at most. An economist may feel fairly safe in predicting GNP three or four quarters ahead. Within this time-horizon he can be wrong by a percentage point or so without looking like a fool. But forecasting models that are reasonably accurate in the short run may easily yield errors of thirty, fifty, or even a hundred percent when pushed forward five or ten years. This sort of result would be intolerable as a *prediction,* though possibly acceptable as a *projection* based on a set of given trends.

A projection, in other words, is a *contingent* statement. It rests on a series of stated or implicit assumptions. It depends on a series of *if*'s. *If* the birthrates of various countries remain at recent levels or decline slightly, *if* no world catastrophe has decimated the population in the interim, *if* current estimates of the population of China and some other countries where there has been no recent census are assumed to be reasonably accurate, *then* by the year 2000 world population can be expected to be on the order of six billion.[8] This is a projection. The assumptions are explicitly stated; their reasonableness can be appraised. The forecasting group gives reasons for making their assumptions. Indeed, the forecasts themselves are modified every few years. A different forecaster may make different assumptions and come up with different results. Both results may be "valid," in the strict sense of correctly describing the projective consequences of the underlying assumptions.

The fact that different forecasters present widely different views of the future should surprise no one. After all, people start out with different perceptions of the past and present and, often, with very different views of the nature of society. At the Club of Rome conference, "Limits to Growth 1975," a number of conferees warned of disaster for the human race if world population, consumption of resources, and environmental damage continue to grow at the rates of the recent past.[9] Yet Herman Kahn, with access to the same data, argued the opposite view,[10] as did Norman Macrae, Deputy Editor of *The Economist* (London),[11] who envisions the possibility of an *accelerated* growth in the output of all the things the world needs, including food, energy, and many of the comforts of life. In their view, the materials and energy will be available, and environmental damage will be controlled.

The way people interpret facts seems to depend, perhaps to a greater extent than commonly realized, on the way they perceive and experience the world. In some instances the forecasts throw more light on the forecaster's religious, educational, and social background than on actual probabilities of future events. This in no way depreciates what the forecaster has to say unless he has failed to be explicit about his underlying assumptions. So long as these are stated clearly, it is possible to evaluate any forecast in relation to others.

One important element of a good forecast is the identification of long-term secular trends. This is a bit like picking out the melody of a song from among the various noises emanating from an AM radio during a thunderstorm. Of course it helps if one has heard the tune before. Thus each forecaster can build to some extent on the insights and analyses of others. It is not necessary, for example, to defend in detail the selection of certain macrovariables—such as population, GNP, food production, and energy consumption—as "significant."

With respect to some of these trends, it is safe to say that the future pattern is not likely to deviate sharply from the past. Many changes are relatively gradual. The physical, political, economic, and social structures of the present have a high probability of persisting and affecting events for a good many years. A considerable proportion of the people who will live on the Earth in the year 2000, especially the future leaders, are alive now. It is not too difficult to make an objective appraisal of what is happening now and to project it into the future. Some trajectories are much more likely than others. Thus total disarmament of all countries by mutual agreement may be possible in theory but almost inconceivable in practice. On the other hand, an agreed limitation of armaments is far from out of the question (as, unfortunately, is a continuation of the arms race).

Of course it goes without saying that forecasters should be flexible and free from mental rigidity, overoptimism, overpessimism, strong advocacy, excessively narrow concerns, ideological dogmatism, the influence of vested interests, and any other orientation that might warp their judgment. Forecasters must be independent-minded and indifferent to outcomes. Since no human can hope to meet all these criteria of the ideal, the perfect, unbiased forecast does not exist and never will. Still, in evaluating forecasts it is useful to keep these hazards and pitfalls of forecasting in mind.

I mentioned "advocacy" as one of the hazards that interfere with making a balanced forecast. Yet there is a role for advocacy — so long as it is explicit. The influence of early advocates of space travel certainly helped bring the United States and the USSR to embark on national space programs in the 1960s. Rachel Carson's *Silent Spring* (1962) galvanized action to impose curbs on the indiscriminate use of dangerous pesticides. Whatever one might think of their premises and arguments, the Club of Rome has "raised the consciousness" of the world about the dangers of unrestrained growth and the pressures on resources. Indeed, there is need for many a new Paul Revere. In one shape or another disaster looms as a possibility for the next half-century. The major pitfall for the passionate advocate of a cause is his tendency to overstate his case. He has trouble seeing both sides, and this, in the long run, can reduce his credibility and injure his cause.

Balance in assessing the future means looking at possibilities and probabilities from the vantage point of all relevant scholarly disciplines. For instance, the people in principle best equipped to assess technological possibilities — that is, scientists and engineers — are seldom qualified to appraise the probability of their widespread adoption or to gauge their social effects. In view of the U.S. Congress' rejection of Federal support for the supersonic transport and the questionable economics of British–French Concorde, it is interesting to reread the forecast in the *Wall Street Journal*'s optimistic study of the future, *Here Comes Tomorrow* published in 1966–1967[12]: "The supersonic transport [SST] has yet to fly. But the forward thinkers in aerospace already are turning their attention to the hypersonic transport. The HST, as it's called, could start commercial service in the 1990s. The first versions of the dart-shaped 250-passenger craft would travel 4,000 miles an hour, fast enough to fly from New York to Hong Kong in two hours. Later HSTs might hit speeds of 6,000 miles an hour." The engineers could do it, no doubt. But does anybody need it? Can the fuel be spared for it? Will the citizens on the ground tolerate it? Actually, there are many examples of "possible" technologies that, for a variety of reasons, are unlikely to be developed in the near future even though scientists and engineers are set to proceed with all possible speed. But economists, businessmen, politicians, and citizens may see things differently.

The business community, notwithstanding its hard-headed pragmatism, often makes poor forecasts. To mention one legendary example: IBM and Kodak both turned down the opportunity to invest in the infant technology of xerography. Bankers and corporate officers are necessarily conservative—they are, after all, responsible for other people's money—and they are sometimes too narrow in vision. Decisionmakers probably should not be held too responsible for failures of foresight (we are all subject to them). It is certainly unfair to laugh at mistakes in judgment—however absurd in retrospect—from the vantage point of a hundred years later. Yet I cannot resist citing the difficulties Alexander Graham Bell had in raising money for launching the telephone. His financial backers, Thomas Sanders and Gardiner Hubbard, believed in the telegraph, not the telephone, and objected to the time Bell was devoting to telephone experiments. Years later, in 1911, Bell had this to say to the Telephone Pioneers of America[13]: "I want to speak now of a very curious thing. In the case of new inventions we are generally led to believe that the public is ready to swallow anything but that grave scientific men are the most skeptical of all. I found just exactly the opposite to be true in the case of the telephone. The public generally and the businessmen were very slow to perceive any value in the telephone. The scientific world, on the other hand, took it up at once."

A lifetime is usually barely sufficient to master one specialty—it seems too short for many of us to do even that. Hence the professional economist cannot be expected to master technology, nor the engineers to be adept in economics, nor the biologist comfortable with sociology, and so on. Each specialist necessarily views the world through the tinted lens of his chosen field of knowledge. He knows better than anyone else what the frontier problems are in his field, but he often has difficulty in relating these problems to those of all the other disciplines that overlap his own at some point. Some of the greatest mistakes in forecasting—and in planning—are made because of this limitation.

The tunnel vision of even the most competent specialists means that the forecasts they make must be taken with some skepticism.

Unfortunately, there are not many "Renaissance men" (or women) capable of combining insights from the many disciplines involved. Only specialists are in a position to know the directions being taken at the leading edges of their respective fields. But someone of broader vision, with a generalist's view, must appraise the specialist's forecasts in relation to forecasts made by other specialists in other fields.

In this book I hope to achieve a useful amalgamation of the specialist's knowledge and the generalist's sense of balance and perspective. I hope also to avoid certain kinds of methodological one-sidedness to which many forecasters are prone. The issue of methodology is considered in greater depth in the first chapter, which follows.

ROBERT U. AYRES

Washington, D.C.
September 1978

1. Gerard O'Neil, "The High Frontier," *The Futurist,* X, No. 1, Feb 1976.

2. J.B.S. Haldane, *Daedalus, or Science and the Future,* Kegan Paul, London, 1924.

3. Robert Prehoda, *Designing the Future: The Role of Technological Forecasting,* Chilton Book Company, Philadelphia, 1967.

4. Arthur C. Clarke, *Profiles of the Future: An Inquiry Into the Limits of the Possible,* Harper and Row, New York, 1958.

5. Clarke, *Profiles.*

6. Sir George B. Thomson, *The Foreseeable Future,* Cambridge University Press, New York, 1955.

7. Harrison Brown, *The Challenge of Man's Future,* The Viking Press, New York, 1954.

8. United Nations Department of Social and Economic Affairs, "World Population Prospects As Assessed in 1973," ESA/P/WP 53, March 10, 1975.

9. Limits to Growth 1975 Conference, Houston, Texas, reported in the *New York Times.*

10. H. Kahn, W. Brown, and L. Martel, *The Next 200 Years: A Scenario For America and the World,* W. Morrow and Company, New York, 1976.

11. N. Macrae, "America's Third Century," *The Economist,* October 25, 1975.

12. The Editors of the Wall Street Journal, *Here Comes Tomorrow,* Dow Jones Books, New York, 1966–1967.

13. Quoted by Thnomas Costain in *The Chord of Steel,* Doubleday and Company, 1960.

ACKNOWLEDGMENTS

It is commonplace, and common courtesy, for authors to mention teachers, colleagues, and close relatives who have contributed in various ways to shaping the ideas expressed in a book. However, in the present case it is strictly accurate to say that my father, John U. Ayres, has actually participated to a significant degree in the research and writing of the book itself. Indeed, he invested several months of his time in doing library research, background reading, and collecting, sorting, and annotating clippings and articles on various subjects with which I was insufficiently familiar. Moreover, he "ghostwrote" initial drafts of two chapters — Chapter 2, Values, and Chapter 9, Scenarios. He wrote according to my outline, and although I have heavily rewritten his sections, the results unquestionably bear his stamp and reflect our lengthy discussions and, in some cases, arguments. I am extremely grateful for his assistance and support.

It is customary to thank colleagues "too numerous to mention," which I now hasten to do. I must, however, mention Herman Kahn, whose wide-ranging intellect and discursive brilliance I particularly admire — though, nowadays, from afar.

Other friends who have read and helpfully commented on early drafts include Robert Aten, David Devlin, Ed Hudson, Erika Iakson, Milutin Peritchich, William Persen, Martin Stern, Rolande Widgery, and Philip Wyatt. My wife, Leslie, has been a very acute critic (as well as assistant proofreader). My former secretary, Frances Calafato, typed the manuscript impeccably at least three times. To two ex-employers, International Research and Technology Corporation, and Delta Research Corporation, I also owe thanks for their tolerance of my preoccupations.

R. U. A.

CONTENTS

CHAPTER 7   MEASURES OF MAN—
TECHNOLOGY (II)

CHAPTER 8   MEASURES OF THE
ENVIRONMENT—NATURAL
RESOURCES

CHAPTER ONE

METHODOLOGICAL ISSUES

INTRODUCTORY REMARKS

Methodology is not interesting or fun. The word is both dreary and offensive. Its ability to induce sleep can be verified by any lecturer in the social sciences. The word is offensive because it reeks of jargon. (Physical scientists speak of *method,* not *methodology.* Why must social scientists be so pompous?) Having said this much, I have given almost everybody grounds for feeling abused.

My apologies, then, to you all. A little adrenalin will help keep you alert. Method or methodology—take your choice. The key point is this: if you wish to assess the remainder of the book *critically,* you should be aware of the range of choices an analyst must face and the criteria that can reasonably be applied to help select among alternative approaches. This chapter tells something about how I think about these problems. To others who are engaged professionally in similar pursuits, this material may be of interest. To more casual readers who are interested in "the future," but not in the applicable processes of analysis, feel free to skim lightly. I do advise, however, that you try to read the first few paragraphs of each section before passing on.

WAYS OF CLASSIFYING FORECASTS

Forecasts proliferate nowadays in every variety and form. Some envision future technological marvels, some utopian societies, some doom and disaster. To read a selection of forecasts covering the full range of the available literature is enough to leave most readers in a state of frantic confusion. They are marvelously inconsistent. They cannot all be right—even in the broadest sense, taking it for granted that events and dates are not intended to be precise. Which ones (if any) should be taken seriously? How can one judge?

Forecasts can be looked at in a number of ways. It would seem helpful as a means of imposing some order on the chaos to start from a systematic set of criteria for comparing and evaluating them. I would like to focus particularly on three "dimensions" for classifying possible approaches. The first of these is the conservative/radical *orientation* of the author. A conservative would be one who sees the future primarily as an extension of the familiar recent past. A radical, on the other hand, would be one who sees the future in terms of the emergence of potent new technologies and/or new and sharply different kinds of social organization. A second way of classifying forecasts is by their use (or (nonuse) of *quantitative* data. Some are based largely on quantitative analysis; some are strictly qualitative. A third classification of some importance is in terms of the explicitness of objectivity. Is the rationale of the forecast largely *subjective* or is it *objective?* An objective method is one that can be repeated by others, yielding the same results. Although this strict test is seldom imposed outside a laboratory, a minimal criterion of objectivity is that the procedures used can be explained and evaluated by other investigators. Before proceeding with actual forecasts, I think it is helpful to look more closely at these three aspects of the discipline of studying the future.

Conservative versus Radical

(Alpha-Omega) Forecasts

The conservative and radical designations are merely convenient ways of referring to two extremes of orientation, each representing a particular way of looking at the world. Because conservative and radical have irrelevant (and misleading) political connotations, I prefer to introduce an alternate set of value-free labels, viz., alpha and omega, which will be characterized in a moment. Neither of these extremes is very helpful to people who must make decisions in the real world. Each is one sided and limiting. Both are widespread in the "futures" literature.

The *alpha* forecaster believes, essentially, that the future will be very much like the past, only "more so." He sees the secularization, (sub)urbanization, centralization, economic growth, and technological conquest of nature characteristic of the past century as established permanent features of industrial societies. He expects no major change in these trends—only minor adjustments in *rates* of change. Thus he projects that personal incomes, electricity consumption, automobile use, and so on will continue on their more or less exponentially rising curves. He sees the kinds of appliances people use in future homes — and the homes themselves — as being much as they are now, but with more automatic devices, more "push buttons," with perhaps more remote control and programming capabilities. He sees automobiles as being a trifle smaller, more economical of fuel and probably more automated in various ways, but otherwise much as they are now. He sees the "American Way of Life" of the mid-twentieth century translated with little change to the twenty-first century. In short, the alpha forecaster foresees an unending series of human inventions and improvements of services and products along lines fairly well worked out already. It is characteristic of the alpha position that it sees a continued substitution of mechanical and electronic devices and systems for human functions. This, if carried to a logical extreme, would imply that our descendants would have very little to do but direct the activities of batteries of automated machines. Yet the alpha forecaster foresees no social consequences of that fact.

Forecasts by official government agencies tend to be of this nature.[1] All modern industrial economies depend on continued growth; without growth they would stagnate. This produces unemployment and uncertainty and multiplies social tensions. An end to growth is political anathema. Its continuation is unquestionably at the core of alpha forecasting. Thus State and Federal highway-planning engineers map new highways to accommodate an assumed continuation of historical growth in automobile traffic. Utilities plan their investments in new capacity on the basis of an assumption of steady exponential growth in electricity demand. (Events since 1973 have shaken their confidence in this assumption, however.) Not many highway planners think in terms of the possibilities of providing alternate means of transportation to reduce dependence on the private car with its waste of energy resources. Nor do electric utilities concern themselves with the possibilities for radical changes in the distribution pattern, such as the introduction of many small on-site electric power generators with local use of by-product heat (so-called total energy systems) to supplement the giant "base load" generating plants of today.

The forecasts made by nongovernment establishmentarian groups such as the Edison Electric Institute, the Conference Board, or the National Petroleum Council[2] typically fall in the alpha category. Alpha forecasts often have an element of vested interest hidden in them. Petroleum companies sell oil products, and this cannot but affect the hidden assumptions — shared within the industry — that underlie their forecasts. Despite honest attempts to be objective, the basic thinking is alpha, whence the result is alpha. Many illustrative examples might be cited, but one will suffice. It exemplifies the alpha position rather neatly.

Donald C. Burnham, President of Westinghouse Electric Corporation, criticized the demand forecasts adopted by the Ford Foundation's Energy Policy Study as being substantially too low.[3] He gave the following reasons:

> First, the base case used a period in which significant *structural changes* to the energy supply were taking place; railroads shifted from coal to diesel, reheat turbines allowed dramatic increases in electric generation efficiency, coal was replaced by oil and gas for space heating, and glass wool insulation was introduced. These significant increases in end use efficiencies had the effect of masking the growth in the amount of "useful work" performed, and thus understate the true historic growth.

> Second, since energy utilization has historically included a constant stream of energy efficiency improvements, the failure to eliminate that portion of projected savings which would have occurred in due course, double counts the savings.

> Third, inadequate provision was made for new energy using devices. There are no equivalents of jet planes, air conditioning plastics, fertilizers, or any other similar significant new energy uses projected in the report.

What Burnham's criticism boils down to is that major ("structural") innovations that reduced energy consumption in the past cannot be expected to continue, whereas innovations that increase energy use in the future cannot be expected to stop! This is a vintage example of alpha thinking.

A variant of the alpha position, which at first glance appears to be its opposite (but is not), is exemplified by the "Limits to Growth" hypothesis put forward a few years ago by the Club of Rome.[4] This approach focuses on the problem of exhaustion of the Earth's resources due to an exponential growth of consumption and various associated consequences thereof. The Club of Rome initially recommended rather strongly that growth policies be replaced by reduced growth or no-growth policies.*

This is not the appropriate place to comment at length on the central thesis of "Limits to Growth." The major issues of resource availa-

*This position has since been modified.

bility and scarcity are addressed in Chapter 8. I classify the "Limits" argument in the alpha category because it depends, at bottom, on the idea that a resource today is a resource for all time, and that the resources we use today will be as essential in the future as they are now. The similarity to Burnham's line of reasoning is unmistakable.

So much foir the alpha position which forecasts the future essentially as extrapolation of the familiar past, changes being primarily quantitative (bigger, faster, etc.) rather than qualitative.

The opposite of the alpha position is the *omega* position. This position is characterized by a tendency to minimize (or even overlook) institutional and psychological rigidities and political-economic constraints. It visualizes a utopian future and leaps over all the difficulties and problems of getting there from here. It ignores the complex dynamics that characterize the real world. I gave some examples of visionary thinking in the Preface. The omega viewpoint, essentially, is that almost anything which the mind of man can envisage (as long as it does not violate natural laws) can be implemented by a sufficiently concentrated engineering effort. The argument is often heard that, "because Man can land on the moon," we should also be able to design and produce an efficient nonpolluting automobile or a good public transport system, or build adequate housing for the poor, or irrigate the deserts, or solve this or that problem. What is overlooked too often by this kind of rhetorical argument is the interaction of nontechnological factors that are invariably involved. Most of the problems that plague mankind, including the problem of feeding the world's expanding population, are *not* primarily technological, as I pointed out earlier. They are social, political, cultural, and administrative.

When a problem is narrowly defined and technological in nature, it is institutionally possible to bring sufficient resources (funds and trained personnel) to bear to overcome the difficulties. The Manhattan Project in World War II, for example, produced the nuclear reactor and the atomic bomb, based on physical principles that had barely emerged from the laboratory. The United States sent astronauts to the moon by mounting a ten-year national program (Apollo). Unfortunately, it often takes an external threat to bring about this kind of concentrated effort. When objectives are unclear or in dispute, when central authority is lacking, and when financing is uncertain (as, for example in a typical metropolitan rapid transit program), progress is likely to be very slow and painful at best.

Among the more interesting recent examples of the omega viewpoint is the vision of Princeton physicist, Gerald O'Neill,[5] who advocates colonizing the region of space around the Earth by stationing satellites in space where they would be held in stable points of the combined gravitational fields of the Earth, Moon, and Sun. Such satellite colonies could theoretically become self-sustaining as to food and energy and could export energy-intensive industrial products to the Earth—meanwhile providing accommodations for millions of residents and tourists from the Earth. Moreover, they could, O'Neill says, be built largely from materials mined on the moon, not brought up from the Earth. This is a fascinating conception—a real "mind bender." However, it is of little help to Earth-bound planners because the proposal says almost nothing about the path from here to there: who would pay the immense front-end costs involved? Would the project be national or international? If the former, would it have military significance? If the latter, how would costs be allocated? How would such a colossal project be organized and administered? O'Neill does not really deal with the important question of whether human beings would want or consent to live permanently off the Earth (unless things got so bad here that anywhere else might seem better). It is not inconceivable that—after the novelty wore off—compulsion or some other strong incentive might be required to get people to join the colonies. And how would such incentives be created?

Another striking example of omega-type thinking is architect Paolo Soleri's dream city "Arcosanti" which was proposed to be constructed in Arizona. Displays based on the underlying "Arcology" concept made a great impact at the Corcoran Gallery a few years ago, and some science fiction writers have freely implanted Arcosantis in imaginary future landscapes. But cities are not ordinarily built as a whole, by a single architect. They grow from small beginnings through the uncoordinated efforts of thousands or millions of individuals. Why should this historic pattern be set aside? The question of whether city dwellers *want* this kind of city does not seem to have been addressed seriously. Omega visionaries often prescribe what they believe people *should* have, but consistently fail to inquire deeply enough how people or institutions would react to the innovations being put forward on their behalf.

It is relatively easy, of course, to obstruct a visionary project by raising practical objections. Virtually every innovator must overcome deeply rooted barriers of skepticism, of the kind described by Alexander Graham Bell, quoted earlier. A forecaster must be cautious about writing off visionaries based on the arguments of conservatives, especially established experts. It is important to remember that visionaries have been responsible for many of the developments that have fundamentally altered the shape of man's world. And "experts" are very often wrong, especially when they argue in the negative.

Arthur C. Clarke introduces his book *Profiles of the Future* with a list of astonishing failures of foresight by outstanding scientists and thinkers of their time.[7] These include the famous pronouncement by Simon Newcomb, a well-known astronomer, to the effect that sustained mechanical flight was theoretically impossible—published just before the scientifically untrained Wright Brothers took off! Clarke also mentions an article by a Professor Bickerton in 1926 saying that rocket flight off the Earth was "basically impossible" and an assertion by the eminent Dr. Richard Van deRiet Woolley, Astronomer Royal of England (made one year before Sputnik I went up) that "space travel is utter bilge." To cite yet another example, Clarke quotes Dr. Vannevar Bush in testimony before a Senate committee on December 3, 1945, as follows[8]:

There has been a great deal said about a 3,000 miles high-angle rocket. In my opinion such a thing is impossible for many years. The people who have been writing these things that annoy me, have been talking about a 3,000 mile high-angle rocket shot from one continent to another, carrying an atomic bomb and so directed as to be a precise weapon which would land exactly on a certain target, such as a city.

I say, technically, I don't think anyone in the world knows how to do such a thing, and I feel confident that it will not be done for a very long period of time to come. . . . I think we can leave that out of our thinking. I wish the American public would leave that out of their thinking.

What Vannevar Bush was dismissing so lightly was nothing less than the ICBM—the key weapon in the United States military arsenal for the last fifteen years and (very likely) for the next fifty.

I feel a little bit apologetic about using quotes like these; anyone can back the wrong horse, and practically everyone does. But we also can learn from these examples not to be too cocksure about what is, or is not, in the cards. Whereas visionaries are often much too optimistic, skeptics are sometimes much too pessimistic. The forecasters' hardest task is to find the right balance between these two types of error.

With full allowance for the power of visions, however, a forecast of a specific future scientific or technological development ought to contain, as an integral part, a consideration of the social, political, and economic, and cultural factors impinging on it. I referred earlier to the problem of food production in India and to the dead weight of traditions, customs, lifestyles, laws, religious beliefs, government policies, and the system of land ownership that, together, make agricultural efficiency in that country extremely difficult to achieve. India keeps coming to mind because it is a land of such vast potential and so little flexibility for adapting to necessary change. Consider another beautiful technical opportunity: in the Himalaya Mountains of Tibet near the border of India exists perhaps the world's greatest potential hydroelectric power source. There is a place where a major river—the Tsangpo-Brahmaputra—drops 10,000 feet between two points only forty miles apart as the crow flies, although the river actually follows a much longer loop around the mountainous massif of which the highest peak is 26,000-foot high Namcha Barwa. A 40-mile tunnel connecting the upper river (Tsangpo) with the lower river (Brahmaputra) could provide enough hydroelectric power for a significant part of the present and future energy needs of three adjacent countries: India, Tibet (China), and Bangladesh. In addition to being an important renewable energy source, such a dam could partially control the catastrophic floods that now ravage Bangladesh. The project would, however, require close political and economic cooperation between India and China—since the dam would have to be in Tibet, whereas the generating plant would be across the border in India. Obviously, until the governments in question are ready to drop their quarrels and work together, the dam (I am tempted to call it "Omega Dam") will never be built.

Incidentally, the Aswan Dam built in Egypt with Soviet help has not met expectations. The lake has not filled up completely because of excessive evaporation into the dry desert air, plus substantial seepage into the ground. Hence electric power output is lower than anticipated. There have been some unfavorable effects on agriculture in the Nile Valley—more synthetic fertilizers are needed than formerly. Irrigation has also resulted in the spread of parasites including bilharzia, not formerly a problem there. Some of these problems have arisen because the dam is not optimally located. The proper place for the project from an engineering and ecological viewpoint is much further south, within the territory of the Sudan. However, the location was dictated by the fact that Egypt wanted the dam under its exclusive political control. As a result, the benefits of Aswan are substantially below what they might have been if political rivalry had not been a factor.

To take still another example of the intervention of nontechnological factors, consider weather modification or "rainmaking." This is technically feasible today under certain circumstances, but it is much less widely used in practice than was originally thought likely. Why? Because, although artificially induced rain helps one area or one set of people, it may simultaneously damage the interests of others. The farmers in a dry area need rain—but nearby, perhaps, is a resort where the people want to swim, sun bathe, and play golf. It is not possible to pinpoint the rain so it will fall gently on the farms and avoid the fairways. If the rain falls on a resort, the owner may sue the rainmaker for damages. Our system of laws makes no provision for maximizing the general public good in a case like this, nor is there any mechanism whereby the resort owners may be compensated by the farmers. Consequently, only a government agency can, in practice, safely undertake to modify rainfall. Forecasts of the widespread use of climate control must be tempered by such considerations.

Perhaps the most extreme omega forecast I can cite is the following quotation from "Designing the Future" by Robert Prehoda[9]:

> Science may be on the threshold of greatly extending your life span to 100 years, 200 years, or more. If all causes of biological aging are discovered and cured, man eventually may have an indefinite life span extending for many centuries.
>
> Some of you may bypass the immediate future, finding a door through and via human hibernation. Total suspended animation at very low temperatures is a more distant possibility. The winter of your lives may be spent as cold slumber, allowing the sleeper to awaken in a golden age of perpetual spring; then this metamorphosis may include further biological transformations, curing past ills and restoring the vigor and the appearance of youth.

Despite the apparently cautious "may," practical considerations are not considered in the slightest degree. Prehoda never deals with obvious questions such as the basis for selecting the people who are to be awarded this near-immortality (and who will be denied it) or how the world would adjust to the population growth that would automatically result if extended lifespans became general without a corresponding decrease in birthrate. Considering the explosive effects of population growth that relatively modest public health advances of the past have had, the population impact of doubling the human lifespan would be staggering. The science fiction writer Larry Niven has taken Prehoda's forecast seriously enough to postulate a few interesting (possible) implications. Niven envisions a world population stabilized at 18 billion, enforced by rigid controls on having children, "Mother hunts" to track down violators of procreation restrictions, and organ banks to replace worn-out (or accidently destroyed) limbs, eyes, and so on. Since the demand for replacement parts would inevitably exceed the supply, Niven goes on to suggest a blackmarket in human spare parts, run by "organleggers" and supplied by kidnap/murder on a large scale and other bizarre implications.[10] Omega forecasters do not like to deal with awkward questions like these, but someone other than writers of fiction must do so. Forecasts that evade such questions tend to be disregarded — as they should be — after an initial "gee whiz" reaction.

It is appropriate here to quote one last omega thinker, Lewis Mumford[11]:

> Plainly, the ability to translate mathematical theorems and subatomic or molecular forces into new inventions, without encountering either technical delays or sobering human inhibitions, has turned our dominant technology itself into the equivalent of science fiction. Whatever appears in scientific fantasy the night before may appear next morning or next year in actual life. . . .
>
> Now we are faced with just the opposite situation. The obstacles to immediate acceptance have been broken down; and the latest technical proposal, instead of having to establish its right to be recognized and accepted, rather challenges society to take it over at once and at any cost; whilst any reluctance to do so immediately is looked upon as reprehensible, or, as Ogburn once naively put it, a cultural lag.

Mumford is an omega precisely because he sees no barriers between a technological possibility and its implementation — a state of affairs he finds objectionable. Mumford's negative feelings about technology may have substantive justification, but he is demonstrably wrong in asserting that new technology is "automatically" accepted. What he was really thinking about, of course, was the military-aerospace community and its uncritical eagerness (in the 1950s and 1960s, especially) for new "high-technology" weapons. In the civilian sectors of our society one could make a much better case for the reverse of Mumford's argument. In fact, badly needed new technology, for example, for more efficient and less polluting motor vehicle propulsion systems, is unreasonably and irrationally resisted, to the great detriment of society as a whole.

There have been few, if any, explicit attempts by forecasters to chart a deliberate path between these two extremes: the alpha and the omega. It is my hope to map such a middle course in this book. I hope to avoid being entrapped either by the assumption that the future will be a simple extrapolation or magnification of the past or by the view that whatever is technically possible in coming decades will actually come to pass. This book focuses less on technical possibilities than on institutional and policy-regulated constraints that will, ultimately, determine the outcome. To give weight to these constraints without falling into the "alpha trap" of predicting a future much like the present is admittedly difficult. Institutions may look rigid today, yet they can sometimes change almost overnight. When institutions change, they do so because of external forces. People's views and preferred lifestyles can also change, but only in response to a changing environment. To escape from the alpha trap it is essential to try to identify and take into account the underlying pressures which "drive" the system. I return to this topic later.

Qualitative versus Quantitative Forecasts

A second characteristic by which the "futures" literature can be classified is whether the forecasts are based on the analysis of *quantitative* data or draw largely on *qualitative* judgments, insights, and values. These, like the alpha and omega types, represent two diametrically opposite ways of approaching the subject—two contrasting styles of thought. The people who use these different approaches are concerned with different things, and one gets the impression that they scarcely listen to, or hear, each other.

This situation was well expressed by C. P. Snow in his famous analysis of the "two cultures."[12] Snow found the intellectual world of England (circa 1960) split into two groups that did not understand each other and had virtually ceased to communicate: the scientific-technical community on one hand and the artistic-literary-humanist community on the other. Snow, whose interests spanned both worlds, felt a deep frustration that these groups—both of which, he felt, made major contributions to modern life—were so far apart in goals and values. Each went its way almost as if the other did not exist. The situation in the United States and elsewhere in the Western World was, and still is, substantially similar.

There is a comparable cultural split between quantitative and qualitative forecasters. On one hand are the people who make quantitative forecasts, full of facts and figures on population, labor force, gross national product, agricultural production, energy consumption, automobile use, gross pollution output, and the like. Typical of these are the alpha forecasts already mentioned, by such organizations as the United States Office of Management and Budget, the Office of Education (HEW), the Bureau of Labor Statistics, the Federal Energy Administration, the Bureau of Mines, the National Petroleum Council,

Resources For the Future, Inc., and so on. Also, "Limits to Growth" and other recent world models are of this type. Such forecasts measure trends, formulate relationships between variables, and attempt to interpret what will happen in the future in terms of amounts and sizes. Magnitudes are attached to income, urbanization, resources, health, life expectancy, and a variety of other variables. The future is charted in terms of shifts between these variables.

At the other extreme are many studies of the future that quantify little or nothing. They focus on *qualitative* factors, often emphasizing a perceived decline or a radical change in the quality of life. One subgroup, the technological optimists (C. P. Snow, A. C. Clarke, Robert Prehoda, Dennis Gabor, Sir George Thompson, and Herman Kahn) concentrates attention on the capability of technology to solve "problems" such as good health, housing, and transportation/communications. Another subgroup (mainly pessimists) is preoccupied with psychological states such as "anomie" and "alienation," with crime, increasing social disorder and dissent, the decline in the work ethic, the overpreoccupation of the society with material comforts, "dehumanization," and so on. Authors with this orientation include Lewis Mumford, Gordon Rattray Taylor, Jacques Ellul, Victor Ferkiss, Rene Dubos, Charles Reich, and Alvin Toffler, among many others.

Some writers of the qualitative school envision a better future for mankind as a result of social changes which they propose or believe they see on the horizon. Some, like Reich, see the possibility of a "flowering" of human potential, a growth of the arts and sciences, a recapture of the feeling of life as an existing and meaningful adventure. Others, such as Mumford, Taylor, and Ferkiss, believe a happy outcome is possible only by the abandonment of the present excessive preoccupation with growth, material progress, and "runaway" technology.

Each of the qualitative authors has important things to say and makes a contribution by focusing on factors very likely to be neglected or overlooked in the quantitative projections.

Yet each of these ways of looking at the future—the quantitative and the qualitative—has a basic weakness. Each approach grasps a part of the whole. Neither approach, by itself, is comprehensive enough to be really useful to decision makers in charting a course into the future. On the quantitative side, inhabited by people who know how to build a computer model, the temptation seems to be irresistable to spend most of their time "improving" it. Once such a model is constructed, it seems to take over—like the magic broom and bucket of the Sorcerer's Apprentice. The model dominates the discussion, and those elements of the real world that do not fit the model tend to be ignored. Thus questions of political organization, institutional structure, social relationships, psychological needs—even significant technological details—tend to be set aside. Only those factors that can conveniently be quantified and put into the model are considered. The key failure of most modelers is that they fail to explain to the audience the shortcomings and inadequacies of their brainchildren (leaving this task to specialist-critics who are often competing modelers). Lay readers seldom know what to make of the models, and they can hardly be blamed for taking a skeptical attitude toward "black boxes" whose inner workings are obscure.

At the other extreme, the people who eschew models and quantification—whether by choice or because of an inability to handle the requisite mathematical tools—often fail to appreciate important trends that can and do powerfully affect the qualitative factors about which they are explicitly concerned. Relative economic growth rates are one of the factors that tend to be overlooked by the nonquantitative futurists. The quality of a person's life does not depend solely on money income—Man surely does not live by bread alone—but at the same time, lifestyle cannot be totally divorced from considerations of wealth. The amount and distribution of income must be considered in any realistic discussion of the quality of life. I think Mahatma Gandhi once said, "To a starving man, God appears in the form of bread."*

Those who refuse to be interested in quantities run the risk of missing other important—indeed vital—qualitative factors. A large quantitative change, after all, *is* a qualitative difference. For example, much is being made today of the approaching overpopulation of the Earth and the inability of our Earth to feed its teeming billions. World population is now growing at a rate of about 2% a year. This does not sound particularly alarming; but a 2% annual increase will double the world's population in thirty-five years—about half the lifetime of an average American. At this rate, the world's population will *quadruple* within the lifetimes of babies born this year.† It will multiply *eight times* within the lifetimes of their own children. No wonder the population increase is called an "explosion" and is creating real consternation among all who consider its implications!

Yet there are profound changes taking place in the world today that are occurring far more rapidly than the growth in population.

---

* The quote may be quite inexact. I have been unable to locate its source.
† Assuming, incidentally, that Prehoda's forecast of an extended lifespan does *not* come true.

Gross world product (GWP) is increasing faster; its rate of growth averaged 5% per year for the period 1950–1973, which would mean a doubling in only fourteen years. This trend alarms some observers, who question whether the consequent drain on material and energy resources can be long sustained. There are differences of opinion, of course. Some experts believe that this rate of economic growth can even be accelerated, for a while, although in time it must begin to decline slowly. Herman Kahn, for one, believes that, by 100 years from now, average income per capita, *for the world as a whole*, may be between twice and five times today's American level[13] — which is already roughly fifty times higher than the present average income in India and seven times higher than that in neighboring Mexico.

A number of factors that affect human lives are increasing far more rapidly than population. They include the use of radios, TVs, telephones, computers, electricity, automobiles, and air transportation. Another is the destructive power of military weapons in national stockpiles. Another is the number of nations possessing nuclear reactors and a capability to manufacture nuclear weapons.

A particularly compelling example of rapid growth is that of computer use, which has been doubling consistently every three or four years (depending, of course, on how "use" is measured) for more than two decades already. The impact which this continued development will have on human lifestyles by the year 2000 is, quite literally, inconceivable. We cannot anticipate the impact with any exactitude. Unquestionably, it will be enormous. We need not consider the implications here (they are discussed later in any event), but the essential point is that a *quantitative* change of such magnitude is surely *qualitative* in its importance.

Subjective versus Objective Forecasts—Indeterminacy and Causality

I now come to the third way of classifying forecasts: the extent of their objectivity. Some forecasts are largely subjective. By this I mean, essentially, that the forecaster *cannot* really explain how he reaches his conclusions, nor would another individual necessarily arrive at the same ones. They arise out of a "gestalt," an intuitive, holistic vision, which is itself a natural consequence of the inherited nature and accumulated life experiences of the individual. The forecast is a kind of work of art.

A subjective forecast can be illuminating or revealing (or not), depending on whether the vision of the forecaster-artist resonates with the consciousness of the reader-viewer. A person capable of achieving this kind of communication-by-resonance is, by definition, a genius. The audience knows immediately and instinctively that the picture is —at least in some essential aspect—"right," but not why this is so. Immediate acceptance is its great virtue. The scarcity and irreproducibility of suitable forecasting geniuses constitutes a fairly fundamental barrier to systematic analysis of policy alternatives based on subjective forecasting. Hence I lay considerable stress on the element of objectivity in the methodology adopted in this book.

To carry this line of thought further, it seems to me that an explicit paradigm or "world model" is almost essential at this point. Most people who read this book presumably share a common set of basic concepts and assumptions about the relationship between thought and reality, although they may not be consciously aware of it. At bottom, the world view that comprehends my forecasting methodology is essentially common to all Western science. This is not a trivial remark, especially in view of the fact that not all Westerners accept the scientific method, as formulated by Francis Bacon and generations of more recent philosophers, and its underlying framework of axioms and assumptions. In particular, many "humanists" do not accept it.

I am going to state the paradigm of science to which I subscribe in a rather concise unqualified form, with full knowledge that to do so opens one of the deepest chasms which divide Snow's "two cultures." Because I was trained as a scientist and speak the language of science easily, I expect to be immediately understood by most scientists. I also expect to be initially misunderstood by many humanists because of habitual differences in the way in which certain key words are understood. If the nonscientists will bear with me for a few paragraphs, however, I will make an attempt to construct a language bridge across the gulf.

The paradigm of science is, in very brief form, as follows: scientists believe the observable (and measurable) phenomena in the universe can be understood *as if* the universe were a kind of large and complex *machine*—although not quite a piece of clockwork mechanism—that has evolved over eons in accordance with a set of knowable (but never fully known) physical principles. All phenomena are assumed to have definite causes, at least in the sense of being explainable in terms of these principles. Living organisms, including man, are viewed as parts of this great evolving system. The biological and social evolution of Man is assumed to be understandable in terms of this larger context.

In short, the current paradigm of science is *mechanistic**** and *materialistic* in the exact dictionary meaning of those words.

What all this means for the purposes of this book is simply this: that trends or events will not be projected in the absence of ascertainable and understandable connections between cause and effect. Historical trends, for example, will not be extended *indefinitely* without a positive reason for doing so—contrary to many alpha forecasts. A trend line is not necessarily an indication of a continuing cause-effect relationship. I do not make forecasts based on desirability or possibility (the omega position) in the absence of a conceivable and plausible cause-and-effect mechanism for achieving the end result.

So much for the bare statement. Many, if not most, nonscientists tend to be offended by this kind of statement, because it seems to rule out any role for "human" values or for the intuitive, artistic, and spiritual natures of Man. But that is a misconception arising from a strictly semantic problem: it is due to the fact that many humanists use words such as "mechanism" and "materialism" in a rhetorical, or poetic, rather than an analytical sense. These two words—and others of the same flavor—are often used by humanist writers as names for "unacceptable" categories of attitudes or ideas.

The trouble arises from the ambiguities of our common—but not quite shared—language. Indeed, on reflection it is inconceivable that science could function without intuition or aesthetic considerations. Science—an activity of creative thinkers—does not exclude the mind or thought (or, for that matter, feelings) from its province. Although neurophysiologists and cyberneticists have not yet achieved a detailed understanding of the nature of the sensory-cerebral interaction which we call "thinking," most of this activity can now be physically located in the brain. Indeed, much of the associated electrical and chemical phenomena have been monitored, and some key relationships have been traced.[14] As long as the current paradigm of science is accepted, scientists will continue to search for explanations of mental processes within its stated limitations. To admit that a phenomenon such as "thought" is not fully understood now is not to deny the possibility of understanding it better when more evidence is gathered. Only when all possible explanations (within the paradigm) have failed will the paradigm itself be subjected to serious challenge and revision, as T. S. Kuhn has so forcefully argued.[15]

Clearly, one reason there has been little credible scientific research on extrasensory perception (ESP) and other "paranormal" phenomena

---

*But no longer *deterministic;* I return to this point in a later paragraph.

is because the phenomena — assuming they exist — cannot (yet) be understood within the currently accepted paradigms of neurophysiology and psychology. If enough scientists are convinced that the phenomena in question are "real," they will, eventually, develop a paradigm within which they can be fitted. This may or may not require a relaxation of the mechanistic and materialistic characterizations noted above.

The paradigm of science has undergone one major change within the last century. In the Newtonian system of mechanics, which prevailed until the great discoveries of Planck and Einstein, the universe did appear to be a machine in which cause and effect were linked precisely and unalterably, like a clockwork device. In this view, which was generally accepted by nineteenth century science, human free will had to be an illusion, for a human being was presumed to be subject to the same cause-effect linkage as everything else in the universe. Even the psychology of that century, culminating in the works of Freud, gradually abandoned the concept of human will and looked for explanations of human behavior solely in terms of childhood traumas and external conditioning. Thus nineteenth century scientific determinism gave a curious kind of intellectual support to the waning religious concepts of fatalism and predestination.

In the twentieth century, this deterministic view has been substantially modified. Newtonian mechanics were superseded by both Einsteinian relativity and quantum mechanics. The latter, in particular, is the keystone of modern physics. In quantum mechanics, causal relationships exist on a macro scale, for example, in the motions of stars and planets. Cause-and-effect relations become probabilistic (i.e., statistical) in nature as one views the basic phenomena under greater and greater magnification.

An absolutely basic implication follows from this: one cannot know everything about the past, present, or the future even *in principle.* Indeed, the limitations on such knowledge have been expressed precisely as the so-called "Heisenberg uncertainty principle," which states that the product of the statistical uncertainties of complementary variables (say, momentum and position) can never be less than the fundamental physical "unit of action," known as Planck's constant.

Philosophers of science have made much of the principle of indeterminacy because it has truly fascinating implications. Thus beyond a definite limit one can determine the track of a particle with very great precision only by sacrificing knowledge of its speed on that track! Similarly, it might be suggested that to know every relevant detail about the historical trajectory — or path — of any social or economic variable

of possible consequence would require such intensive—and disturbing
—scrutiny as to cause significant and unpredictable changes in its
trajectory. (Indeed, most forecasters of "doom" are quite candidly in
the position of trying to create so much disturbance as to invalidate
their own forecasts.)

Two comments seem pertinent at this juncture. The first comment
is that the physical science paradigm does not imply that the world
future is completely and absolutely determined by the past. Absolute
determinism of the "clockwork" variety is incompatible with the principle of indeterminacy, which is part of our current understanding of
the laws of physics, as well as our predominant Western (i.e., Judao-
Christian*) cultural and religious attitudes regarding individual free
will and the malleability of social relationships.

A second point, related to the first, is that *indeterminacy* is not the
same thing as and does not imply *unpredictability*. It means merely
that predictability has intrinsic limits. Just because we cannot know
everything does not mean we know nothing at all! (Actually the notion
of impossibility of prediction would hardly occur to anybody except a
philosopher, since it is so manifestly contradicted by everyday reality.)

The two comments just noted, in the light of the basic paradigm of
science, lead to a basic conclusion with regard to forecasting methodology. Since it is a fundamental tenet of the paradigm of science that
every event has a set of real causes, the problem seems to be to structure the causal relationships in a useful way. That is, one would like to
sort out the consequences of unidentifiable, unmeasurable, and predictable ones. And one would like to concentrate attention on the
latter.

This abstract statement of objectives becomes clearer with the help
of a simple example. Consider a bolt of lightning generated by a thunderstorm. This is an event that can be of significance for human activity. Its causes are well understood in the sense that it can be fully
explained in terms of basic electromagnetic and meterological theo-
ries. However, the exact time and path of a particular strike depend on
random events having to do with the exact details of the distributions
of positive and negative ions in the air, which depend, in turn, on
"micro-scale" patterns of wind turbulence, particulate matter, humidity, water droplet size and density, and so on. To measure all these
variables exactly at any moment of time would require such elaborate

---

*It can hardly be said that Christianity was always fundamentally incompatible with
doctrines of predestination, but its post-Renaissance form seems to have evolved in this
direction.

(and *perturbing*) monitoring systems that the values at the next instant of time would inevitably be influenced by the measuring process itself. Thus the principle of indeterminacy comes into play.

Each of these microscale phenomena has a cause, to be sure, in the sense that it corresponds to a physical state of distributed matter that evolved from previous states of matter subject to the physical laws governing transformations of matter and energy. We know these laws to a reasonably good approximation insofar as they apply to "ordinary" matter at temperatures and pressures that occur on the surface of the Earth. We can even predict the probable occurrence of lightning in certain areas at certain times in terms of associated macrostates of matter. Weather forecasters do this routinely when they predict thunderstorms.

However, the prediction of thunderstorms in practice is strictly in the language of probability. For instance, a forecast might call for "75% probability of thunderstorms occurring during the next foiur hours" over a specified region that might be a hundred square miles in size. This is helpful in warning golfers and picnickers to stay home, pilots to avoid the area, and forest fire watchers to redouble their alertness. Such a prediction is of little value to a photographer who is interested in obtaining a photograph of a tree in the process of being struck by a bolt. Even with the help of the weather forecast, his chances of picking the right tree are negligible on an absolute scale.

It is illuminating to ask how much social benefit would be gained by improving our monitoring and computational capabilities to the point of being able to predict *which* tree will be struck by lightning, say 30 minutes in advance—assuming for argument's sake that such a degree of precision were compatible with the indeterminacy principle.

Needless to say, even if it were technically feasible, the information input and computer requirements and the cost of processing the data to produce the forecast would be staggering. Apart from amateur photographers, the major potential beneficiaries would be people (or animals) who could be warned not to shelter under the wrong tree and forest rangers who would be able to deploy fire fighting equipment more efficiently.

Only a few people per year are struck by lightning, and even fewer could be saved by a hypothetical warning system based on this degree of forecasting capability. (After all, hikers and golfers do not normally carry portable radios tuned to the weather forecasts.) Thus the potential benefits are measured largely in terms of a certain number of hundreds or thousands of acres of trees that might otherwise burn as a result of lightning strikes. Without doubt, far cheaper means exist of achieving this same benefit — although even the cheaper approaches might still cost much more than the value of the potential savings.

The lesson to be drawn from this example is obviously much broader. In the first place, some things are difficult or impossible to predict in detail because the underlying phenomena which govern them cannot be monitored to the requisite degree of precision without interfering with the outcome. That is, they are subject to some sort of uncertainty principle. In the second place, many such detailed predictions would have little practical value and would certainly not repay their cost.

The example used to make this essential point was deliberately derived from the realm of physical science. Other events on a larger scale — such as volcanic eruptions, earthquakes, droughts, or epidemics — could also have been chosen as examples. Yet a more pertinent, but possibly more treacherous, illustration could have been taken from the realm of human behavior. In social science a principle of indeterminacy seems to operate with regard to "measurements" of the behavior of individual persons or even small groups. Thus indeterminacy is by no means an ultimate limit without practical significance. On the contrary, the principle operates whenever the act of observation by an experimenter unavoidably interferes with the outcome of the experiment. It is virtually impossible to obtain detailed meaningful data about individual humans without significantly interacting with them and thus affecting their attitudes, reactions, perceptions, and behavior.

So-called double-blind experiments in clinical psychology are feasible in certain limited situations, but these are necessarily aimed at determining behavioral characteristics common to significant groups of people or to the human species as a whole. At best they can offer hints as to how most people might be expected to behave in certain critical situations (usually rather artificial ones). There is no objective technique for determining by observation alone, whether conducted "at a distance" or close at hand, the likely reactions of a given individual to given external stimuli. Psychoanalysis is a relatively primitive discipline, with very limited capabilities even if a highly trained investigator and a cooperative patient spend years together.* Despite var-

---

*Admittedly, the diagnostic phase does not take nearly as long — most of the time is used in the therapy phase. Then again, the analyst is usually only concerned with diagnosing pathological (e.g., neurotic) conditions that interfere with the patient's ability to function. This is a much easier task, in principle, than constructing a complete psychological profile with general predictive value.

ious highly publicized attempts, it seems clear that "remote" psychological analysis can never be more than a poor substitute.

Suppose we suspend judgment on the issues of cost and effectiveness and simply consider the consequences of constructing a full-scale psychological profile of every political leader in a position to have a significant influence on events, for the purpose of improving sociopolitical predictability. Of course, if the information were published it would also be accessible to the general public. There is a possibility, for instance, that psychotic personalities, such as Adolph Hitler, might have been excluded from power if comprehensive psychological information about them had been available at an earlier date. (Would the German electorate have cared? Or was Hitler an attractive candidate in the circumstances, in part, *because* of his neuroses?) What seems beyond doubt is that the psychologists themselves could not remain strictly observers. They would inevitably become part of the power equation, thus interfering with and influencing the historical process. The objective of trying to make politics more predictable might, in fact, be achieved, but only by changing the political system at the same time.

The purpose of the lengthy discussion of uncertainty and indeterminancy is to justify an assertion that the appropriate methodology for forecasting involves sorting the inherently unpredictable from that which is more or less predictable in principle.* This distinction requires elucidation.

In the unpredictable category, it now appears, we would first include events arising from physical processes that can never be monitored in sufficient detail for complete predictability (for various reasons) and can therefore be regarded as random in some sense. As already noted, storms, volcanic eruptions, earthquakes, droughts, and epidemics fall naturally into this category.†

It is also clear that many human decision processes—especially where a few individuals are especially influential—are essentially unpredictable. This is because of the inherent impossibility of an outsider

---

*Of course, the practical problems of forecasting are formidable, and progress can only be made step by step. The state of the art is still relatively undeveloped.

† I do not deny the possibility of forecasting the pattern of periods of peak activity of known volcanos or earth tremors along known tectonic faults by close monitoring of preliminary signals. In a similar manner, one can forecast when and where a hurricane will reach land after it has already been observed somewhere in midocean. This is useful because it may provide a valuable few days of warning, but it is not the same thing as predicting the *creation* of the storm or the occurrence of a major volcanic eruption or earthquake.

knowing enough "at a distance" about the factors that will affect the thinking of decision makers. These factors are only partly visible, at best, to the nonparticipants. Personal ethics, prejudices, idiosyncracies, fears, and ambitions all play a significant role in decisions, even at the very highest levels.*

"Normal" politics is not the only arena in which personal decisions can have global significance. Assassinations have occasionally changed the course of history, at least marginally. The assassinations of Presidents Lincoln, McKinley, and Kennedy; of Robert Kennedy; and of Martin Luther King are obvious cases. The famous assassination of the Archduke Ferdinand at Sarajevo in 1914 was the immediate excuse for World War I, although hardly the real cause. For centuries Japanese internal politics has been influenced by assassinations (and the threat of assassination), although the conspirators have generally been political insiders rather than outsiders. A number of assassinations were carried out by Japanese Army plotters in the period 1931–1939 to secure military control over the government. However, I see no prospect of forecasting future assassinations or their consequences.

Another interesting question that has concerned several forecasters is whether scientific or technological "breakthroughs" can be predicted. Again, I take it for granted that usually they cannot. The basic question to be addressed has to do with the *role* of individual crusaders, philosophers, spiritual leaders, discoverers, inventors, and innovators. To what extent has recent history been changed by individuals such as Charles Darwin, Karl Marx, Sigmund Freud, Gustave Hertz, Alexander Graham Bell, Thomas Edison, Henry Ford, Mahatma Ghandi, or Albert Einstein? In a certain sense, the answer must be that these people did, in fact, "make a difference." It is not really plausible to assert — with doctrinaire Marxists, for instance — that every great individual was, or is, no more than a surface symptom of some deeper historical force.†

The question at issue here is, essentially, whether these luminaries really "lit the way" for their contemporaries or whether, and to what extent, their light is actually reflected. To state the matter more prosaically, does invention tend to precede (and create) the demand for itself, or is it more often a response to a need that has already devel-

---

*Which is what makes the private memoirs of major political leaders like Nehru, Churchill, DeGaulle, and Krushchev so fascinating.
† A curious historical sidelight: the Marxist geneticist Lysenko made a major individual difference in the development of Soviet agriculture. His influence was retrogressive, as it happens.

oped? Although folklore persistently asserts the former and glorifies the "great" discoverers, inventors, and innovators, recently gathered evidence seems to point the other way. It is important to distinguish between invention and innovation (or adoption of the invention). It is easy to make a persuasive, but essentially irrelevant, case that inventions tend to occur as soon as supporting scientific research and other technological developments (innovations) make it possible. It can also be argued that invention only occurs in response to a definite need. Either theory can explain why there are so many otherwise inexplicable cases of "simultaneous" inventions in different places at roughly the same time. However, adoption for practical purposes is another matter, and here there is little doubt that needs come first.[16]

The rule has exceptions, to be sure, some of them important. The atomic bomb seems to have been built mainly because it (rather suddenly) was seen to be technically possible: President Roosevelt proceeded with the Manhattan Project because he had been persuaded by Leo Szilard and Eugene Wigner—through the intervention of Einstein—that the Nazis were already proceeding on a similar project. Military use clearly followed from possession of the weapon; it was not specifically planned at the outset, and many scientists opposed it. The laser, invented in 1962, seems to be another example of an invention that was widely developed and promoted before any social need for it was perceived. In this case, applications have followed from technical possibilities. These two well-known, but essentially, atypical, examples seem to be mainly responsible for the spread of the notion in the 1950s and 1960s that technology has a kind of "life of its own," and that anything that is technologically feasible will *automatically* be introduced and accepted.

In any case, it seems reasonable to conclude that the *rate* of discovery, invention, and innovation is to some extent controlled by policy decisions (e.g., concerning the level of research and development funding and the availability of funds for venture capital), but that the *directions* of social and technological change are likely to be determined by straightforward economic and political considerations.

To be absolutely clear on the issues, I think that the shape of the world of 2025 will *not* be primarily determined by the technological possibilities that have been so well described and enumerated by such scientific authors as Arthur C. Clarke and Dennis Gabor. These possibilities are relevant insofar as they prescribe *outer limits* to achievement in certain areas. They in no way imply that the limits will be reached or even approached. What is relevant to the methodological issue is that scientific and technical developments—in the large—probably belong to the "more-or-less predictable" category.

Although it is impossible (by definition) to predict either the timing or the detailed substance of major scientific discoveries or inventions — which is akin to trying to predict exactly when and where a bolt of lightning will strike — to the scientist who is successful (or his competitor who fails), the outcome is crucial. Just as it is probably enough to know in what geographic regions thunderstorms are likely to occur, from a societal standpoint, it is enough to forecast in which areas of technology the rate of progress will be greatest and, roughly, how fast that progress could be for given levels of support.

In the next three sections I discuss the dynamics of change from a slightly more technical perspective. The purpose of this review is to sharpen the analysis which comes later in the book. A small number of mathematical expressions are introduced along the way to clarify the discussion (for those who prefer symbolic language), but these are confined to footnotes and should not be an obstacle to a nonmathematical reader.

DYNAMICS OF CHANGE— GROWTH FUNCTIONS

It would be easy but pointless to forecast in an unchanging world. But the world is changing, which is what makes forecasting nontrivial and worthwhile. The next easiest assumption is that the key rates of change are unchanging. This is common, especially among alpha forecasters. If one takes this view (which I do not), the problem for a forecaster boils down to determining the various rates of change and the correct rule for extrapolation. Thus, if the rate of change of a variable — call it f — is constant, the variable itself must be an exponential function of time.* The variable f can then be extrapolated by plotting its historical values on paper with a linear scale on the horizontal (time) axis and a logarithmic scale on the vertical axis where they should fall on a straight line.[†] The extension of this straight-line trend into future times will show what the future values of f would be. Let me explain this in terms of a specific example.

---

*This can be verified by observing that if $f = A \exp(\mu t)$ then the rate of change is the partial derivative with respect to time, $f = \dfrac{\partial f}{\partial t} = \mu$, which is a constant.

[†] If the assumption of constant rate of change is valid.

The rate of increase of world population in 1970 was almost exactly 2% per year (see Chapter 4). If this value continued steady for fifty years, until 2020, world population at that point would be exactly

$$e^{0.02 \times 50} = e^{1.00} = 2.7183 \text{ times the 1970 level.}$$

That is, the factor of increase in fifty years would be 2.7183.

This kind of calculation is so simple, once you grasp the rules, that a kind of mystique has grown up around the exponential growth function. The electric utility industry in the United States (among others) has been totally entranced by the beauty and inevitability of exponential growth. Between 1950 and 1970 consumption of electric power grew at an average rate of 7.25% per annum. This is equivalent to almost exactly a factor of 2 increase every decade. If it continued for fifty years, this would result in an overall increase of $2^5 = 32$ times the 1970 consumption. Although this seems patently absurd, electric utility industry leaders have not considered it necessary to try to explain why such a massive increase in demand should occur.* Until recent (1973–1974) events affecting the energy industry, they simply regarded the historical rate of growth as a fact and concerned themselves with its implications, that is, how and where to build enough generating capacity to satisfy the expected demand. Figure 1.1 shows a selection of other examples of apparently exponential changes which might make the validity of exponentiation seem plausible (or, perhaps, implausible).[17]

Rather than regarding the exponential function as a useful approximation over short periods of time (which it undoubtedly is), a surprising amount of pseudoscientific mumbo jumbo has been written over the past half century to defend the proposition that exponential growth is a sort of natural law for human progress. Suffice it to say

---

*Donald Burnham, former President of Westinghouse Electric Company, quoted earlier in this chapter, merely insists on "allowing for" new energy-using devices "equivalent" to jet planes, air conditioning, plastics, fertilizers, and so on.

† Sometimes called a logistic curve, for obscure historical reasons. Mathematically the function may have the form

$$f = A \frac{\exp(\mu t)}{1 + \exp(\mu t)}$$

(other forms have also been used.) Its first derivative with respect to time (rate of change) is a function of time, not a constant. The derivative is small when f itself is small, rising to a peak and then declining again toward zero when f approaches its upper limit.

$$f = \frac{\partial f}{\partial t} = A \frac{\exp(\mu t)}{(1 + \exp(\mu t))^2}$$

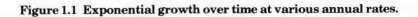

Figure 1.1 Exponential growth over time at various annual rates.

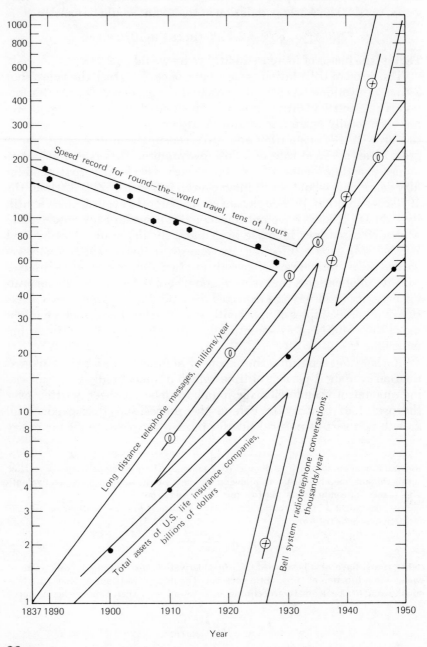

Year

that the evidence really cannot be stretched this far.

Recently a silly controversy has arisen among some futurists as to whether the "true" long-term growth function is exponential (as many have assumed) or whether it is actually slower or faster than an exponential. A favorite example of a slower growth function is the so-called Pearl-Verhulst function,[†] which has the form of a stretched-out S curve. As the growth process begins, this function starts out behaving like an increasing exponential function, but gradually slows down and eventually approaches a fixed upper limit, or asymptote.

This kind of "saturation" behavior that occurs with a logistic function is characteristic of certain biological models, such as the growth of bacteria or yeast in an environment containing a fixed amount of nutrients. When only a few bacteria are present, the environment is relatively infinite in extent, and growth is determined only by the natural reproduction rate of the species — that is, it is exponential. Later, however, as the population grows, it begins to be limited by competition for available resources, and the rate of reproduction is slowed down because of the build up of toxic wastes. Eventually a limiting "sustainable" level is reached. This model of change has also been applied to a number of situations, especially where one technology is substituting for another. Some examples are displayed in Figure 1.2, taken from a recent article on technological forecasting.[18] The corresponding rule for extrapolation in this case is somewhat more complex, involving coordinate transformations, but it is still relatively straightforward.*

It has also been suggested based on some empirical observations that the "true" long-term growth function for several important macromeasures of Man, including population and technological change, is really faster than an exponential function.[19] That is to say, if one looks closely at historical data for a number of macrovariables, it appears that the rates of change have not really been constant, but have recently been increasing. As shown in Chapter 4, a better fit to the historical population data is obtained if one uses a hyperbolic function of time in place of the usual exponential one.[†] A relatively straightfor-

---

*A bit too much for a nonmathematical exposition. If you are deeply interested, see the article by Fisher and Pry, from which Fig. 1.2 was taken.

[†] One convenient mathematical form is $f = \dfrac{A}{t_0 - t}$

The time rate of change is increasing, viz., $\dot{f} = \dfrac{\partial f}{\partial t} = \dfrac{A}{(t_0 - t)^2}$

The usefulness of this mathematical form is limited by the fact that both the function and its derivative become infinite at time $t = t_0$.

ward extrapolation rule exists in this case too. Whereas an exponential function of time can be plotted as a straight line on paper with a linear horizontal (time) scale and logarithmic vertical scale, the hyperbolic function plots as a straight line on log-log paper with logarithmic scales on both axes.

As it happens, the hyperbolic function leads eventually to an impossible result, namely, that the variable eventually becomes infinite in a finite time. In the case of world population, several curve-fitting studies have independently reached the interesting conclusion that world population reaches infinite values close to the year 2025. This does not mean the Day of Judgment is approaching. It merely means that the hyperbolic function *cannot* be a good approximation, at least not as we get closer to the year of singularity — 2025. At some point some other (slower) growth function must take over again.

What does one conclude from all this? Unfortunately, what it boils down to is that no really simple mathematical model is likely to be any

Figure 1.2 Examples of logistic change in modern society.

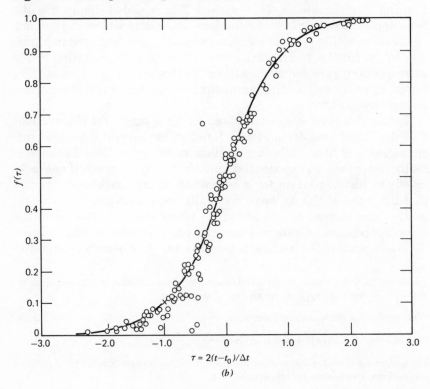

$$\tau = 2(t - t_0)/\Delta t$$

(b)

good at all. The kinds of model that will have to be used to do quantitative long-term forecasting are quite sophisticated and difficult to describe. In effect, each factor depends on many other factors, allowing for some lags (of variable length) in the system. A change in the value of any major indicator from this year to next will affect other indicators later on. Conversely, the change that is occurring now must be attributed to still other changes that occurred in the past. Such a model is classified technically as a multivariable recursive simulation model. All the large-scale economic forecasting models now in use (Wharton, Brookings, etc.) are basically of this type.*

I make some quantitative projections (mainly Chapters 4 and 5) where a purely qualitative discussion seemed to be inadequate. The method I generally use to project population and some economic variables has no formal name. It uses exponential growth functions, but with a key difference. Instead of assuming $f(t) = A \exp(\mu t)$, I have allowed both the coefficient A and the rate μ to vary over time also, viz.,

$$f(t) = A(t) \exp[\mu(t) \cdot t]$$

Such a function is actually quite general even though it does not look at first like a recursion scheme. Defined thus, $f(t)$ can have any behavior at all. If $A(t)$ and $\mu(t)$ vary slowly enough, the growth function is quasiexponential. If $A(t)$ is constant or increasing and $\mu(t)$ is increasing monotonically over time, $f(t)$ grows faster than an exponential, and conversely.

The "real" $A(t)$ and $\mu(t)$ are understood not to be explicit functions of time, *per se,* but functions of other factors which change over time. In practice, I shortcircuit the implicit variable scheme by simply specifying $A(t)$ and $\mu(t)$ based on case-by-case judgments. A more elaborate method could not be justified for a broad-gauge study such as this. There is no further mathematical discussion in this book.

DYNAMICS OF CHANGE — ACCELERATORS AND BRAKES

As I argue in the preceding pages, there is no universally valid growth function—still less one that can be determined by empirical means, that is, by playing around with plotting historical data points on var-

*The equations in the models reflect postulated cause-effect relationships, although they are statistically fitted from observed correlations. Causality can only be imputed, never directly verified.

ious types of graph paper. Each of the three types of time-dependent growth function mentioned has its occasional use; still other types may be needed. Several different simplifying models can be applied, depending on circumstances. What seems to be needed is guidance as to which basic model of change is most appropriate in a given case.

Often an analytic distinction is helpful in such a situation. One that may be helpful is a dichotomy between two seemingly fundamental processes of change: *compound growth* and *substitution*. The terms are more or less self-explanatory. An interest-bearing account in a savings bank is the archetype of the first category. If one shifts money from one investment into another — say, from telephone stock to steel stock — it is clearly a case of substitution.

On reflection, however, one can see that the distinction between compound growth and substitution is not as clear as one would like. Ambiguity is not only possible, it is commonplace. For instance, animal population growth in an unlimited environment is clearly an example of compound growth. However, if two species (or countries) are competing for a limited territory, one can only succeed at the expense of the other. Thus growth in this case is actually equivalent to substitution. These are extreme cases, of course. Almost any combination of compounding and substitution can be conceived.

Evidently substitution involves the element of competition somewhere; it appears that compound growth is actually a special limiting case of substitution where there is no competition between alternatives. In reality there are few, if any, "infinite" environments to accommodate compound growth indefinitely. When the upper limits —because of finite resource availability or demand—begin to influence the compounding process, competition for resources or markets begins to occur. Of course, competition may occur between members of the same industry, community, or species, or between different industries, communities, or species. As resources in their original form are converted into some other form, for example, sugar is converted into biomass by growing yeast cells, the process can be described as substitution (of yeast for sugar). Similarly, as one competitor displaces another in a finite market, a substitution can be said to occur.

Another useful analytic distinction involves the concept of a *feedback loop*. The idea is, simply, that a change in one part of a complex system triggers a change somewhere else in the system which, in turn, either reinforces or opposes the original impulse. These two cases are termed positive and negative feedback loops, respectively. A mechanism with positive feedback is self-accelerating—and inherently unstable—whereas one with negative feedback is self-limiting and inherently stable.

It is easier to think of examples of self-limiting systems in nature than self-accelerating ones. Most biological and ecological systems, for instance, have built-in negative feedback control mechanisms that tend to oppose and compensate for externally induced changes.* For instance, if a warm-blooded animal is exposed to a cold environment, its capillaries contract (to reduce heat loss) and its metabolic rate increases. It may curl up to reduce the exterior surface from which heat can be lost. It will also seek shelter. On the other hand, if it is exposed to a hot environment, it will maintain its temperature by increasing the rate of evapotranspiration of water (through skin and/ or lungs), reducing its metabolic rate, and avoiding the direct sun.

In a complex ecosystem the controls work in a similar manner. For instance, when a fire destroys a forest, the heat often causes long-dormant seeds to germinate, thus speeding recovery. Similarly, a localized insect outbreak attracts insect-eating birds from miles around. The favorable food supply also encourages breeding, and the bird population rapidly increases — until the outbreak is suppressed. The growth of a species in a limited environment — already mentioned in another context — evidences several negative feedbacks. With less food less readily available, growth is slower and breeding rates are reduced. Toxic metabolic wastes build up, and individuals are weaker and less resistant to attack or infection. Thus the death rates rise. Interspecies predation, such as the bird-bug example, involves more complex negative feedbacks. As the prey population grows it attracts a predator population which suppresses it. When the prey in turn becomes scarce, the predators starve or disperse.

Self-accelerating inherently unstable systems seem to be mostly man made. (There may be an unstable feedback system involving CO_2, which will be discussed in Chapter 8, but I do not describe it here.) One of the classic examples is the great stock market crash of 1929. The mechanism was quite a simple but devastating one. Interest rates in the 1920s were kept artificially low by the Federal Reserve Board. Money was "easy." Many people had made use of easy money to purchase stock on margin — meaning with borrowed money — using the stock itself as collateral. When the Federal Reserve Board finally raised interest rates in a belated attempt to slow down the unjustified speculation, they succeeded far too well. As the first large downward price fluctuation occurred, the value of the collateral dropped; worried lenders, wanting to protect their assets, tried to cash in some of the stock they were holding as collateral. Since there were more sellers than buyers, the stock prices were depressed further. This cut into the

---

*This property is known to biologists as homeostasis.

collateral still further, causing more stock to be dumped, causing the price to drop still more, and so forth. Prices eventually dropped to less than 10% of their 1929 highs.

The Great Depression was another example of a positive feedback self-accelerating phenomenon.* It was triggered by the stock market crash, which resulted in a massive contraction of financial assets; people were much poorer in 1931 than they had been in 1921. This disappearance of wealth led to a sharp reduction of consumer confidence and a consequent cutback in spending. Thus demand for goods and services dropped. As a consequence, employers laid off unnecessary workers to reduce payroll expenses and cut back on capital spending for expansion. This reduced consumer buying power still more, resulting in a further erosion of confidence. Demand dropped again. Production and payroll costs were cut back further in response, and so on.

Of course, even a man-made self-accelerating system cannot go on indefinitely. Eventually something must bring it to a halt. In the case of the United States economic system, the downward spiral was finally halted in the mid-1930s by compensatory public consumption activities on the part of the government. However, not until public consumption reached a very high level as a result of rearmament for World War II—which also put an end to the depression mentality—did the economy recover fully.

A consolidation of several of the foregoing ideas seems appropriate at this point. To begin with, one can equate exponential and compound growth. They are mathematically equivalent. Furthermore, the competition and substitution phenomenon, as applied to biological species, communities, nations, industries, or technologies, is clearly an example of self-limiting growth (i.e., subject to negative feedback). Examples are numerous. Indeed, all growth processes must evidently be self-limiting in the very long run, since the solar system is finite.[†]

Are there any examples of self-accelerating growth (subject to positive feedback) over significant historical times? Any trend which is demonstrably faster than exponential for a period of time must presumably have this character. It has been suggested already that world population and some measures of technological capability have been progressing hyperexponentially. If so, a positive feedback must be involved. It is vitally important to understand the nature of this feedback phenomenon *precisely because it must be temporary*—no self-accelerating process can continue indefinitely. This means that every

---

*The acceleration was, of course, in the downward direction.
[†] So, for that matter, is the Universe.

positive feedback loop must itself be subject to some overriding negative feedback with a longer (but finite) response time. Unfortunately, when the upper limit is finally reached, the positive feedback mechanism may again come into play on the reverse slope, as it were, leading to an accelerated decline (or "crash").

Again, the 1929 stock market crash offers a helpful insight. Positive feedback resulting from the built-in financial leverage in the system tended to accelerate the decline of market prices from their peak. How did prices get so high in the first place? It was the same leverage mechanism (stimulated by easy money and low-interest loans) operating in the other direction! As prices rose, the value of collateral increased, and people were able to expand their margin purchases. This process created new demand for stock and kept forcing prices up and up. Many naive investors assumed that the magical process of creating something from nothing would go on forever.* It did not because, of course, it could not. It matters not what precise event tilted the balance. If the Federal Reserve Board had not been the culprit, something else would have triggered the wave of selling that converted a self-accelerating bull market into a self-accelerating bear market.

DYNAMICS OF CHANGE—
ROLE OF CRISIS IN HUMAN AFFAIRS

I have been discussing change as though it always proceeds gradually and smoothly. But, although underlying factors do tend to change gradually, their visible manifestations are often sharp and violent, as though restraining forces are suddenly overwhelmed. There is a great deal of evidence that human institutions do not adjust very readily to small pressures. This is probably because of negative feedback loops which give institutions — like individuals — a built-in capability to preserve themselves in their original form. As pressures build, the institution reacts defensively, hardening its shell, so to speak, to ward off external threats. Not until the pressures become overwhelming and some sort of crisis or revolution occurs is the institution swept away or reformed in a fundamental way.

*The boom in conglomerate stocks in the late 1960s resulted from a comparable case of positive feedback. Aggressive (go-go) conglomerates with high price/earnings ratios were able to acquire stodgy older companies with hidden assets and low price-earnings ratios. The unused assets were then converted into fast earnings, creating new acquisition capabilities for the conglomerates. Not surprisingly, this cycle too culminated in massive financial troubles on Wall Street (1969–1974).

A fascinating example of this phenomenon is occurring in Lebanon as I write. A complex political system was devised in 1943 sharing political power permanently, but unequally, between the then majority Maronite Christians and minority Sunni Moslems and Druze communities. Christians held the presidency, command of the army, and a 6 to 5 ratio of seats in Parliament. Since 1943, however, the Moslem population has increased faster than the Christian population. Most observers think the Moslems are now a majority in the country. Apparently sharing this general suspicion, the dominant Christians refused to conduct a census (the last was in 1932). The Moslems have pressed for reforms, and the Christians stubbornly refused. Recent violence was triggered by the presence of large numbers of armed Palestinian refugees (Moslem) living in camps throughout Lebanon. Palestinians used Lebanese camps as a basis for conducting commando raids into Israel, thus attracting Israeli retaliation against Lebanon. This activity has been generally supported by the Lebanese Moslems, but opposed by the Christians—especially the Rightists—who wanted to disarm the Palestinians. Subsequently, of course, the Syrians intervened to exploit a power vacuum, and a new, probably unstable, equilibrium has been created under effective Syrian domination.

The Lebanese case is only one of many examples that could be cited. The violence in Ulster (Northern Ireland) broke out because politically dominant Protestants refused to concede overdue political or civil rights of minority Catholics, although the United Kingdom government as a whole would like to do so. The Catholics, in turn, are supported by the Eire-based IRA, whose major objective is to eliminate the British "presence" from Northern Ireland and permit reunification of the country. Without doubt, everyone including the Ulster Protestants would be much better off with such an outcome,* but there seems to be no peaceful way to bring it about.

Not all revolutions actually involve physical violence, of course. The violence may be verbal or financial on occasion. Women's rights, civil (i.e., Black) rights, and environmentalist and consumerist reforms also fit the revolutionary description. In each case nothing was done at all for many decades until the pressure built to an explosive level—at which point the resistance to change crumbled and new institutional structures were created. Women got the right to vote only in the early years of the twentieth century after long and violent agita-

*Catholic Eire has never discriminated against Protestants. It has even had a Protestant President. Moreover, Eire is now economically progressive and growing, whereas Northern Ireland is a depressed area, with very poor prospects under its present regime.

tion, primarily in England. (The currently active women's rights movement is much less intense, probably because the remaining inequalities are far less serious.)

Recent (1972–1975) modifications of the world monetary system constitute still another case in point. Although the old (Bretton-Woods) system of fixed exchange rates was no longer working, it took a full-scale "exchange crisis," two rapid-fire unilateral devaluations of the dollar (August 1972 and March 1973), unilateral demonetization of gold by the United States, and a major world recession to convince the nations of the world that a new system was imperative. Even so, progress toward an agreement has been agonizingly slow.

There is an interesting physical analogy to the earthquake phenomenon. The Earth's crust has weak spots, of course. There are cracks, called "faults," and one might think that blocks of crustal material could shift slowly along fault lines to reduce stresses. However, this does not happen because of resistance to change, due to frictional forces. Instead of adjusting gradually, no motion at all occurs until the stress forces exceed a certain minimum threshold level, at which the resistance of friction is overcome. Then, once motion begins, the resistance of friction sharply decreases. Thus the crustal movement occurs suddenly and violently.*

In human affairs, too, stresses and strains, reflecting deep internal instabilities, can build up to enormous levels. Yet the institutions of society – church, unions, government agencies, business, schools, and so on – tend to resist strongly any change imposed on them from outside. Indeed, faced by an external threat, they tend to react by purging any internal sympathizers with the external critics, thus becoming more rigid and unbending than before. The response of the Catholic Church to Protestant critics was to create the Office of the Inquisition for the avowed purpose of rooting out heresy. In all probability, the cause of church reform was set back a century or two by this reactionary response to criticism.

In modern times one sees a similar phenomenon in a number of emerging nations. Landowners and members of privileged elites have frequently embraced reactionary political regimes in the name of international anticommunism in an effort to suppress legitimate dissent

---

*It is a similar phenomenon that leads to skidding in automobiles. The tires roll on the pavement – with no slipping at all – until the braking forces exceed a certain threshold level. At this point the skid begins because sliding friction is less than rolling friction. Then braking action virtually disappears. To regain control of the car, it is necessary to reestablish a rolling motion by taking one's foot off the brake.

forcibly, rather than accommodating themselves to it by undertaking necessary internal political and economic reforms. Since totally effective suppression of dissent is not really possible in this age of mass communication—except in a totalitarian society—the attempt can only increase the pressures and the violence of the ultimate explosion.

In Rhodesia and South Africa, too, we see the typical reactionary syndrome in action. In response to increasing pressures to extend political rights and economic opportunity to a majority Black population, the white minority government has resorted to repression and military action.* This can only make matters worse in the long run. When the forces demanding change ultimately overcome the forces "holding the lid on," the result is likely to be an extremely violent explosion in which much blood will be shed.

Clearly, the type of violent crisis that we have had the most experience with in the past is war. War has occurred primarily between nation states, especially in Europe. Two questions therefore arise. First, will the nation state be the natural "unit," so to speak, in human affairs during the next half century? Or, on the contrary, is the role of nation states declining? Is there any possibility of multilateral institutions being created with an ability to moderate and mediate the frictions between the member states? The second question, of equal importance in the next half century, is whether stresses between neighboring political units—whether those units are nation states or larger groupings—can be relieved by crises short of war? Is it possible that financial crises, depressions, inflations, famines, or perhaps some kind of crisis beyond our historical experience will allow for the necessary relief of stress to occur through mechanisms other than the ultimate in violent conflict?

Perhaps the most important challenge for Mankind is to learn how to design institutions that are self-reforming. I do not know whether this is possible or whether any examples now exist of institutions which have successfully reformed themselves. The U.S. Constitution may be as good an example as there is, at least in the political sphere. Some institutions seem to be more flexible than others, and perhaps we can learn by finding out the difference between the ones that have survived for a long time with changing circumstances (like the churches) and those which are shattered and destroyed entirely when the cumulative stresses exceed the ability of the institution to resist.

---

*Since this was written, the Rhodesian situation has changed, and the era of white supremacy appears to have come to an end. The nature of the next regime is highly uncertain at present.

The fact that societies seem unable to reform themselves gradually, but rather resist change until pressures become overwhelming, also raises the question as to whether a "quasicrisis" of some sort might conceivably be engineered on occasion as a means of deliberately bringing about a set of conditions in which basic reforms could be made.*

Is there such a thing as a major crisis without pain or bloodshed? In the last few years Portugal has provided an illustration of a relatively bloodless crisis, although, by definition, there can be no crisis without some major readjustments and consequently some pain. Some groups gain power, others lose power; some gain wealth at the expense of others. In the most extreme kind of crisis almost everybody loses, but generally speaking there are at least a few winners.

Having said all this, mainly with reference to the Western countries, I think it is appropriate to comment on the nature of the possible crisis in the communist countries. These seem to be a special case. Most have the superficial appearance of being extremely stable, but the appearance of stability in Eastern Europe is somewhat deceptive, since it is mostly enforced by the military power of the Soviet Union. China has not actually been a model of stability, although much of the turmoil has been hidden from the outside world. Stability *within* the USSR has been maintained for a number of decades, but only with the help of intensive internal surveillance of citizens, overwhelming police power, direct governmental control over the movement of citizens, trade, movements of capital, and information flow. These restrictions on personal freedom are pervasive to an extent that is utterly unknown in the Western World and which citizens of the democratic regimes of the West would consider intolerable. Repression has stimulated the development of a very persistent dissident group of intellectuals, as exemplified by Solzhenitsyn, Sakharov et al. Dissidence, in turn, has triggered still more severe repressive measures, which are probably limited only by Soviet concerns about maintaining an image of "socialist democracy."

It is difficult to guess how this kind of conflict might result in an "ultimate" crisis — the kind that could collapse a regime. I suspect that the government can contain the intellectual dissidents more or less

---

*Continuing the earthquake analogy, this would be like deliberately triggering a series of "small" earthquakes to relieve the tectonic stresses and prevent a large and destructive cataclysm. Interestingly, the technology for doing this is in existence today, but the institutional framework that would be required to permit it has not been put into place. Probably nothing will be done until after the next really destructive quake.

indefinitely, although at considerable cost in terms of internal morale and efficiency. A really severe political crisis would probably not occur until or unless there are very severe economic difficulties of some kind. This raises the question as to whether a high level of internal repression against intellectuals could cause the creative "growing tip" of technology to be stultified, leading to economic stagnation, and the inability to compete in foreign markets and to satisfy the economic aspirations of some critical segment of society.

It is not inconceivable that even a technologically advanced society like the Soviet Union could be toppled by a *coup d'etat,* assuming sufficiently widespread dissatisfaction among a critical segment, such as middle-level managers. In the case of the Soviet Union there are further problems arising from unhappy minority groups, such as the Jews (who have been discriminated against in Russia for centuries), and other national or ethnic groups, such as the Volga Germans, Balts, Ukranians, Kurds, Georgians, and so forth.

It would be foolish to expect these national/ethnic groups alone to topple the power of the Soviet central government, but in combination with a crisis of economic origin they might help to do so. It is also pertinent, in this context, that in the case of the Soviet Union there is a critical problem with agriculture. Although spectacular increases in average (and maximum) production have been recorded, there are big fluctuations from year to year, leading to recurrent shortages. Moreover, the Soviet regime has never been able to cope adequately with the agricultural sector as such. It seems not out of the question that a major misallocation of resources, combined with an unfavorable climatic change, could lead to a severe food crisis—or even an agricultural revolt. Some combination of these things could conceivably bring about a collapse and modification of the entire top-heavy system.

In the next seven chapters a number of key measures of Man, measures of technology, and measures of the environment are examined. The purpose is to determine current aggregate quantitative rates of change where possible. In addition, an effort is made to assess the nature of positive and negative feedback mechanisms that can be identified. We look particularly for two kinds of situations designated *short-run unstable* and *short-run meta-stable.*

The short-run unstable case, exemplified by the stock market of the 1920s, is characterized by significant positive feedback that tends to produce excessive changes in the state variables before being limited by overriding negative feedback forces. The result is a series of wild oscillations.

The short-run meta-stable case is exemplified by an institution—

governmental or other—that reacts to threats by hardening its position instead of adapting gradually. Among governments, white minority regimes (Rhodesia and South Africa), anticommunist dictatorships, such as South Korea and Chile, and repressive East European communist regimes are prime examples. Faced by internal dissidence, they escalate repression. Many large corporations faced with challenges by consumerists, environmentalists, or dissident stockholders have reacted similarly by attacking the opposition, rather than by acting to eliminate its major grievances.*

Generally speaking, when an institution refuses to bend or reform itself in response to pressure, the pressure continues to grow. The institutional resistance to change is often itself a factor contributing to the buildup, but not usually the dominant one. The pressures that tend to bring about crises arise from changes in the outside world—increased population, urbanization, prosperity, education, facility of communication, and so forth. In the long run, the human institution must either bend and adapt or be broken. An important aspect of this book is to assess critical institutions in terms of their likely response to foreseeable pressures.

REFERENCES

1. For a good example of this type of thinking, see the U.S. Office of Management and Budget Forecast, published in *The Futurist,* August 1974.
2. For example, "U.S. Energy Outlook," Report of the National Petroleum Council, December 1972; or "National Energy Outlook 1976," Federal Energy Administration.
3. Donald C. Burnham, Appendix, "A Time to Choose—America's Energy Future," Final Report of the Energy Policy Project of the Ford Foundation, Ballinger Publishing Company, Cambridge, Mass., 1974, p. 56. Reprinted with permission.
4. D. Meadows et al., *Limits to Growth,* Universe Books, New York, 1972.
5. G. O'Neill, "The High Frontier," *The Futurist X,* No. 1, Feb 1956.
6. Paolo Soleri, Retrospective Exhibition, "Arcology," The Corcoran Gallery, Washington, D. C., 1968. Also "Ten Elements for Discussion," 1968.
7. Arthur C. Clarke, *Profiles of the Future: An Inquiry Into the Limits of the Possible,* Harper and Row, New York, 1958. Reprinted with permission.
8. Vannevar Bush, quoted by Clarke, *Ibid.*
9. Robert W. Prehoda, *Designing the Future: The Role of Technological Forecasting,* Chilton Book Company, Philadelphia, 1967, p. 5.

*In all fairness, some corporations have reacted positively to challenges. Others seem to have belatedly learned a (costly) lesson. A few seem to have learned nothing.

10. Larry Niven, *The Long Arm of Gil Hamilton*, Ballantine Books, New York, 1976.
11. Lewis Mumford, *The Myth of the Machine: The Pentagon of Power*, Harcourt Brace Jovanovich, New York, 1964, p. 223.
12. C. P. Snow, "The Two Cultures and the Scientific Revolution," Godkin Lectures, Cambridge University Press, 1959.
13. H. Kahn, W. Brown, and L. Martel, *The Next 200 Years: A Scenario for America and the World*, W. Morrow and Company, New York, 1976.
14. For a popular overview, see Carl Sagan, *The Dragons of Eden*, Random House, 1977.
15. Thomas S. Kuhn, *Structure of Scientific Revolutions*, University of Chicago Press, Chicago, 1962.
16. See for example, S. C. Gilfillan, "The Prediction of Inventions" in *National Trends and National Policy*, U. S. Natural Resources Council, Washington, D. C., 1937.
17. L. Ridenour, *Bibliography In An Age of Science*, Univ. of Illinois Press, Urbana, Ill. 1951.
18. J. C. Fisher and R. H. Pry, "A Simple Substitution Model of Technological Change," *Technological Forecasting and Social Change 3*, 75–88 (1971).
19. F. Meyer and J. Vallee, "The Dynamics of Long Term Growth," *Technological Forecasting and Social Change 7*, 285–300 (1975).

CHAPTER TWO

MEASURES OF MAN
—VALUES

INTRODUCTORY REMARKS

Forecasting is history extended: It is the study of the state of mind,
actions, and achievements of Man, through time as yet unborn. In the
study of history (allowing for some uncertainty), we know effects and
can often infer causes. In the study of history extended, we know only
the present and the past—history actual. It is therefore essential to
take man's measure. Hence the running title of this and the five chapters that follow: "Measures of Man." Measures of Man has been divided into a group of natural categories: sociopolitical, international,
demographic/macroeconomic, microeconomic, and technological.

This division is more than merely arbitrary. It is somewhat astonishing, but easily verifiable, as mentioned in Chapter 1, that one group
of forecasters—notably "humanists"—has concerned itself almost exclusively with the sociopolitical factors discussed in this chapter and
the following one. Another group, including the quantitative modelers,
has concentrated almost exclusively on the demographic-/economic di-
mension considered in Chapters 4 and 5. A third distinct group has
focused narrowly on the scientific and technological prospects (and
threats) taken up in Chapters 6 and 7. Each group has virtually ignored the others.

This trichotomy of different orientations is the more significant in
light of the fact that the topics considered here and in Chapter 3 and
again in Chapters 6 and 7 are almost all qualitative, whereas the
issues in Chapters 4 and 5 are more quantifiable. I have already commented on the fact that people who are accustomed to thinking quantitatively tend to avoid dealing with qualitative issues, and vice versa.
Evidently the human mind tends to work in watertight compartments.
Although disciplinary compartmentalization can be understood, it cannot be tolerated in a serious forecast. All kinds of issues belong among

the Measures of Man and to overlook any of them can unbalance a forecast to the point of irrelevance if not outright falsification.

HISTORICAL BACKGROUND

An interesting paradox immediately encountered in the study of socio-political matters is the fact that the concerns which matter most to us as human beings are precisely the ones about which we have most difficulty being objective. In any period of history, the issues that are central to peoples' lives provoke intense — even violent — discussion and controversy. Thus 300–400 years ago in Europe people were deeply aroused by differences on points of religious doctrine. Religion was a dominating passion of the times — to a degree that is difficult to comprehend today. Individuals not conforming to the prevailing religious practices and beliefs ran the risk of social ostracism, economic discrimination, physical persecution, and sometimes even martyrdom.

In the eighteenth and nineteenth centuries, religious institutions and feudal dynasties declined markedly in their power to command allegiance and were replaced to a considerable extent by another center of attraction. Nation states increased in power, cohesion and self-consciousness during these centuries, and much of the energy that people had once devoted to the defense and propagation of religious doctrine they now gave to the building and defending of "their" countries. Patriotism became a primary emotional driving force for much of the world.

Yet close on the heels of the growth of loyalty to the nation, came another form of allegiance: loyalty to one or another political ideology. Political movements such as a democratic republicanism (modeled on the United States) or socialism (mainly in Europe) have developed a powerful impetus and affected great numbers of people.

The key manifesto of democratic republicanism was, of course, the *Declaration of Independence* of the American colonies of Great Britain. It was written by Thomas Jefferson in 1776, two centuries ago. The most quoted words in that document are

> We hold these truths to be self-evident, that all Men are created equal, that they are endowed by their Creator with certain unalienable Rights, that among these are Life, Liberty and the Pursuit of Happiness, that to secure these Rights governments are instituted among Men . . .

The philosophy of government expressed in these immortal words derives, originally, from the notion of the "social contract," which was evolved mainly in monarchic France by Jean-Jacques Rousseau, Voltaire, and others, as a substitute for the discredited "divine right of kings." In the new United States of America, hereditary rulers were rejected from the start. Men were to rule themselves through permanent institutions operated by replaceable elected officials. Liberty— meaning many things, but particularly freedom from oppression by kings or their representatives—was perhaps the central theme of the *Declaration,* and it was a powerful one.

In an era in which power and position were determined by birth, it must have seemed a considerable effrontery to the established order for a group of unsophisticated farmers, shopkeepers, and lawyers to claim the right—and the ability—to govern themselves. In the prevailing ideology of the eighteenth century the rights of life and liberty only belonged to the Crown, which, according to ancient tradition supported by the established church, derived these rights from God. Thus the American *Declaration,* from the viewpoint of this tradition, is close to both sacrilege and blasphemy and so it was viewed, not only by the crowned heads of Europe, but also by a considerable number—possibly a majority—of the American colonists as well.

The divine rights of kings is, of course, no longer a live issue in most of the world. Emperor Haile Selassie, one of the last "divinely appointed" monarchs, was finally overthrown only a few years ago. In Europe, the remaining monarchies are, in reality, social democracies retaining the king or queen as a powerless ceremonial head of State to maintain historical continuity and tradition. However the claim of an individual right to liberty or personal freedom, superior to the rights of the State—as stated in the *Declaration of Independence*—remains a focus of fierce controversy even in the United States. Americans of the present generation do not agree on how much liberty ought to be allowed or to whom (To women? To unborn children? To teenage children? To the dying? To students? To homosexuals? To reporters and publishers?) or even on whether liberty itself is necessarily a good thing. Libertarianism is actually an epithet in many quarters.

The *Declaration of Independence* also promised every individual an equal right to "the pursuit of happiness." This has been restated more succinctly as the right to "equality of opportunity." This phrase was originally interpreted somewhat narrowly and not initially extended to women, Black slaves, or native American Indians. (It is probably fair to suggest that most of the signatories of the *Declaration,* and particularly the Federalists, regarded the key words as merely a pretty but meaningless sentiment.) However, the populist Jeffersonians and Jacksonians who came to power in the early nineteenth century took the idea of equality of opportunity quite seriously and did much to give it meaning.

Nevertheless, equality of opportunity has been an elusive goal. With growing disparities in wealth to compensate for such innovations as universal education, it is hard to say whether opportunity is distributed more equally in twentieth century America—apart from progress in eliminating legal discrimination for reasons of race, sex, or religion —than it was in the original thirteen colonies. In any case, "equality of opportunity" in the United States was never intended to mean actual equality of status or income. However, this notion was soon introduced in Europe.

On the heels of the American Revolution came the French Revolution (1789–1792) with its famous slogan *"Liberté, Egalité, Fraternité."* Fraternity, or brotherhood, is not an idea that evokes much response today. In eighteenth century France it was probably intended to remind the rural peasants and urban workers, artisans, and shopkeepers of their common French nationality and their common interest in throwing off the yoke of an intolerable oppression by entrenched privileged classes. The explicit addition of "equality" to the American political ideal of liberty was truly radical. Even though the word was perhaps more narrowly interpreted at the time than later on, it went far beyond the position the vast majority in both Europe and America of that time was prepared to take.

Liberty from an oppressive and unresponsive foreign government was the American colonists' chief objective. They wanted the right to make their own laws, levy their own taxes, pursue their legitimate business in peace, speak their own minds, and worship as they pleased. Equality was envisioned only in terms of treatment under the law (Blacks, Indians, and women excepted), and equality, of property, income, or position in society was no part of the colonists original concept. Nor for that matter did the majority in revolutionary France demand or expect real equality in all things. The independent French peasant wanted clear title to his land and freedom from onerous taxation and repression by clerics and aristos. The shopkeeper and factory owner, too, wanted to be left alone (*laissez-faire*) without interference by a corrupt and captious bureaucracy headed by an incompetent king and his lavish parasitic court. The French Revolution was far too radical for its time.

Egalité was vigorously pursued for a few months by applying the equalizing guillotine mercilessly to "aristos"—and later to the chief Jacobins themselves. When the blood stopped flowing, inequality still remained both de facto and de jure. *Fraternité* brought the French people enthusiastically together to fight off a series of Royalist invasions and later to undertake major foreign conquests, but within a few years of the Revolution, Napoleon Bonaparte was crowned Emperor of France, and, after Waterloo, even the despised Bourbons were restored in name, if not in full panoply of power. The French were back to hereditary monarchy for six more decades.

The United States, on the other hand, gradually consolidated a shaky voluntary Union of thirteen sovereign states under the world's first written democratic constitution. A remarkably stable form of government finally emerged which, apart from the temporary secession of some states during the Civil War (1861–1865), has survived intact and in the same form for 200 years. This is longer tenure than that of any other modern government except that of Iceland.* For most of its history the United States has been a beacon of liberty for the oppressed peoples of the world, attracting some 46,700,000 immigrants from nearly all countries in the period 1920 through 1974. Today, as former United States Ambassador to the United Nations, Daniel Patrick Moynihan has observed in many forums,[1] the democratic ideal is under heavy siege; other ideologies have arisen that seek to displace it. One of the burning questions about the future is whether democratic government as we know it can or will survive the wrenching challenges ahead. If not, to what form of government will the hitherto democratic nations of the world turn?

A system or an ideology is open to attack when it fails to deal effectively with major problems. America's major failure may have been in not confronting effectively enough the need for social justice—the French *Egalité*, or what I prefer to call "equity." Slavery, to be sure, was abolished by the Emancipation Proclamation in 1864, but the Black population of the United States remained badly educated,

---

*At first glance, the oldest uninterrupted system of government (after Iceland) might appear to be that of Great Britain. However, the British government only achieved its modern form during the premiership of David Lloyd-George after the death of Queen Victoria. At that time the hitherto rampant and uncontrollable House of Lords was finally demoted to its present strictly advisory and ceremonial role. That the change was bloodless (and almost unnoticed by the body politic) does not mean that it was not of enormous significance. Britain had previously been a constitutional monarchy governed by a small aristocracy, which controlled both the House of Lords and the House of Commons. After Lloyd-George, it became a parliamentary democracy in fact, although not in name.

discriminated against, and sunk in deep poverty. There developed in the United States, as in industrialized Europe, enormous gaps between the large-scale farmers, merchants, bankers, and factory owners and the rest of the population forced to sell its labor by the hour or the day for an uncertain living. Power inexorably migrates into the hands of established wealth. This has left the industrial democracies incresingly vulnerable to attack by ideologies that promise "social justice" ahead of all else.

The problem of unequal distribution has existed throughout the ages, but it was made acute by the great accumulation of wealth in a few hands since the industrial revolution. Capitalism has been a fantastic success, in its own terms, since it was invented in Tudor England in the sixteenth century. However, what began as a device to facilitate trade with the Levant and India turned out to be far more relevant to the organization of manufacturing at home. By the early nineteenth century, English industrialism had already created some very severe social problems, especially the creation of noisome factory slums, such as the Midlands in England. Abetted by a corrupt political system which denied votes or effective representation to all but a small minority of property owners, small farmers and tenants were dispossessed and disenfranchised to become urban workers. In the slums of the cities they were unmercifully exploited. With the cards of power so blatantly stacked in favor of employers and owners (the "bourgeoisie") and against the "proletariat," it is hardly surprising that the notion of "class interest" and "class warfare" took root in the nineteenth century. As expressed in the words of Marx and Engels,[2]

> The modern laborer . . . instead of rising with the progress of industry, sinks deeper and deeper below the conditions of existence of his own class. He becomes a pauper, and pauperism develops more rapidly than population and wealth. And here it becomes evident that the bourgeoisie is unfit any longer to be the ruling class in society, and to impose its conditions of existence upon society as an over-riding law. It is unfit to rule, because it is incompetent to assure an existence to its slave within his slavery, because it cannot help letting him sink into such a state that it has to feed him, instead of being fed by him. Society can no longer live under this bourgeoisie. In other words, its existence is no longer compatible with society.

This theme was new, fresh, and attractive in the 1830s and 1840s. Millions were converted to the siren song of socialism. Faith in the

Marxist creed as the route to a promised land of social justice and abundance for all took on much of the emotional power of a religion. Like other religions, it transcended national boundaries, as was expressed in its militant rallying cry, "Workers of the world, unite!" This slogan never became a reality, of course. Socialist internationalism, based on a fairly theoretical brotherhood between members of a class, has never been capable of overcoming the narrower but stronger ties of language, culture, and religion. However, it has somewhat weakened the loyalties of at least one important segment of the population of the nation-states of Europe and America.

The conflict between nationalism and international socialism (and its variants) produced a horrifying pattern of political pathology in the years after World War I. Fascism in Italy and National Socialism (Naziism) in Germany were disguised as attempts to create a viable form of socialism in a purely nationalist framework. Stalinism followed a similar path in Russia after the fall of Leon Trotsky and Stalin's cynical conversion of Trotsky's Communist International (COMINTERN) into an instrument of Russian national policy. In every one of these cases socialist ideals were quickly sacrificed to nationalist aspirations, and the rhetoric of social justice became an Orwellian parody of itself.

Very possibly the present generation is tired of political ideology. Americans begin to show indications of growing skeptical of the politics of promises without performance. At the same time, United States moral leadership on behalf of the old ideals of freedom and democracy has declined, more or less, as United States political and economic power have increased. From the first American entry into imperialist adventures in the 1890s (however minor in scale) to the cynical military alliances of the 1950s and 1960s with reactionary and undemocratic regimes—as long as they were "anticommunist"—the role of ideology in the United States has become increasingly negative. Once admired as the seat of democracy, the United States has reached a point at which it is actually regarded as an enemy of social progress by many liberals within its own borders and by most intellectuals in the less developed countries.

Marxist ideology, too—which looked at one time as if it were about to sweep Europe—also seems to be suffering from hardening of the arteries. Although the Communist Party remains numerically strong in Italy and France, it appears that for most of Western Europe a communist vote is primarily a means of political protest against existing government policies rather than an expression of faith in the Communist Party program. The reduced dynamism of the communist-socialist movement is clearly related to the failure of the "flagship" of Marxism—the USSR—to pursue the original communist goals of social and economic justice and its lapse into Czarist habits of totalitarianism and territorial aggrandizement at the expense of neighboring countries. Many idealists who once embraced Marxism as the hope of the oppressed working class are now (reluctantly) beginning to see the USSR (like the United States) primarily as a nationalist and imperialist power. Some are even beginning to notice that the USSR also has a dismayingly repressive regime. Some European Communist parties—notably those of Italy, Spain, and France—have publicly commited themselves to work within the parliamentary framework. The Italian communists have even disavowed any intention to nationalize more of the economy than Mussolini's Fascists and the Christian Democrats have already done. Some formerly socialist intellectuals have even become disillusioned with socialism as an economic system.

Capitalism, however, has not emerged as a sufficiently satisfying answer to human needs, and it now attracts few (if any) passionate defenders, for reasons to be explored shortly. The nonsocialist labor movement, too, although still very much alive, has become institutionalized and is beginning to look like just another special interest concerned mainly with self-perpetuation and institutionalization of the hard-won rights and privileges of its immediate membership, rather than with meeting the needs of the working population at large.

These setbacks of ideological movements that once attracted such hopeful enthusiasm have left vast numbers of people, especially in the Western countries, groping for something to believe in. Many are apparently returning to some sort of evangelistic religion as an outlet for their energies and a center for their lives. But others cannot accept this answer, and many people today are left psychologically high and dry—in a state of "anomie"—with little to cling to. It is important to consider what effects this psychic void is likely to have on the society of the future.

Nationalism remains a major—if diminished—force, and its influence on the world in the next half-century also seems likely to be important. However, there are interesting indications that the force of nationalism in the older, more established nations may have lost some of its earlier potency. In any case, it seems less evident on the surface and is much less strident. I will take a closer look at the phenomenon in the next chapter. For the remainder of this chapter, I would like to examine, one by one, the principal domestic sociopolitical issues that may have important impacts over the next five decades.

COMPETING SOCIAL GOALS
AND IDEOLOGIES

The competition between the several sociopolitical ideologies of today can be better understood by examining the social goals embodied by each. What appears on the surface as a conflict of political systems can be interpreted rather as a competition between four paramount social goals which in practice have proved difficult to reconcile. These are

- Equity or social justice
- Economic efficiency (creation of wealth)
- Personal freedom
- Stability or order

In limiting the discussion to these four goals, I do not mean to suggest that others I have left out may not be more important — even dominant — for some individuals. Actually, the noneconomic aspects of equity could perhaps be omitted from the list, not because they are unimportant, but because they do not appear to be in fundamental conflict with other goals. I do not believe there is any serious obstacle to gradual but steady elimination of religious, racial, or sexual discrimination in Western society. Our descendants will be amazed that we (and particularly our parents and grandparents) discriminated on the basis of skin color alone. Race relations are likely to be very important in African affairs during the next half-century. On the other hand, Africa is not an especially important part of the present world, considered in a larger context.

Our ancestors would certainly have included virtue, or some equivalent, in the list of basic social goals. Our descendants may very well subtract one or more of the goals I have listed and add others. (For example, one might consider wisdom, civilization, or manners.) However, my list does not seek to achieve completeness, but rather some degree of clarity. I think the four goals I have listed are the most important ones for the majority of existing human societies. The chief point I want to make is that there are inherent contradictions between them. In most societies the pursuit of one or two goals to an extreme degree has resulted in sacrificing others.

At first glance there seems to be no reason why equity, efficiency, freedom, and stability need be in conflict. An enlightened society presumably should be able to enjoy all four. However, in historical fact, few (if any) countries have been able to do so for extended periods. To enjoy all of them at once the large majority of a society's members must have personal qualities of compassion and tolerance for others and respect for their rights and "the law," combined with self-discipline, some kind of work ethic, and the capacity to postpone immediate satisfactions for future well-being. The reasons become apparent as one examines how these goals are expressed in different political-economic systems.

Let me discuss the problem of stability first, since it is, to some extent, different in kind from the others. First, it can be argued that stability is not a goal *per se,* since an otherwise intolerable situation is not ameliorated by being made permanent. To say the least, stability and order are positive goals *only when other positive social goals are met at the same time.*

Another difference is that social instability or disorder is to some extent an automatic consequence of conflict between other social goals, viz., equity/efficiency, efficiency/freedom, and freedom/equity. (I discuss these conflicts later.) On the other hand, it is not necessarily true that stability is automatically promoted by satisfaction of other social goals. Although many social theorists, especially liberals, passionately believe that respect for law and order will follow from achievement of social justice, the truth may be the other way around, which is much less comforting. In any event, it would seem that there is probably an inherent contradiction between high levels of personal liberty and high levels of social stability.

To state the obvious, a high degree of institutionalized protection for the rights of individuals, such as exists in the United States,* is likely to interfere to at least some degree with the practical implementation of an orderly and safe society. Some individuals rights, such as the right to possess and carry handguns, may create temptations and opportunities that tend to increase both the frequency and level of violence of certain types of crime. By the same token, it can also be argued that the widespread ownership of handguns in the United States is mainly a symptom, rather than a cause, of social disorder and instability that springs from deeper roots. I think there is some truth on both sides.

The conflict between freedom and order is more fundamental than I have implied above. It is not merely a question of efficient police work or misuse of guns. The fact is that individual rights in many spheres, *if exercised,* may create infringements on the rights of others. The smokers' "right" to smoke infringes on the nonsmokers' right to breath pure uncontaminated air. The right of a chemical company to manufacture

---

*For example, rights of privacy, security against "unreasonable search and seizure," *habeas corpus,* protection against self-incrimination, and so forth.

and sell its product (say, Kepone) may create pollution that will destroy the livelihoods of thousands of innocent fishermen or oystermen. The right of a landowner to erect a large ugly billboard on his property conflicts with the rights of passers-by to see the scenery. And so on.

Only an orderly society can possibly adjudicate and compromise these complex and competing rights. Without order, social justice is impossible, freedom exists only for the strongest, and wealth cannot be accumulated, except by theft. Nor can it be protected or enjoyed. Order is, in a real sense, the most basic social goal of all.

I therefore discuss the other three social goals — equity, efficiency and freedom — in relation to each other. Historically, societies have fairly often achieved one of these goals. They have sometimes been able to combine two of them, but generally at the expense of the third and seldom for more than a few decades. Let me consider in turn the three possible combinations of two goals:

1. *Personal freedom and efficiency* (sacrificing equity). Ideology: *laissez-faire* capitalism. Examples: Britain before the Boer War; the United States before 1929; Japan, West Germany, France, Belgium, Italy, Switzerland, Brazil, and Mexico from World War II to the early 1970s.
2. *Equity and efficiency* (sacrificing freedom). Ideology: "hard"* socialism (=communism). Examples: USSR before World War II; East Europe and China since World War II; Cuba since Castro.
3. *Equity and personal freedom* (sacrificing efficiency). Ideology: "soft"* socialism. Examples: present-day Britain, Denmark, Sweden, Israel, Sri Lanka, New York City.

All these combinations have been tried repeatedly in human history. All three, over a period of time, have generally proved unstable in various degrees, tending inevitably to change into something else. In most cases the original goals were, in the end, eroded.

There are a few plausible examples I can think of in which all three political values have been simultaneously achieved to a significant degree in combination with each other over a significant period of time. Most are in Western Europe: Norway, Sweden, Holland, and Austria since World II; the other is Israel.

Norway, Sweden, Holland, and Austria have managed to combine strong economic growth and soft socialism for a couple of decades, but

---

*By "hard" socialism, I mean socialism imposed by a disciplined central cadre using the police powers of the state to suppress dissent and enforce central policy decisions. By "soft" socialism, I mean the systematic use of punitive or "soak the rich" taxation and a variety of social welfare schemes to redistribute income.

all except Austria are small, staunchly Protestant countries with very well-educated, homogeneous, and traditionally frugal populations. All except Norway are closely linked to the booming economy of West Germany,* and Norway sits on a major part of the North Sea oil. Israel is a very unusual case: It has benefited since its founding as a state by a tremendous influx of well-educated Jewish refugees, plus substantial capital grants from West Germany and the United States. On the other hand, it has been forced by Arab hostility to devote an extraordinary amount of its GNP to national defense, which certainly inhibits ordinary economic development.

The first combination (freedom and efficiency) seems to work well in the first generation following a new frontier when everybody starts from "scratch," as in the United States in the nineteenth century or Japan after World War II. However, it quickly leads to entrenched self-reproducing concentrations of productive assets in a few hands, which effectively denies economic opportunity to the majority. In later generations even the most creative and potentially productive individuals find themselves victimized and exploited and their upward mobility blocked by the predatory practices of entrenched wealth.†

---

*West Germany, Switzerland, Italy, and France have essentially the same strong record of economic growth and respect for human rights in the postwar period as the four countries mentioned, but they have not so far undertaken any explicit program of egalitarian "soak the rich" taxation. On the other hand, most of these countries have social programs nearly as ambitious (and costly) as those of Sweden et al.

†The most extreme proponents of capitalism, such as Ayn Rand and her "objectivists," have a peculiar blind spot on this point. Miss Rand idolizes the Men of the Mind, such as John Galt and Hank Rearden, the heros of her famous novel *Atlas Shrugged.* One of her favorite real life examples has been Thomas Alva Edison, inventor of the incandescent light and many other valuable electrical devices, including the phonograph. Miss Rand fails to provide a convincing explanation of why real wealth admittedly produced by the genius of scientists and inventors never seems to remain in their hands. Edison made no fortune. Nor did Alexander Graham Bell, inventor of the telephone. Nor did Charles Steinmetz of General Electric. Nor did Charles M. Hall who invented the aluminum reduction process. Nor did the progenitors of hundreds of other major discoveries and inventions that have shaped our society. A very few scientists or inventors have become truly rich: E. L. DeGolyer (an oil geologist of some renown), Charles F. Kettering of General Motors, and Edwin Land of Polaroid are the chief examples. But for each scientist-entrepreneur like Land there are many others who have been essentially robbed of their inventions by systematic infringement, or paid a meager pittance in royalties, often only after extensive and expensive litigation. The DuPonts, Rockefellers, Mellons, and Fords invented nothing: they made their vast fortunes by exploiting technology developed by others. Ayn Rand bitterly complains about "legal theft" by the government. But legal (or illegal) theft by entrenched corporations is probably a more common occurrence.

The second combination (equity and efficiency) rules out freedom, because individual enterprise is forbidden by law in countries practicing "hard socialism," and individuals cannot dispose of the products of their own labor or inventions. Equity in hard socialism is eventually sacrificed through the creation of a self-perpetuating managerial elite lacking the idealism of the original revolutionaries, as in the USSR.

The third combination (equity and freedom or "soft socialism") is often very inefficient in practice, lacking either the explicit discipline of the police state or the implicit discipline of the free market. Basically it depends on "good will" or "law abidingness," especially in terms of the average citizen's continued willingness to work hard at his job and pay taxes at punitive rates for the benefit of highly visible parasites as well as those who are truly needy. Since altruism is scarce to begin with and tends to wither rapidly when it is abused, soft socialism usually does not work for any length of time. A country that tries this as a national policy will generally begin at some point to live off (i.e., to depreciate) its accumulated assets, as Denmark, the United Kingdom, and New York City have most probably been doing for a number of years.

In establishing the United States of America, equity was not considered to be a relevant political goal given the prevailing (Protestant) ideology of the time. Virtue and morality, on the other hand, were thought to be a proper concern of the state. Religious and political freedom were particularly valued—although the slaves were obviously not beneficiaries—and this resulted in a general acceptance of *laissez-faire* competition with free markets. This has proved historically to be an economically efficient system of allocation of resources.

In the economic realm, free market capitalism corresponds roughly to Darwinian "survival of the fittest" in the biological realm. The system can be harsh—individuals often get hurt—but it has produced goods and services in remarkable abundance. Thus 150 years after its founding, the United States became the wealthiest nation in the world in material terms. Its only rivals in per capita wealth today are staunchly capitalist West Germany, France, and Switzerland, plus Norway, Sweden, and Holland (see Table 4.5 on page 135). Capitalist Japan, too, appears to be catching up fast.

However, little by little, the original *laissez-faire* system was altered in ways that have been reducing both efficiency and freedom. Evidently capitalism has hidden within it a tendency to self-destruct. Since unsuccessful competitors drop out of the race—often by merger or absorption by the more successful—unbridled competition rapidly leads to the creation of cartels or monopolies. Huge aggregations of privately owned wealth arise, and their possessors acquire the power to control markets and limit competition by those who are less wealthy.

To counteract the weight of private monopoly power, government may intrude with antitrust or other forms of stultifying regulations. This, too, destroys the discipline of the free market. Prices, instead of being determined by supply and demand, are increasingly set in corporate board rooms or by regulatory bodies. Free enterprise ceases to be free, and the free market vanishes in more and more areas of the economy. What evolves is an administered economy controlled by giant self-perpetuating corporate entities in effective collaboration with government agencies. The system tends to operate increasingly outside the control of representative government. Hence the ordinary citizen feels powerless to alter its course, although what happens in the economy affects him more directly than does government. In a real sense, freedom (in textbook economic terms) has been eroded.

The system of administered markets is certainly less efficient from an economic perspective than *laissez-faire* capitalism, because the "invisible hand" of competition has been largely removed. This is seen in numerous ways; in the cost-plus contracts negotiated between giant aerospace manufacturers and the Defense Department, in excessive wage settlements between oligopolist producers and monopoly unions where the costs are simply passed on to the consumer, in unemployment benefits so generous that people do not have to be employed to live comfortably, in sharp increases in prices in the teeth of a severe drop in demand, and so on. The United States is still an enormously rich country, but the cumulative effect of many such inefficiencies in the economy can (and will) erode the basis of that wealth. If economic efficiency declines further and the standard of living of Americans begins to drop in absolute terms, the pressures against the system at its weakest point — the gap between the rich and the poor — will intensify to the point that there may be a question of the system's long-term viability. At times of business recession and high unemployment, political pressures to put human welfare ahead of economic rationality become more and more difficult to resist.

One of the ways in which the capitalist system can destroy itself is exemplified by the recent history of the United Kingdom. The great accumulation of wealth (i.e., productive capital) that occurred there during the early part of the Industrial Revolution and subsequent imperial expansion of Victorian times was very unevenly distributed. The vast majority of people in the United Kingdom own very little of the national asset pool. But they all have votes and many of them also

belong to trade unions. The militant unionized workers feel themselves to be engaged in a power struggle which now, for the first time
in history, they actually have a chance to "win." Their object is to take
power (and wealth) from the "bosses" or the "rich" by disruptive practices, and wage demands having no relationship to increased productivity. To meet these demands, enterprises must divert funds that
should properly be used for maintenance and reinvestment. Thus plant
and equipment becomes progressively worn-out, obsolescent, and less
productive—it is "used up." This amounts, of course, to confiscation of
property from its owners without reimbursement. Many people who
are perfectly honest in their daily affairs see nothing wrong with this
method of redistribution (and destruction) of wealth. It is too seldom
pointed out that the major victims are not the very few remaining rich
individuals, but large numbers of moderate-income persons, such as
retired people, and educational and philanthropic institutions which
have in good faith invested in these businesses.

The private owners of capital have few weapons to combat these
practices, and their voting strength is much smaller than that of the
organized workers. Hence more and more businesses chronically lose
money and eat into their capital assets. Of course, they cease to attract
investors (or even creditors). When an industry in the United Kingdom, such as shipbuilding or auto manufacturing, loses so much
money that its properties become relatively worthless, the labor-con-
trolled government of the United Kingdom takes it over (nationalizes
it) as the price of providing loans or subsidies. Stockholders receive
nothing—their investments having long since lost their value. Back-
door nationalization of major industries has been an openly avowed
objective of a powerful element in the labor unions all along. It is a
step toward full socialism—ownership of the means of production by
the state—which is the political goal of Fabian as well as Marxist
socialists.

However, the firms which the state takes over in this manner are
no longer viable enterprises, and state ownership *per se* does not make
them so. After nationalization, as a rule, they become even more inefficient than before. Their operating deficits must be made up out of
general tax revenues (like the deficits in most public enterprises, such
as the Post Office). Large infusions of new capital are needed, also
necessarily from public funds. The latter can come only from taxes on
personal incomes or on profits of such profitable enterprises as remain
in the economy. These are fewer and fewer. The capital assets of the
nation as a whole are thus depleted. The nation is losing not only its
productive capital but its investment in educational institutions, hos-

pitals, and research laboratories—the whole array of institutional structures that organize human thought and effort.

There is no incentive for anybody to save from current income to reinvest in any business enterprises in an economy like this. If allowed to do so, people with capital take it elsewhere, or they spend it on current consumption. The government becomes the investor of last resort, but its revenues are so stretched by a plethora of competing demands for politically popular welfare (consumption) schemes that it is forced to ration capital or resort to the printing presses or both. The consequence of a few years of this is that the country's credit collapses, leading to uncontrolled inflation and some kind of societal crisis. The end result is likely to be a dictatorship of the Right or of the Left. Thus in sacrificing efficiency for equity and freedom, the outcome is likely to be the loss of all three values.

Is the United States following this route? There are ominous but still inconclusive signs that it may be. Still, the United States has not yet gone past the point of no return. A reversal is possible. Perhaps even the United Kingdom can also find a way out, although with every year of continued profligacy its chances of survival grow slimmer. If the Labor Party left wing of doctrinaire militants brings down the present Callaghan-Healey government and embarks on a new round of profligate "social" spending, the last hope may be gone.

An example of the same tendencies operating in the United States can be seen in the recent fiscal crisis of New York City. New York City —in common with many other cities, some states, and the Federal Government itself—has been caught in a constantly rising spending pattern consistently exceeding its revenues, thus throwing a rapidly rising debt burden on future generations. At the same time New York's relatively lavish welfare policies* were attracting nonproductive residents to the city, raising costs, reducing the quality of services provided to citizens, and reducing the capacity of its economy to produce tax revenues. Businesses are rapidly fleeing the city,reducing the tax base. Between 1965 and 1975 over seventy large corporations formerly headquartered in Manhattan moved to Fairfield County, Connecticut. New York State's rent control laws, in effect since World War II, have also resulted in the deterioration of assets (equivalent to the consumption of capital) because landlords who cannot expect to make a profit on their existing investment will naturally not carry out any except bare minimum maintenance and repairs. Thus housing units in

---

*Admittedly, these policies were not exclusively invented in the city itself, but this is beside the point.

the city are being steadily abandoned. (As of 1977 there were over 100,000 abandoned housing units in New York City.) This process tends to accelerate because of positive feedback: As apartment houses deteriorate and are abandoned, they cease to pay taxes to the city, which thereupon is forced to raise taxes or cut back services to the remaining taxpayers, driving them to the suburbs in their turn.

The crisis was compounded when, in the mid-1960s, a myopic city administration, afraid to offend the municipal workers unions by cutting costs and afraid to exacerbate the economic decline by raising taxes further, found a temporary expedient for deferring the day of reckoning. They went into debt to finance short-term operating costs. The banks cooperated by looking the other way until the short-term debt had grown to the point at which it obviously could not be paid off. Suddenly the lending institutions self-righteously refused to lend more, and the threat of massive bankruptcy loomed. When the dimensions of the threat were finally assessed, it became clear that the creditors included hundreds of small banks around the country, and that many of these, in turn, might fail if a part of their assets were wiped out overnight.

When, in late 1975, the State of New York stepped in to "rescue" the city, it became clear that the state, too, is in a very shaky economic condition. A bankrupt city could lend to a bankrupt state, with even more massive ramifications. Thus the Federal Government has already had to intervene to save New York State to keep the national economy on an even keel. However, it can only do so by taxing other regions and diverting resources from productive purposes to consumption at a time when it would seem that the rate of investment is already much too low.

Evidently there is some tendency for a society that has grown wealthy under *laissez-faire* capitalism to move voluntarily in the direction of soft socialism and thence toward economic collapse. Why is this?

One of the factors tending to push a capitalist state toward socialism is the so-called "business cycle." Because of the operation of positive and negative feedback mechanisms in the absence of government intervention, there is a periodic recurrence of business recessions accompanied by high unemployment. Since the people affected are voters, there are political demands for relief of the suffering. In response to these demands there begins a long, slow accumulation of "social" legislation to remove, one by one, the principal hazards of life: loss of income through unemployment, sickness, old age, industrial accidents, deprivation via racial discrimination, and so on.

Every one of these reforms is humane and defensible in a narrow context. But the process of legislating perfection develops its own dynamic. For every hazard removed, a dozen new problems are uncovered which people had formerly not worried much about: correcting inequitable voter registration laws, inequitable tax "loopholes," ensuring welfare recipients' rights, ensuring legal representation for the poor, correcting maldistribution of government funds between geographical districts, providing consumer protection, enforcing antitrust, eliminating corruption in the granting of government contracts, eliminating discrimination in the pay and promotion policies of government agencies and private businesses, and so on. The list is literally endless because equality is an ideal that cannot possibly be achieved in practice. It can only be roughly approximated, and there are forces perpetually magnifying old inequalities or creating new ones of various sorts.

So the legislative mills keep grinding. The costs of the programs keep rising. Yet the unmet "needs" seem to grow faster than the programs can meet them, because they are constantly redefined. (Legislators need something to keep them occupied, after all.) The perpetual redefinition of impossible objectives and redeployment of resources in their pursuit engages the constant attention of increasing numbers of functionaries, administrators, bureaucrats, educators, social workers, lawyers, union leaders, and researchers.

What happens, then, is that an increasing proportion of the population becomes engaged in kinds of work that are focused on the more equitable distribution of wealth or services but not on their *production.* Moreover, most of the people who benefit from these shifts of income are indifferent producers or nonproducers of wealth, and their number constantly increases as the work week gets shorter, retirement age is reduced, "disability" pensions become easier to get, and so on. The ultimate effect of withdrawing so many people from productive activities is a decline in the productive efficiency of the society as a whole, that is, its ability to create wealth for people to consume.

Thus soft socialism comes into being, "not with a bang, but with a whimper," to borrow a phrase from T.S. Eliot. It happens so gradually that people are not really aware of it. And it happens for the best of moral reasons: to provide aid for the poor, the oppressed, the old, and the helpless. However, the end is a decline in the productive capability of the whole society. It can be argued (and some do so argue) that this ought to occur: that the economies of the wealthier nations have been too exclusively concerned with increasing private wealth and too negligent of the need to help their poorer citizens and the poor of the rest of the world. There are persuasive people like Schumacher[3] and Illich[4] who argue forcibly that, for the sake of humanity, Americans and

Europeans should reduce their standard of living, stop buying luxury goods, and restrict their consumption levels to "essential needs." Yet what is a luxury in one country or century is regarded as essential in another. Who—in a Schumacher/Illich world—is to decide on priorities? Presumably the state would, in the end, have to undertake to define human "needs" and to determine whose needs deserve to be met. Such an all-powerful state is, by definition, totalitarian. To me it is curious and ironic that such a program should be advocated by liberal humanitarians who, in theory, believe strongly in freedom and democracy. However, I do not dig further into this distracting and contradictory topic for the moment.

In 1967 Pope Paul VI issued a widely acclaimed Encyclical, *Populorum Progressio*,[5] ("On the Development of Peoples"), which places the Catholic Church squarely in the soft socialist camp and, incidentally, spells out the soft socialist position on goals and values in explicit detail. Reiterating the historical position of the Catholic Church, it specifically rules out profit as an ethically acceptable motivation for human conduct (labeling it "avarice"). The highest goal is "to furnish each individual with the means of livelihood and the instruments of his growth and progress"; it does not specify what "needs" are, who should define them, or how they are to be met, except that *the means of livelihood are a paramount right of every human person** and "all other rights whatsoever, including those of property and free commerce are to be subordinated to this principle." Moreover, it asserts that those who have *must** give to those who have not. It quotes St. Ambrose: "You are not making a gift of your possessions to the poor person. *You are handing over to him what is his.** For what has been given in common for the use of all, you have arrogated to yourself. The world is given to all and not only to the rich." This echoes Jesus' admonition to accumulate no possessions and to give what you have to the poor. It obliquely addresses the problem of how to organize society so that people do this by saying "it pertains to the public authorities to choose, even to lay down, the objectives to be pursued, the ends to be achieved, and the means for attaining these, *and it is for them to stimulate all the forces engaged in this common activity."**

Ayn Rand follows the implications of *Populorum Progressio* to their logical conclusion: "Totalitarian control (by nations) of their citizens' economic activities" and "a global state with totalitarian control over global planning."[6] This would follow simply because, deprived of either economic incentives *or the moral right* to invest, people would no

*My italics.

longer save voluntarily. The government would therefore have to take over all means of production and supply all capital—obtained from the citizens by taxation. This can only be done by transfer of all economic planning and decision making to the state (which the Encyclical specifically recommends), eliminating any opportunity for an individual to benefit from his own inventions, initiative, or creative work of any kind. Every citizen would finally be reduced to being a functionary of a bureaucracy.

Indeed, the Encyclical is so full of inherent contradictions that one may raise the question—as Miss Rand does—as to whether its pronouncements were really supposed to be workable. She believes they were not intended, in fact, to relieve suffering or abolish poverty in the real world, but rather to increase the intensity of feelings of guilt among men by being accepted as morally right and then (inevitably) failing in practice. Having helped increase the human burden of guilt, the Church can step forward with its time-tested prescriptions for relieving the bad feelings by receiving confessions and offering benedictions in exchange for adherence. However, this is speculation and, certainly, digression.

The classic example of "hard" socialism, of course, is the USSR, which entered on its Communist course after the Bolshevik Revolution in 1917. It is easy to see that the Soviet system has been built on the pursuit of equity and efficiency (at least for the state) with the sacrifice of freedom. Equity was the great ideal: an egalitarian workers' state with the total elimination of the "exploiting" class (property owners). However, some degree of efficiency was also essential after the revolution of 1917 and the Civil War that followed, because the Russian economy was in a state of total collapse—much of the population was facing imminent starvation—as a result of incompetent administration and the enormous loss of lives and wealth in World War I. To build the Communist Society in the face of near anarchy and many dissenting elements, Lenin justified the "dictatorship of the proletariat;" this meant, in practical terms, dictatorship by the leaders of the ruling Communist Party.

The sacrifice of freedom, in the theoretical formulation of Marx and Lenin, is intended to be temporary, until the class struggle is completed. Then the state is supposed to "wither away." What actually happened was the exact opposite: the Soviet State has become a monstrous entrenched bureaucracy, stifling dissent, discouraging diversity, and great limiting personal freedom for its long-suffering citizens. An elite, privileged class has emerged comprised of senior party functionaries, military officers, high-level bureaucrats, managers, scientists, engineers, and skilled technicians. For these people, incomes and perquisites far surpass anything the ordinary workers can ever hope to attain. Thus equity, in its original formulation ("From each according to his ability, to each according to his need"), was never achieved or seriously attempted. It is doubtful if the Soviet regime today has any intention of promoting it further.

However, although industrialization has been achieved, together with a high level of technical sophistication and military power, economic efficiency, too, has eluded the USSR from the start. Growth in total output has been achieved by rigorously limiting consumption to the lowest possible level and investing the forced savings in added industrial capacity—according to the requirements spelled out by the central planners. The system, by its bureaucratic nature, does not reward innovation or individual enterprise. The discipline of competition is limited to the bureaucratic framework, and free markets are nonexistent except for handicrafts and garden produce. In some jobs, where the possibility of promotion in the hierarchy is vanishingly small or unrelated to job performance—as in collective agriculture— workers become time-servers, and managers are drones selected and promoted for political reliability. Moreover, there is a tendency in the Soviet system to rely heavily on threats and police compulsion to enforce conformity. This compounds the problem of inefficiency. Outside of a few prestigious research institutes, people have little personal incentive to do anything beyond what they must to survive and to stay "invisible." Original and imaginative ideas tend to dry up because they are likely to be nonconformist.

The result, I think, is evident in the fact that the Soviet economy in recent decades has become very unbalanced. It has not grown nearly as fast as it should have in agricultural and consumers' goods, housing, and service sectors. The principal growth has been in so-called heavy industry such as hydroelectric power, cement, petrochemicals, metallurgy, and military hardware, where it is possible even for a clumsy bureaucracy to build huge factories and marshal work forces to operate them. The production and distribution of consumers' goods and services require more diversity of design and more individualized attention and is less easily organized on a giant scale. In this area, the Soviet regime has its most serious deficiencies.

The agricultural sector in the USSR suffers from the fact that traditional peasant skills have been lost or suppressed,* whereas indus-

---

*In the 1920s, Stalin tried to stamp out resistance to collectivization by a bloody campaign of repression against the Kulaks (small farmers). Millions were killed or starved as their crops and livestock were confiscated.

trial skills and specializations have migrated to the cities where wages and living conditions are better. Of course, it is to be expected that sons and grandsons of peasants tend to resent both the regimentation and dehumanization of vast collective farms. Such a deeply ingrained human urge as attachment to one's own land is not easily eliminated. Agricultural output per worker in the USSR is shockingly low by United States, or European standards and seems likely, under present policies, to remain so.

The stifling weight of bureaucracy is felt most keenly by intellectual workers such as artists, writers, scientists, engineers, technicians, and managers, because the qualities most needed for the work they do are precisely the ones regimentation and collectivization tends to suppress, namely, independent ideas, new approaches, and creative solutions to problems. Apparently, the only way the USSR has been able to use these kinds of workers effectively* has been to make them an elite class, exempt from many of the limitations applicable to the rest of the population. This has necessitated a blatant repudiation, in practice, of the theoretical egalitarian ideals of Marxism — an ironical development, considering that the avowed purpose of the Revolution was to abolish privileged classes!

Not much is known quantitatively of China's economic development, but it is conceivable that China may be ultimately more successful in making the Marxist formula work than is the USSR. The Chinese have a very long history of subordinating the individual to a collectivity, especially the family and the clan. The Chinese tradition through the centuries has been one of deference and obedience to elders, which the Chinese are taught as small children. Hence Chinese peasants are probably better material for Marxist "social engineering" than Russians ever were. Moreover, the Chinese Communist leaders have deep roots among the peasantry — unlike the Russian Bolsheviks, who were strictly urban — and instead of attempting to convert peasants into industrial workers, they have sensibly woven traditional peasant skills and life patterns into the new fabric.

China's troubles, as Russia's, probably stem from dissatisfaction on the part of intellectuals, scientists, and technicians who do not always fit smoothly into the prescribed communist mold. The first official response to growing pressures for greater intellectual freedom was Mao's injunction to "let a thousand flowers bloom." However, even a little freedom is dangerous for a totalitarian regime. It is not clear exactly what happened, but apparently the "cultural revolution" of 1966–1968

---

*For example, in its nuclear and space programs.

was triggered by—if not a reaction to—this brief and feeble renaiss-ance. Super-Maoist ideological zealots purged many urban intellec-tuals and overturned and revamped the entire system of education to ensure that educated Chinese remained strictly conformist and obe-dient to the official egalitarian doctrine.

Following the death of Mao in 1976, the uneasy balance shifted again. The "gang of four" (including Mao's fanatic wife) are now offi-cially banished, and the functionaries, managers, and administrators seem to be in control. The ripples on the surface of the pond have momentarily subsided, and uneasy tranquility prevails for the mo-ment. The long-term prognosis is not at all clear, but my guess would be that the repression of dissent will ultimately fail. The ideological regimentation of people whose work requires that they *innovate* has never succeeded anywhere for long. The reasons have been mentioned earlier: The qualities needed for original and creative thought are simply incompatible with collectivization. If China is to move ahead economically and technologically it will be forced eventually to give its brain workers freer rein and higher status. Probably because they regarded this as an unacceptable price, the rural-oriented radical Maoists apparently adopted an "antigrowth" stance. However, events since the death of Mao suggest that the moderate pragmatists, that is, the urban-oriented managerial class, may have finally won the long internal struggle for power in China. If so, we can expect less concern with egalitarian ideals and more concern with economic growth and military power.

Is there any reasonable possibility of combining all four of the listed goals: equity, efficiency, freedom and order? Some, including Ayn Rand and her followers (the objectivists), insist that equity is inherently in conflict with freedom, but that efficiency (and wealth) will follow automatically if freedom is protected. Others, who agree with the Papal Encyclical, *Populorum Progressio,* quoted earlier, name equity as the highest goal. These people advocate freedom only subject to the limitations imposed by demands of equity. They regard wealth as inherently bad, whence efficiency—the prerequisite of wealth—becomes irrelevant at best. A third group, including prag-matic nationalists of all colors (both capitalist and communist), disa-gree utterly: To them, national power (i.e., efficiency) is the highest value. Equity and freedom may be desirable also, but can (and must) be sacrificed whenever they interfere with the implementation of the goals of the state.

My personal view is that mankind can and *must* try to discover a recipe for combining all four goals. This is intrinsically difficult. The conflicts between them are real and will not disappear. A balance must be achieved. There are a number of avenues worth exploring. But we will never succeed as long as we allow ourselves to focus on any one goal to the exclusion of others.

COMPETING PERSONAL VALUES

The preceding section discussed four important and, to some extent, competing goals of a society: freedom, equity, efficiency (or wealth) and stability (or order). Now I want to focus on values held by individuals in a society, as distinguished from goals pertaining to the society, recognizing, of course, that there is some overlap. Personal values that tend to characterize a large element of an entire population merge into social goals. Societal goals are closely related to personal values for many individuals. A curtailment of political freedom is immediately felt as personal oppression. An absence of equity is perceived directly as personal discrimination or injustice. An absence of stability or order leads to personal insecurity. And, of course, individual poverty is less common and easier to overcome in a society that is wealthy than in one that is not.

Still, the social goal that is least directly understood in relation to its underlying structure of personal values is, without question, efficiency. For a society to achieve wealth, it must be economically efficient. And the attributes of a productive worker and generator of societal wealth are quite different from the attributes of a dedicated consumer of wealth! That is why this, of all the social goals, is in the greatest danger of being undermined in democratic societies. When economic efficiency declines, as can happen for a variety of reasons, the people of a country experience that decline as a puzzling and dismaying series of symptoms, such as prices rising faster than incomes, protracted unemployment, business failures, soaring interest rates, falling stock prices, shortages of goods, oppressive and constantly rising taxes, and deteriorating public services. People feel the impact of these disturbances in their personal lives, but do not trace them to their root causes. Instead of trying to restore the functioning of the economy as a whole, they demand symptomatic remedies which often exacerbate the problem. Typical examples include price and rent controls, inflationary wage increases, increased job security, unemployment relief, public service jobs, and the like. This is ineffectual (or worse) tinkering with the economic engine. At most, such measures help one segment of the population by taking wealth or income from other segments. When the total economy of a nation (or of the world) is not growing, any improvement in the economic well-being of one group can only be at the expense of other groups. This is elementary logic. A moment's reflection should make it obvious that there is only one way in which improvements can be experienced by all groups at once: when the economy as a whole is growing. This fact, although simple and easily understood, is broadly ignored by politicians in nearly all non-communist countries.

This is not to imply that no redistribution of incomes is justified at any time or for any reason. People who have no way of defending themselves — such as the aged and sick who cannot work and the very poor, many of whom are functionally illiterate or otherwise not qualified for available jobs — need assistance. This should be provided within limits of what is available, primarily for humanitarian reasons perhaps, but also to give these people an opportunity, if possible, to become productive and self-supporting. But when a society does this, its leaders and people are not always fully aware of what they are doing and its long-term effects. In a stagnant economy, "redistribution" may amount to taking assets away from investors and producers — who could make the economy grow — for the benefit of the unproductive. If public policy carries this beyond a certain point (which is difficult to define in advance), economic efficiency suffers irreparably and the gross wealth of the entire society begins to dwindle. Although clear statistical evidence is not available, I think this process has been occurring for some years in the United Kingdom and that the United States and Canada are now teetering close to the brink.

Labor leaders, who often talk as though they are protecting the interests of the poor, ignore the fact that when they demand (for their members) wage increases and other benefits exceeding the rate of productive growth of the economy, they are simply using monopoly power to increase their share of a fixed pie at the expense of other groups. Those hurt worst are the truly poor, who are not protected by political influence or union wage contracts. Such "gains" by organized labor also reduce the shares of retired people and many members of the middle class — such as small shopkeepers — who are already under heavy pressure from large retail chains. The organized workers themselves ultimately suffer, too, but the process is slow, so that what is happening is not clearly observed. It took New York City many years to reach the brink of bankruptcy, and the mechanisms mainly responsible for this are not understood by most New Yorkers — or other Americans — even now. While ritually condemning New York for profligate "welfare" policies, politicians in other cities are busily enacting similar ones. One of the first acts of Washington, D.C. as a self-governing city was to pass a rent control act which may turn out to be even more counterproductive than that of New York State.

Modern society is in an unsafe condition because its economy has grown too complex to be readily understood as a whole. The labor leader understands one set of mechanisms from his point of view, the businessman another set of mechanisms, lawyers and politicians still other sets of mechanisms. Each has a tendency to think that if the mechanism he is familiar with works well, the whole system will necessarily work well. A former Secretary of Defense and Board Chairman of General Motors, "Engine Charlie" Wilson, was once quoted "I thought what was good for the country was good for General Motors, and vice versa." This sentiment illustrates a kind of corporate myopia that does in fact exist. The catch-phrase (and movie title) "I'm all right, Jack" neatly encompasses a similar myopia on the part of British (and other) trade unionists.

In some earlier and simpler societies the importance of economic efficiency seems to have been more clearly understood than it is now. There is not much margin for misunderstanding the economy of a primitive society; the consequences of mismanagement are experienced quickly in terms of starvation and social collapse. As John Maynard Keynes put it, *"the struggle for subsistence always has been hitherto the primary, most pressing problem of the human race* — not only of the human race but of the whole of the biological kingdom from the beginnings of life in its most primitive forms."[7] Only after some of the pressure is off the subsistence struggle (as a result of increased efficiency in the tasks of producing food, shelter, and other needs) can mankind afford to be concerned with such goals as freedom and equity. In the long perspective of history, freedom and equity have been luxuries compared to wealth and stability. Quite possibly this hierarchy of priorities still holds today.

It is important to understand the personal values that contribute to economic efficiency. Wealth, the product of economic efficiency, does not come into being by accident or magic, nor is it created automatically by virtue of language or culture: in any society only certain types of people are wealth creators. Productivity demands specific personal attributes and attitudes that not all people share even in the most efficient societies. These values are not universally accepted or applauded. Ominously, many of the wealth-creating values are denigrated, or even attacked, by the humanitarian (soft) left in the democratic societies.

The values in question are not at all peculiar to the white races — a comfortable illuson of the empire builders of Europe in the nineteenth century. The Japanese obviously hold the wealth-creating values to a formidable degree, as do the Chinese. Where these values appear to be largely missing or only partly developed is among formerly subject peoples recently emerged into nationhood or among people whose lives are dominated by an "other worldly" religion. They also tend to be missing in tribal societies in which animist superstitutions and other irrational elements predominate. New or newly independent nations are likely to face serious difficulties in building workable economies, not only because they start from a low level, but also because the needed personal attitudes and values are not highly developed in the population and their importance is not given adequate recognition in schools.

Table 2.1 sets forth six key personal values which, in my judgment, are closely related to economic efficiency and the creation of wealth, together with their opposites. The several wealth-creating values merge somewhat into each other and tend to form a package. An individual who holds any one of these values tends to hold some or all the others as well, although there are certainly exceptions. Note that I distinguish values — which can be changed — from inherent qualities of mind. Imagination and creativity, for example, are not on the list because they depend on inherent qualities. Although they often contribute to the creation of wealth, such qualities are not actually necessary to it.

The selection of wealth-creating values, of course, must be a matter of personal judgment. Yet I doubt if many readers will disagree strongly with the selection, though some will want to distinguish finer nuances, whereas others may prefer different distinctions or aggregations. It seems to me important to identify as clearly as possible these values and their related attitudes and feelings, because the future outlook for economic efficiency in different countries rests on the outlook for the preservation of these values among ordinary people. What are the prospects? If I can begin to answer that question, there may be a basis for forecasting the future of democratic societies.

To begin with, it is an interesting exercise to look at the opposites of the wealth-creating values, considering them as a group. It may be significant that five of the six value opposites (apathy, helplessness, chronic withdrawal, despair, and failure to consider consequences) are among the attitudes and feelings regarded by psychiatrists as symptoms of emotional disorder. In extreme form, these are specific characteristics of many mental hospital patients. They are clearly associated with an incapacity to deal with life effectively in Western society. This may be dismissed as irrelevant by those people (such as some humanists and social critics) who look with disfavor on Western social norms. However, the humanists who despise industrialism and disdain "The Establishment" do not seem to have fully accepted the contradictory fact that they deprecate that system which allows them to live in relative comfort and think great thoughts without worrying about securing the means of personal survival.

Looking at the wealth-creating values as a package, it is significant that these values, for the most part, seem to have preexisted in the populations of the countries of Northwestern Europe (and their colon-

Table 2.1 Wealth-Creating Values and Their Opposites

Wealth Creating	Non-Wealth Creating
Motivated	**Apathetic**
Life is felt to be meaningful, to be worth living, to have purpose.	Life is felt to be without purpose or meaning.
Positive Attitude to Work	**Negative Attitude to Work**
Having an urge to achieve, to overcome difficulties, to acquire knowledge, abilities, and skills. Pride in results of work.	Thief or "dropout" mentality; work seen as a necessary (or unnecessary) evil, something any "smart" person avoids.
Integrity and Personal Honor	**Lack of Integrity**
Can be trusted and cares about reputation for dependability or "word of honor."	Cannot be trusted; indifferent to reputation for dependability or "word."
Reality Orientation	**Escapist**
In close touch with reality; able to attack problems, seek rational solutions, and keep control over emotions.	Tendency to flee from harsh realities, to withdraw into an imaginary world of dreams, fancies, cults, or magic. Lack of emotional control.
Concern With Future	**Concern Only with Present**
Willing to accept responsibility, not only for oneself but for children, family, community, and the nation. Willing to sacrifice some immediate pleasures for long-term goals.	Tendency to avoid responsibility, to be impulsive, and live for the moment with no thought for consequences. (Extreme example: psychological addiction to gambling, alcohol, or drugs.)
Optimistic	**Pessimistic**
Hopeful for the future: confident something can be done to make future better.	Hopeless or despairing attitude about the future: believe nothing can be done to make it better.

ial outposts in North America) before the Industrial Revolution began. Max Weber traced the close connection between that momentous event and a set of attitudes produced by the Protestant Reformation, especially the teachings of John Calvin and John Knox.[8] The doctrine of predestination, in particular, asserted that the ultimate destiny of a person's soul after death is revealed during life by his success in earthly endeavors. The cause-and-effect relationship between them is controversial, but there is no doubt that the spreading of Protestant religious doctrines and capitalist industrial development went together.[9] Certainly the Industrial Revolution was not brought about by any deliberate plan or action on the part of the leaders of the countries in which it occurred. Quite the contrary, it developed spontaneously through the independent actions of a large number of individuals – far below and invisible to royalty, aristocracy, and Parliament alike. According to C. P. Snow, the Industrial Revolution was either ignored or deplored by the intelligentsia and the defenders of traditional culture:[10]

(It) crept on, without anyone noticing what was happening. It was, of course – or at least it was destined to become, under our own eyes, and in our own time – by far the biggest transformation in society since the discovery of agriculture. In fact, those two revolutions, the agricultural and the industrial-scientific, are the only qualitative changes in social living that men have ever known. But the traditional culture didn't notice: or when it did notice, didn't like what it saw. . . .

Almost none of the talent, almost none of the imaginative energy (of the country's academic and intellectual leaders) went back into the revolution which was producing the wealth. The traditional culture became more abstracted from it as it became more wealthy, trained its young men for administration, for the Indian Empire, for the purpose of perpetuating the culture itself, but never in any circumstances to equip them to understand the revolution or take part in it. . . .

The academics had nothing to do with the industrial revolution; as Corrie, the old Master of Jesus (college), said about trains running into Cambridge on Sunday, "it is equally displeasing to God and to myself." So far as there was any thinking in nineteenth-century industry, it was left to cranks and clever workmen. American social historians have told me that much the same was true of the U. S. The industrial revolution, which began developing in New England fifty years or so later than ours, apparently received very little educated talent, either then or later in the nineteenth century. It had to make to with the guidance handymen could give it — sometimes, of course, handymen like Henry Ford, with a dash of genius.

If ever a great event occurred because a large number of ordinary people shared a certain kind of common values, this was it.

Another curious aspect of wealth-creating values is that these are the same attitudes that lead to conspicuous success in war. It is interesting to observe how wars have sometimes accelerated the development of these values. Eighteenth century France, under the declining Bourbon dynasty, did not show evidence of any strong development in wealth-creating values among the population at large. After its egalitarian antimonarchist, anticlerical revolution, Republican France was attacked by its Royalist European neighbors. Under military pressure, France coalesced into a modern nation. The peasants and workmen were not much interested in fighting wars of dynastic succession, but they discovered a tremendous unifying purpose in fighting for "La Patrie."

Later, unified under Bismarck, Germany too experienced a nationalist outburst and embarked on a series of militaristic empire-building adventures, beginning with Frederick the Great, that coincided with a period of rapid industrial development in Germany itself. Italy's nationalist resurgence — or Risorgimento — occurred during the same period, as Italians chafed under the weak but arbitrary rule of the Austrian-based Hapsburg dynasty. Japan's nationalist movement was triggered by Commodore Perry's naval "visit" in 1853 and culminated in the Meiji Restoration of 1867 and the abolition of feudalism in 1871, the first step in the creation of a modern constitutional monarchy. Japan too embarked on a militarist-imperialist course beginning with the Chinese-Japanese War of 1894 and the Russo-Japanese War of 1904 and culminating in World War II.

Probably one of the reasons why nations such as Japan, the countries of Western Europe, and the USSR have been able to make such rapid recoveries and rebuild their economies so quickly after devastating wars is because the values required for effective war effort are the same as those needed to create wealth (capital). The values already shared by the population were simply directed at different goals.

Examination of these values individually reveals other interesting relationships:

Motivation.   This is an obvious prerequisite for wealth creation; some form of motivation must exist in the population or too few people work to accumulate anything beyond minimal subsistence requirements. One very strong early source of motivation has already been mentioned: the Calvinist and related doctrines of the Protestant Reformation. The notion that achievement of wealth on Earth would also guarantee later rewards in Heaven was probably a factor in the industrial rise in the United Kingdom, Germany, Switzerland, the Scandinavian countries, and the United States.[11]

Another powerful source of motivation is national pride, often stimulated by war. I mentioned the experience of France after the French Revolution. The mood of the French people became nationalist and patriotic, they marched under the tricolor to the strains of the "Marseillaise," and the spirit of their leaders and troops made the French armies almost undefeatable until Napoleon made the mistake of challenging the Russian winter — and incidentally kindled a nationalist surge of feeling in that country. National pride is certainly a factor in the high motivation of the Japanese, the Chinese, and the Russians, as well as the countries of Europe and the United States. It tends to be weak or absent, on the other hand, in countries that have been "liberated" from colonialism by voluntary withdrawal of former occupying powers, unless the liberation was clearly due to the struggles of the people themselves.

Brazil is a case in point. Although separated more or less amicably from Portugese rule in the early nineteenth century, it has only recently begun to develop a strong sense of national identity — a prerequisite for national pride. The building of a new capital (Brasilia) in the interior was conceived as a focus for emerging Brazilian nationalism. Although Brasilia can be criticized as inflationary and grandiose, it may well prove to be the effective catalyst for internal development that its original sponsor (Rafael Kubitschek) envisioned.

A third source of motivation is the ordinary secular desire to consume more of the things that money can buy. This is reinforced by the award of respect and high social prestige to people on the basis of their apparent success as measured by consumption expenditure. "Keeping up with the Jones" is a motivation not to be dismissed lightly in consumer-oriented societies.

Economic competition is probably spurred by fostering a competitive attitude. Emphasis on individual achievement is an important aspect of this process. Sports and schools provide experience in intense individual competition in most countries. (Communist countries, where private accumulation of wealth is quite difficult , seem to put special emphasis on sports.) Communist countries seem strongly motivated to prove, by excellence in sports or in cultural activities, that the communist system is superior to that of the West.

As a value, achievement orientation for individuals conflicts with the social goal, equity. In the United States, for example, schools which once laid heavy stress on scholastic achievements are increasingly forced to admit and promote students without regard to their qualifications. Many state and municipal institutions of higher learning have been required to accept virtually all students who apply — at least for the first year — with a consequent dilution of resources and erosion of standards. The introduction of gradeless courses, inflated grades, automatic promotions, and open enrollment has lowered quality standards in many schools. In Washington, D. C., a "track" system, which once permitted bright students to progress faster than slower ones, was successfully attacked in the Federal Courts as disciminatory against Blacks and finally had to be abandoned.* All these developments are antithetical to achievement orientation and are symptomatic of its decline.

In the United States and the United Kingdom, the moves toward discouragement of individual achievement are increasingly ominous. Plumbers, truck drivers, or dockworkers typically make more money than many university graduates or even professors. Why bother getting an expensive education? In both countries the route to economic reward is shifting away from personal merit and toward such circumstances as having the "right" social or political connections or belonging to a powerful union with a restricted membership. In any society in which rewards are not based on merit, motivation to achievement inevitably declines.

Incidentally, it is important to realize that motivation is greatly reduced by malnutrition, especially protein deficiency, and by excessive use of alcohol or other drugs. In countries in which food is scarce, alcohol, analgesics, or narcotics are commonly used to mask the pangs of hunger. Because of food scarcity, betel nuts and hashish are widely used in India and other nations of South Asia; the Indians of Paraguay and Bolivia chew coca leaves; others take peyote or marijuana for the same reason. In any society, the rise of a drug culture is likely to inhibit the motivations of people to achieve. The urge toward consciousness altering by means of drugs, such as has recently occurred in some elements of American society, suggests a dissatisfaction with the modes of consciousness associated with striving and struggling and weakening of the motivations which hitherto have driven people toward specific goals.

*With catastrophic results for the city school system, incidentally, since most middle-class families with school-age children promptly moved out of the District to nearby suburbs.

Positive Attitude to Work. This attitude requires motivation, but is not an automatic consequence of it. It is perfectly possible to be motivated to achieve success (or an appearance of it) while scorning actual work. The heroines of thousands of romantic novels achieve success by marriage to a suitable handsome, rich, and titled—non-working—man. One of the deepseated problems of Britain is that its middle- and upper-class children have been taught for generations to admire the amateurish and casual Gentleman of Leisure who lives on inherited wealth, while deploring the striver who works "in trade." Unfortunately, the United Kingdom probably exported too many of its hard-working Presbyterians and Puritans to the American Colonies. The highest cast of India, the Brahmins, are equaly scornful of work, at least of the kind that requires getting one's hands dirty. Among Arabs, the trader, the banker, or the lawyer are admired, but not the farmer or the mechanic who produces something tangible.

Of course, many societies have also admired the acquisition of wealth by conquest, piracy, or theft from some (despised) victim-group —usually "unbelievers." The Vikings lived for centuries by stealing from people in warmer climates. Much of the portable wealth accumulated in Europe in the fifteenth and sixteenth centuries was stolen from "infidels" in the Middle East, the Moguls of India, the Aztecs of Mexico, or the Incas of Peru. In exchange for being relieved of their excess wealth, the victims were generally given an opportunity to give up their evil ways and adopt Christianity. The Spanish and Portuguese originated this form of accumulation, but the British and Dutch did very well stealing in turn from the Spaniards. Catholic Europeans also systematically confiscated the worldly goods of Jews.

Evidently productive labor is not universally respected as an occupation. Although a few societies have made a virtue of hard work for its own sake (as, for instance, the so-called Protestant ethic), this seems to be unusual.* Even the hard-working Japanese are apparently motivated primarily by a sense of obligation and a combination of personal and national pride. However, it is probably fair to say that the Japanese and Chinese, along with most Western Europeans and Americans, are positive, or at least not negative, toward work as a way of life. This is much less true for Latins, Moslems, and Indians—especially Brahmins. I hesitate to characterize the average Russian's basic attitude toward work for lack of solid evidence. The extreme efforts of Stalinist propaganda to glorify labor and heros of labor might be indirect evidence of negative attitudes. This would seem to be con-

---

*The kibbutzim in Israel also value work essentially for its own sake.

firmed by reports of Western visitors who have encountered nonworking functionaries in hotels, shops, and restaurants.

Integrity or Positive Self-Image. Integrity is a value that is rather difficult to pin down. In most cultures it appears to arise from an implicit (or explicit) code of honor. The code of honor that underpins the Western economic system is the *validity of spoken or written promises.* At first glance one might assert that contracts are observed only to the extent that they are legally enforceable. This is nonsense. The great majority of contracts in the business and financial worlds are observed precisely because it is a part of the businessman's code to honor his commitments, and he expects and is expected to do so. The enforcement is indirect but effective: if a businessman gets a reputation for not honoring his promises, people will not trust him and will refuse to do business with him. Honoring commitments strictly is recognized by successful businessmen to be a good business practice.

The immensely complex exchange economies of the industrialized nations (and, indirectly, the world economy) are based squarely on trust. Without trust, no industrial economy could long survive. The legal system is a hopelessly clumsy, slow-moving, and expensive instrument for enforcing agreements. Imagine the chaos that would ensue if more than a tiny fraction of all contracts had to go to a law court for adjudication! In the United States contractual disputes of this sort normally require several years for settlement; if courts become clogged with such cases, most would never reach final judgment at all. Businessmen know this. In a modern economy, a great majority of undertakings to buy and sell are made by letter or verbally; prices and schedules for payment and delivery are agreed on in the same way. Individuals, too, overwhelmingly honor their personal financial commitments without legal enforcement. If they did not, the consumer credit industry — and much else — could not exist.

Cultures and countries vary widely in the codes they follow and consequently in what they regard as integrity. People accustomed to functioning in Western commercial-industrial circles take for granted such matters as arriving for work on time. Those not accustomed to this habit — such as many who were raised in Black ghetto communities in American cities — have great difficulty in understanding why one should go to work on time (or appear for work at all if inconvenient). Threats of dismissal to such people create fear and insecurity but often have surprisingly little effect on actual behavior. This has been the frustrating experience of many corporations like General Motors or the New York Telephone Company that have hired minority workers under pressure from government agencies concerned with countering discrimination. In some cases, adults from ghetto backgrounds simply could not be trained to change their habits sufficiently to hold a job.

The American experience reflects the difficulties faced by multiethnic societies in which the codes of honor (or duty) of different ethnic groups do not coincide. If there is no strongly shared code applicable to all, there is no social glue. Societies that are relatively homogeneous have less difficulty in this respect. Germany and Japan are examples of societies in which personal integrity and dependability are exceptionally high, as is Switzerland, despite its several distinct language groups. The Arabs have a highly developed personal code of honor which can facilitate certain kinds of transactions, although not others. India, on the other hand, does not: Promises made in India between people of different religions, languages, or castes are not always taken seriously; the concept of a complex economy resting on trust has yet to be fully developed there. Businessmen tend to deal exclusively with others of their own group. Dependability as a cultural trait varies widely among the various ethnic groups of India: Gujaratis, Punjabis, and Tamils are regarded as more trustworthy than, for instance, Bengalis.

Some nations such as Japan have a highly developed code for interpersonal relations that is widely understood and accepted within the nation itself, but not equally understood in relations with outsiders. Westerners, for example, have had difficulty in grasping the importance of "face" in dealing with Orientals. Orientals, on the other hand, have difficulty understanding such public school notions as "sneakiness." The Japanese did not regard their military attack on Pearl Harbor in 1941 as a violation of any ethical or moral norm—since the United States had actually issued a diplomatic ultimatum. To Japanese, the sudden attack without warning was simply good military tactics, given the inevitability of war.

Reality Orientation. This has to do with the extent to which rational thought processes supersede nonrational or emotional responses in controlling human actions. It is now known that these two modes of mental activity are seated in different parts of the brain: the various parts of the human brain possess different functions and interact with external reality in different ways. The left half of the neocortex is the center of what we commonly call rational activity: planning, calculating, reasoning and problem solving. The right half of the neocortex is the center of intuitive and imaginative functions. These halves of the brain are apparently developed somewhat unequally in different people: engineers, scientists, accountants, computer programmers, and others who do analytical work usually have a greater development of the left side of the brain; artists, poets, mystics, and others who rely more on their imagination have (according to this hypothesis) a greater development of the right side of the brain.

Some societies tend to stress left-brain functions much more than right-brain functions, and conversely. Anthropologists have referred to the two kinds of societies as Apollonian and Dionysian. An Apollonian society puts greater emphasis on the logical, analytic functions of the left hemisphere. Puritanism is an example of an extreme Apollonian ethic — in which emotionalism was actively suppressed — and the Industrial Revolution was clearly an Apollonian process. Marxism, too, is strongly Apollonian. On the other hand, all "other worldly" religions and most primitive societies are fundamentally Dionysian in orientation.

Although most major societies today are predominantly Apollonian insofar as they have glorified science and technology and "scientific" ways of thinking and acting, it seems that Dionysian elements are now increasing in the West. This is exemplified by the rise of evangelical fundamentalist forms of Protestantism and the continuing strength of the counter-culture with its antipathy to scientific rationality and its interest in consciousness-expanding drugs, sexual liberation, "hard" rock music, astrology, occultism, Eastern religions, and so forth.

If this were only a correction of an unhealthy imbalance due to past overemphasis on the rational, analytic, left-brain functions and their emphasis in Western education systems, it might be welcome. However, reactions against extremes tend to go to opposite extremes which are equally undesirable. The Dionysian worldview is essentially a glorification of irrationality, a seeking for ecstatic or "mind-blowing" experience, emphasis on "getting high" and on enhancement of emotions like fear, awe, and pain. It is congenial to supersititious beliefs, witchcraft, sexual orgies, torture-murders,* use of hard drugs, and other excesses. I cannot help, therefore, but regard the current spread of Dionysian elements in Western societies with considerable apprehension. In any case, Dionysian attitudes are clearly incompatible with promoting economic efficiency and the creation or preservation of wealth. Nations like India and Nigeria, in which Dionysian elements are deeply embedded in the underlying culture, are going to have great difficulty in surmounting the economic difficulties they will encounter in the decades to come.

*For instance, the murders of the Manson Cult.

That Dionysian attitudes are antagonistic to the creation of wealth is obvious when one looks at the people who most nearly personify them in our own culture: the people formerly called beatniks and more recently hippies. They are footloose, rootless, living only in the present, eking out a marginal existence with a minimum of discipline or hard work. They are deliberate dropouts from the workaday world and are, in a true sense, parasites—for they live on what others create. One of the great problems of modern liberal, democratic society is its tendency to accumulate parasitic elements just as the submerged hull of a ship accumulates barnacles. I return to this topic later.

Concern With the Future of This World.   This is related to achievement orientation. Achievement of any kind, of course, requires training and preparation aimed at the future, but the future concern I have in mind looks at the very long term. Comparing different societies, it is clear that religious beliefs have had a powerful influence on this value.

A society in which the predominating religion is preoccupied with some sort of afterlife is *not* future oriented in a temporal secular sense. People whose thoughts are on Heaven are not concerned with the future of the society in which they live while temporarily on Earth. People who believe strongly in immortality or reincarnation are future oriented only in the sense of looking beyond their present—often miserable—day to day existence. They do not consider, or care, what kind of earthly lives their children and children's children will have, whether their descendants will have enough to eat, or whether the Earth itself will be fit for human habitation.

In nearly all religions (Christian, Jewish, Moslem, Hindu, or Buddhist), the most traditional religious teachings, that is, the teachings that are considered most orthodox or fundamentalist, are essentially other-worldly. They emphasize not the material well-being (or even the survival) of mankind on this Earth, but rather doctrinal beliefs, adherence to practices sanctified by scriptures, obedience, and/or the pursuit of a mystical "higher" state of consciousness. These attitudes are not oriented to the future of this world. They do not help either individuals or societies to engage in the rigorous thinking and hard decisions necessary to overcome such massive threats as overpopulation, starvation on a mass scale, nuclear war, environmental deterioration, and social collapse.

Most religions urge their followers to the comforting belief that if they follow "the way" or "do God's will" (as directed by their sacred texts and religious instructors), they will be rewarded in afterlife and need have no personal worries about the future. The future would presumably be "in God's hands." Fortunately, most religious groups also have "liberal" elements that are more concerned with the here-and-now than are the orthodox believers and are less bound to literal interpretation of sacred texts. These people, along with unbelievers of various degrees — including strict Marxists — can be and sometimes are future oriented. One of the elements bearing on any social forecast, then, is the trend in the relative strengths of religious versus secular attitudes and of the orthodox or fundamentalist vìs-á-vìs liberal or reform elements in the principal religions of the world.

Unfortunately for the long-term prospects of mankind, however, the most influential of all religions, in practical terms, is the Roman Catholic Church. Here orthodoxy is entrenched and rampant, whereas the liberal fringe is small, disorganized, and apparently unrepresented in the highest councils of the Vatican. All concern for the problems of achieving a decent life for future generations on this Earth was scorned by the late Pope Paul VI.

Papal doctrines insist on the absolute authority of a strictly celibate male priesthood and encourage large families without any consideration of the availability of means to support the children. They condemn artificial means of birth control and forbid abortion and divorce — a set of directives that, if strictly followed, will ensure mass poverty, social unrest, and starvation in a few decades because of inability of the world's resources to cope with its present rate of population growth. As a result, Catholic countries such as the Latin American nations have birth rates among the highest in the world. Some of these countries, such as Argentina and Brazil, still have the space and the land resources to absorb a sizeable population increase above the present level. Other countries are already in deep trouble, and no Latin country can support such a rate of increase for more than another generation or two at most. Nor can the deus ex machina "technology" provide for a perpetually expanding population on a finite resource base. Technology does not achieve miracles (see Chapters 6 and 7). It cannot convert stones into loaves of bread or fish. The Catholic influence, even in the richest countries, will, if not countered, ultimately exhaust the country's (and the world's) resources and bring unimaginable poverty and suffering. The Catholic Church declines all responsibility to the living — now or in the future. Its present role is, essentially, architect of future disaster for mankind on Earth in the name of "eternal" values that can only be enjoyed by the dead.

In European countries such as Italy, Spain, and France, where Catholic influence has been strong for centuries, other forces have fortunately arisen which, to some extent, offset the effects of Church doctrines. Secular and anticlerical influences are strong; even Catholics do not always follow the teachings of their own Church, and there are pressures from the political left and intellectual competition arising from other systems of thought.

The official Catholic view is summed up in the Papal response to the attempt by liberal Catholics to persuade the Vatican to reverse its stand on birth control. The Pope was not blind to the importance of the problem:[12]

The changes which have taken place are in fact noteworthy and of varied kinds. In the first place, there is the rapid demographic development. Fear is shown by many that world population is growing more rapidly than the available resources, with growing distress to many families and developing countries, so that the temptation for authorities to counter this danger with radical measures is great. Moreover, working and lodging conditions, as well as increased exigencies both in the economic field and in that of education, often make the proper education of a larger number of children difficult today. . . .

Still the church remains oriented to eternal rather than temporal values, and its position on birth control is correspondingly unchanged:

. . . we must once again declare that the direct interruption of the generative process already begun, and, above all, directly willed and procured abortion, even if for therapeutic reasons, are to be absolutely excluded as licit means of regulating birth.

Equally to be excluded, as the teaching authority of the Church has frequently declared, is direct sterilization, whether perpetual or temporary, whether of the man or of the woman. Similarly excluded is every action which, either in anticipation of the conjugal act, or in its accomplishment, or in the development of its natural consequences, proposes, whether as an end or as a means, to render procreation impossible.

Another religious belief that hinders planning and action aimed toward the future is Moslem fatalism—the belief that the future is preordained by God (Allah) and cannot be changed by man's actions. This belief, referred to earlier in this book, has unquestionably been one factor responsible for the painfully slow economic growth of countries like Pakistan, Bangla Desh, Egypt, Tunisia, the Sudan, Morocco, and the other non-oil-producing Arab countries.

In many poor countries, such as India, such future orientation as exists among the most rural population takes the form of wanting large families so that at least one or two sons may survive to take care of the parents (and any unmarried daughters) in their old age. This custom originated at a time at which medical care was extremely primitive and most babies died soon after birth. When progress in public health improved the survival rate of children, the need for large families decreased, but the tradition was unaffected and still continues, even though large families now menace the capacity of the country to feed itself. Future orientation, when it takes a narrow form such as this, can be counterproductive.

Marxists are not all atheists, but Marxism is basically incompatible with most orthodox religions. It is centrally concerned with the future of mankind in this world. Marx and Engels predicted a certain series of historical stages through which a society would pass and postulated these stages as *historically inevitable.* Capitalism, they argued, was headed for an ultimate crisis resulting from its internal "contradictions"; the bourgeoisie would first acquire all the wealth; the proletarians, united in misery to their "class interests," would revolt and overthrow the corrupt system; a socialist state would then be established with the workers in common owning all means of production (capital). After the working class' final triumph in the class war and the total elimination of the capitalistic classes, the state would "wither away" and a classless (communist) society would naturally evolve. This scheme provides a specific framework of ideas for evaluating actions in the present and plans for the future. This book is not the place to present a critique of Marxist doctrine, but its future orientation is beyond argument.

The future orientation inherent in both capitalist and socialist thought is one of the reasons why the Catholic Church is antagonistic to both ideologies. To the Church, both are secular movements that place earthly values ahead of eternal ones. Both, from the Church's point of view, are to be condemned. This is a very basic conflict, the outcome of which will have a great effect on the future of human societies in coming decades.

Optimism.   This is an essential ingredient for the realization of all the other wealth-creating values. There is an old saying that "hope springs eternal." But does it? Some people have very little optimism, and with reason. Yet optimism actually has little to do with reason.

My concern is not with hopefulness as an attribute of mind (like imagination) but with optimism as a value arising from a culture and affecting the individuals in that culture. This ultimately seems to depend on the prevailing concept of the nature of man. Is Man a "fallen angel" as Catholic doctrine insists or a "risen ape" as modern biology suggests? This was the riddle presented in Aldous Huxley's famous novel, *Point Counter Point*. If Man is a fallen angel, there is little philosophical basis for hope, for human nature is far indeed from being angelic. But if Man is a risen ape, there is certainly reason for hope — for civilization has been upward bound through the ages of recorded history and can conceivably rise still further. Philosophically, then, humanists and theologians who contrast man as he is with what he "ought to be" are often pessimistic in outlook. Many writers, artists, and moralists feel despair about the future of mankind as expressed in works like H. G. Wells' *Mind at the End of Its Tether* or George Orwell's *1984*. They see the abyss beneath more clearly than the sky above. Scientists, on the other hand, with few exceptions, tend to be optimistic. To many, Man is a "risen ape," and society can be further improved by suitable "engineering."

Countries which raise science to high status tend to be essentially optimistic, willing to look far ahead and make plans for a distant future. The United States and the USSR are probably the most optimistic countries in the world today. Western Europeans and Japanese are less optimistic, probably because they are less strong and less self-sufficient. Other cultures tend to be pessimistic in varying degrees. Moslem fatalism is mildly pessimistic, as are the Chinese, with their long history of cyclic ups and downs. The incomprehensible Hindu pantheon of Gods, in jealous conflict with each other and interfering more or less whimsically in human affairs, is thoroughly pessimistic. There is no rational strategy for "winning" (i.e., assuming favorable Karma) in such a situation. Nonrationality also characterizes the "wheel of life" concept — the unending series of reincarnations that, for most low caste Hindus, can lead down, for example, to life as a dog or cockroach, as easily as up to a higher caste.

Tribal cultures like those of the Black African countries are also deeply pessimistic. Although Christian or Moslem on the surface, they have Animist roots, and much effort goes into propitiating an enormous number of minor deities. Basically, tribal people are at the mercy of these deities, many of whom are whimsical or cruel. Optimism cannot take root in such soil.

Is there any way to appraise the directions in which these six wealth-creating values are moving in today's world? My summary would be this:

1. *Motivation* is high but probably declining in most of Europe, the United Kingdom, and the United States as the old impetus provided by the Protestant ethic and national pride wanes. Motivation

is still strong in Germany, Japan, China, and the USSR. It is low in India and many other poor countries and may even decline further because of malnutrition. It may increase in Brazil and other parts of Latin America as a sense of national identity grows.

2. *Positive Attitude to Work* (achievement orientation) is declining in the United Kingdom and the United States, because of an unresolved conflict with equity issues. It is quite strong in Northern Europe, Japan, and China; much less strong in Latin Europe, Latin America, the Moslem world, and the USSR; weak in India because of the caste system and in Black Africa because of a tribal cultural heritage.

3. *Integrity and personal honor* are high among the middle class in all Western countries, is less strong among the poor, very strong in Japan, strong in Arab countries, and not highly developed in the USSR. These traits are weak (but possibly increasing) in Latin America. They are variable but generally weak in India and undeveloped in ex-tribal societies like Nigeria.

4. *Reality orientation*; in Western countries, especially the United States and United Kingdom, the trend seems to be away from the strong rationalistic (Apollonian) position of the past toward some nonrational emotional (Dionysian) attitudes. If it goes too far, this trend could seriously reduce the capacity to produce wealth. The communist countries are strongly Apollonian and are likely to remain so under their present regimes. Nonrational elements are very strong and likely to hinder the economic progress of India and some African states. The Catholic and Moslem religions also contain significant nonrational elements.

5. *Concern with the future* is still strong in the Protestant countries and in the United States. It is also very strong in all communist countries. It is weaker in the Latin countries—despite anticlericalism—due to Catholic doctrine, especially in Latin America. It is weak or nonexistent in Moslem countries because of fatalist religion and in India because of both religion and the caste system.

6. *Optimism* is strong in science-oriented countries—both Western and communist—although it is slipping. (America went through a pessimistic phase in the last decade, although optimism appears to be on the rise again.) It is weaker in the Moslem world, China, India, and the countries of Black Africa. It is also weak in strongly Catholic countries.

This is a rather somber appraisal, on the whole. A number of wealth-creating values may be declining in the United States, which bears a key economic relationship to the rest of the world. Nor is there much hope for a rapid rise of wealth-creating values in Latin America, the Moslem World, India, and Black Africa. However, I am not yet ready to write off the economic future of the United States or the democratic countries of the West. These countries are still very strong and possess and value personal freedom to a considerable degree. If they can draw on the strengths of individualism without succumbing to the siren calls for an impossible egalitarian ideal, they may continue to generate new wealth while propagating the wealth-creating values that the rest of the world needs to progress.

REFERENCES

1. Daniel P. Moynihan, "Capitalisms' World Struggle For Survival," (interview), *Nations Business,* February 1976.
2. K. Marx and F. Engels, *Communist Manifesto,* Henry Regnery Co., Chicago, 1949.
3. E. F. Schumacher, *Small is Beautiful: Economics as if People Mattered,* Harper and Row, New York, 1973.
4. Ivan Illich, *Energy and Equity,* Harper and Row, New York, *1974.*
5. Pope Paul VI, *Populorum Progressio,* "On the Development of Peoples," Encyclical Letter.
6. Ayn Rand, "Requiem For Man" in *Capitalism, The Unknown Ideal,* Signet Books, New York, p. 314.
7. J. M. Keynes, "Economic Possibilities For Our Grandchildren" in *Essays in Persuasion,* Harcourt, Brace and Company, New York, 1932.
8. Max Weber, *The Protestant Ethic and The Spirit of Capitalism,* English Translation by Talcott Parsons, G. Allen & Unwin, Ltd., London, 1930.
9. R. H. Tawney, *Religion and the Rise of Capitalism,* Harcourt, Brace and Company, New York, 1926.
10. C. P. Snow, *The Two Cultures and the Scientific Revolution,* Godkin Lectures, Cambridge University Press, 1959.
11. R. H. Tawney, *op cit.*
12. Pope Paul VI, *On the Regulation of Birth,* Encyclical Letter, July 25, 1968.

CHAPTER 3

MEASURES OF MAN
–INTERNATIONAL

INTRODUCTORY COMMENTS

Mankind is highly diverse in language, religion, culture, and in the level of development of political and social institutions. This diversity is beneficial in many ways. Without it, there would be little purpose in international intercourse, apart from purely commercial activities. The diversity of Man enables a variety of different kinds of societies to coexist, and political competition and social interaction create the mechanisms for the most successful of the various institutions and social systems to prosper and survive. As in competition between biological species, the weakest and least fit tend to lose out. But, also in analogy with the biosphere, there is room for many survivors because there are many specialized "niches."

Certain nations – like certain species – are destined to be major actors in the world scene because of their large populations and/or area, their access to critical resources, their exceptional internal discipline and cohesion, or their exceptionally advanced technology. Examples of each of these special advantages are obvious and need hardly be cited here. Other nations survive and prosper by finding and exploiting a specialized need – like Switzerland and Luxembourg in Europe, Hong Kong, and Singapore in Asia, and Lebanon (until recently) in the Middle East.

However, there are also a good many countries in today's world that appear to belong in neither group. Since nineteenth century colonialism is now at an end, most of these leftovers, such as the island principalities of the Indian Ocean and the Caribbean or the "banana republics" of Central America – can expect to be left alone to stagnate or starve quietly. In some cases, a group of them may voluntarily merge into a larger, more viable unit – as the countries of Europe have begun to link themselves via the EEC and as a group of Latin countries have formed the Andean Pact. Another possibility is for micro states to unilaterally join larger ones for mutual benefit, as the Mariana Islanders recently voted to become a United States territory.*

More important for the world as a whole, however, is the fate of the larger and more important countries and their future relationships with each other. This is the topic of the chapter.

NATIONALISM AND NATION STATES

Nation states have been proliferating in recent decades as peoples in Africa, Asia, and the Pacific Islands have emerged from colonial status. The large number of tiny new poverty-stricken totalitarian and impotent "nations" has altered the atmosphere and tone as well as the membership of the United Nations, has complicated many problems of international negotiation by increasing the number and shrillness of the interested parties, and has resulted in some erosion of the power and influence of the older, stabler, more developed, and more democratic states. Nationalism, obviously, has achieved a new lease on life at a time when the world's needs would be better served by larger political and economic aggregations.

At one level, nationalism is an integrative force in countries; it supersedes tribal and local loyalties, submerging them in a larger loyalty. The rise of modern Germany is a case in point. Two hundred years ago what is now Germany was a collection of feudal leftovers, not a nation state in the modern sense. Loyalties were to the church and to the local baron or margrave, not to the Habsburgs or to the ancient Holy Roman Empire. A citizen would have viewed himself as a Württemberger or a Thuringian or a Bavarian, but not necessarily as a German. During the nineteenth century this view changed: under Frederick the Great and Bismarck, Germany became a cohesive nation of German-speaking people. The Italian-speaking provinces of the Aüstro-Hungarian Empire were similarly unified during the nineteenth century to create the modern nation of Italy.

Nationalism is not so effective, however, where neither religion nor

---

*It cannot be taken for granted that small, poor countries will be accepted as merger partners by larger richer neighbors, or even former colonial rulers to whom they would be burdensome. Some of the smallest and poorest new republics were cut loose against their wishes.

language unifies. The Austro-Hungarian Empire and the Ottoman (Turkish) Empire collapsed under nationalist pressures compounded by the stress of World War I. Catholic Ireland finally succeeded in separating itself from Great Britain—minus the six Protestant northern counties—at more or less the same time.

India—unified by the British—was partitioned into primarily Moslem and primarily Hindu parts soon after independence in 1947. British Palestine was also partitioned into Jewish and Arab parts after the British departure. The same kind of thing has happened more recently in Cyprus and in Lebanon. The problem is even more acute when a nation incorporates many traditionally hostile tribal groups, as in Nigeria, for example. The Ibo tribesmen of Southern Nigeria recently attempted to secede and form a separate country (Biafra). This secession was only ended by a bloody civil war. Other examples are easily cited. The Kurdish rebellion in Iraq was recently suppressed, but perhaps only temporarily. Even in the West, Basques want autonomy from Spain, the Scots are agitating for more autonomy within the United Kingdom, and Quebec has voted into office a party dedicated to autonomy, if not independence, from Canada.

At the international level, nationalism is often a disintegrative force. It divides the nations at a time when the major problems of the world (food distribution, monetary stability, capital flow to undeveloped areas, energy supplies, pollution of the biosphere, etc.) are worldwide in scope and require for their solution a high degree of international cooperation. A key question about the future, then, is whether the integrative or the disintegrative aspects of nationalism will tend to prevail.

As nationalism emerges among a people and enables them to weld themselves into a coherent national state, its emotional intensity seems to follow a rising curve. When a nation is young, the tone of its patriotism is apt to be jingoistic and even xenophobic. There is much flag waving, patriotic speech making, praise of the armed forces, and the like. A threat of war raises the pitch higher still.

All the older nations experienced this kind of nationalistic fervor in their nation-building phase. It tends to persist until some excess produces a counterreaction. In Europe, the last great orgy of nationalism was World War I. Emotionally and spiritually, people responded, at first, with rousing inspirational speeches, marching, songs, recruiting hysteria, and all the rest of the familiar blarney. Duty to country was touted as a supreme virtue—to die for one's country the ultimate achievement. Tear-jerking, patriotic sentimentality was the style. One cannot help recalling the famous words of soldier-poet Rupert Brooke (1887–1915):[1]

> If I should die, think only this of me:
> That there's some corner of a foreign field
> That is for ever England ...

Brooke did not go so far as to glorify death in battle (although some did), but his lofty verse certainly conveyed nothing of the fear, filth, or futility of the war. To people at a distance, and even to some of the combatants, the war was a tremendously exciting experience. To the infantry soldiers in the trenches, of course, it was simply an extended horror, ending more often than not in asphyxiation, maiming, or meaningless, impersonal extinction.

This emotional intensity kept World War I going long after it should have been evident that the war's cost was out of all proportion to any gains either side could be expected to win. However, almost no-one—public or private—dared to say that the war had ceased to serve (if it ever did serve) any rational purpose. When it ended in general exhaustion, none of the victorious Allies could point to any solid benefit derived from it except the defeat of the Kaiser and his armies. Even this benefit was a sham, since the arrogant but sane Kaiser was replaced in a very few years by Hitler and the Nazi madness. It was not the "War to End All Wars," nor did it "make the world safe for democracy" as the citizens of England, France, and the United States had been led to expect. It achieved nothing, really, except the end of a relatively civilized era and the beginning of an unprecedentedly barbaric one.

This disaster created, as it were, an "antigen" for the disease of patriotic nationalism in England and France, at least. Indeed, a famous Oxford Union debate held only a few years before the outbreak of World War II approved the proposition "that this House will under no circumstances fight for King and Country." Such sentiments would have been unthinkable two decades earlier. Pacifism had certainly become respectable, at least among intellectuals, in the England of the 1930s. These attitudes may have influenced both Hitler and Chamberlain in the crucial Prague negotiations of 1938. (There was little or no antiwar sentiment in Germany due to resentment of the Treaty of Versailles.) When World War II broke out in 1939, the patriotism of the contending nations, other than Japan, was much more subdued. There was desperation, there was fear, there was willingness to risk death if necessary, but the exalted notions of glory and duty to country had lost much of their power to move men. The war was experienced instead as a grim, dirty, dreadful, appalling, but necessary, ordeal to be faced. Bill Mauldin's cartoon characters Willy and Joe expressed the attitudes of the citizen-soldiers in that holocaust.

A most impressive difference of attitudes between World Wars I and II was shown in the contrasting treatment of the defeated nations at the wars' end. World War I ended with the vengeful Treaty of Versailles — an attempt to crush Germany, to keep her hopelessly in debt, and to destroy her capacity to wage war in the future. The policy failed, obviously. Its main result was the catastrophic inflation and its resulting pauperization of the middle class, which ended by bringing Hitler to power. World War II was followed by a much more humane and rational policy, permitting (and assisting) the defeated nations to rebuild their shattered governmental institutions and industries. In particular, the temperate and enlightened policy followed by the United States toward Japan resulted ultimately in that country's rise to become an economic giant and a solidly democratic society in which personal freedom and respect for civil rights seem to have taken healthy root.

These are significant changes which go part way toward explaining the anomaly of the Vietnam War in which a great power — the United States — was held to a military stalemate, politically defeated, and badly humilated by a small nation. Yet there was no governmental collapse* no divisive McCarthyist witchhunt or search for a scapegoat to blame. Most Americans merely felt relief. The older form of patriotism would have led to bitter accusations of treachery and demands for retaliation against North Vietnam and the resignation of the governmental and military leadership. In fact, the American people were sick and tired of the war and relieved to get out of the quagmire, even at the cost of considerable loss of national pride and prestige.

Is nationalism declining in the older nations? I think, on the whole, it is not (yet), but its manifestations are changing. Its rationale remains: race, common language and institutions, common experiences of triumph and suffering, and special links to a particular geographic territory (the homeland). All these factors seem to be involved in group identity and justify insistence on retaining control of the major decisions affecting the group (sovereignty). To some extent, this notion of retaining control or sovereignty is illusory. Governments, even in democratic countries, rarely consult their people in detail about the deci-

---

*Except for Nixon's resignation, following Watergate, which was traumatic enough.

sions they make. Even so, people prefer to have decisions made by *their* government (even an oppressive or a dictatorial one) than by foreigners. Irrational this may be, but it is a powerful feeling and it is at the heart of nationalism. The idea of sacrificing any national sovereignty in the interest of a vaguely defined international community—which is not a true community in any sense—is still anathema in the United States, as in most other countries. This situation is likely to change but slowly. In fact, it has been recently discovered that an impulse to identify with and defend territory is biologically innate, not culturally acquired. This tends to suggest that nationalism in some form is a very deep rooted force that will not be altered in a fundamental way by any conceivable political changes.

Yet forces now developing may bring about an eventual shift toward some partial sacrifice of sovereignty even by the United States. Such forces have had visible effects in Europe in the gradual establishment of the European Economic Community (EEC) and in the belated action of the United Kingdom to join after first scornfully refusing and later being excluded by Gaullist France. This suggests the possibility of irrational barriers gradually giving way under pressure of economic realities, for it is clear that a fragmented Europe cannot compete successfully, either economically or politically, with the superpowers, the United States and the Soviet Union. Whether this kind of rationality can be brought to the questions of monetary stability, competition for raw materials, equalization of the rich-poor gap in the world, and the equitable distribution of food and energy are other questions. Much hinges on the answers.

One near certainty in the decades to come is that competition between nations for access to raw materials, especially fuels, will intensify. In times past, this kind of competition took the form of colonialism, but the colonial era is dead and cries of "neocolonialism" or "economic-imperialism" from the third world nations are echoes of the beating of a dead horse. Competition for resources now is taking—and will increasingly take—the form of bilateral agreements between producers and consumers with nations and/or giant corporations bidding against each other for preferential treatment. To whatever extent they are able, the producers of raw materials will use OPEC* as a model and attempt to form cartels to keep prices high. In rare cases, especially where the supply is limited to a few regions (e.g., bananas, sugar, coffee, bauxite), they may partially succeed. The competition, then, will not only be between the consuming nations themselves but

*The Organization of Petroleum Exporting Countries.

also between the consumers as a group and the producers as a group. Will the consuming nations be able to subordinate their diverse interests enough to function as a cohesive unit? The response of the consuming nations to OPEC's recent oil price boosts gives little encouragement for thinking so. More likely, existing international bodies such as the OECD or UNCTAD will play a gradually larger role in negotiating and ultimately settling trade policies and prices.

INTERNATIONAL COMPETITION

Economic competition between nations for export markets has a dynamic that, if understood, can be helpful in forecasting what is likely to happen in future decades. There is a useful analogy between international economic competition and the competition between products or materials in a particular industry. When a new product is beginning to compete against an established older one, it is axiomatic among sophisticated market researchers that, once the substitute captures 10% (more or less) of the market, the key barrier is breached and only inertia remains in the way. A complete takeover is usually only a matter of time. The 10% threshold is enough to assure that the new product is a real alternative and that it is either better or cheaper than the old one. The 10% penetration level is beyond the reach of a fad or curiosity.

The reason for the market researchers' rule of thumb is quite straightforward. A new product must have captured the first 10% of the market *without benefit of savings due to economies of scale in production and distribution.* Thus, as its market share rises further, its cost will drop, whereas the old product is now in a position of declining sales, increasing overcapacity (or underutilization of capacity) and increasing capital write-off per unit of output. Thus the new product can continue to cut prices, whereas, even at the old price, the old one merely becomes unprofitable and eventually unviable.

This frequently observed pattern seems applicable also to competition between nations, allowing for the fact that there are many more competitors and the terms of competition are often obscured by political, geographical, and other factors. The same mechanism that operates in the narrow case would also apply in the broader one, namely, that once a new entrant has obtained a foothold in international markets, even if that foothold is achieved by subsidy for small-scale production, its costs are likely to drop thereafter as output rises. I think history shows that once a new competitor enters the scene and begins to penetrate international markets, successfully taking markets away from an older exporter, there is very little that the latter can do* to change the direction of the trend. It is not until some still newer challenger comes along that the pattern will change again.

Thus in the last 700 years we have seen the Venetian Republic — the first modern trading nation — overtaken by Portugal, which perfected the arts of long-distance navigation and dominated international trade in the fifteenth century. Shortly after Columbus' Spanish-sponsored voyages to the New World in 1492–1498, Portugal lost primacy to Spain for ninety years until the dispersal of the great Spanish Armada (1588). Thereafter Spain also declined slowly as Holland and Britain battled for trading supremacy. The Dutch — inhibited by dynastic and religious conflict with Spain — began to fall behind in the late seventeenth century, and Britain took over undisputed trading leadership of the world early in the eighteenth century. Napoleon's challenge in Europe was contained on land and defeated on the seas. Of course, in those days trade was accompanied by colonial expansion, and British hegemony lasted until the early part of the twentieth century, passing its zenith at the time of the Boer War. Trade in the later period of British dominance was mainly in textiles, cheap manufactured articles, hardware, industrial and agriculture raw materials, and arms.

In the late nineteenth century, Germany and the United States began to challenge British economic leadership. Starting from a less developed situation, Russia and Japan also began to make their moves. Japan defeated Russia in the Russo-Japanese War of 1904 and expanded into Taiwan, Korea, and Manchuria. Germany competed directly with Britain for colonial territory and markets in Africa and the Middle East (especially Turkey and Iraq) and would undoubtedly have prevailed in straight economic competition — especially in arms, machinery, and chemicals — had it not been for World War I, which temporarily disrupted the German economy and raised the United States prematurely to superpower status. World War I also shattered Czarist Russia and paved the way for the Bolshevik revolution in 1917. Thereafter, until the 1950s, Russia was preoccupied with internal development, and later with defeating Hitler. It has not yet entered into world trade to a significant degree. The United States did not consolidate its competitive trading advantages in the twenty years between World War I and World War II, being also preoccupied with internal development and domestic problems. Germany recovered from the aftermath

---

*Presumably one thing it cannot do is lower its labor or raw material costs.

of World War I in the 1930s, only to embark on a second futile round of military conquest, as did Japan, which lost all the overseas territories it had grabbed earlier.

Following World War II, Germany and Japan, having finally turned away from militarism, concentrated their efforts intensively on economic growth, and both countries succeeded amazingly well in building export markets for chemicals, pharmaceuticals, automotive equipment, and electrical equipment. Temporary United States political/military dominance after World War II resulted in an inflated dollar. This, plus United States preoccupation with the Cold War and political military competiton with the USSR, gave Germany and Japan a great advantage in establishing a strong trading position. As of the mid-1970s, Germany and Japan are undisputed champions in the export competition, but their success is creating problems. They are awash with excess dollars, and domestic labor costs are rising quite fast. Both countries are controlling domestic inflation to a significant degree by allowing their currencies to become more and more overvalued, thus reducing the apparent cost of imported raw materials and food. This mechanism obviously cannot work forever. Eventually it will cost both countries some of their overseas markets, particularly in the United States. In addition, when the enormous trade surpluses begin to shrink, and the Deutschemark and the yen end their long postwar climb against the dollar, the same mechanism will work in reverse, to the benefit of the United States. The United States will be buying oil and selling food, computers, and arms with an *appreciating* currency that will hold domestic inflation rates down and accelerate the process of recovery.

CORRUPTION AND EFFICIENCY IN GOVERNMENT

In the previous chapter in the discussion of values I spoke of honesty and integrity as being wealth-creating values. The converse—that dishonesty and corruption tend to undermine productivity—was also touched on. Indeed, there are some parts of the world in which deeply rooted corruption is thought to constitute a major obstacle to economic development. This is particularly true in noncommunist developing countries with fairly advanced social programs "on the books" and correspondingly onerous taxes—on those (few) who pay. Indonesia, India, and Latin America come especially to mind. To accumulate, or even retain, wealth in such countries, political patronage and protection are vital ingredients. These are purchased with bribes, direct or indirect, which can, in themselves, constitute significant transfer of wealth. The law is not uniformly applied to rich and poor, which undermines its legitimacy and creates cynicism among the better informed citizens. In a country ruled by an oligarchy of wealth, where virtually every public official is on the take, effective social reform, even effective administration of public policy, through constitutional channels is impossible. Hence reform movements in most of Latin America (except Mexico) and Africa tend to take the form of military-backed *coups d'etat,* which are themselves quickly corrupted.

The fact that idealistic "soft socialist" programs put forward by most regimes are seldom and badly implemented is not in itself an obstacle to economic development. On the contrary, private sector development probably takes place much to the extent that entrepreneurs find means to evade the intent of such laws and programs. The problem is not so much that corrupt governments get in the way – although they do so increasingly – but that corrupt governments are inefficient. They offer too little of a positive nature in exchange for the overhead costs they impose on productive enterprise.

For example, less developed countries (LDCs) usually have state monopolies on water, electric power, communications, and transportation services, which are almost invariably operated grossly inefficiently. (Each service breakdown is a new opportunity to extract further "mordida" or "baksheesh" from the helpless customer.) Public sector investments such as roads, dams, irrigation projects, and the like are subject to so many contrary political winds that it is unduly risky for a prudent private sector enterprise to commit its own funds on any investment that is contingent on timely completion of such a project. Corruption – big and small – is perhaps the major reason for crippling governmental inefficiency in many less developed countries and as such constitutes a major impediment to progress.

There is, of course, a significant difference between "big" corruption – the nephew of the minister is appointed to the directorship of the state gas monopoly, and, in turn, noncompetitive contracts are awarded to the firms which contributed most to the political war chest of the party in power – and "small" corruption. The latter is exemplified by the ten dollar bill which persuades the traffic cop not to write a ticket, or the 100 peso note which speeds official approval of an electrical connection. To a rigid moralist the two are equivalent. To an ethical relativist the former is likely to seem far worse. (The bribes are bigger, obviously.)

However, in terms of governmental efficiency, the opposite may be true. Actually, big corruption (in a country like Indonesia) does not stop socially useful things from getting done (it may be the only way to expedite them), whereas small corruption in the mordida or baksheesh tradition is a form of sand in the politicoeconomic works (see next chapter). It tends to slow everything down. Paperwork proliferates, since the more paper work and approvals a project requires, the more money gets spread around among clerks and inspectors. Thus the cancer grows.

I do not want to leave the impression that I favor big corruption. I do not. However, it is ironic that the most effective answer to it, in practice, seems to be the decentralization of power and the proliferation of bureaucracy. The more diffuse the network of power, the less it can be abused by a small number of people. Big bribes are only offered to individuals who have a great deal of real power, which means power to get things done. The major reason big corruption is now relatively rare in the developed countries is not because of high morality. It is due to rampant bureaucratization: to the fact that very few (if any) individuals in the public sector have the power to make things happen, and those few are under constant scrutiny by legions of reporters, accountants, auditors, and contract officers who are answerable to other, often rival, authorities.

What of the less developed countries? Leaving morality aside, it is not big corruption that impedes economic development, except insofar as it undermines public support for the policies of government. It seems outrageous to a middle-class American that an Indonesian general of no particular educational attainments can become a millionaire more or less overnight. Is Indonesia worse off with a new class of millionaire generals and a fast-growing petrochemical industry than it would be with an incorruptible but massive and inefficient (and expensive) bureaucracy? If these were the true alternatives I would, with some reluctance, choose the first.

What of the future? I suspect corruption — big or small — will not be eliminated from government in the next half century. As governments become more complex and bureaucracies grow, it seems likely that opportunities for really massive corruption — such as in Indonesia today — will gradually disappear. From the standpoint of inhibiting economic growth, small corruption is worse and probably harder to stamp out. This will not, however, penalize or favor any one country or group of countries over the rest.

INTERSECTORAL COMPARISONS

The question now is, in the light of this analysis what can we expect in the next fifty years? That question can only be explored intelligently by subdividing the world economy into distinct sectors and examining national comparative advantages one sector at a time.

In the *agricultural* sector, it seems clear that, despite substantial progress in the European Economic Community's becoming much more nearly self-sufficient in food, the United States has actually strengthened its competitive position in world food markets. It has only two significant competitors—Canada and Australia—both of which are much smaller producers, although similar to the United States in terms of geopolitical and economic perspectives. Competition from Argentina, which might have been intense under some different circumstances, has been virtually nonexistent in the past twenty years. Indeed, Argentina has declined in relative economic importance since the nineteenth century. Brazil, on the other hand, which may in the future become a major competitor in this field, has not yet begun to approach its potential, and it is not by any means certain whether Brazil will achieve significant progress in its agriculture. Thus it seems safe to project that during the next twenty-five years the United States will continue to dominate the world scene in agricultural production, providing about 75% of exportable agricultural commodities and probably continuing, at least for some time, to increase its relative dominance in this area.

In regard to *raw materials other than agricultural products,* dominance belongs to the countries with the cheapest remaining unexploited reserves. The countries of the Persian Gulf are extraordinarily well endowed with high-quality hydrocarbon resources. They will obviously convert this asset into substantial economic wealth of other kinds during the coming decades. This topic is more conveniently discussed in connection with resource problems (Chapter 8), so I do not pursue it here.

As regards other sectors, world trade can reasonably be divided into three categories. The first is *low technology* manufactured goods such as basic iron, steel, or other finished metals, basic chemicals, textiles, paper, wood products, ships, automobiles, tractors, simple machine tools, products assembled from mass-produced parts, and so forth. The second category, *high technology* manufactured goods, includes electronic equipment, computers, telecommunications, precision machine tools, jet engines, nuclear power plants, chemical plants and oil refineries, sophisticated military equipment, jet aircraft, radar navigation equipment, satellites, scientific instruments, pharmaceuticals, and perhaps some other things. The third category is nonmaterial *services,* such as banking and credit, insurance, education, administrative and business services (economic consulting, legal, scientific, technological research and development, etc.) and tourism.

It is quite clear that countries tend to specialize in different areas. Japan and West Germany have concentrated since World War II mainly in the first area (low technology products), where they have competed very successfully against Britain and the United States in world markets. In particular, Germany has been very successful in exporting specialized steel products, chemicals, pharmaceuticals, machine tools, electrical quipment, and automotive equipment. Japan has been successful since World War II in exporting textiles, steel, ships, motor vehicles, radios, TVs, cameras, and watches. (Textile products and electronics have already moved on to Korea, Taiwan, Hong Kong, and Singapore.)

In the high technology category (computers, aircraft, nuclear power plants, sophisticated weapons, and so forth) the United States holds a dwindling lead, but Japan has strongly challenged United States dominance in some fields, especially electronics. France is also competing quite well in selling military aircraft, nuclear power plants, and even urban transit systems. Germany is the capital goods champion. It might also be noted that France is the world's leading exporter of certain sophisticated consumer products like glassware, wine, liqueurs, cheeses, patés, perfumes, and high fashion clothing, which contain a very large component of skill that is difficult to acquire.

In the third area (services), Britain still maintains a substantial foothold in the market for business and financial services, particularly investment banking and insurance. Lloyds of London remains the world's leader and chief innovator in marine and certain other kinds of insurance. The British investment banks are still important in some areas; consulting engineering is another area in which Britain is still quite strong (although the United States is dominant). Britain has viable communications, publications, and entertainment industries, as does the United States.

There is a rather obvious connection between the service industries in which Britain is preeminent and their dependence on the use of the English language. English is now (probably past the point of no return) the universal language of science, business, and technological communication. This gives English-speaking countries a built-in permanent advantage in such fields as business services, insurance, and finance which other countries will find it very hard to overcome. This also explains Britain's continued international strength in publications, advertising, and research and development, all of which are closely tied to the use of language. Other business and business-related services are concentrated in the United States; for example, major international financial dealings are primarily consummated on

Wall Street or at least by United States-based international banks. The world's chief stock and commodity exchanges are in New York, London, and Chicago, and it is difficult to see why any of these activities would ever find it advantageous to move their centers of operation outside the English-speaking countries.

The United States also shares with the United Kingdom a world leadership in television programming, movie making, music recording (at least for the international market), and other components of the entertainment business. Television shows, movies, songs, and records originating in the English-speaking world are played or shown in almost all other countries, whereas non-English-speaking countries primarily produce only for their own domestic market. Similarly, the English language is the only one in which there are many publications (newspapers, magazines, and books) in countries in which a different language is spoken. Japan for example, has several English language newspapers, English language television for several hours per day in Tokyo, and an English language book publisher. All national newspapers and magazines in India are in English — indeed, it is the official language of government. In Europe, the Paris *Herald Tribune* is perhaps the only all-European newspaper. In Mexico City and Teheran there are several English language newspapers. It goes without saying that these publications are read not only by local residents or expatriates from the United States or Britain, but also often by resident Germans, French, Japanese, and businessmen from other countries who may be more adapt with English than they are with the local language. For similar reasons, English will probably continue to be the dominant language of most of the "information" industries, including business consulting. English is the major language of all significant international organizations, belonging both to the United Nations and others. It is incidentally the basic language of computers, nuclear energy, aviation, and space travel.

So many of the new technologies are so intimately involved with the English language in their terminology and literature that the people for whom English is a native tongue have a very important competitive advantage. This does not apply in manufacturing, to be sure, or undertaking hardware-related engineering, but it is certainly relevant in terms of the documentation, software development, and information-related services pertaining to these technologies.

Tourism and related personal services are available in many countries, but they have been particularly highly developed in and around the Mediterranean and more recently the Caribbean, Mexico, and Hawaii. For tourism, of course, countries with attractive beaches or mountains, interesting historical monuments or "ruins" and cultural resources, and interesting cuisine will always have built-in advantages—provided the government is reasonably stable and hospitable. There is no reason to suppose that the present mix of these resources will change much in the future. However, North and Northwest Africa, the west coast of South America, and possibly the east coast of Brazil and the Polynesian Islands of the Pacific offer very substantial tourist potential that has not yet been realized. Clearly, tourist potential exists in other parts of the world also, notably India and Ceylon (Sri Lanka), but tourism is not likely to become an important part of the economy of southern Africa, south Asia, or Southeast Asia in the next half century unless transportation costs drop substantially and politics in those areas becomes less volatile.

Returning to the sector of *low technology* manufacturing, the "assembly" kinds of industries seem almost sure to move into the countries in which labor costs are still very low and there is not much chance of them rising substantially in the next fifty years. That would seem to indicate countries like India. By low technology in this context I refer to the assembly of things, devices, components, products, appliances, and so on from mass-produced parts, but in a range and variety of sizes and styles which require a degree of personal attention that is difficult to program into a mass production system. This also applies to certain handicrafts. The high-quality end of the market for furniture, home furnishings, and clothing is now (and will probably continue to be) reserved for handcrafting. This market could be increasingly captured by low-wage countries with highly skilled craftsmen (such as India), provided the craftsmen can be taught new styles and designs—which may not be their traditional ones—to satisfy tastes in other countries.*

In some of the other areas of low technology manufactured goods, such as iron and steel products, agricultural equipment, machinery, and motor vehicles, it seems probable that the Soviet Union and Eastern Europe, along with Taiwan, Korea, and Brazil, will make a major challenge to the West Germans and Japanese. On the other hand, the USSR will probably not compete effectively in producing other consumer goods, at least in the relatively near future, because of problems in design and marketing. Textile manufacturing, of course, is already moving into South Asia where labor costs are the lowest, and it is

*Yet it is curious that such craftsmanship seems to be on the wane, rather than on the increase. Despite the growing demand for high-quality craftsmanship, young people in India, Iran, Mexico, and so on seem uninterested in learning the necessary skills.

likely that India and Pakistan will have a much bigger part of the world textile market in thirty years.

Japan will probably willingly give up a good part of its present large share of the world's exports of iron and steel products, ships, and automobiles. This is because Japan is an overcrowded country, with severe environmental degradation and rising resistance from local residents to the use of increasingly scarce coastal land for factory sites. I think that as these trends evolve, Japan will deliberately move more into the area of high technology manufactured goods where the environmental impact is less, especially telecommunications, satellites, electronics, computers, and also high-quality consumer goods (cameras, watches, appliances, furniture, and furnishings). Japan will probably not make any major impact on the business and other nonmaterial services, except for a modest amount of tourism.* This is mainly because of its very difficult language and communications problems. Indeed, Japan will become an increasingly large service importer.

Germany is likely to try to move more into the high technology area than it has and will probably enjoy some success. For example, Germany has made a strong move into the nuclear fuel processing business and has developed technology which is already scheduled for export to Brazil and elsewhere. Germany will not succeed in exporting business or entertainment services to any great extent because of inherent language problems.

It would seem that the United States is likely to continue to phase out of the low technology manufactured goods and will begin to lose much of its current advantage in the high technology area as well within the next twenty years and certainly within the next half century. The United States will continue to be dominant in business, technical, communications, and entertainment services for many decades to come. The United States is also becoming more attractive to foreign tourists.

Some countries, of course, have advantages in possessing material resources not easily duplicated elsewhere. An example of this is the ability to grow hardwood trees very rapidly. This ability is uniquely concentrated in the humid tropics, notably the Amazon and Central Africa, and in Southeast Asia. By the same token, large parts of these areas are not suitable for permanent agriculture due to the hilly terrain, erosion, and problems of soil leaching. Consequently, these regions should become specialized producers of wood products, at least up

*Japanese tourists will spend much more outside their own country than foreigners are likely to spend visiting Japan.

to the level of finished materials and possibly some subassembly work. Depending on the price of transportation, the final assembly and manufacturing of finished wooden furniture, house components, and so on might well be carried out in low-wage countries such as India, as previously noted.

As more and more countries get into the competition, the world seems to approach nearer and nearer to an "equilibrium" situation characterized by each country having dominance in that particular market in which it has an intrinsic advantage, such as the United States has with respect to food products and language-intensive services. The Middle East has the major petroleum reserves and will probably build a petrochemical industry on that base. The Soviet Union will become a dominant source of basic materials, such as cement, iron and steel, and other metals, mainly because it has good sources of them in Siberia, plus a highly disciplined workforce. There can be no question of "work stoppages," for example, at least under the present government. The USSR can also compete in certain high tchnology areas, especially aircraft and sophisticated weapons. The big question marks are Europe and Japan, which probably have nowhere to go except into ultrahigh technology products, where they must compete with the United States and the USSR. But Europe and Japan will retain some cultural advantages from high-quality elitist educational systems, strong basic and theoretical science, and strong traditions of craftsmanship.

INTERDEPENDENCE

It is a truism that the further the world moves toward industrialization and urban living, the more interdependent it becomes. Only an agrarian society in which people consume products made locally or by themselves can be in any substantial degree self-sufficient—and only at very primitive subsistence levels. The interdependence of the modern world already leaves virtually every nation (with the partial exception of continental ones like the United States, the USSR, Brazil, and China) highly vulnerable to the disruption of channels of supply. This interdependence is growing inexorably, decade by decade.

If every nation in the world behaved in strictly rational fashion and acted always in terms of its own best long-term interests, the fact of growing interdependence would persuade nations to draw together and set up international agencies with the power to provide some protection against possible breakdowns of the international order on which all depend. Is this likely to occur in reality? Any objective observer is forced to conclude that, as of the present moment, it is not.

How does the realization of its dependence on the outside world affect a country? To get some clues to this, one might look at Japan. Japan is interesting because — once one of the most isolated and xenophobic of nations — it is now perhaps the country whose economic survival is most completely dependent on trade relations with other parts of the world. Although it produces its major staple (rice), it is probably no more than three-quarters self-sufficient in food overall, and any improvement in diet must come by increased imports (especially of meat or animal feed). It has virtually no metals and must import nearly all its fossil energy. Of course, Japan pays for all this by exporting low technology manufactured goods, which it now does very efficiently.

Japan is not unique in the world; most of the smaller European countries are in comparable situations. Taken as a whole, the EEC is self-sufficient in agricultural terms, except for animal feedgrains, and is likely to continue so. However, the EEC too must import much of its meat (or feed), metals, and petroleum, notwithstanding the oil discoveries in the North Sea. The United States is also increasingly dependent on the outside world for some metals, and nearly half of United States petroleum requirements now come from abroad. Against this, the United States is by far the major exporter of food, producing about 75% of all agricultural commodities in world trade. The autarkic goal of "Project Independence" was always unrealistic on economic grounds and, if taken seriously as a national policy, would have set in motion very damaging counterreactions in other countries.[2]

At the present time only the Soviet Union and China are truly self-sufficient to a very large extent, although the USSR seems unable to feed itself at a Western standard, and China functions close to the subsistence level. To upgrade its national diet, the Soviet Union is inevitably moving into a closer trade relationship with the outside world. This is undoubtedly one of the factors that made "dètente" possible. The same is gradually becoming true of China. For those two countries, the trend toward interdependence could still be reversed, at least temporarily. The Soviet Union could conceivably again shut the door on the outside world, as Stalin once did. This would involve an increase in repression and would be very painful for the Russian people; it would certainly involve some decrease in their standard of living. China could probably do it also, but only by sacrificing any possibilty of rapid economic development through industrialization. In the long run even these two communist giants cannot turn back the clock.

The world is moving into a condition of mutual interdependence far beyond the present comprehension of insular Americans—although Japanese and Dutchmen live with its implications every day.

Interdependence is not necessarily good or bad. It is simply a fact of life. Some will find it encouraging that in an obviously interdependent world it would be irrational for any country to "rock the boat." On the other hand, I have not yet seen convincing evidence that national leaders are ready to behave rationally in all circumstances. Interdependence can result in serious problems for everyone arising out of the narrow passions or fixations of tiny minorities. The terrorist groups that currently abound persistently attempt to achieve abstract political objectives by deliberately hurting or killing completely innocent hostages. The opportunities for sabotage and terror will doubtless increase steadily as time goes on. It remains to be seen whether political institutions and instrumentalities can be developed to cope with this problem before our most cherished values are sacrificed in a spasmodic "law and order" reaction. I return to this problem in other contexts.

POSSIBILITIES OF VIOLENT CONFLICT

Whatever new forms of crisis the world may experience in the next fifty years, there is no evidence that the world has passed beyond the need for relieving tensions occasionally by means of violent conflict. I might as well say at the outset that the possibility still exists for large-scale nuclear war. For obvious reasons, this is precisely the contingency which attracts the most attention among sophisticated "think tanks" as well as among ordinary citizens. But it is not this kind of war which, in my view, is most likely to occur. In fact, one could argue that if a full-scale nuclear war between the United States and the USSR (or China) occurred, it would probably be because of some kind of grisly accident or plot and not as a result of deliberate (or quasideliberate) political-military "escalation" of the kind which led to World Wars I and II.[3]

On the other hand, smaller wars between other powers have been occurring regularly over the last thirty years. In the context of any of these conflicts, the superpowers have had the ability to destroy each other and minor antagonists. The United States, one of the superpowers, has actually engaged in direct conflicts with both North Korea and North Vietnam without being too seriously tempted to use nuclear weapons, even though such weapons were available to the United States and not to its adversary. This is a very important lesson. If we had not actually lived through the situation, many people would still doubt that a major power would allow itself to be frustrated and militarily defeated without using weapons which it had in its possession and which it stood in no danger of having used against it in its homeland.

I think that, for the same reasons that the United States did not use nuclear weapons in Korea or Vietnam, the use of nuclear weapons by major nations in the next fifty years is unlikely. If the United States, the USSR, or China are themselves involved in military conflicts in any part of the world, these conflicts are likely to be of a so-called "conventional" nature, using foot soldiers, armament, high explosives, rockets, and other nonnuclear weapons. There are two possible exceptional contingencies, however.

One contingency is that one of the superpowers believes it can completely knock out the nuclear capabilities of the other by a single preemptive stroke — *and that this opportunity is unique and will never recur.* The other is that a power about to be defeated in conventional warfare may resort to nuclear weapons to protect its own territory. Both contingencies involve such enormous risks of world destruction that a leader advocating such a course would necessarily have lost touch with humanity, if not with reality. Nevertheless, the emergence of "mad" leaders cannot be ignored totally, especially in a world that has produced Hitler, Stalin, Kim Il Sung, Idi Amin, and others. Nor can we altogether dismiss the possibility that a weak leadership could find itself helpless to control a war-oriented bureaucracy that, through a series of fateful low-level decisions, blunders into major nuclear war.*

Despite these possibilities, it is my belief that there probably will not be a nuclear conflict between the great powers in the next several decades. The vital interests of all great powers are overwhelmingly perceived to be in avoiding such a conflict, and the national leaders of major nations are typically subject to many checks and balances which enforce a certain element of rationality in decision making.

Such restraining influences, on the other hand, may not apply to small countries and even less to terrorist groups. Many ministates and extragovernmental groups have an extremely narrow view of their objectives. They also have fanatical leaders in some cases and might

---

*This is pretty much the way Japan got into World War II. The early moves (in China) were actually decided on by middle-echelon military leaders and presented as *faits accompli* to the top brass, who were then forced to take the logical confirmatory actions or risk calamitous loss of face.

well be tempted to use nuclear weapons regardless of wider ramifications. If some of the more extremist members of the Palestine Liberation Organization, for example, had an opportunity to plant a nuclear device in Tel Aviv, what are the odds that it would forego the opportunity on either political or humanitarian grounds? Would an extremist African nationalist group hesitate to plant a nuclear device in all-white downtown Salisbury or Johannesburg? Or, for that matter, might not a member of the "provisional" wing of the IRA be willing to "sacrifice" the lives of a million Londoners to the cause of Irish unification?

These nightmarish possibilities pose a grave threat. One nasty possibility arises if the victimized nation is a great power or the ally of one. Might one of the nuclear powers (mistakenly or not) attribute the disaster to a rival and be maneuvered into retaliation? The present lack of any effective planning to forestall such contingencies and to limit the spread of nuclear weapons raises a question as to how much thought, at decision-making levels, is being devoted to safeguarding the world's future.

Even some of the more sophisticated small powers might, under certain circumstances, resort to nuclear violence. There is, for example, little doubt that Israel would use nuclear weapons to defend itself against an overwhelming military threat from its more fanatic Arab neighbors even if the latter were strictly conventional. Nor can we assume that India, which possesses nuclear weapons, would necessarily resist the temptation to use those weapons in the event of a possible conflict with Pakistan. Obviously such use would be deliberate, and one could imagine the government of India deciding that the so-called threat from Pakistan is "intolerable." Finding itself, conceivably, unable to overcome an efficient Pakistanian military establishment by conventional means, it might resort to the use of a nuclear bomb to destroy Rawalpindi or Karachi in the hope of achieving instant hegemony over the entire subcontinent. These seem to be the most likely places in which a nuclear weapon might be used, at least in the next decade or two.

One can certainly make a much longer list of "hot spots" around the world where nonnuclear fighting is reasonably likely. First, in the Western Hemisphere, the possibility of border skirmishes clearly exists between Brazil and some of its neighbors to the west. The most likely single point of conflict would be on the border with Peru, probably because of disputes over the ownership of recently discovered petroleum resources. (Brazil badly needs domestic oil to fuel its industrial expansion, which is being seriously hampered by balance-of-payments difficulties brought about by the rapid increase in international petroleum prices.) Again one must not overlook the possibility of the continuation of some of the historical disputes in Latin America such as between Bolivia, Peru, and Chile, Argentina and Chile, or Uruguay, Paraguay, and Bolivia. Colombia might conceivably be tempted to recover its lost northern province of Panama, and Guatemala has threatened to take over the territory of formerly British Honduras. In much of Latin America, the possibility also exists of a left-oriented revolution (such as the one in Cuba) attempting to export its ideology across its borders, leading to violence. Nicaragua is a candidate.

Moving to Africa, conflict within and between many countries is virtually a certainty. The Sudan, Rhodesia, Zaire and Angola are all in the midst of civil war as this is written. Ethiopia is currently fighting with Somalia. Morocco and Algeria have teetered on the edge of conflict over claims in formerly Spanish Morocco. Libya is encroaching on territory in Mauritania to the south. Uganda is perpetually on the brink of revolution or civil war. It is a sad fact that virtually every Black African country which has become free of colonial government during the last thirty years has suffered at least one military *coup d'etat,* and many countries have suffered multiple changes of government, mainly violent, since their independence. Wars between countries have been less frequent, but the possibilities clearly exist, for example, between Algeria and Morocco, between Kenya and Uganda, between Rhodesia and its neighbors, or between South Africa and its neighbors.

The Middle East is also a natural cockpit of violence. In recent years this has pitted Israel against its Arab neighbors, particularly Egypt and Syria. There have also been serious civil conflicts within countries, particularly Jordan, Cyprus, and recently Lebanon. Syria and Iraq are violently antagonistic. The same is true of North and South Yemen. Iraq threatens Kuwait. Iran casts a shadow over the entire Persian Gulf, especially the feeble emirates and sheikdoms.* The Palestinians constitute a threatening minority within most of the Arab states. The causes of these conflicts remain unsettled, and unless one side or the other should achieve total victory — which would probably be impossible without total annihilation of the loser — one can only assume that the causes of the conflicts will remain indefinitely and that the conflicts themselves will tend to recur at intervals. The problem for the rest of the world would seem to be containing these

---

*A chilling recent best-seller, *The Crash of 79,* is predicated on an Iranian "Blitzkrieg" to take over the Persian Gulf.[4]

conflicts and not allowing them to spread or escalate too high in level of violence.

The Persian Gulf is a particularly critical area. It has been relatively calm in the recent past because the Persian Gulf sheikdoms are small and were ruled for practical purposes by the British. That situation has ended, and now the Soviet Union and the United States, as well as Iran, Iraq, and Saudi Arabia, are actively contending for influence in the region. One can only speculate whether this competition can be restrained to submilitary levels of intensity. In addition, it would not be surprising if further conflicts should occur within or between Iran, Iraq, and Turkey, possibly involving the Soviet Union, as a result of the perpetual irritant of Kurdish nationalism. The recent "pacification" of the region resulting from withdrawal of Iranian support for the Kurdish rebellion in Iraq may not prove to be a permanent solution. Iranian civil war is also a possibility.

A long-festering quarrel between Pakistan and India over the ethnic Moslem states of Lakakh and Kashmir has recently been "settled" by a clear demonstration of Indian military superiority, but the situation could easily become unsettled again in a variety of ways. Problems of a similar nature may arise in the remote areas of South Asia, including Iran, Afghanistan, and Pakistan, and possibly including southern Russia and western China. The Baluchis and Pakhtoons are currently causing difficulty between Pakistan and Iran, on one hand, and between Pakistan and Afghanistan on the other. Those areas are very remote, and communication is extremely bad. They are ruled by military dictatorships whose centers of power are located at a considerable distance from the rebellious tribesmen. Southern Russia is ruled from Moscow by people with nothing in common ethnically with the peoples of Central Asia. Much of Afghanistan may not be ruled at all in any real sense. Pakistan is ruled from the Punjab by plainsmen who have historically been very antagonistic to the Pathan tribesman in the hills. Western China is ruled from Peking by northern Chinese who again have little in common with the Tibetans, Tadjiks, Mongols, Turkmen, or other peoples of the western mountainous regions; the latter are very proud and independent and are linguistically and culturally distinct from the Chinese. Thus, it is not difficult to imagine a successful rebellion against the governments of Afghanistan, Pakistan, or Iran, and I think it is quite easy to project continuing trouble in the areas.

I have already noted the possibilities of conflict between India and Pakistan. This perhaps deserves some additional comment. The government of India views itself as a multireligious, multiracial/ethnic, multilanguage government. There is no doubt that the Indian nation has succeeded in demonstrating an unusual degree of religious and racial tolerance. Most Indians of the intelligentsia and the upper levels of government deeply resented the British-sponsored partition in 1947 that created the state of Pakistan as a separate Moslem country. Many Indians would like to put an end to this division, which they regard as artificial and having been imposed by a colonial ruler. This explains their constant antagonism toward the government of Pakistan and their irritation with the United States for providing Pakistan with weapons. It also explains their policy of dividing East and West Pakistan and supporting the new state of Bangladesh, even though Bangladesh is anything but a viable country and will prove in the long run to be a severe drain on Indian resources.

The situation in South Asia is further complicated by the fact that India is also extremely antagonistic to China. Indian pride was deeply wounded by the humiliating defeat of Indian armed forces at the time of the Chinese incursion on the Tibetan border in the mid-1960s. There is still a deep "revanchist" sentiment in India today, which partially explains why India has devoted so much of its limited resources toward building up major military capabilities. India has also made it clear that it intends to dominate and eventually annex all the Himalayan states, starting with Sikkim (annexed in 1975), to be followed by Bhutan and eventually Nepal. If any of these small principalities resists an Indian takeover, an opportunity for conflict will arise rapidly, particularly if the Chinese choose to intervene.

The borders between China and Burma and the disputed territories of Indo-China also offer potential for conflict. There is a long history of conflict between the Khmers (Cambodia) and their neighbors the Vietnamese to the east and the Thais to the south and west. North Vietnam and South Vietnam communist regimes in Laos and Cambodia are already sponsoring insurgent groups in Thailand, which is also involved in border conflicts with Malaysian ethnic groups. Thailand thus would rank high on most lists of likely trouble spots, as would Malaysia, primarily due to continuing disaffection by its Chinese ethnic minority. However, ethnic Chinese support of communist insurgency will probably tend to keep the Moslem Malays in the noncommunist camp (as in Indonesia). Malaysia also has potentially troublesome territorial disputes with Indonesia and the Philippines. The discovery of oil in the South China Sea and the Gulf of Tonkin will intensify ancient unresolved disputes over the ownership of some otherwise useless islands. Vietnam and China are already arguing over offshore drilling rights. However, these quarrels are more likely to result in delaying effective integration of the countries in the region into an effective regional economic-political force than they are to lead to direct military conflict between the countries in question. Physical separation between Malaysia, Indonesia, and the Philippines is an important safety factor here.

Finally, one must mention four other very critical conflict points, one of which has already led to a serious shooting war in the last thirty years (which could be renewed at any moment), namely, that between North and South Korea. Another has led to a protracted military and political stalemate, viz, that between Taiwan and mainland China. The third, which for the moment is quiescent, but which, in principle, could be the most serious of all, involves possible conflicts between China, Japan, and Russia. Japan has fought with China for a significant part of the past fifty years. Indeed, the Japanese entry into World War II arose from an attempt to dominate North China. Japan also fought against and humiliated Russia in 1904. Then, in the waning days of World War II, the Soviet Union took advantage of Japan's impending defeat to seize a considerable amount of territory, including Manchuria — which it turned over to the Chinese communists — and Sakhalin and the Kurile Islands, which it retained. The USSR has refused to negotiate on the possible return of the Kuriles.

For the moment, Japan is not in a position for military adventure, since it relies entirely on the United States for its military protection. However, now that Japan has grown into a mighty economic power, there is a growing feeling among Japanese that Japan should no longer rely so completely for its defense on its alliance with the United States, especially in view of the fact that the United States and Japan do not see entirely eye to eye on trade matters. Then, too, the militarist sentiment in Japan was not totally wiped out by Japan's defeat in World War II. The Japanese are very proud people. It is by no means out of the question that some of the quasifascist religious parties in Japan (such as Soka Gakkai) could, under some circumstances, become strong enough to take over political control of the country. Even if that should not occur, nuclear rearmament cannot be ruled out. Conventional rearmament (to a point) is a virtual certainty in any event.

If Japan should become a major military power — which it could do rapidly, once having made the necessary commitment --relations between Japan, China, and Russia would become exceedingly tense and complicated. The fact that China and Russia are generally antagonistic toward each other would not necessarily prevent those two countries from burying their differences in a combined front against Japan. Of course, one must also consider the opposite possibility, that Japan will continue to opt for a low profile or even ally itself with China. This might result in an escalation of border conflict between China and Russia arising from ancient Chinese grievances against nineteenth century Czarist incursions. Several skirmishes took place in 1969 along the Sinkiang-USSR border in the west and on the Ussuri River in the far east, with reports of dead and wounded on both sides. Protracted border talks have been held from 1970 onward, but (to date) there have been no territorial concessions or adjustments. Armed conflict could recur at any moment or even escalate into full-scale war. This is certainly the most likely of any of the obvious conflict situations to escalate to the level of full-scale conventional or nuclear war between major powers.

INTERCOUNTRY COMPARISON

In this brief section I want to focus on a limited number of key countries (including individual members of the EEC) on which I have fixed attention for purposes of writing this book.

Since World War II the countries of continental Western Europe have enjoyed consistently high rates of economic growth. Several factors contributed to this, varying in importance between countries.

West Germany (EEC). This country embarked on its high-growth trajectory under allied occupation with a new constitution that corrected the glaring faults of the Weimar constitution. It had a conservative free enterprise-oriented government led by Konrad Adenauer and his successor Ludwig Erhard dedicated to the reconstruction of industry as an essential prerequisite to achieving ambitious social goals. It had and has nonmilitant, noncommunist labor unions and a highly disciplined and competent work force including many refugees from formerly German territories in the eastern area now ruled by Poland. Germans, having experienced a catastrophic inflation within living memory, have been unusually willing to tolerate deflationary measures. Marshall Plan aid was helpful in the initial stages of reconstruction after World War II. In the 1960s Germany fueled its domestic industrial growth by importing unskilled contract labor from Italy, Yugoslavia, and Turkey, but retaining most skilled jobs for German nationals. This has created social dissensions in some German cities, and the practice will probably be gradually discontinued. Thus West Germany will have to live with slower economic growth or domestic labor shortages during economic upswings, probably resulting in a more rapid rate of domestic wage increase and, ultimately, substantial capital outflows.

In the past twenty years Germany has also benefited substantially by rapid world-wide growth of the motor vehicle market which is not expected to continue at the same rate in the future. Also, the somewhat inflated value of the Deutschemark* will hamper the future growth of exports. Even if labor becomes available, industrial growth in Germany will be limited by the scarcity of appropriate sites. Although Germany has some domestic energy resources (coal), the coal is not particularly cheap to extract or convert into clean fuel, especially with a scarcity of miners. It does not share in the North Sea bonanza. Thus, despite its excellent past record of economic growth and management and its superb infrastructure, West Germany will have serious difficulties to contend with in the coming decades.

France (EEC).   France achieved unusually high growth after the end of the Algerian War by renovating its constitution to rationalize its government and by exploiting its natural advantages. These are excellent farm land and a highly productive agriculture, architecturally attractive cities and established tourist attractions, acknowledged leadership in producing high-quality luxury-grade consumer goods (especially food products and wine), an efficient civil service, and excellent technical schools. France is now the high technology leader of Europe having invested heavily in nuclear power, electronics, and aviation, and has displaced the United Kingdom in this regard. The domestic labor supply was increased sharply by significant mechanization of agriculture and by a substantial inflow of former French Algerians. The mechanization of farming and the rationalization of the excessively labor-intensive service sector will continue to release some additional productive labor for the next few years. Thus France is not yet approaching the condition of acute domestic labor shortage which characterizes Northern Europe. France has also benefited in the past from growth of the world motor vehicle market, but the French economy is the most diversified in Europe and can replace motor vehicle exports by others. Paris is overtaking London as the major metropolitan city and corporate headquarters city of Western Europe. France will probably, once again, be the wealthiest nation in Europe by the year 2000 despite its lack of domestic petroleum resources, but France

---

*The Deutschemark is overvalued precisely because Germany's success as an exporter leads to an accumulation of foreign currency. However, domestic prices in Germany are also higher than in other countries with a comparable degree of industrialization.

can pay its oil bills by selling its food products to its northern neighbors.

Italy (EEC). This country has achieved rapid economic growth in the recent past by utilizing relatively cheap contract labor from the undeveloped south in the modern industrial environment of the Po Valley. Italy has been fortunate in having a group of progressive and dynamic industrialists who have successfully integrated private and public interests to a surprising degree. However, the northern industrial cities are now seriously overcrowded (and very badly polluted), and the industrialization of the Po Valley has cut into Italy's ability to feed itself. Hence the government is increasing pressure on firms to build new factories in the southern part of the country. Unfortunately, this is proving to be difficult (and unprofitable) because of inadequate infrastructure, corrupt and inefficient local government, and strong Mafia/Church influences. Also, Italy suffers from a chronically unstable and inefficient central government and a society that is deeply polarized between the communists and the Catholic Church. Radical left-wing terrorist groups like the Red Brigade have seriously reduced the effectiveness and credibility of the existing governmental structure. The worst immediate problem is a total dependence on foreign energy resources (oil), which makes the Italian economy highly vulnerable to the vicissitudes of world oil prices. A significantly reduced economic growth rate must be assumed until (or unless) oil prices drop or large domestic energy sources are discovered.

Benelux Countries (EEC). These countries are individually small but cumulatively important. They have succeeded, in general, by virtue of efficient government — a benefit of smallness — and by specialization. Holland is still heavily agricultural, yet it is the home of several very large multinational corporations. Rotterdam and Antwerp are two of the three chief sea ports of continental Europe with major refineries and petrochemical industries. The Dutch have benefited from the discovery of natural gas which currently supplies much of Holland's domestic energy needs. Brussels, the seat of the EEC, is now a major corporation headquarters city (along with London, Paris, and Geneva). These countries live mainly by trade and will prosper more or less in parallel with their larger EEC neighbors, especially Germany and France. Unfortunately, Holland has a serious problem with Moluccan and Guianian ethnic minorities, and Belgium is chronically split between Catholic French-speaking Flemish and Protestant Dutch-speaking Walloons.

The United Kingdom (EEC).   This was once the richest country in Europe, basically due to its early industrialization and protected trade with a large empire. It now lags behind Germany and France, and without the discovery of North Sea oil it would soon have slipped behind Italy. The United Kingdom survived World War II with slight physical damage to its industrial plant, but because of a low rate of investment, its factories are now obsolete. The social innovations of the "welfare state" have done little to ameliorate old class antagonisms. Nor has belated entry into the Common Market (EEC) provided the competitive stimulus that was once thought to be the answer. British labor unions are among the most disruptive and undisciplined in the world, and industrial mangement is inbred and probably less competent than in any other advanced country. Government in the United Kingdom, regardless of party, seems incapable of resolving these problems, and consequently the poor economic performance of the past twenty-five years is more than likely to continue for some time. The North Sea oil wealth and London's continuing role as the financial capital of Europe will (unfortunately) allow the British to continue their bad habits a little while longer. For one thing, the oil bonanza will artificially prop up the British pound, making imports cheaper than they should be. By 1990, when the North Sea oil is past its peak production, a very severe economic crisis is probably in store for Britain.

United States.   The United States economy grew at a modest but healthy rate during the 1950s and early 1960s, despite the overvaluation of the dollar, but the growth rate has slowed down considerably since 1965. Slow growth in recent years can be attributed to an unprecedented increase in public sector expenditures—only partly due to the Vietnam War—and a consequently low rate of nonhousing investment. The large United States investment in the high technology of the 1950s and early 1960s has heavily emphasized military and aerospace technology. Although providing some export potential (military electronics, weapons, aircraft) these technologies have contributed little to upgrading the overall productivity of industry. The large overseas United States military commitment (increased by the Vietnam War) was a serious drain. In addition, the United States developed its industrial system on the basis of exploiting cheap, high-quality domestic resources. These are now becoming scarce and are no longer adequate. Thus a major readjustment to the new situation (requiring the use of capital to "substitute" for cheap resource inputs) is needed, but the necessary investments have not yet been made.

On the other hand, the United States is still relatively rich in many resources, such as coal, as well as the renewable resources of agriculture and forest products. Labor supply is ample, with substantial (illegal) immigration from Mexico and the Carribean providing a cushion.* Transportation facilities are good (although the rail net is aging), and communications are excellent. Wage rates have not risen as fast as in other industrial countries, and a declining dollar means that imports are becoming expensive while exporting is increasingly attractive. This is attracting significant amounts of foreign investment into the United States for the first time in many decades. Also, the United States is exceptionally strong in the areas of technology needed to improve productivity, especially automation, chemical processes, and computers. Thus, although it has become fashionable to assert that many other countries will soon overtake the United States in productivity, it seems not unlikely that the United States may be able to embark on a new period of significant economic growth in the 1980s following the recent period of domestic economic (and social) troubles. The limiting factor will be capital investment, which, as I discuss later, will have to be increased substantially over its levels of recent years.

Canada.   This country is and will continue to be closely linked to the United States economy by virtue of geography, language, and interlocking financial interests. It has the resources to grow somewhat faster than the United States in the next fifty years if the private sector is not unduly discouraged by short-sighted government policies. Much of this growth will be in the undeveloped eastern and northern areas of the country. A major unresolved problem for Canada, however, is the future of Quebec, where separatist sentiment is extremely high. Currently, the Quebec uncertainty is having a very adverse effect on the entire Canadian economy. If Quebec does secede (which still seems unlikely), the future of English-speaking Canada as a separate nation is very dubious.

Japan.   Postwar Japan has institutionalized high economic growth. Many people have predicted that Japan's high growth rate would "soon" come to an end. Generally, they have been proven embarrassingly wrong.[5] The lack of natural resources has not turned out to be a limitation, nor has lack of land or excessive pollution. However,

---

*Depending, of course, on one's point of view. This illegal immigration also constitutes a very heavy welfare load on certain overburdened cities, such as New York.

the situation facing Japan in the next several decades is significantly different from that of the 1950s or 1960s. By the early 1980s Japan will have a level of per capita income as high as any in the world, and it will be largely urbanized. The pool of "convertible" rural labor in Japan will have pretty much dried up, and, in any event, land for new industrial sites on the two southern islands is virtually unavailable.

Thus Japanese investment in the future will increasingly be in Hokkaido or outside of Japan. This trend is already well established. Korea, Taiwan, Singapore, the Philippines, Indonesia, and Australia have already absorbed large amounts of Japanese capital, as have Hawaii, Alaska, Canada, Mexico, and Brazil. These investments are generally designed to secure access to needed raw materials (such as coal or soybeans) or simply to acquire real estate in attractive resort areas (e.g., Hawaii, Polynesia). Korea, Taiwan, and Singapore have also been developed as large-scale "subcontractors" to Japanese manufacturers, supplying finished materials (such as textiles) or electronic components.

However, as Japanese business interests spread across the world, they will encounter unfamiliar problems, not the least of which are employees less well disciplined than the Japanese. As Japan becomes richer it will also encounter increasing political resistance to its export drive—especially in its biggest existing market, the United States. It is too early to predict how this resistance will make itself felt, but there is little doubt that stronger efforts will be made to maintain United States/Japanese trade in rough equilibrium. Eventually, therefore, Japanese economic growth will tend to be constrained by the rate of growth of its chief export markets.

The Soviet Union (and its satellites).   The communist countries of Eastern Europe* are linked tightly by a political and economic system centered in Moscow and backed up by Soviet military power. It is unlikely that this sytem will disintegrate during the next several decades, although strains are likely to increase. East Germany, Czechoslovakia, and Hungary are still culturally Western countries†with little or no Slavic tradition. Poland, although Slavic, has a long history of resisting Russian encroachment. Its alliance with Soviet Russia is very uneasy and is propped up mainly by Russian military power plus a

*Excluding Yogoslavia.
† Czechoslovakia has a Slavic province (Slovakia), but the most dynamic and advanced part of the country has always been Bohemia (Prague) and the German-speaking Sudeten (Brno, Pilsen).

residue of fear and distrust of German reunification and possible "revanchism." The final peace treaty to settle World War II and formal acceptance of the Oder-Neisse Line by West Germany will probably soothe Polish concerns about Germany, to some extent at least, and thus magnify, by contrast, Polish dislike and fear of the USSR.

The increasing disillusionment of all the Eastern European communist regimes with the "Soviet connection" can be expected to grow. In the first place, economic growth in the East has lagged behind the West, and the discrepancy in standard of living is becoming more apparent to ordinary East-bloc citizens as a result of easing travel barriers in both directions. A decline in Cold War rhetoric also contributes to a better understanding of the economic realities. More important, however, the Soviet Union has made it clear that East European satellites cannot expect favorable (or even equitable) terms of trade — including prices on natural gas or petroleum — as long as their domestic living standards are higher than levels in the USSR. This effectively forces East Germans and Czechs to lag behind neighboring West Germans and Austrians while waiting for a hundred million rural Russians to catch up with them.

The USSR can be expected to continue in its present political pattern for several reasons. First, Russians are extremely — perhaps excessively — security conscious. Their eastern land borders have repeatedly been invasion corridors from Mongolia, Central Asia and the Caucasus, and Northern Europe. Memories of the "Hitler-War" are still very much alive. Russian national security strategy from Napoleon onward has been to build successive buffer zones around the Muscovian Heartland. Under the Czars, Russia expanded into Central Asia and Siberia and took advantage of Chinese weakness to extend control over several remote territories that were historically Chinese; Russia also probed into Afghanistan until stiff British resistance from India became evident. Under Stalin, during and after World War II, the recently independent Baltic states were peremptorily returned to Russian control, and slices of border territory were demanded from Finland, Poland, Czechoslovakia, and Rumania (as well as Japan). Of course, all these border territories now incorporated into the Soviet Union also constitute a "minority" problem. Indeed, close to half the population of the USSR is non-Russian.

From the Russian viewpoint, to maintain effective physical control over this vast territory, as well as over satellite nations, and to suppress all potential internal "national liberation" movements virtually necessitates a continuation of the centralized one-party police-state apparatus with its censorship and restriction of liberties. In addition, having sponsored and assisted a communist insurrection in neighboring China, the Soviet Union now has a politically unified, militarily powerful, and economically successful rival in Asia. The rivalry is a very unfriendly one, and the antagonism is not purely ideological.

The Chinese are resentful of nineteenth century Russian territorial aggrandizement in the Far East at the expense of China. China, being militarily inferior to, and perhaps even more cautious than, the Soviets, has not yet attempted to enforce any of its territorial claims, except in Tibet. Even the disputed offshore islands of Quemoy and Matsu remain, for the time being, in Nationalist hands. However, the threat remains real, and the Soviets give every indication of trying to reduce tensions on their western (NATO) borders to beef up defenses against China in the east.

Nixon and Kissinger contributed to this diversion of Soviet worries from west to east by initiating a process of normalizing United States relations with China and accelerating détente with the USSR. Thus neither country has much to fear from the United States, and each is encouraged to compete for United States support against the other. Since it is clearly not in Western interests for either communist giant to ultimately defeat the other, the process of forging new trading and diplomatic links with both Moscow and Peking can be expected to continue. It should accelerate now that the divisive Vietnam War is finally over.

Economically, the East European countries will probably continue to stay somewhat ahead of the USSR (despite the latter's favorable mineral resource position) because of more flexible political systems, better infrastructure—such as internal transportation and communications—better agricultural land, and the Western cultural tradition. These countries are mostly homogeneous (except Czechoslovakia), and they do not have large unassimilated, technologically backward ethnic minorities within their borders. Also, external security is not a problem for them, and they can afford to minimize military expenditures. Internal security is mainly a question of maintaining communist political control and suppressing liberal movements that could lead to open dissent and invite Soviet repression. The USSR will continue to grow economically because demand continues to outrun supply for most types of consumer goods. However, its economic system is functioning increasingly badly, as basic urban infrastructure is now largely in place and satisfying the complex and diverse wants and needs of consumers (especially in rural areas) becomes relatively more important.

The problem is, essentially, a rigid centralized planning system. The basic trouble—inflexibility—is probably inherent in the Soviet system. To decentralize meaningfully would be to permit a much higher degree of local political and economic autonomy, to allow market pricing of products and labor, and allocating resources by competitive bidding rather than by decree. Given the extreme security consciousness of the Russians and their very real internal and external security problems, it seems unlikely that they will voluntarily change the present centralized system, at least until the economic penalties associated with it become too obvious and painful to accept.

Brazil.   One of the wealthiest countries in the world from a resource point of view, Brazil moved into a very rapid growth trajectory after the fall of the Goulart government in 1964 and the accession of a new constitution in 1967. For a time, inflation was sharply reduced (although not eliminated), and enormous amounts of foreign capital were attracted into the country. The recently opened Trans-Amazon Highway is already stimulating a boom in the interior comparable to the gold rush in the United States. Brazil has also became a successful exporter of several categories of manufactured products. Since success tends to breed more success, there is every reason to suppose that Brazil will continue more or less along its present path for at least the next two decades. Eventually, the south central highlands of Brazil should become a big food-producing area. The Amazon basin offers a temptation to strip the timber and clear for agriculture, but this could be an ecological disaster. The other major problems facing Brazil are the shortage of domestic hydrocarbon resources, necessitating heavy imports, and the growing disparity in wealth between the (relatively) prosperous industrial cities of the south and the dry, poverty-stricken northeastern region. Also, Brazil's development has historically been concentrated too much on the coastal zone, ignoring the rich interior. A major oil strike, either in the Amazon basin or offshore, is regarded as a strong possibility.

India.   This country is potentially an industrial powerhouse despite its poor economic performance in the past twenty years. There is no reason to assume that the intractable social problems of India (including its excessive birth rate) will be "solved" in the next decade or two. However, there are reasons to believe that a significantly faster rate of industrial growth can be achieved rather painlessly simply by eliminating some of the bureaucratic constraints and decentralizing economic decisions. India has a highly developed indigenous science and technology base and a highly developed political system. Transportation and the communications infrastructure are far more advanced than in most other countries at a comparable level of average income. Actually, India should be regarded as an *urban* country of 100,000,000 and a *rural* country of 400,000,000 which happen to coexist in the same territory. Unfortunately, only the urban country offers potential for economic growth, but the potential is still significant.

From an industrial standpoint, India's major problem is securing an adequate domestic energy supply. This can be done by opening more coal mines – already in progress – and, hopefully, by offshore drilling for oil in the Bay of Bengal and in the straits between India and Sri Lanka (Ceylon). The Indian railway system can eventually be reconverted from oil to coal burning, if necessary. New fertilizer plants will certainly be coal based, also. These adjustments will require a number of years, but having made them, India could conceivably embark on a much faster economic growth trajectory. The recent political eclipse of Indira Gandhi may well prove to be temporary. If, as I suspect, she returns to power within a year or two, it will be with a stronger mandate than she had before. Given such a mandate, it is (barely) possible that some of these problems can be attacked successfully. However, in view of the immense inertia of the massive Indian government bureaucracy and the dead weight of the primitive social system, only rather cautious optimism seems warranted at present.

Nigeria.   A former British colony specializing in tropical plantation crops (such as palm oil) and the most populous country in Africa, Nigeria is now one of the major oil exporters and, consequently, a beneficiary of substantial capital accumulation. Despite the legacy of British rule and a very enlightened policy toward encouraging domestic entrepreneurs, it is likely that the political system of the country will not be equal to the task of successfully managing a rapid industrialization. Nigeria is still fractured among a number of regions and tribes: the northern tribes are Moslem, the southern ones are Christian. There are over 220 languages in the country. The most advanced tribal group, the Ibos, attempted to secede from the rest of Nigeria to form an independent state (Biafra). This attempt led to a bloody thirty-one-month civil war ending in 1970 with over 2 million dead. The subsequent period of reconstruction has not healed the old tribal antagonisms. It would be surprising if rebellion or war do not break out again within a decade. Based on the resources available, physical development of the country is bound to occur at a reasonably rapid rate, but the country is lacking in modern administrative, social, political, and economic management skills. It will in all likelihood develop a layer of urban entrepreneurs providing some of the basic goods and services needed by the economy, but themselves largely living on imported luxury goods. The country will not, for many decades, become industrially significant in its own right.

China (PRC).   Little hard data are available about China. What is known tends to be more or less "common knowledge" (or opinion). The most notable characteristic of the Chinese model of industrial development is that it has proceeded independently since the withdrawal of Russian aid in the 1950s. At least a moderate level of economic success can be presumed from all reports, although detailed statistics are almost totally unavailable. Evidently the factional political strife and turmoil of the 1960s has abated, and the rules under which internal disputes are settled seem to have been established fairly firmly. China also seems to be committed at present to a moderately increasing degree of cultural and technological interchange with the West, including trade relations. The reasons for this are, at least in part, certainly related to China's rivalry with the Soviet Union. Having successfully survived the problems of the last twenty-five years and the death of Mao, there is no reason to suppose that the present regime cannot continue to do so for some decades to come. I expect that it will.

REFERENCES

1. Rupert Brooke, "Soldier," in A. Quiller-Couch, ed., The New Oxford Book of English Verse, 1250–1918, 2nd ed., Oxford University Press, 1939.
2. M. Kaplan Ed., *Isolation or Interdependence? Today's Choices for Tomorrow's World,* The Free Press, New York, 1975.
3. H. Kahn et al. *On Escalation: Metaphors and Scenarios,* New York, Praeger, 1965.
4. M. Erdman, *The Crash of '79,* Simon & Schuster, Inc., New York, 1976.
5. H. Kahn, *The Emerging Japanese Superstate: Challenge and Response,* Prentice-Hall, Englewood Cliffs, New Jersey, 1970.

CHAPTER FOUR

MEASURES OF MAN
—DEMOGRAPHIC AND
MACROECONOMIC

INTRODUCTORY REMARKS

In this chapter (and the next) there is a shift of emphasis from the
general to the specific. The focus is now on a small number of key
Measures of Man, which can be assessed and projected quantitatively.
The methodological issues involved were taken up briefly in Chapter 1,
and I do not elaborate on that discussion further. The choice of measures also seems relatively obvious. Whether these measures have been
used extensively (by others) because they are easily quantified or
whether they have been quantified because of their fundamental significance matters not. The fact is, where quantitative assessment is
feasible, as it is for these measures, a merely qualitative discussion
would be inadequate. As I said previously, quantitative changes may —
and often do—have qualitative significance. To understand that significance one must look at the numbers.

POPULATION GROWTH

Population is certainly the most easily quantifiable of all the measures
of Man. There can be no fundamental difficulty in deciding what is (or
is not) included in a given category. No sophisticated measurement
systems are needed for counting, only a tally sheet or the equivalent.
Population counts have been conducted since (at least) Roman times
and probably much earlier. The word census comes from Latin. Is it not
curious, then, that at least a quarter of the population of the world
today has never been counted? There are no reliable data at all on

China, Indochina, Bangladesh, Sri Lanka (Ceylon), Afghanistan, Saudi Arabia, Ethiopia, or Lebanon. Data on India, Pakistan, Indonesia, Nigeria, and Egypt, to name only some of the larger countries, are of poor quality, to say the very least.

Even where counting is carried out on a regular basis with sophisticated controls, surprisingly large errors creep in. For instance, in the United States, published "final" figures are always quite a bit higher than "raw" counts. What seems to happen is that people in certain age-sex-racial groups, such as teenage Black males, "disappear" only to reappear again in later census reports when they are older. When anomalies appear in the age-cohort data, corrections can be introduced for people the census takers failed to find for various reasons by comparing cross-sectional samples with longitudinal series (over time). Of course, this kind of adjustment cannot be used in countries in which less detailed data are available or certain groups of people are *always* undercounted.

Using such methods of adjustment, United Nations demographers have developed means of interpolating and extrapolating sketchy data to synthesize a reasonably complete picture of the world's population in the recent past. Moreover, they have regularly undertaken to project population trends into the future. Unfortunately, these projections have not been particularly accurate, as Figure 4.1 shows.[1] In fact, all the United Nations forecasts from 1951 to 1966 have been below the actual trend.

The reason for the forecasting lags can be inferred in Table 4.1, taken from the same source. The United Nations forecasts displayed in Figure 4.1 essentially assumed that future growth would continue at the same *rate* as current growth adjusted a bit up or down, whereas the growth rate has been continuously increasing since 1650 (and probably long before that). Hence even the "high" estimates were always too low.

A faster than exponential growth model can easily be constructed. As I noted in connection with a discussion of growth functions in Chapter 1, the rate of growth can be fitted to an increasing curve, instead of being regarded as constant. For example, using the data points in Table 4.1, the hyperbolic function

$$P = \frac{\exp{(11.3)}}{2026\text{-}T}$$

fits quite well for historical years. However, this function has a

Figure 4.1 Forecasting lags.

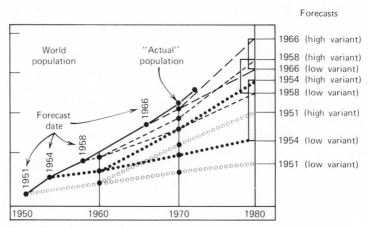

"Actual" population: solid line
Forecast population: dotted or dashed lines

singularity: it becomes infinite in the year 2026, which obviously makes no sense.

If the exponential functions do not fit the data, and the hyperbolic function cannot be realistic during the time period of interest, what reasonable forecasting procedure remains? An answer must be based on an analysis of the reasons for each of these failures. The likely reasons are not hard to discover. First, the exponential function failed to explain what has happened in the last 300 years because it omitted a key factor that was rapidly changing: life expectancy. The rate of population increase, after all, is the *net* birth rate less the *net* death rate. If both remain constant, the net rate of population increase will also be constant. Although birth rates probably have not changed much, death rates have dropped sharply as modern medicine and public health techniques have taken hold. Whereas only a few generations ago most babies died before reaching childbearing age, now the contrary is true. And though childbirth was once frequently fatal to the mother, this is now seldom the case, even in the less developed countries. Hence the *rate* of population increase has increased continuously. United Nations demographers erred because they conservatively assumed an equilibrium level had been reached when it had not.

Will the rates go still higher in the future? It is possible, but better insight may be available from comparing the growth rates of countries with each other, as I have done in Table 4.2.[2] Whereas the average

Table 4.1 Acceleration of Population Growth

Year	Population (millions)	Yearly Rate of Growth (%)
1972	3782	2.03
1971	3706	2.02
1970	3632	1.97
1960	2982	1.82
1950	2486	0.91
1930	2070	0.86
1900	1600	0.62
1850	1070	0.52
1800	900	0.44
1750	720	0.31
1700	620	0.27
1650	540	

world growth rate for 1970 was 2.0% per annum, the *range* in Table 4.2 is from a low of 0.4% (Belgium) to a high of 2.8% (Brazil). Actually some countries of Africa, Central America, and the Carribean (not specifically listed) are growing even faster, at 3.2% per annum.

An important observation leaps to the eye: As of 1970, the regions with the best public health did *not* have the highest growth rates. Indeed, rather the contrary. Hence there is no reason to suppose that further major decreases in death rates are in the offing as a result of further progress in public health. On the contrary, a major focus of public health efforts in the next fifty years is likely to be on family planning and birth control, rather than on death control. If any success at all is achieved, some of the higher birth rates should begin to decline. In fact, the latest figures suggest that this may have begun to happen.

Of course, on the other side of the coin, the faster-growing regions will continually constitute a larger share of the total, thus driving the world average up—assuming that each region's average growth rate remained constant. It must be remarked that Central America, with the highest population growth rate, is relatively small potatoes compared to South and East Asia. What really affects the world as a whole is what happens in China (1.7%) and India (2.4%). Both of these rates have, incidentally, been adjusted downward by about 0.1% between 1969 and 1973. Notice that a population-weighted average of these two

Table 4.2 Population Summary, 1970

Region or Country	Population 1970	1970–1975 Population Growth Rate (%)	Years to Double	Percentage of Population Under 15 (1970)
North America	226.4	0.90	77	30
(two countries)				
United States	204.9	0.86	81	30
Canada	21.4	1.26	55	33
Latin America	283.0	2.71	26	42
Brazil	95.2	2.84	25	43
Europe, Total	459.1	0.6	115	25
EEC (six countries)	242.0	0.5[a]	139[a]	24[a]
Belgium	9.7	0.43	165	24
France	51.1	0.87	80	25
Germany (Fed. Rep.)	58.6	0.32	220	23
Italy	53.7	0.54	125	24
Netherlands	13.0	0.85	82	28
United Kingdom	56.0	0.34	210	23
USSR	242.8	0.99	70	28
Oceania	19	2.0	35	32
Africa	351.6	2.64	27	44
Nigeria	55.0	2.67	27	43
Asia	2056.0	2.2	32	40
China	771.8	1.66	42	35[b]
India	543.1	2.43	30	41
Japan	104.3	1.26	56	25
World, Total	3610.0	1.89	37	37

[a]Estimated by weighted average of individual countries.
[b]Estimated on the basis of growth rate.

countries would have a combined growth rate very close to the 1972 world average of 2% per annum.

Summarizing, then, although the United Nations demographers did consistently underestimate for twenty years, the reasons for the underestimates now seem clear (at least in retrospect), and the likelihood of future underestimates arising from the same error seems to be small. Thus, rather than blindly adopting a hyperbolic population function despite its very good apparent fit to data from the past, I am inclined to accept the latest United Nations projections as the most realistic available. It is obvious, of course, that rates of growth will *not*

Table 4.3 Population Growth Projections, 1972–2025

Region or Country	Growth Rates (% p.a.)			Population, Millions			
	1972	2000[a]	2025[b]	1970	1972	2000	2025
North America (two countries)	0.90	0.69	0.3	226.4	230.5	289	328
EEC (six countries)	0.50	0.40	−0.2	242.0	244.5	278	286
Japan	1.26	0.51	−0.2	104.3	106.9	139	145
USSR	0.99	0.67	0.3	242.8	247.7	314	355
Brazil	2.84	2.42	2.0	95.2	100.7	210	363
China	1.66	1.04	0.6	771.8	797.7	1175	1445
India		3.00[c]	3.0[c]			1193[c]	2500[c]
(three cases)	2.43	1.77	1.2	543.1	569.8	1033	1500
		1.10[c]	0.0[c]			954[c]	1101[c]
Nigeria	2.67	3.15	2.8	55.0	58.0	128	267
World	1.89	1.64	1.0	3610.0	3747.7	6150	8600

[a] Year 2000, United Nations median projection (1973).
[b] Year 2025, author's projection.
[c] Hypothetical cases, discussed in text.

remain constant for the decades ahead. The best guess is that rates will continue to rise (but not much) in a few regions, but that they will soon peak and begin a protracted decline—if such a decline has not already started. My estimates for the next fifty years, strongly influenced by the United Nations projections, are shown in Table 4.3. (Note negative growth rates by 2025 for Western Europe and Japan. Continued growth in North America will be partly due to immigration.) Corresponding populations are also shown in the table.

It is clear that quite a wide range of possibilities still exists, and the future population trajectory is by no means preordained. Upper and lower limits are difficult to define meaningfully, and I hesitate to try. However, it is worth pointing out how much difference a serious and well-conducted birth control program might achieve. Taking India as an example, in one extreme case population growth rates might rise from the 1970 value of 2.5% per annum to, say, 3% (as a result of an unforeseen food production breakthrough, for instance). Assuming a continuation to the year 2025, the population at that time would be 2656 million. On the other hand, given a reasonably well-administered birth control program starting immediately, a decline of 0.5% per decade might not be out of the question. This would lead to a zero net growth rate by 2025 at a (near-peak) population level of 1117 millions.

In the first case the 1970 population would increase nearly fivefold in fifty-five years, whereas in the second case it would merely (!) double.

At present it is extremely difficult to see how India or Western Africa could support a population increase of 3% per annum (or close to it) for five more decades. Some kind of societal collapse would seem to be inevitable. The problem in forecasting such an apocalypse is that — apart from the Irish potato famine — the Western World has no recent experience for guidance as to the likely sequence of events. In the case of the potato famine the differences are surely greater than the similarities, since the excess population of Ireland after 1845 escaped largely to the United States and other countries of the British Commonwealth. Even so, famine and associated diseases (notably typhus) may have killed outright several hundred thousand people from 1845 to 1850. Emigration is not a feasible outlet in the event of a future large-scale famine in Africa or Asia.

Comparatively speaking, most of tropical and temperate America is not yet close to a critical density of population. Brazil, with greater area than the United States (excluding Alaska), still has less than half the United States population. Several of the other Latin countries — especially Argentina, Uruguay, Paraguay, and Venezuela — are probably also still underpopulated, if anything. High rates of growth can be tolerated for a time and may even be officially encouraged. However, the Andean countries, Central America, and Mexico appear to be facing serious problems in the coming decades from absolute overpopulation. Even so, these problems are of a much less critical nature than the population problems of Asia, and there is at least an outside chance that rising standards of living will solve the problem in much the same way as has happened in Southern Europe (which is culturally somewhat similar).

URBANIZATION

Apart from the basic problem of feeding people, which is clearly related to the total number that must be fed, most of the problems that people attribute to population density are actually related to urbanization. Rural populations are normally self-supporting. Until — and even after — they reach enormous densities, as in Asia, they are also nearly "invisible" from a political and cultural standpoint. They demand and receive few public services. They initiate no changes. They do not threaten the *status quo.*

Urbanization goes hand in hand with industrialization and economic development. In the most primitive societies, towns were often located at natural stopping points for traders, such as oases, river conjunctions, or good harbors. As established trade routes and markets developed, artisans and cottage industries clustered around the towns to supply services to merchants. Trading provided most of the "hard money" revenue opportunities for local rulers (e.g., through taxes and customs duties) so administrative and governmental functions also became naturally linked to towns. Governments or rulers also became natural clients for urban services, especially the manufacture of weapons for defense, household items, clothing, tools, and luxury items for the wealthy. Accumulations of trade-goods and artifacts made cities into stores of portable wealth and therefore subject to attack for purposes of looting. However, being compact, they were also intrinsically more defensible than rural tracts. Thus towns acquired walls, storehouses, arsenals, reservoirs, and other structural installations—becoming cities in the process—which, in turn, required new skills and created new industries. As cities grew in size and wealth and their defenses became more sophisticated, they gradually became immune to military threats from the hinterlands. With rare exceptions, a strong city can only be successfully attacked by another urban-based power.

To feed themselves, cities have always had to grow food for themselves or buy it from the surrounding countryside. On occasion they did both. Gradually, as cities grew larger, they evolved more extensive trade relationships with rural hinterlands, exchanging tools, draft animals, vehicles, seeds, and, more recently, farm machinery, fertilizers, pesticides, and household goods for agricultural commodities. Always the cities have dominated in the exchange. Increasingly, most of the products manufactured in cities have been destined for urban rather than rural consumers. Although the rural areas only sell their products to the cities, cities sell largely to themselves and to each other.

Because of these changes in the relative wealth and power of city vís-à-vís countryside, the fraction of the human population living in urbanized areas has increased. At first the increase was gradual and slow. In recent decades the migration from farm to town has become quite explosive. At the beginning of the nineteenth century no country was significantly urbanized. Today the most industrialized countries are also largely urbanized. Although definitions of an urban area differ from country to country, the European countries which began to industrialize in the nineteenth century are now typically 75–85% urban. This process has taken place in roughly a century, give or take a few decades. These countries generally have highly efficient, capital-intensive agricultural sectors. In many cases they also import a significant fraction of their grain, mostly from North America. By comparison, at the other extreme of the scale are the so-called less developed countries (LDCs) in which urbanization can be as low as 17% (Indonesia).

Of course, these trends need not follow the historical pattern. It is interesting, however, to see in Table 4.4 how the situation in 2000 – as seen by United Nations demographers – might compare with 1970 if the recent trends continue more or less unabated.[3] Again, I extrapolated the trends roughly to 2025.

It will be noted that the most and least urbanized regions are likely to change (relatively) the least. The middle-range countries, which have a substantial industrial base and also a large but still inefficient agricultural sector, should experience the most rapid urbanization. It must be emphasized that this picture probably presumes a significant rate of worldwide economic development and would necessarily be somewhat modified if economic growth slows down sharply, for instance.

Two questions must be answered. First, why are these numbers important? If they are, how can we expect them to change? The answer to the first will help in giving a sensible answer to the second.

The connection between urbanization and economic development has already been pointed out. In one sense urbanization is a *symptom* of development: a very advanced industrial country tends to have an industrialized form of agriculture that does not require many people actually working on the land. (Many more are likely to be involved in

Table 4.4 Urban Growth Projections

Region or Country	Urban Percentage of Population			Urban Population		
	1970	2000	2025	1970	2000	2025
North America (two countries)	72.7	83	88	164.6	239.8	288.2
EEC (six countries)	75.0	83	85	181.5	230.5	242.8
Japan	53.3	83	88	55.6	115.3	127.5
USSR	57.1	78	85	138.6	245.0	301.9
Brazil	56.5	85	88	53.8	178.5	319.8
China	25.5	54	70	196.8	634.7	1011.3
					357.9	1248.9
India (three cases)[a]	19.6	30	50	106.4	309.9	748.6
					286.3	550.3
Nigeria	22.8	40	60	12.5	51.3	160.4

[a]The high and low cases for India correspond to the three hypothetical population growth trajectories shown in Table 4.3.

supporting industries such as the production of agricultural machinery and the processing of raw commodities into finished food products.) These people tend to live in towns and cities.

Urbanization is also an indication of the development potential. A large urban population—even in a less developed country—means a large labor pool and large existing markets for consumer goods. These factors permit economies of scale in both production and distribution of goods and services. The latter point is particularly important because one of the key services associated with economic and technological development is education. In poor countries—for that matter, even in the USSR—the rural population simply does not receive much education. Although village schools may exist in name, the quality of education they are able to provide is extremely low. This is true for obvious economic reasons and for another less obvious reason: good young teachers, being educated themselves, resist being stationed in rural areas where there is nothing to do after work and nobody interesting (i.e., educated) to talk to.

In practice, education of the standard necessary for individuals to function in an industrial society requires educational facilities that are too expensive for duplication in tens of thousands of small village units. Thus education (beyond the minimal requirement for bare literacy) is an urban service, and the best-educated people naturally congregate in the larger cities. Being educated, they also demand specialized services, such as offices, communications media, printed publications, and libraries. These services, too, exist only in cities, since the demand in rural areas is not sufficient to justify them because rural people are both poorer and less mobile than their urban cousins.

These brief comments begin to suggest some of the reasons why rural development is so difficult—virtually an empty phrase. Ideally, it means to bring urban services to the countryside rather than attracting rural population to the cities. Although a widely distributed low-density population is conceivable (for a *very* rich country), the transportation, communication, and educational infrastructure needed to make it work must first be created by an industrialized—hence urbanized—society!

Thus a postindustrial society such as the United States or Western Europe may be beginning to abandon its large cities and spread out over the landscape. This is feasible up to a point, because factories will be largely automated, and employees, with access to cars and fuel for them, can commute to work from quite long distances. The projections in Table 4.4 do not reflect this (possible) trend, however, because there is no real evidence that large numbers of people want to move into truly rural areas. Instead, the smaller cities and remoter suburbs of large cities are doing most of the growing. This pattern is irrelevant for countries like India, Mexico, or even Russia, where the modern transportation and communications facilities are limited to major towns.

A final argument for the relevance of urbanization to other issues concerns the basic structure of society. The differences in lifestyle and personal and social relationships between rural and urban settings is too obvious to require elaboration. Many humanist writers have taken sides on this, often idealizing the qualities of a rural or small town existence — typically modeled on New England or perhaps Iowa — while piling up moral and sociological arguments against the very existence of large cities. Those who argue so vehemently that urban life is dehumanizing forget that our industrial wealth was created by such cities. One of the favorite arguments of the anticity writers is that high population densities actually *cause* antisocial types of behavior. I think this argument is weak and strained, but that is really beside the point. The key point is simply that urbanization is very relevant to the state of society and Man.

What about the future of urbanization and (economic) development patterns? Although development and urbanization are closely related, and *neither can take place without the other*, it cannot be assumed that they always occur in tandem or at the same rates. In particular, it is possible that urbanization can also be a consequence of rural overpopulation, changing agricultural technology (as in the United States*), or changing land-tenure patterns, as in sixteenth and seventeenth century England.

Thus, although peasants in most poor countries normally will not voluntarily sell or leave productive land — their means of livelihood — there are a variety of circumstances that can and do lead to dispossession. Actually, many of the world's peasants do not legally own the land they occupy. It may be owned by individual landlords, by tribes in common, by collectives, or by governments or hereditary rulers. A landlord, tribal council, or government may opt for alternative uses or decide to sell land to outsiders to raise cash. Industrial sites, housing, roads, hydroelectric or flood control dam sites, or assembly of large tracts for irrigation or plantation development inevitably result in

---

*The great migration of rural Southern agricultural workers to the cities of the North in the 1950s and 1960s was largely due to a shift of cotton production from the Southeast, where the soils were exhausted, to newly irrigated lands in the Southwest.

some people being dispossessed. Often unable to find alternative agricultural land, these people either become landless agricultural laborers or migrate to cities.

If industry is expanding, rural immigrants find jobs as manual laborers at the bottom of the urban employment hierarchy. If not, they become beggars, petty thieves, or wards of the government—or they starve. When too many of these displaced people accumulate in one city, as in Calcutta or New York, the ability of the core city to function is seriously impaired. Not only are local resources necessarily diverted to unproductive welfare, law enforcement, and custodial functions, but crime rates and traffic congestion rise, increasing the direct costs of productive enterprises in the city, and the city becomes an unpleasant and dangerous place to live. Managers, executives, and professional persons who have a choice begin to leave the city for other locations where life (for them) is easier, provided, of course, such locations exist.

The decline of a city in trouble, then, is a process with positive feedback: a self-accelerating phenomenon. On closer scrutiny it can be seen that this also applies to the rise of a city. If a city is prosperous and growing and has a reputation as a pleasant place to live, it attracts the most affluent and mobile types of people. For instance, it may specialize in clean, high technology engineering industries which are not closely tied to any particular market area or set of raw materials, selling to a market that is very broad—national or international in scope. The more such industries are attracted, the more attractive and prosperous the city becomes.*

In North America the rising cities of the 1960s were Washington, D.C., Toronto, Atlanta, Miami, Houston, Dallas, Phoenix, Denver, and the cities of the West Coast from Vancouver to San Diego. Houston is seemingly the biggest winner of the 1970s; Atlanta, Los Angeles, and San Francisco have probably peaked. The most notable declining cities are Newark, New York, Buffalo, Cleveland, Detroit, and St. Louis. A few cities, including Boston, Chicago, and Montreal, have recovered somewhat from earlier declines, which offers some hope for the future. Those older cities based on heavy industry or on water or rail transportation will have the most difficulty finding an alternative economic base. The very fact that they are old (and heavily built up) makes it especially difficult to provide the easy access by freeway and air that light manufacturing and service industries require.

In Western Europe, the major cosmopolitan cities have never been

---

*National capitals are obviously somewhat special cases, especially in countries with very centralized governments, such as France.

centers of heavy industry except perhaps for Milan. Otherwise, manufacturing industry has been scattered among a large number of medi-
um-sized cities, such as Birmingham, Glasgow, Manchester, Sheffield,
Essen, Mannheim, Stuttgart, Lille, Barcelona, Antwerp, Rotterdam,
Turin, Göteborg, and so on. The great capitals—London, Paris, Berlin,
Vienna, and Rome—were and are primarily administrative centers.
Brussels, Geneva, Dusseldorf, Frankfurt, Munich, and Zurich (financial and administrative cities) have been rather conspicuously rising
in recent decades. Glasgow, Berlin, and Vienna have unquestionably
declined, each for a special reason. Western Europe—except for the
United Kingdom—enjoyed such a rapid economic growth rate from
1950 to 1970 that most cities have done fairly well. The same is true in
Japan.

Rises and declines are evident elsewhere in the world. Beirut was
conspicuously rising until the recent civil war. Its successor as the
"headquarters" city for the prosperous Middle East is uncertain. In the
absence of a plausible alternative, Beirut may conceivably regain its
former importance. (Athens is a possible, but non-Arab, alternative.)
Teheran is still rising but running into serious congestion problems.
Cairo, on the other hand, seems to be in a decline, along with Istanbul.
In India, Calcutta is clearly declining, and Bombay has probably
peaked. The rising cities are New Delhi and Bangalore (where the
major science and advanced technology industries are located). Singapore is still rising spectacularly, but Bangkok, Manila, and Hong Kong
may have peaked. Rangoon, Pnom-Penh, and Saigon have declined
sharply. Lagos is the great boom city of West Africa, although it is
choked with congestion. In Latin America the greatest attractions
have been Buenos Aires in Argentina, Rio de Janeiro and Sao Paulo in
Brazil, and Mexico City. The last three may have passed their peak
attractiveness, however, due to problems of congestion. Buenos Aires
has assimilated its growth and remains potentially attractive. Other
continuing major growth centers are Brazilia, Belo Horizonte, and
Caracas.

These are all statements about the present. As a general rule, the
trends noted can be expected to continue for some time. However,
slower economic growth in Europe and rural population pressures elsewhere will greatly reduce the number of rising cities and increase the
number of declining ones. If this happens—as I expect—many more
cities all over the world will begin to lose their "progressive" and
"modern" images and will increasingly become refugee camps for the
dispossessed rural poor. One of the most disturbing aspects of this
prospect is precisely that, once located in an urban setting, the poor

and unemployable may pose a significant threat to the rest of society. In the United States, the problem largely takes the form of individual crime and random violence on city streets. In Latin America and the Middle East organized terrorism and urban guerillas have emerged as a more serious political force. It is still unclear how the increasing pressures will make themselves felt in India, Indonesia, and other countries of Asia.

Looking further ahead, one wonders how the existing central cities can hope to survive the continuing shift of heavy manufacturing to areas with lower population density and better access to highway and air transportation. The characteristic urban pattern for industrial (and postindustrial) countries of the twenty-first century seems likely to revert to the nineteenth century pattern in some respects. In the central core area will be found a cluster of high-rise offices housing financial institutions, corporate headquarters, government offices, and business services, plus hotels and apartment complexes (including shopping centers and schools). Major universities will have active downtown centers.

Nearby and interspersed will be an area of restaurants, specialty shops, and small businesses interspersed with townhouses, usually restored (as in Georgetown, Capitol Hill, Society Hill, Beacon Hill, Murray Hill, and so on). Old warehouses and factories located near railroad yards or piers will be abandoned and replaced by housing or, in some cases, by arts/crafts centers or recreational facilities.*

Low- and lower-middle-income housing will tend to move further away from the core to the outer fringe of the central city or the inner suburbs, either in subsidized "new-towns-in-town" utilizing abandoned urban industrial sites or in aging apartment buildings and development housing built in the 1950s and 1960s. Except for restored townhouses, most pre-World War II urban multifamily housing will have been torn down by the end of the century and replaced by offices or new luxury complexes. With smaller families, the demand for low-density single-family dwellings far from the city will dwindle, and some of the suburban tract housing built after World War II will deteriorate to semi-slum status.

Oil refining, chemicals, metallurgical, and heavy manufacturing industries will mostly be located in industrial enclaves some distance away from the core area, but still convenient to freeways, railroads, container terminals, and air terminals. These industrial parks will employ relatively few people on-site. They will be linked by high-

---

*Old warehouses or piers sometimes make excellent indoor tennis courts, for instance.

capacity information channels to administrative, design engineering, and other functions in the central city or in other suburban office-park locations.

The major difference between the land-use pattern characteristic of cities of the industrialized countries and cities of the developing countries is that the latter tend to be surrounded by barrios or squatter communities, whereas in the United States (at least) the worst slums are the aging tenement areas around the inner city, built in the days before the automobile became a feasible means of transportation for the middle class. The advent of the motor vehicle has been particularly traumatic for the older cities of North America, since it has enticed many of the more affluent people away from the urban core to the (formerly) green countryside. However, the era of the low-density middle-class suburb is probably passing, and the well-off will often prefer to have a city apartment (or townhouse) for weekdays and a more distant retreat for weekends. Thus I foresee a gradual but definite return to city living, with some convergence between European and American urban patterns. That is, European cities will spread out somewhat, reducing core densities, and American cities will tend to coalesce and become denser along well-developed transportation corridors, leaving some remote suburban bedroom communities to decline in importance.

ECONOMIC GROWTH PROJECTIONS

Once national power was crudely measured in terms of the size of standing armies and the number of capital ships in fleets. The irrelevance of these simple measures became clear in World War II, the outcome of which was determined solely by the superior industrial capability of the United States, not by its initial fleet of battleships or its standing army.

In recent decades we have become addicted to measuring national power in terms of the intensity of economic activity (as measured by GDP*). Figures are reported, with considerable fanfare, several times a year. It may be surprising to some readers that this is a practice that was essentially initiated in the United States after World War II,

*The more familiar term is GNP, which is short for Gross National Product; it is defined as the sum total of all goods and services produced for sale by a national economy, including foreign subsidiaries of domestic enterprises but excluding domestic subsidiaries of foreign enterprises, plus public (government) services. Recently, a close relative GDP (or Gross Domestic Product) has come to be preferred. GDP for a country is the total of goods and services produced *within* the national territory.

when the Council of Economic Advisors was first created by President Truman.

Without commenting at length on the many conceptual deficiencies of GDP as a measure of economic performance, it is probably fair to say that there is—at present—no better indicator available. Hence I use this measure freely, with occasional qualifying remarks.

The most important thing to note about GDP is not its absolute size —which is meaningless to most people—but its rate of change from year to year. Naturally this increment fluctuates, but since World War II the progression has been steadily and rapidly upward for most of the world. For the key countries, average rates of GDP increase from 1960 to 1972 are shown in Table 4.5, taken from United Nations National Account Statistics.[4]

Table 4.5 World Economic Summary, 1972[a]

Country	Average GDP Growth Rate (%) 1960–1972	Average GDP/Capita Growth Rate 1960–1972	Total GDP (billions) 1972	GDP per Capita
North America (two countries)	4.3	3.3	1232	5560
EEC (six countries)	4.8	4.1	713	2920
Japan	10.6	9.3	316	3000
USSR	7.1	6.1	378	1500
Brazil	6.6	3.8	50	500
China[b]	7.0 (est)	5.3	146	185
India	3.6	1.1	56.5	100
Nigeria[c]	1.6	-1.0	9	160
World	5.5	3.5	3800	1030

[a]Based on 1970 exchange rates between national currencies, expressed in 1972 dollars. This method of calculation may conceal quite large differences in the real cost of living, e.g., between countries (like Japan, Germany, or the USSR) with strong or deliberately overvalued currencies and countries (like Italy or Brazil) with chronic balance-of-payments difficulties. Adjustments to take account of these factors are difficult to make accurately and consistently. However, it is likely that the comparison in Table 4.5 somewhat overestimates the real standard of living of the USSR and significantly underestimates the relative standard of living of the poorer countries. See further discussion in text.

[b]Official data for China are almost nonexistent. Figures shown represent published UN estimates, where available, supplemented by private estimates by Business International Corporation.

[c]Data for Nigeria are unreliable at best, but to complicate matters further there was a destructive civil war in the mid-1960s which set back both actual growth and the collection of statistics.

In this discussion I stick to so-called constant dollars, which are
corrected for inflation, that is, increases in the general price level. I use
1972 (the latest United States Census of Manufactures year) for con-
vience. In comparing figures given in dollars of different years, one
must remember that in each successive year inflation has increased
the number of dollars in circulation, which means that each dollar is
worth intrinsically less. Thus the GDP for any year in dollars is considerably larger than the GDP for the same year in (say) 1958 dollars.

One thing tables 4.5 and 4.6 do not reflect accurately is the relative
standard of living between countries with sharply different per capita
GDP's. This is because countries with high per capita productivity also
tend to have higher wage and price levels. As a very rough generalization, commodities that are easily transported and traded across national boundaries tend to have similar prices in all countries. However
commodities that are too bulky or perishable to transport may have
quite different prices, depending on local availability; the same is true
of most services. In practice, low wage countries also have much lower
costs for housing, food, public transportation, medical services, and the
like. When official exchange rates are adjusted for relative purchasing
power (prices) it turns out that the "real" standard of living in India in
1970 was actually 3.34 times higher than the "nominal" standard as
measured in U.S. dollars.[5] For Nigeria the 1970 ratio was about 2.46,
while for Brazil it was about 2.23. Ratios in 1970 for more advanced
countries were smaller, but still well above unity: Japan (1.45), U.K.
(1.38), Italy (1.35), Netherlands (1.23), France (1.23), W.Germany
(1.16), Belgium (1.13), and Switzerland (1.09). Only Canada and
Sweden (1.01) were essentially identical to the U.S.*

It must be emphasized that the total GDP numbers in Table 4.5 are
national aggregates. They have some significance as measures of overall national power or economic weight. In many respects GDP per
capita is more meaningful. (When the small GDPs of China and India
are divided among their enormous populations, their true status is
revealed more clearly.) Changes in GDP from year to year thus reflect
both changes in GDP per capita and in population growth. These figures are also shown in Table 4.5. Subtracting current (1970–1975)
average population growth rates from the 1960–1972 GDP growth

*Based on this comparison it might be argued that the 1970 U.S. Dollar was significantly
overvalued with respect to the currencies of the other advanced countries. By the same
token, exchange rate changes since 1970 have pushed the Dollar sharply down with
respect to other currencies. The German and Swiss currencies, in particular, have appreciated too much.

rates yields the approximate actual rate of *productivity increase.** The gravity of the problems facing countries with high population growth rates is more clearly seen when the figures are projected.

The projection (shown in Table 4.6) is a comparatively straightforward exercise in which economic productivity is assumed to increase either slightly faster than in the past (the less developed countries) or slightly slower (the advanced countries). Most economic theorists shy away from offering any fundamental explanation of the phenomenon of productivity increase *per se.* I try to deal with this difficult question as best I can a little further on. Note that the projections are in constant dollars, assuming constant 1970 exchange rates. In the long run, exchange rates presumably vary, reflecting differential inflation rates. In the short run, exchange rates can vary much more dramatically, reflecting balance-of-payments problems and speculative pressures. If 1975 exchange rates had been used, the EEC projections would have been around 30% higher and Japanese projections would have been around 40% higher, relative to North America. Using 1978 exchange rates, even more dramatic shifts in the same direction would be seen. Evidently, short-term exchange rates can and do fluctuate much more widely than long-term inflation differentials would seem to justify, and long-term projections are sensitive to whatever one assumes in this regard. Clearly, the projections in Table 4.6 *must* be regarded as merely one (relatively optimistic) "scenario" that seems superficially plausible based on recent past history. It undoubtedly contains some elements of wishful thinking, and very little of deep analysis. (For the present, it shouldn't be taken too seriously.)

The most important thing to observe about Table 4.6 is that the world average GDP per capita increases only slightly faster than per capita output in North America—despite a substantially higher absolute growth rate. A faster-growing population absorbs virtually all the differential. The gap in relative wealth hardly narrows at all in this scenario.

A second point of note is that the EEC countries together in 1972 had twice the GDP of the USSR, although they were and are militarily much weaker. On the other hand, they were still well behind the United States in economic strength. (Dollar devaluations since 1972 have narrowed the apparent gap, but these exchange adjustments reflect

*To pacify the professional economists, I concede that this is a very sloppy and inexact definition of productivity. Population growth rates are not constant, for one thing. Also, productivity should be defined in terms of the *labor* force, not the whole population. But, for the purposes of this book, greater precision is not needed.

Table 4.6 Baseline Economic Projections

Country	Per Capita GDP Growth Rates			Per Capita GDP (1972$)			Total GDP (billions of 1972$)		
	1960–1972	1975–1999	2000–2025	1972	2000	2025	1972	2000	2025
North America (two countries)	3.2	2.8	2.2	5562	11,024	18,994	1232	3135	6220
EEC (six countries)	4.1	2.8	2.0	2920	5993	9832	714	1664	2300
Japan	9.3	4.5	2.0	2385	7647	13,176	255	1062	1900
USSR	6.1	4.0	2.0	1526	4782	7846	377	1502	2700
Brazil	3.8	5.0	4.0	507	1985	5293	51	417	1900
China	5.3	6.0	5.0	183	822	2785	146	966	4000
India (3 cases)	1.1	1.0	1.0	103	171	219	53	199	535
		2.5	2.5		193	357			
		4.5	6.0		198	506			
Nigeria	−1.0	2.5	2.5	166	350	649	96	45	175
World	3.5	3.2	2.7	1100	2700	5300	4130	16,600	46,000

balance-of-payments relationships somewhat more than cost of living. At present exchange rates, the German Deutschemark and other currencies tied to it seem to be moderately overvalued in terms of relative buying power as compared to the dollar.) Yet, despite the fact that EEC countries grew somewhat faster than North America during the period 1950–1970, I doubt if this differential can be sustained. The superior resource base of North America, its agricultural self-sufficiency, and its relative homogeneity and political stability should give it the edge in the next five decades.

A final point worth remarking on is that the economies of some of the less developed countries are so comparatively tiny that even exceptionally high rates of productivity increase—which are not realistically likely—can hardly bring them into the "developed" category within the next three decades. China and Brazil are the two possible exceptions. Thus, if Brazil could cut its population growth rate gradually from 2.8% per year to 1.5% per year and maintain the *same* rate of GDP growth it had from 1960 to 1972, for example, it would be able to achieve the performance suggested in Table 4.6. This would be a fairly remarkable performance, but, given the natural resources Brazil has available, not impossible.

Of course, North America—continuing at its historical growth rate—would also continue to double every twenty years, thus reaching a GDP per capita level of around $33,000 by 2025. Here a significantly lower growth rate seems much more plausible for many reasons. (A *much* slower growth rate can hardly be ruled out either!) Similarly, if Japan continued to expand its economy at the dizzying pace of 1960–1972, it would double every 7.5 years, multiplying its 1972 level by a factor of $2^7 = 128$ by 2025. At this rate each Japanese citizen would have to produce—and consume—about $375,000 worth of goods and services, based on 1972 prices! This figure is sufficiently incredible to dismiss out of hand. But even assuming a dramatic slowdown, as shown in Table 4.6, the Japanese will be the world's second wealthiest people by 1985 or so.*

Are extrapolations like these of any use at all? Some respected forecasters do take them quite seriously, based on the implicit argument that productivity increase is essentially *habitual* and therefore likely to continue. Herman Kahn provides an example of especially fearless ultra long-range extrapolation of growth rates.[6]

Our analysis leads to projections which tend to focus upon a world

*Disregarding oil shiekdoms and emirates.

population leveling out near the end of the 21st Century at about 10 to 28 billion people with an average per capita from $10,000 to $20,000 derived from a GWP of $100 to $300 trillion (as compared with current Gross World Product (GWP) † of around $5.5 trillion).

Actually the projections of Table 4.6, if extended to the year 2100, would not be so different from those of the Hudson Institute (which probably used a similar methodology). Nevertheless, I am doubtful that the historical mechanisms of economic growth can be trusted to work reliably that far ahead, as I now explain.

LONG-TERM CYCLIC PHENOMENA

Up to now I played the projection game as most alpha forecasters do, on the basis of a very dubious assumption: that economic growth, based on steadily increasing productivity of labor and capital, will continue for many more decades in a relatively stable fashion. In view of the dramatic changes that seem characteristic of the real world, however, the basic reasonableness of such projections can be questioned.

Of course, business cycles of relatively short duration, such as the forty-two-month (Kitchin) cycle and the eight to ten-year (Juglar) cycle are a well-known phenomenon in market-oriented economies. Marxists assert that such cycles are fundamental to capitalism, being absent in centrally planned economies, and go on to make the sweeping claim that their elimination is a primary objective and benefit of "social" ownership of the means of production. This proposition does not stand examination, however, in the light of what has been learned through detailed analysis of many actual business cycles by economists such as C. Wesley Mitchell, Joseph Schumpeter, and Jan Tinbergen, since the 1920s.

The culprit in the business cycle is not, it would appear, private *ownership* as such, but decentralized economic decision making by imperfect decision makers. Evidently expectations play a major role. Consumers and investors both tend to defer spending plans during periods of economic uncertainty and decreasing activity (the down side of the cycle), while accelerating expenditures when aggregate demand and economic activity begin to rise again. Ideally, of course, they should do the reverse. Businessmen in particular should invest during

†Gross World Product is the sum of all national GDPs (or GNPs).

slack periods when labor and credit are more readily available, rather than waiting until shortages begin to develop. In a manner of speaking, the cycle occurs precisely because people do not understand that peaks are always followed by valleys and vice versa. That is to say, most consumers and most economic enterprise managers always make the error of assuming that each short-term fluctuation is a long-term trend.

In very brief and simple terms the typical sequence is as follows:

"Boom" Period

- High demand backlog resulting from previously deferred spending
- Declining inventories
- Stable prices
- Rising employment (decreasing unemployment)
- Rising capacity utilization

Turnaround – Inflation Heats Up

- Selective shortages of capacity and labor
- Inventories reach bottom
- Increased investment to relieve shortages (resulting in *added* demand)
- Rising labor costs and commodity prices
- Consumer price increases

"Bust" Period – Deflation Begins

- Reduced demand as consumers again start deferring purchases due to uncertainties in the economic outlook
- Inventories rise
- Cutbacks in investment (resulting in further demand reduction)
- Cutbacks in labor force, increasing unemployment (resulting in still further demand reduction)
- Increasing excess capacity

Turnaround – Deflation Ends

- Prices stabilize
- Inventories reach peak
- Demand begins to rise as backlog of deferred spending reaches peak

Regrettably, the occasionally destabilizing role of capital spending in the business cycle has led to some widespread misunderstandings of the relationship between consumption, capital investment, and capitalism. Many critics of capitalism seem to have misconstrued the accelerator/decelerator function of capital spending — which is responsible for the short business cycle, as I have just noted — and jumped to a much more radical but erroneous conclusion, namely, that continuous economic growth is necessary in a capitalist society to avert depression and unemployment. A typical assertion is that of Robert L. Stivers.[7]

> In blunt terms, our private economy is on a treadmill. To avert mass unemployment, consumption and investment must continually increase. We cannot even stand still.

Governments have increasingly intervened since the 1930s to try to ameliorate the downs in the cycle. The great British economist John Maynard Keynes suggested that governments should undertake deficit spending during periods of slack consumer demand, cutting back spending during boom periods to reduce inflationary pressures. Unfortunately, this procedure does not work as well as one might wish. Quite apart from political factors which make cutbacks difficult, the bureaucratic process is so slow and cumbersome that a public works project conceived and approved during a slack period is likely to come "on stream" just in time to add to inflationary pressures during the recovery period, rather than significantly softening the pain of recession.

Monetary interventions are quicker but probably not much more helpful in the long run. Central bankers try to stimulate demand during slack periods by lowering interest rates and vice versa. However, cutting interest rates and increasing the money supply does not in itself create demand, so the stimulative impact is slight. Similarly, when interest rates are raised, the effect on long-term business decisions (e.g., capital investment) or consumer decisions is slight, and the main short-term impact is likely to be on inventories. Higher short-term interest rates encourage manufacturers to liquidate inventories by restraining output, thus tending to add to unemployment, create unnecessary shortages, and feed inflation. This is probably one of the reasons why unemployment and inflation have been increasingly correlated during recent decades.

Of course, other policy instruments can also be brought to bear on the problem of short-term business cycles. Investment credits and unemployment insurance are two of the principal ones. I return to this topic in the final chapter.

Far more relevant to this book, however, are long-term fluctuations. Although less thoroughly studied—because there have been fewer to study—there is fairly compelling historical evidence of the existence of long cycles. These were first noticed by a Russian economist, Nicolai Kondratieff, in the 1920s. The most identifiable feature of the so-called Kondratieff cycle is a sharp peak in the wholesale commodity price index that occurs at roughly fifty-year intervals.[7] The first peak for which reasonable price data exist occurred just after the Napoleonic Wars (1814 to be exact). The next price peaks occurred in 1864 and 1919–1920.* The latter two also followed major wars but by slightly different intervals. However, no similar peak occurred after World War II, although a small peak occurred in 1953 (Korean War). The most recent commodity price peak may have occurred in the fall of 1974. This would be a little later than the pattern suggests but understandably so in view of the continuing inflationary pressures of the Vietnam conflict and the major OPEC oil price increase in 1973.

Actually, commodity prices may be symptomatic of other aspects of the long cycle. Jay Forrester of MIT believes that the Kondratieff cycle is attributable to natural fluctuations in the size of the stock of productive capital relative to the overall size of the economy (GDP). Forrester argues that during long boom periods there is a tendency for capital investment to gradually outpace demand for goods, resulting in a long-term decline in rates of return on invested capital. Then, when net returns are too low, there is a fallow period of underinvestment (and very slow growth) while excess capital stocks gradually depreciate. Finally, a new boom starts for some reason—often a war—and a new investment cycle begins again.

In any event, wholesale commodity prices or rates of return or capital do not rise and fall subject to the movements of the planets or sunspots; more mundane explanations are needed. To identify the existence of an apparent cycle in history is merely interesting, not necessarily significant. The fact that commodity prices have risen and fallen several times with some regularity from the late eighteenth century through the late twentieth century is not sufficient evidence that the pattern will continue, given changing circumstances.

Yet I believe there is a moderately good chance that the fifty-year cycle which has already played itself out four times (that we know of) in United States history will repeat itself at least one more time, from

---

*The peak price levels were (in 1958 dollars), in sequence, 62.3 (1814), 74.7 (1864) and 84.5 (1920), as compared to an index of 100 in 1957–1959. The troughs were, respectively, 24.5 (1843), 25.4 (1896) and 32.7 (1933).[8]

1975 to 2025. If it does so, the sequence might possibly be something like this:

Carter Boom (1977–1982). A half decade (more or less) of gradually increasing prosperity, characterized by generally high employment, generally declining (real) commodity prices, declining long-term interest rates, and (after 1979) inflation rates, increased profits, and increased price/earning ratios for stocks. The dollar finally begins to regain some ground against the Deutschemark and the yen, as the latter now (1978) appear to be overvalued. Capital gains tax relief is also in prospect. All this could create a short but spectacular stock market boom after the current slump, analogous to that of the late 1920s. A "Dow" of 2000 is not inconceivable.

Of course, the shorter (three to four-year) business cycle will be superimposed on the longer one. The year 1975 was an unusually depressed trough. The next dip, probably shallower, is expected in late 1978 or 1979, with subsequent recovery years peaking in 1981 or 1982, driven by a temporary capital investment upswing. This would coincide with the first two years of a (likely) second term for President Carter. However, the 1980–1982 recovery will be weakened because of reduced capital spending combined with continued high rates of personal saving and a low rate of new household formation. This will be unnoticed by most people at first because of an ebullient stock market and the creation of much speculative (paper) wealth.

The Crash of 1983–1984. Stock market booms eventually peter out when stocks are overpriced, and the booms of 1979–1980 or 1981–1982 could come to a sticky end in a major liquidation (crash) by 1983. The increased profitability of 1975–1980, attributable to declining commodity prices and stabilizing wages, culminates in a severe cost-price squeeze as the normal downswing of the business cycle drives many producers (with older, high-cost facilities) to the wall. These marginal producers will tend to be mostly in the urbanized Northeastern and Great Lakes states. The recession could become a full-scale depression as many older plants are closed permanently and bankruptcies and unemployment rise. Some of the big cities and several major states might be forced to declare bankruptcy, resulting in a world-wide financial crisis.

Another factor contributing to the possible depression might, ironically, be the long awaited (but ultimately unwelcome) collapse of OPEC in the early 1980s. This could result from a glut in world-wide petroleum production coming from a number of newly developed (on-

and offshore) fields, especially in South and East Asia, Mexico, Alaska, and the North Sea. If this event occurs, it will not cause universal joy, as some have suggested. On the contrary, it will trigger severe financial stress to many tanker operators, offshore drilling equipment producers, and refiners locked into long-term high-cost contracts. Many big oil companies will have to write off enormous investments in costly projects, such as the North Sea and North Coast Alaska developments, predicated on the high oil prices of 1973–1980. Investments in coal gasification plants, shale and tar-sand recovery, nuclear power, and other capital-intensive energy technologies will also be sharply depreciated, and many electric utilities will also face severe financial difficulties and huge write-offs.

1985–1990.   To combat the effects of the 1983–1984 depression, a heavy program of deficit spending for unemployment relief would be the natural response by a lame duck Carter administration in 1984 in an attempt to save the 1984 election for the Democrats. However, the distressed Northeast and Midwest might vote for a liberal Republican (Percy?) who promises a sharp increase in unrestricted federal aid to states and local governments, plus a lavish public works program to help "restore the cities." By exchanging their obsolescent principles for more palatable political fare, the Republicans could quite easily win on such a platform with a suitably dynamic candidate.

Stabilization and Recovery.   After 1986 a recovery of sorts would presumably begin. The bankrupt cities and states in receivership should be able to shift some of their financial burdens to the federal government. Other high-cost debts would be refinanced at lower interest rates, and major public works projects, such as the modernization and automation of the New York subway system, and the Northeastern rail network, would become financially feasible. The recovery would still be feeble at this stage and set back by short-term business recessions (around 1987 and again in 1991). The cost-price squeeze for industry would continue until around 1995, when the excess capacity overhang should finally be worked off. (A war or a really big natural resource discovery would accelerate this process, of course.)

Commodity prices and long-term interest rates would probably hit bottom just after the turn of the century, around 2005, but they would probably remain low until a new long-term wave of consumer spending and industrial expansion begins to compete with government borrowing for funds and a new cycle of energy shortages begins to drive up commodity prices again. This will end the deflationary part of the long-run cycle and initiate reflation which should continue until 2025, the end of the long cycle, interrupted by occasional brief recessions.

Obviously, the interrelationships between the various parts of the world economy make the scenario quite complex. Peaks and valleys in economic growth rate, inflation rates, commodity prices, stock prices, long-term interest rates, unemployment, and so forth do not coincide neatly. They never have, nor ever will. (If they did, economics would be easy, but not interesting.) In a book like this it is not possible to treat all these factors separately in detail, and I now shift attention to another topic.

GOLD-BUGGERY

I have, up to now, neglected a persistent, if minority, view of the world economy. There is a non-negligible subculture in our society that fervently believes in the existence of an intrinsic "store of value." To most of these people, *gold* is the ultimate measure of value. It is an article of faith with them that sound money must therefore be based on the so-called "gold standard" and freely convertible to gold.

The demonetization of gold and silver began in the depths of the Great Depression, when gold coins were removed from circulation and private citizens were forbidden to own gold, except as jewelry. The government became the only legal buyer for gold and silver mined within the country, and it set the price at $35 per Troy ounce. Gold and silver were stockpiled by the United States Treasury at Fort Knox, Kentucky. The Federal Reserve Bank of New York also kept large stocks of gold in its vaults as "backing" for its Federal Reserve Notes. Until 1945 Federal Reserve Notes were underwritten by 40% of their value in gold; the requirement was dropped to 25% for the next 20 years and eliminated entirely in 1965, although gold retained (and still retains) a major role in international monetary arrangements.

The world price for gold was determined by the United States price ($35/oz.) for several decades. Whereas United States citizens could not own gold privately, foreign producers and/or governments could sell gold to the United States Treasury for dollars at that price. (Governments can also buy.) During the Depression, World War II, and the first few years of postwar recovery, there were more sellers than buyers, because the United States had a massive trade surplus with the rest of the world. In effect, many countries exchanged gold for the

United States manufactured goods, weapons, or food. As a consequence, the gold hoard at Fort Knox grew to monstrous proportions.

Not until the United States balance-of-payments became consistently negative in the 1950s—reflecting massive capital outflow as well as growing raw material imports—did the long influx of gold begin to reverse itself. The outflow grew slowly at first, but it began to accelerate in the 1960s as France (under DeGaulle), Switzerland, West Germany, and other European countries began to rebuild their gold reserves at the—by then, cheap—price of $35/oz. Yet the price remained at the old level through 1971, rising to $38 for 1972, then to $42.22 in 1973, for intergovernmental exchanges only. These increases were far too little and too late, however, as the free market for "private" gold (not yet accessible to United States citizens) rose far higher. The obvious answer was to suspend convertibility—at least temporarily—even for intergovernmental monetary transactions and to treat gold like any other commodity. The prohibition against ownership by United States citizens was finally lifted in 1976. Since then the price has fluctuated (like any other commodity price), breaking the $200/oz.level in the summer of 1978.

So much for recent history. It is the contention of the most prominent Gold Bugs that this trend represents a "devaluation" of the dollar against gold, and that the devaluation will proceed until at least the level corresponding to 1932 prices, allowing for inflation. This equilibrium price, they insist, will be in the range of $300–400 per ounce.

Gold Bugs argue, in effect, that inflation is caused by expanding the money supply faster than the gold supply. Professional economists generally sniff at this rather narrow view of the world, pointing out—with impeccable logic—that what really supports the money supply is productivity, not gold. It would be ludicrous to limit the growth of the world's money supply to the rate at which new gold can be mined. More than that, it would be silly to deprive jewelers and industrial users of a metal that is both beautiful and useful.

But the clincher is that remonetization of gold would also put the health of the world economy entirely in the hands of the world's two major gold producers, which happen to be the Union of South Africa and the USSR. Beyond being economically ludicrous, it is also politically impossible for the United States or other majorWestern democracies to permit such a thing to happen. Thus it should be quite safe to predict that the gold standard is really dead—not just waiting in the wings for a triumphant return to stage center.

However, the Gold Bugs constitute more than a minor aberration of the financial scene. For one thing, some of them are highly placed in financial institutions—especially in Switzerland. Then, too, if logic ruled the world there would be more astronomers than astrologers. It may be irrational to believe that gold is the ultimate "store of value," but quite a few people do believe it, and they preach it with great intensity. Worse, the recent sharp rise in the marker price of gold—coupled with persistent "stagflation" and other disconcerting economic phenomena—appears to confirm their thesis. What better evidence could anyone ask for? If somebody tells you that the price of kumquats is about to quintuple, and it does, it is natural to assume that that person actually knows something about kumquats!

Actually, I'm afraid that what the Gold Bugs know, that economists have not properly appreciated, is the breadth and depth of the popular yearning for *SOMETHING* eternal to believe in. It is, in fact, the religious impulse translated into financial markets. Because so many people want to believe in the ultimate value of gold, it gains value in uncertain times. (The fact that the price of gold can go down, as well as up, has not yet penetrated the consciousness of the new legion of true believers. This, too, will happen in due course.)

There may be a positive element in this phenomenon. It is perfectly true that, as the Gold Bugs point out, a gold-backed currency would impose "discipline" on central bankers and governments. In a world characterized by the underutilization of resources due to inadequate demand, as happened in the 1930s, the strict discipline of a gold standard is a serious economic drag. Partial demonetization of gold was really part and parcel of the Keynes' prescription for economic reflation by deficit spending.

On the other hand, given the world of 1978, even the most liberal Keynesians are now coming around to the belief that more deficit spending is merely inflationary. Whereas the gold standard probably made it harder than necessary to *REFLATE* in the 1930s, a return to the gold standard—perhaps in some disguised form—might be the easiest way to *DEFLATE* in the 1980s. Given the propensity of politicians to choose the easiest solution, I wouldn't rule this out.

On the other hand, the political difficulties I noted earlier remain very much in the way. How will it all come out? The world seems ripe for some new monetary accomodation during the next decade. Anybody who could predict its final shape and content in detail could also become very rich on currency speculation during the interim period, which will certainly be financially turbulent. I have no advice along those lines, except to be very cautious!

PRODUCTIVITY: GROWTH OR DECLINE?

The underlying dynamics of economic growth must be examined in greater detail to permit any rational assessment of future prospects. A point that is not implicit in the World Economic Summary (Table 4.5) or the Baseline Projections (Table 4.6), but which is nevertheless of critical importance is this: *economic growth is, essentially, a recent historical phenomenon.** Until the onset of the industrial revolution, average annual GDP per capita had never exceeded about $200 for any country at any time in history (the range was roughly $50–200). The most developed countries are generally the ones that have been industrializing for the longest time. † Bearing this fact in mind, why should we assume that it will continue indefinitely? §

It may help to state more precisely what "increasing productivity" actually means. Strictly speaking, it means that output increases for the same input of labor. Why should this happen? Economists once attributed the phenomenon of increasing productivity exclusively to investment (from savings or profits): that is, capital accumulation. Technology was regarded as playing a contributory but subsidiary role until recently. Older economic doctrine (Ricardo, Schumpeter) regarded technological innovation mainly as a means for increasing *demand* by creating new products and services. More recently, the importance of developing production-related skills and techniques has been recognized. In the last two decades detailed econometric studies have been carried out to elucidate the relationships more clearly. In a landmark statistical analysis of the United States from 1929 to 1957, Edward Dennison[9] concluded that three variables contributed significantly to per capita growth: he attributed about one-third of the observed United States growth to education, two-ninths to "straight" capital investment, and the rest (four-ninths) to other technological

---

*This point has been properly emphasized by Kahn.[6]

†This is true in a broad sense, although there are some obvious discrepancies. The industrial revolution is usually said to have begun in Britain. Actually, it probably began more or less simultaneously in England, Belgium (Flanders), and Bohemia, although Britain industrialized most rapidly in the seventeenth century. Until 1960 or so, the United Kingdom was still the richest country in Europe (except for Sweden), but it has lagged behind the rest of Northern Europe and is barely ahead of Italy.

§I beg the question as to whether continued growth is really desirable. There are some who argue strongly to the contrary. I comment further on this issue in the Epilogue (Chapter 10).

improvements. The comparative unimportance of capital investment *per se* is perhaps the most surprising result of Dennison's work.

In developed countries both capital and technology obviously must be accumulated internally for the most part, since sufficiently good sources are not available anywhere else. On the other hand, less developed countries can (sometimes) attract capital and technology from the more advanced countries. High growth rates in South Korea, Taiwan, Singapore, Mexico, Brazil, and Spain, among others, are largely attributable to capital and technology investments from the United States, Japan, and Western Europe. Capital/technology transfers of this kind tend to decrease the internal growth rates of the lending or investing countries and increase the growth rates of the recipient countries—other factors remaining equal, of course.

Some less developed countries can also capitalize—literally—on stocks of valuable natural resources* such as petroleum, if these can be sold for hard currencies (or bartered for capital goods) at prices significantly above the cost of extraction. Again, the money to buy these resources comes from the industrialized countries.

From this observation it is clear that the industrially advanced countries will—one way or the other—have to supply most of the capital not only for their own continued (?) growth, but also for the growth of the poorer countries. Some capital can, of course, be created artificially by a cartel selling natural resources at prices much higher than competitive markets would dictate. This is not a form of savings to the consumer of the resources—only to the seller—so it is unaffected by the efficacy of the usual accumulation mechanisms, such as thrift institutions. † The remainder of the needed capital must be explicitly saved, however, by private individuals, corporations (out of operating revenues), or governments (indirectly out of taxes). Repayment of loans must also be financed out of savings.

Clearly some investment is necessary simply to replace existing capital that is depreciated by age, wear and tear, or technological obsolescence. Obviously, some types of capital depreciate much faster

*The danger in this is that revenues from the sale of exhaustible resources come to be regarded as if they were a self-perpetuating form of income rather than depletion of a fixed asset. But this is another topic (see Chapter 8).
† It is affected, however, by the general level of prosperity in the consuming country. If demand is slack, it is hard for a cartel to maintain internal unity, and prices are likely to slip back toward the competitive free-market equilibrium level. Again, this is another subject.

than others. At one extreme, land and liquid assets (e.g., cash) do *not* depreciate (in principle) at all. Canals, harbors, tunnels, and roads may depreciate very slowly, depending on detailed circumstances, of course. A century would not be an unusually long lifetime for this type of infrastructure. Bridges, railroads, and steel structures may last thirty to fifty years or longer. Heavy machinery may last fifteen or twenty years. Automobiles last about ten years. Some types of tools and dies might only last three or four years or even less.

No one knows exactly the "true" average depreciation rate for a whole economy. It certainly varies from country to country and from period to period. A rough estimate would be 5% per year for the United States. Thus, although the United States has consistently reinvested about 15% of its GDP, about one third of this is simply replacing depreciated capital assets. The current rate of *net* capital accumulation in the United States is about 10% p.a. in the industrial and public sectors. Accumulation of household assets (houses, automobiles, furniture and furnishings, appliances, etc.) may well have been even faster, notwithstanding more rapid depreciation.

The depreciation rate of non-household capital tends to rise as the rate of growth increases, due to accelerated obsolescence. A rapidly growing city, for instance, will have to demolish perfectly serviceable older facilities to make way for urgently needed newer ones with higher capacities. In the past twenty years Tokyo has been almost totally rebuilt; many of the arterial streets had to be widened, and a number of limited access motorways were constructed to accommodate heavier motor vehicular traffic. This would not have been necessary if Japan had had a stagnant economy. The same kind of experience applies to industrial plants and facilities. In a rapidly growing economy, older plants cannot be justified economically and are rapidly replaced, whereas in a stagnant economy they are retained. Thus Japan, with its exceptionally high growth rate, now has the youngest capital stock in the world. The Japanese growth machine has been powered by an extraordinarily high rate of reinvestment: 29% of GDP was reinvested in nonhousing capital during the 1960s. Obviously, in Japan, too, some of this is for replacement (probably above 10%), but there is enough left over for a very substantial rate of net accumulation.

The situation in West Germany and France is consistent with this picture. Both countries have, for the past two decades, consistently reinvested about 20% of GDP, and both are clearly accumulating capital on a net basis faster than the U.S. although far less rapidly than Japan. The rate of capital depreciation in these countries must be slightly higher than in the United States because of faster recent growth, but doubtless it is lower than in Japan. In the stagnant United Kingdom, on the other hand, reinvestment in nonhousing capital has been only about 13.5%.

A curious fact emerges. It is indisputable that non-housing capital stocks have been growing considerably faster than national incomes, at least in the advanced industrial countries. Moreover, as Dennison showed, such income (GDP) growth as has occurred is largely attributable to factors other than investment. It is not surprising that returns on investment have been declining, while returns to labor—that is, wage rates—have been rising in real terms. In other words, productivity gains have benefitted wage-earners in recent years, at the expense of investors. The flight of investment money away from the stock market and into real estate, works of art, coins and other 'collectibles' is a reflection of this trend. But in aggregate terms the talk of 'capital scarcity' seems to be off the mark. The evidence suggests, if anything, a surplus of capital and a scarcity of profitable opportunities. This is consistent with Forrester's explanation of the Kondratieff cycle noted earlier.

If not from capital investment *per se* what are the likely sources of future economic growth? I suggest the following three:

1. Discovering and substituting more effective but less capital-intensive processes or methods of production
2. Improving the skills, training, or motivation of the labor force (effectively replacing capital)
3. Changing the mix of goods and services to decrease the importance of capital-intensive inputs

Method 1 lies in the realm of technology. I discuss specific opportunities to save capital (and energy) through technological innovation in Chapter 7. For the present it is enough to say that many such opportunities do exist, particularly through the increasing use of automation and computers. However, it is not likely that technology will come to the rescue automatically, without specific encouragement.

Method 2 is partly an aspect of education. This is dealt with at greater length in a section of the next chapter. In terms of the problem of securing continued increases in productivity, however, I anticipate the conclusions of that discussion by saying that the United States— like all the advanced developed countries—has already exhausted most of the benefits to labor quality that can be derived from the introduction of universal public education through the age of 14–16 plus relatively easy access to higher education for a significant fraction of the population. As far as the United States is concerned, the *quality* of public school education appears to be declining sharply, with grim implications for the future productivity of workers in industry. Further improvements in the quality of the labor force will be achieved slowly and somewhat painfully, to say the least, unless there is some totally unexpected technological or organizational breakthrough in the process of education.*

The question of motivation is deeper. Although it is highly doubtful that personal *values* can be affected on a wide scale by a deliberate act (or acts) of policy, it is just conceivable that an innovation in the area of industrial *organization* could have a major impact on productivity. There has been much talk about the effectiveness of modern "management" methods, for example, as taught by the prestigious business schools, and the relative success of United States-based multinational corporations was widely attributed, for a time, to the use of such techniques. There is also a wave of attempts to improve productivity in the advanced countries by various job enrichment schemes, or in a few cases by converting employees into owners. Quoting Norman MacRae[10]

> In three successive waves of efforts to solve their "people problem" (or "alienation problem"), rich northern countries have (a) imported more amenable workers from the poorer south, (b) sent multinational factories down to the poorer south, (c) tried to persuade native workers to love factories more through worker participation. None of these three systems is conceivably going to work. . . .
>
> Incentives to make workers happier will have to become much more individual, and be geared to allowing each human to choose his lifestyle—because choosing one's lifestyle is what freedom in future must mainly mean. . . .
>
> The marrying of job specifications to the individually-varied and constantly-changing patterns of lifestyles demanded—with the lower wages going to those who say they choose the less productive or more popular lifestyles—cannot efficiently be attempted by a hierarchical corporation, but will be a matter for constant experiment. . . .

*There have been flurries of excitement at times in the past decade over the potential of computer-assisted programmed-learning devices, "tele-schools" using satellites or cable TV, and so on. None has had any lasting impact to date. Nor will the current "back to basics" movement prove to be a panacea if it is conducted in a mechanistic manner.

Dynamic corporations of the future should simultaneously be trying several alternative ways of doing things in competition within themselves, and have on their payrolls a lot of individuals and group cooperatives of workers who are part-entrepreneurial sub-contractors and part-salaried staff but wholly neither. . . .

Method 3 for increasing productivity relates to the pattern of final demand and the fact that all highly industrialized countries seem to be shifting gradually toward service industries and what has been called by Daniel Bell the "postindustrial society." Intuitively, it would seem that services can be more labor intensive and less capital intensive than extraction and manufacturing. I think there is much potential in this area.

Of course, the outcome depends in great part on the way in which the services are provided. Education is a service that may be provided in a little red schoolhouse as in the nineteenth century or in a luxurious country-club setting with expensive physical plant and facilities of every kind, as exemplified by many recently constructed suburban schools in the United States. Similarly, health services can be provided by a district nurse or midwife or by space-age hospital-institutes equipped with every diagnostic and therapeutic device known to man. It is not clear in either case how much the extra capital investment contributes to the education or health service rendered. There are grounds for suspicion, at least in some of the more extreme cases, that the contribution may actually be negative. In effect, the luxury might be for the benefit of the teachers or doctors more than for the benefit of the students and patients.

Services comprise more than public school education and health. What services will expand if economic growth does continue? Presumably more of the kinds of services that people now provide for themselves or each other with their spare time and money. Repair and maintenance, even household cleaning and cooking, is one such area. Education for adults is evidently a growth sector. Entertainment of all kinds, including sports, movies, TV, music, and theater, will certainly continue to grow in economic importance, as will the arts and handicrafts. Games and gambling will doubtless do the same (professional bridge or poker partners will become more numerous, for instance). Tourism and travel will certainly expand. Environmental protection and conservation activities will employ more people. Mental health and social rehabilitation of misfits, criminals, drug addicts, and the mentally ill will also occupy more people. In principle, most of these activities can be carried out without heavy investments in expensive machinery and equipment. In view of the increasing capital requirements per unit of output projected by other sectors (such as energy production), the growth of the service sectors is an important safety valve for the economy.

The issue of capital accumulation and its relation to economic growth cannot be wrapped up without considering another important (and often overlooked) factor. I refer to the contribution that has been made in the past by the availability of cheap, high-quality natural resources, many of which are now becoming seriously depleted. The truth — which we (as an industrialized society) have not really faced — is that these exhaustible resource stocks have constituted a form of nonrenewable capital which we have been depreciating by extraction. One economist who has stated the problem very well is E. F. Schumacher[11]:

> The illusion of unlimited powers, nourished by astonishing scientific and technological achievements has produced the concurrent illusion of having solved the problem of production. The latter illusion is based on the failure to distinguish between income and capital where this distinction matters most. Every economist and businessman is familiar with the distinction, and applies it conscientiously and with considerable subtlety to all economic affairs — except where it really matters: namely, the irreplaceable capital which man has not made, but simply found, and without which he can do nothing.

> A businessman would not consider a firm to have solved its problems of production and to have achieved viability if he saw that it was rapidly consuming its capital. How, then could we overlook this vital fact when it comes to that very big firm, the economy of Spaceship Earth and, in particular, the economies of its rich passengers?

The equivalence between underground nonrenewable resources (e.g., petroleum) and man-made capital is quite exact for the simple reason that as the most accessible high-quality pools of oil or ore are pumped out or dug up we must continually find replacement sources. These are progressively deeper, further away,* harder to extract, and

---

*Oil from the North Slope of Alaska cannot be utilized in the United States without a very expensive trans-Alaska pipeline, for instance. Oil from the North Sea would be far too expensive to exploit at pre-1973 prices due to the high cost of drilling from offshore platforms in a stormy ocean.

more difficult to process. It is perfectly true, but irrelevant, that in the past century improved technology has more than kept pace, resulting in an actual decline in most crude energy and material prices from 1870 to 1970. (The reader is referred to Chapter 8 for further discussion and justification of this surprising statement.) The point is that both man-made capital and energy requirements to extract and process crude materials keep rising as the best-quality sources are exhausted. To go on consuming the same quantities of such resources even without any increase, the amount of capital devoted to extraction and processing will continuously rise, without any visible limit.

There is a kind of equivalence, too, between technology and capital. The better our technology, the less capital will be needed, and conversely. It has become fashionable in recent years for industrialists and resource economists to argue against the "limits to growth" thesis on the grounds that technology will come to the rescue. Many people, including too many technologists, seem to be imbued with the notion that technology can do anything, given enough financial support.* Although technology has wrought a few miracles, it has its share of failures, too.

As I note in Chapters 6 and 7, there are definite limits to what can be expected from technology, and the failure list is likely to lengthen considerably in the next half century. In any case, it seems to me that technology is expected to fill too many gaps in other areas, especially in view of the declining public and private support for developing new technology.

I come now to the other side of the coin. There are, as it happens, some strong arguments for thinking that productivity may *not* continue to grow for much longer in the advanced industrial countries. These can be collected together and boiled down to

- "Sand in the works" (institutionally speaking)
- Economic parasitism

The two overlap and interact a good bit, but they are not quite the same. It is probably worthwhile to discuss them separately.

By "sand in the works" I mean a variety of institutionalized factors that tend to inhibit progressive change. Remember, economic growth depends on *increasing* productivity, which cannot be done without changing existing ways of doing things. There is no way to secure

---

*Not to mention the even stronger position of the Mumford school that technology *will* do anything its practitioners decide, unless positively stopped!

higher productivity without continued substitution of machines for men in those jobs that machines can do better than men, especially the repetitive tasks involving the moving and processing of energy, materials, and physical objects. For productivity to grow, machines (such as electronic computers) *must* also eventually replace humans in repetitive functions such as operating other machines, as well as in clerical tasks.

When the economic engine is working properly, substitutions of this kind yield increased revenues to the industries taking advantage of them. The extra income will be spent either to increase capacity (generating immediate new jobs in the capital goods sector), increase dividends to stockholders or wages to employees, or to decrease prices —or some combination of all four. Regardless of the allocation, the result is reflected in spending. This eventually results in a greater demand for all goods and services, which creates more jobs.

The point is, however, that the new skills needed are not the same as the old skills that were replaced. The jobs created by the applications of computers are not the same as the jobs eliminated by computers. They may be in the computer industry itself, or in retail trade, tourism, or a thousand other places. The jobs eliminated might be factory jobs traditionally held by men. The new jobs created might be more open to women, for instance. But there is no way to have a growing economy and simultaneously protect everyone's existing jobs —still less increase the number of unproductive jobs.

Of course, those who lose jobs as a result of technological changes are much more likely to be aware of it than those who may ultimately benefit. Many people who are threatened in this way are already organized in labor unions. If not, a perceived technological threat is a strong inducement to unionize. Unions in the United States and Europe are increasingly devoted to only two objectives:

1. Increasing real wages and benefits *without* justification by increased output
2. Preserving existing jobs, job descriptions, and work rules *without* change.

In very many cases unions have used their monopoly power to negotiate the preservation of unnecessary or obsolete jobs such as the firemen on a diesel locomotive, the hod carrier, the plumber's helper, the engineer on a jet airliner, who is actually a third trained pilot, or the elevator operator who pushes the buttons in an automatic elevator.

Hardly anyone in our liberal enlightened society views this kind of job preservation as inherently bad – and so it continues to be tolerated.

Recently, some unions have escalated their demands. A major bargaining objective of organized labor* in 1976–1977 was to *increase* the number of man-hours required to produce a unit of output, *at no decrease in wages,* as a device to create even more unnecessary jobs. In any industry – for example, steel manufacturing – in which this union objective is met, productivity must, *by definition,* decrease. If organized labor succeeds in forcing employers, in general, to create a greater number of jobs (at no decrease in wage rates), the automatic consequence will be to increase the cost of producing everything without producing *more* of anything. Prices will rise while output remains constant. This is a formula for inflation without economic growth – the exact opposite of what we should be trying to achieve. In practice, since unionized workers can protect themselves better than the unorganized poor or the elderly, it is also a formula for subsidizing well-paid organized workers (who do not work very hard) at the expense of those who cannot protect themselves.

Another kind of "sand in the works" is excessive bureaucratic regulation. In this area, the United States probably leads the world. There are literally thousands of regulations – propounded in the name of high ideals such as eliminating discrimination, enhancing the public health and safety, or preserving the environment – affecting every phase of economic activity. These regulations are often complex, running to scores, hundreds, or even thousands of paragraphs. ✝

Each such regulation requires some response by whomever is being regulated, whether a private sector business or a public institution, such as a school or hospital. Compliance is expensive enough, but

---

*The steel workers and longshoremen have been particularly candid about their objectives lately.

✝HEW's newly promulgated regulations to eliminate illegal discrimination against handicapped persons took three years to draft and ran over 200 pages in length. The cost of compliance, to the economy, will be astronomical, certainly in the billions of dollars per year, and this is only one example.

A particularly absurd instance of regulatory overkill is the recent case of TRIS, a chemical flame retardant used in children's sleepware. TRIS has been banned, at great cost to many small clothing manufacturers, because of laboratory tests showing that it has carcinogenic properties. It was introduced in the first place in response to another government regulation designed to reduce the number of children killed by accidental fires! Meanwhile the onus of bearing the costs of this government reversal was placed by the regulators not on the government or the manufacturers of the chemical or of the fabric, but on the manufacturers of the garments *per se* who had no control over the choice of flame retardant that was used nor any technical expertise in the subject.

providing evidence of compliance to satisfy the regulatory bodies is a major hidden cost of regulation. Noncompliance—sometimes inadvertent—may result in extensive and costly litigation, which adds to the cost burden without adding anything to the output of the economy. From simple inspection to assure the cleanliness and sanitation of meat packers and food processors, the regulatory mania has progressed to the point at which regulatory authorities are now legally empowered to prevent new products from being marketed (or delay them indefinitely) or even to retroactively ban products (like saccharine) that have been manufactured and marketed for many years. †

The cumulative impact of this is, unquestionably, to add to the cost of technological innovation. The impact on the United States pharmaceutical sector has already been quite adverse—some say catastrophic. The number of new drugs developed and introduced per year since the FDA obtained authority to impose extensive prescreening and testing requirements has dropped by 40%. New drugs are now rarely introduced in the United States until they have been on the market for some years in other countries—hardly surprising in view of the fact that $40 million and 200,000 pages of documents may be required to get approval for one new drug. Apart from adverse impact on the ability of United States firms to compete (for instance) with German, Swiss, or Italian manufacturers, the public is also the loser insofar as it is deprived of beneficial drugs that would otherwise be available. For every thalidomide incident avoided, one must count the cost of missing the undiscovered equivalents of penicillin or aureomycin, many of which could not have succeeded in passing the rigorous tests of safety that have now been established.

In the chemical industry the recent (1976) TOSCA legislation, regulating production and use of toxic chemicals, will undoubtedly have an equally far-reaching impact on innovation. Again, the rate of introduction of new technology will decline (in the United States), giving an advantage to less-regulated producers overseas. Equally important, in the long run regulatory legislation of this kind discriminates against the smaller, more innovative firms and favors the larger firms with a greater stake in the status quo.

These two industries are not the only ones on which the stifling hand of regulation lies heavy. Utilities and transportation are others. Between recalcitrant unions on one side, and government on the other, railroads and shipowners have little scope for technological innovation. When innovations do occur in such industries, it is usually because they constitute a device to bypass a particularly entrenched roadblock. Containerization of ocean freight to reduce vulnerability to theft of cargo by corrupt longshoremen is a case in point. Obviously, the technology involved is otherwise of trivial significance.

Union rules and government regulation constitute "sand in the works" because they reduce flexibility, slow down the pace of change, increase overhead costs, and generally reduce efficiency. Above and beyond these phenomena, however, there seems to be an increasing number of economic activities that contribute nothing of value to the economy as a whole, while consuming ever-increasing resources. Some of these activities are relatively immune from the operation of the laws of supply and demand in that they are able to create a synthetic demand (or, to use a more accurate word, *addiction*) for their services. A number of so-called professions are parasitic, in this sense, to a significant degree.

Advertising is an obvious example: advertising professionals promote, first and foremost, their own services. It can be argued with some justice that many products are advertised only because their competitors advertise—with no net advantage to either producers or consumers. This is particularly noteworthy in the areas of household products, sundries, and cosmetics, where actual differences between rival brands are insignificant or very difficult for consumers to assess.

Organized medicine is also parasitic. The sanction to practice medicine is, in a real sense, power over life and death. In the United States —more than most countries—this implicit power over the lay public has been exploited for the pecuniary advantage of the doctors. It is regarded as a requirement of medical "ethics" (*entirely determined by the doctors themselves*) that doctors should not compete with each other by offering definite services for fixed prices. Doctors seldom suggest a variety of alternative therapies or drugs with different advantages and disadvantages (and different costs to the patient). Almost invariably, the doctor, in his carefully cultivated role as sole expert, specifies a single "optimum" treatment—regardless of inconvenience, discomfort, pain, or cost to the patient or the patient's family. The prescribed treatment is often elaborated with superfluous and costly laboratory tests, using exotic diagnostic equipment, and prescriptions for costly drugs which may be mere placebos. Patients are sent to the hospital far too often for too many unneeded operations and too many "observations"—at enormous cost to the patient (or, indirectly, the public) and enormous profit to the doctors.

Notwithstanding the great sins of the medical doctors, the legal profession is probably the most parasitic single group in the United States, which is saying a lot. This is so by virtue of lawyers' unique ability to create demand for their own unproductive services through effective control over both the law-making and the law-enforcement processes. Again, the helpless victim, caught in the toils of the legal process, seldom has any practical alternatives. In part, the artificially inflated demand for lawyers happens inadvertently as a natural consequence of the sheer complexity of regulatory law, which requires each government agency and each private enterprise of any magnitude to have a staff of lawyers simply to interpret the existing corpus of legislation as it applies to specific cases. Tax law is one specialty that exists essentially because the accumulation of relevant legislation is too complicated for the average person to understand.

Another less innocent way in which lawyers create socially unproductive employment for themselves is by framing new laws in such a way as to create unnecessary disputes that can only be settled by costly litigation requiring more lawyers. Divorce and settlement of insurance claims are two notable examples. "No fault" insurance could theoretically cut insurance costs to the public by as much as one-third, but it has been bitterly—and quite successfully—opposed by trial lawyers who have been living off the system. "No fault" divorce is also perfectly feasible—indeed, it exists in a few states—but, again, the trial lawyers have opposed it. Worse still, the legal profession refuses to reform the cumbersome and costly system of civil litigation that permits endless delays at each stage—with several successive levels of appeal—and often delays decisions for the injured party in a dispute for many years, with no provision for the final winner to recover his ever-mounting legal costs. On balance, delay only benefits the lawyers, rarely the litigants.

A third way that lawyers guarantee maximum income with minimum effort is through the use of an elaborate probate process for settling estates, with executor fees based on a legally fixed percentage of the estate, and legally fixed fees for transferring property. When large estates are probated, the legal fees can run to millions of dollars, although the work involved may be slight. Another abuse is the so-called title search, which is unnecessarily done anew for each transfer (usually by a clerk) and which entitles some attorney to collect a fee bearing no relation to the work actually done. The fee is normally fixed by the local Bar Association. Largely unnecessary legal fees constitute a major fraction of the costs of buying and selling all kinds of real property, especially housing. Settlement costs constitute a heavy burden for the house buyer and a significant barrier to many who would like to own their homes, but cannot because of the front-end costs involved.

A fourth way that some less scrupulous lawyers use to make money is to encourage citizens to file lawsuits for accidental injury or damages or medical malpractice, with the legal fee contingent on a settlement and based on a percentage of the award. This practice has resulted in wildly escalating awards (and legal fees) in the past two decades. Naturally the costs are passed back to the public, directly or indirectly, through higher insurance rates.

Because they are so busy with their various "get rich quick" schemes, most lawyers have too little time for such unremunerative tasks as representing poor people harassed by bureaucracy, tricked into fraudulent "home improvement" rackets, or otherwise in difficulties.

For reasons I cannot fathom, legal parasitism is far worse in the United States than in most other advanced countries. Apparently the problem *can* be brought under control, as it has been (for instance) in the United Kingdom, where the number of lawyers per capita is probably no more than one-tenth of what it is in the United States. I am optimistic, therefore, that some reforms will be made eventually.

If the trends I have noted do not change and if technology does not obviate the problem by compensating for short-sighted economic policies, the recent era of fast economic growth for the advanced countries must soon come to an end. Unfortunately, the end will not announce itself clearly, nor is a smooth transition from "growth" to "no growth" at all likely. Inevitably, many actors — especially producers — will not get the message until it is too late for rational planning.

What happens next? The real economic future is indeterminate, of course. There are many possible paths (or scenarios) from here. However, a systematic exploration of the policy options is beyond the scope of this book.

SERVICES VIS-A-VIS GOODS

Historians have long recognized three distinct stages of organized society. A fourth has recently been suggested (by Daniel Bell, among others), as shown in Figure 4.2. The first stage is subdivided by general agreement into the nomadic hunting-gathering stage characteristic of most truly primitive tribes such as Eskimos, Australian aborigines, Papuans, African bushmen, or Amazonian indians. This is followed by the herdsmen stage of culturally more advanced nomads such as the Laplanders, Berbers, Bedouins, Kurds, or Mongols of Central Asia.

Settled agriculture represents the next major stage, and most historical civilizations have represented agricultural societies gradually

Figure 4.8 Stages of economic development.

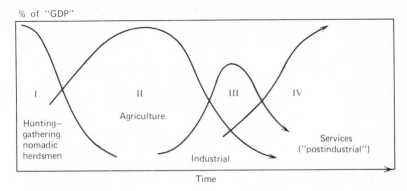

extending their cultivated and irrigated domains at the expense of neighboring hunting-gathering tribes or herdsmen, often invidiously labeled as "barbarians." The series of outbreaks of the Mongol hordes under Ghengis Khan and Tamerlaine was the last (and temporary) major resurgence of the nomads. Since then, they have been pushed gradually but inexorably toward cultural extinction. For five millennia, from the earliest known centers of agriculture in the valleys of the Indus, Mekong, Tigris-Euphrates, Nile, Yellow, and Yangtze Rivers, through the nineteenth century, the world economy has been primarily based on agriculture. The only countries with an absolute majority of workers engaged in nonagricultural pursuits in 1890 were Great Britain, Belgium, Germany, and the United States—the first countries to industrialize. Like their hunting-gathering predecessors, the agricultural stage is primarily rural based.

Primary emphasis on the manufacture of goods represents the third major stage: industrial. The industrial revolution coincided with development of the technology for exploiting external sources of mechanical and heat energy to supplement human and animal muscle power and charcoal. Although several other factors were also involved (as discussed to some extent in Chapter 2), the basic technology of energy conversion was an essential prerequisite. The first phase of the industrial revolution was water and wind power. The invention of sailships capable of tacking (to sail against the wind), windmills, and water wheels were of major importance, but the biggest single impetus to industrialization was the use of coal to replace charcoal for smelting iron and firing bricks and clay. Coal also made steam engines practicable, resulting in the first mobile "prime mover," or source of controlled mechanical power. For purposes of transportation *per se,* the steam engine has been replaced by internal combustion engines and gas turbines.

Obviously, one of the first major beneficiaries of this new source of mobile power was agriculture, which had been technologically almost static for the previous thousand years or more. (The development of harnesses, yokes, and iron plows adapted to the use of draft animals occurred in Europe in early post-Roman times.) In the nineteenth century a general substitution of machines for human and animal labor on farms began slowly. In the twentieth century the substitution of machines for human and animal labor was greatly accelerated, as Table 4.7 shows.[12] In fact, the number of horsepower available in "prime movers" in the United States quadrupled from 1950 to 1970.*

As a result of the increase in available horsepower, less labor was required to produce agricultural products, and surplus was released to the cities to work in the expanding manufacturing (and service) sectors. In 1890 agriculture accounted for 42% of United States employment as compared with 58% for goods- and service-producing industries combined.[†] By 1980, according to the United States Department of Labor, agriculture will probably occupy a mere 2.3% of the work force, as shown in Table 4.8.[13] Manufacturing employment, too, is in a steady decline. Norman MacRae, of the Economist (London) has predicted that less than 5% of the labor force will be required for manufacturing by the middle of the twenty-first century.[14] I agree with that prognosis, give or take a decade. In other words, the service-producing sectors are already predominant and are absorbing all additions to the employed labor force in addition to displaced agricultural and manufacturing workers.

What kind of society does this suggest? It has been called the "post-industrial society" by sociologist Daniel Bell.[15] The label carries many extraneous connotations, some of which were discussed in Chapter 2. For the present, its significance seems to be that as incomes rise beyond a certain point, a society's appetite for nonmaterial services increases faster than its appetite for material goods. Added *quality* — of goods, of services, of life — becomes more important than additional *quantity*. In the United States activities that cater to the demand of quality of life will expand most during the next fifty years[§]: education, entertainment, health services, tourism, recreation, and so on.

---

*It is noteworthy that private automobiles account for 95% of the total. In effect, the household sector has become mechanized.

[†]The exact breakdown in 1890 is not available for labor categories that are currently used, but manufacturing seems to have outweighed services by a significant margin at that time.

[§]After basic needs (food, energy, housing) are met.

Table 4.7   Horsepower of All Prime Movers (United States)
(In millions. As of January, except as indicated.)

Item	1950	1955	1960	1965	1970	1972[a]
Automotive[b,c]	4404	6632	10,367	14,306	19,325	21,738
Nonautomotive	464	526	641	790	1,083	1,177
Factories	33	36	42	48	54	58
Mines	22	31	35	40	45	47
Railroads	111	60	47	44	54	57
Merchant ships	23	24	24	24	22	21
Farms	165	212	240	272	290	305
Electric central stations[c]	88	138	217	307	435	508
Aircraft (pvt. and commercial)	22	26	37	55	183	181
Total horsepower	4868	7158	11,008	15,096	20,408	22,915

[a]Preliminary.
[b]Passenger cars, trucks, buses, and motorcycles.
[c]As of July 1.

As of 1970 only a few countries—the United States, Canada, Switzerland, and Sweden—were postindustrial by Bell's criteria. By 1985, however, the EEC as a whole and Japan will certainly join the club, and the USSR almost certainly will do so before the year 2000 (despite its inefficient and labor-intensive agriculture). On the other hand, none of the other important countries of the world has any hope of reaching this stage even by 2025, with the possible and unlikely exception of Brazil. China will probably be classified as "industrial" (stage III), but it is doubtful whether India or Nigeria will have graduated from stage II.

PUBLIC VERSUS PRIVATE SECTOR EXPENDITURES

One of the most dramatic trends since World War II (in the noncommunist developed countries) has been the growth of public sector spending as compared with the private sector. Expenditures by government roughly parallel employment. In the case of the United States (Table 4.8) public employment has grown from 6.9 million (10.5% of the labor force) in 1955 to 13.3 million (15.5%) in 1977. It is projected to rise to 18.8 million (17.5%) by 1985.[13]

Government spending is not limited to wage and salary payments to public employees, of course. It includes purchases of equipment and commodities, grants and contracts to the private sector cov-

Table 4.8 Total Employment for Selected Years 1955–1972 and
Projected to 1980 and 1985 (United States)
(thousands of jobs)

| | Percent Distribution | | | | | |
| | Actual | | | | Projected | |
	1955	1960	1968	1972	1980	1985
Government	10.5	12.1	14.6	15.5	16.4	17.5
Total private	89.5	87.9	85.4	84.5	83.6	82.5
Agriculture	9.8	7.8	4.7	4.0	2.3	1.8
Nonagriculture	79.7	80.0	80.6	80.4	81.4	80.8
Mining	1.3	1.1	.8	.8	.6	.6
Construction	5.4	5.3	5.0	5.1	4.8	4.8
Manufacturing	26.3	25.0	24.9	22.5	22.6	21.8
Durable	14.9	14.1	14.6	13.0	13.4	13.2
Nondurable	11.5	10.9	10.3	9.6	9.2	8.7
Transportation, communication, and public utilities	6.6	6.1	5.6	5.5	5.2	5.0
Transportation	4.4	4.0	3.5	3.3	3.2	3.0
Communication	1.3	1.2	1.2	1.3	1.3	1.2
Public utilities	.9	.8	.8	.9	.8	.7
Trade	20.1	20.6	21.6	21.5	21.4	20.8
Wholesale trade	4.7	4.8	4.8	4.9	4.9	4.8
Retail trade	15.4	15.8	15.8	16.6	16.5	16.0
Finance, insurance, and real estate	4.0	4.3	4.6	5.0	5.3	5.5
Other services	15.9	17.6	19.2	20.0	21.5	22.2
Total	100.0	100.0	100.0	100.0	100.0	100.0

ering such items as munitions, navy ships, aircraft and missiles, vehicles, food, fuel, and clothing for the military, construction of roads, harbors, school buildings, hospitals, and so on. It also includes welfare payments, medicare and medicaid, social security benefits, veterans benefits, pensions to government workers, and interest payments on the national debt. Thus many private citizens (and businesses) receive part or all their income from the government.

The effect on ordinary citizens has been that payments for taxes and social insurance have risen from 8.9% of all personal income in 1955 to 15.1% in 1972; it is expected to be 16.7% by 1985. The effect on employed workers who pay taxes—in contrast to beneficiaries of social insurance payments—has been much more dramatic, since a growing fraction of all personal income now comes from various transfer payments, rather than from earnings, interest, or dividends. In 1965 an average factory production worker with three dependents earned about $130 (1972 $) before taxes, or $107 after taxes were paid.[16] Although his nominal pretax income increased significantly in the following decade, taxes and inflation consumed all the growth in income. After-tax take-home pay in 1974 was actually slightly below the 1965 level.

The United States is not the world leader in this trend toward expanding the public sector at the expense of the private. The quasi-socialist governments of Scandinavia and the United Kingdom probably lead the way. Government spending as a percentage of GDP in all the EEC countries is now higher than in the United States. Only Japan among the major industrial countries leaves more money in the private sector.

Where does the public sector spending go? Primarily, it buys social services, notably, education, security (defense, police, fire protection, and criminal justice), and health and welfare. Housing, transportation, environment protection, resource development and conservation, recreation, science, and other public purposes receive, by comparison, a pittance. Even welfare spending (in the United States) is not mainly for the chronically very poor but for special categories such as retired persons, veterans, or the temporarily unemployed.

In view of the grave social problems of today and the obvious scarcity of resources to cope with them, it seems odd that as recently as ten years ago some serious (or semiserious) authors actually suggested that the biggest problem facing the United States was to create a synthetic demand for intrinsically useless artificially depreciating products. It was argued that this was necessary to keep the economy growing because of the impending saturation of demand for real goods. It was quite widely believed in some circles in the mid-1960s that the obsolescence of cars, for example, was programmed* simply to keep the factories humming.

It may also surprise some readers, on reflection, how little in the way of "social services" all this spending actually seems to buy. Has

---

*In the case of cars there was, in fact, a modicum of truth in this. GM's policy of periodic model changes was, in fact, designed to stimulate sales of new vehicles and prompt trade-in of older ones, even though the older cars were not discarded nor designed to "fall apart," as has been widely conjectured. The average car, then and now, runs nearly eleven years before being scrapped.

the quality of schools increased in the United States during the past two decades, while school spending has skyrocketed? Has the quality of health care in the United States increased significantly—or at all—during the two decades of soaring Medicare and Medicaid expenditures? Has housing improved? Are the streets safer? Some qualifying details are discussed later, but a preliminary general answer to these and similar questions would have to be negative. Indeed, the failure of government intervention to cure social ills via bureaucratic organizations appears to be virtually total. Few, if any, examples of successful social programs run by civil servants anywhere in the world can be cited as a basis for justifying a continuation of this basic approach.

Of course, one major difference between the United States and Western Europe is that the United States spends a larger proportion of its GDP for military purposes than do Europe or Japan. The proportion as of 1976 was about 8–9%, but it was a few percentage points higher during much of the 1950s and 1960s. At the present United States level it may not pose a serious problem. However, when 15% or more of a nation's output is used to support a military establishment,* there is little doubt that severe distortions can and do occur. President Eisenhower warned of the existence of a "military-industrial complex" in his farewell address to Congress, and the real, if sometimes exaggerated, potency of this establishment has attracted hostile attention from liberals over the last decade and a half. Indeed, the resources devoted to the military (and associated activities such as the CIA) have been cut back sharply as a reaction, in part, to this criticism.

The level of United States military spending for the next decade undoubtedly depends principally on two factors: (1) the level of tension in the world generally and (2) the military posture of the USSR in particular. As to the first, there is every reason to suppose that tension will continue, but there is little reason to think it will be as high as during the period of the Cold War or the Vietnam War, unless one or more major powers becomes involved somewhere in another "brushfire" war. My guess is that the essential lesson of Vietnam will not be forgotten soon by most Americans, although Russians may still have to learn how extremely limited tanks and guns really are as instruments of national power and influence.

*For the USSR the proportion is apparently higher than for the United States. In fact, the latest (upward revised) CIA figures suggest that United States costs to duplicate Soviet military programs would exceed actual United States military outlays in 1975 by more than $30 billion, or 40% of United States spending.[17] In effect, the USSR spends as much or more than the United States, with a GDP only one-fourth as large. According to the CIA, somewhere in the neighborhood of 14% of the Soviet GDP goes to military purposes. But if Soviet expenditures exceed US outlays in absolute terms, the percentage of GDP must be much larger.

As to the USSR, the sad fact remains that a vast, bloated self-perpetuating military-industrial complex *does* exist there. It is an open question whether even the tightly organized Communist Party apparatus supported by other elements of the Soviet system that have been starved of resources can ever bring the Russian military establishment to heel without a crisis of some sort. The most likely such crisis would be an attempt to intimidate China (without resorting to nuclear weapons), resulting in a costly and inconclusive conventional war with that country, fought in scattered locations along thousands of miles of desolate frontier. The USSR might conceivably be tempted to bite off another chunk of Chinese territory — as it has done so often in the past — resulting in a frustrating and difficult "pacification" program. Yet total conquest of China would be exceedingly difficult. Indeed, even if China were occupied, it would serve no long-term purpose. The outcome of any protracted fighting would probably be a strengthening of the political fabric of China (the "underdog," after all) and a corresponding weakening of the political fabric of the USSR. The end might even be a "Second Russian Revolution" of some sort. These possibilities are explored briefly in one of the scenarios of Chapter 9.

Unless or until some such sequence of events occurs, however, the USSR can be expected to continue to spend a great deal of its national output on its armed forces. The United States will almost certainly try to maintain some sort of rough parity, which means continuing to spend at least 8% of its GDP for military purposes. The fraction could rise in many conceivable circumstances.

Is it possible that the electorates of the democratic countries are approaching the end of their tether, and that they will soon (within a decade, say) demand a *reversal* of the trend of the last generation toward public sector spending and bureaucratization? This is a vital question indeed. The answer depends on decisions yet to be taken, both by private citizens and by politicians. Such a reversal appears to me to be possible, but somewhat improbable, from the perspective of 1978.

In suggesting that containment of megabureaucracy may be *possible,* I must emphasize that it would be very difficult. In the United States, for instance, the dismantling of Big Government is probably an impossible task for a doctrinaire conservative Republican, such as Ronald Reagan.* If it is to be done, it must be done by a "converted" liberal Democrat with a strong influence over his party colleagues in Congress. (The same rule applied in reverse to the problem of ending

*Incidentally, Reagan made virtually no real progress in limiting expenditures or containing the bureaucracies of his home state, California, during two terms as governor. Some progress has been made, curiously, by his Democratic successor, Governor Brown.

the Cold War between the United States and the USSR and normalizing relations with China. Only a conservative Republican like Nixon could silence the chief potential critics of such a policy, who were rightwing Republicans.) For the same reason, only the Labor Party in the United Kingdom could effectively cut back on the welfare state, first put in place by the Attlee government in 1945.

DEFICIT FINANCING AND INFLATION

Accompanying the historical increase in government spending, but fundamentally unrelated to it, is the increase in deficit financing by government, private business, and individuals. The Federal Government debt—$533 billion in mid-1975, as compared to $286 billion in 1960—gets most attention, but this is only part of the total. For instance, short-term consumer credit outstanding amounted to $56 billion in mid-1960 but had increased to $186 billion by mid-1975. This does not include mortgage debt on housing. State and local obligations rose from $21.7 billion in 1950 to $206.6 billion in 1974. Corporate borrowing—the largest chunk—increased from $142.1 billion in 1950 to $302.8 billion in 1960 and then zoomed to $1306 billion in 1975. During this period interest rates have also risen steadily; thus the cost of servicing the debt load has gone up far faster than even the debt itself. Here is a fairly shocking statistic: In 1947 United States corporations earned enough in profits to "cover" their debt service twentyfour times. In 1950 the coverage ratio was 17. By 1975 this ratio had dropped to about 3.[18] To the extent that all these kinds of debt, taken together, less savings of all kinds, increase *faster* than the GDP, it means that money is being spent faster than it is being earned and faster than goods are being produced. The imbalance must eventually be reversed somehow to avoid a credit "supercrunch" or a monetary collapse. Fortunately, banks and corporations substantially increased their liquidity during the recent recession (1974–1975). However, the problem of unchecked credit growth has not been finally solved by any means.

In most countries, including the United States, banks make loans only in proportion to their deposits. Both the loanable proportion and the interest rate are determined by the Central Bank. (In the United States, the Federal Reserve Board is responsible.) If rates are low and banks are allowed to loan a high proportion of their deposits, debt rises rapidly and the economy is stimulated. And vice versa. The economic prescriptions of John Maynard Keynes called for easy money and deficit spending by government during periods of unemployment, high private savings, and underutilized industrial capacity (all of which tend to coincide). On the other hand, Keynes prescribed reduced government spending and tight money policies during periods of full employment, full capacity utilization, and inflationary pressures.

Unfortunately, only the stimulative side of the Keynes prescriptions have been followed consistently by the United States and most other industrialized countries in the post-World War II years. (West Germany and Japan are exceptional in that they have also resorted to fairly rigorously deflationary policies at times.) This, in combination with the low savings and investment rates discussed previously, has produced the persistent—and recently accelerating—devaluation of the United States dollar in relation to other currencies. However, as noted elsewhere, the undervaluation of the United States dollar will eventually correct itself.

Will creeping inflation be brought under control? Will it continue more or less as in the past? Or will the situation deteriorate more and more rapidly until it culminates in a total collapse of paper currencies, as some of the "Gold Bugs" suggest? This is another vital question for the future. Again, it is easy to discern some signs of public impatience with continuing inflation and willingness, even eagerness, to do whatever is necessary to end the threat. Unfortunately, there is no agreement whatsoever on the correct policy to adopt. Industrialists ask for wage restraint and reduced government spending. Unions and many consumer groups tend to insist on price controls as a prerequisite for holding back on wage and salary increases. They oppose "tight money" policies because of the impact on unemployment. Still, governments tend to rely excessively on monetary policy (tight money), since fiscal policy is too cumbersome and slow. However, tight money raises interest rates and depresses the economy, thus reducing tax revenues and increasing the Federal deficit. It also tends to expand the demand for uncontrolled "Eurodollars," thus progressively reducing the ability of central banks to regulate the world's money supply.

There seems to be no easy solution to the conundrum. Nevertheless, inflation is evidently in the realm of public policy, and a sufficiently intelligent policy, firmly applied, should be able to bring inflation under control. On the other hand, short-sighted policies, designed, for instance, to generate preelection "booms" to maximize the reelection chances of a party in power,* can only lead to eventual disaster. In this

---

*The Nixon boom of 1973 was an absolutely classic case of cynical maneuvering for short-term political advantage, regardless of the longer-term consequences.

context, the date of a hypothetical collapse of the world monetary system is somewhat irrelevant, but if such an event occurs it seems unlikely to be deferred much beyond the next few years.

SOCIAL JUSTICE AND THE POVERTY CRISIS

It has been suggested by a number of writers that chronic poverty — meaning inequitable distribution of wealth (or income) — may cause some sort of crisis in the coming decades. A crisis would have to arise either from changing attitudes with regard to the equitability of the present highly skewed income distribution, or from changes in the income or wealth distribution *per se*. The first possibility was discussed explicitly in an earlier chapter under the subhead Competition Between Ideologies. The second possibility properly belongs here.

Is there any evidence that the distribution of wealth and/or income is becoming more unfavorable to those at the lower end of the social order?

One can start from the historical fact that very few persons arrived on the shores of North America with significant property. There were some sizeable land grants along the Eastern Seaboard, but almost any European immigrant could — and many did — acquire a chunk of virgin forest or prairie to farm for himself. Large industrial fortunes were accumulated later — mostly in the nineteenth and early twentieth century — and as of 1953 only 0.5% of the population held about 23% of all capital assets.[19] This rose to 33% by 1965 due to disproportionate rises in stock prices. In fact, the bulk of this asset wealth is owned by only the richest 0.1% of the population, most of whom inherited it. On the other hand, half the population had only 8.3% of the total assets in 1953, and these people, on the average, had estimated gross "estates" (including cars, homes, and life insurance) of less than $3500 in that year. Evidently the wealth created in the United States over the past three centuries has been distributed very unequally, with late arrivals and minority groups acquiring a disproportionately small share of it.

Statistics on other countries are scarce and unreliable, but a few data are available. According to one source, in the years 1911–1913 in the United Kingdom only 0.63% of the adult population owned 57% of capital assets, and 1.53% owned a full two-thirds of the property in the country.[20] Thus, although Britain was called a "nation of shopkeepers," evidently the merchants did not own their shops. By 1946–1947, the wealth of Britain was only slightly less concentrated, with the richest 1.84% owning 51.9% of the assets and the richest 4.56% of the people owning 63.3% of the property. This vast discrepancy in wealth undoubtedly contributed to the deep-rooted egalitarianism and "soak the rich" philosophy that has permeated the British labor movement ever since.

In India, too, notwithstanding the deposing of all Maharajahs and native rulers, a mere 1% of the population still receives 50% of all the money income. This admittedly omits the income "in kind" of the rural population (which is 80% of the total) and thereby exaggerates the real situation considerably. It might be noted that average urban populations in India receive between two and three times as much per capita money income as rural populations. The extreme discrepancies here, too, probably account for the egalitarian rhetoric in Indian politics. In both the United Kingdom and India concern with the redistribution of income has taken precedence over — and has seriously interfered with — economic development and increasing the overall national wealth.

I do not have solid data on other major countries. Rather superficial observation suggests that the distribution of asset wealth in Italy, France, and Germany is similar to that in Britain, despite France's relatively few rich industrialists and many prosperous "petits bourgeois" (farmers and shopkeepers). Indeed, OECD statistics show that France has the greatest income differentials among major Western countries. In Germany the chaos of the 1920s and 1930s and the period of drastic societal reconstruction after World War II broke up some of the older concentrations of wealth and created opportunities for many new entrepreneurs. The same thing happened in Japan in the aftermath of World War II. In these two countries, interestingly, the appeal of egalitarianism seems to be distinctly less strong. In Russia, reliable income statistics are totally unavailable, but even if the data existed they would not be meaningful, since goods and services are not equally available to all segments of the population. Major differences exist in terms of *access* to important things such as universities, housing permits in major cities (especially Moscow), or special stores carrying high-quality goods for the elite. There are dramatic differences in effective living standards between rural workers and city workers.[21]

To return to the original question, is there evidence that maldistribution is increasing? Statistics on this point are scarce and not clearcut. Despite much propaganda to the contrary, maldistribution may in fact be getting worse in the United States, primarily because of the recent wave of concentration of industry and agriculture into larger units. Each merger eliminates some top managerial jobs and reduces the number of "effective" owners (those whose ownership share is large enough to provide a measure of control over the use of assets).

The United States has long since ceased to be a country in which every man could start his own business and hope to succeed by dint of hard work. Although many businesses are still started each year, the vast majority are retail shops or small contracting or repair enterprises, and most of these fail in a few years due to undercapitalization and the inability of the small businessman to combine in his individual person all the necessary skills and specialized knowledge that he needs to compete on reasonably even terms with a larger established enterprise. Consistently rising interest rates over the past two decades and generally falling stock prices since the mid-1960s* have also caused venture capital to become scarce and further increased the odds against new enterprises. The average lifespan of a private business in the United States is about six years. America has become a nation of employees, most of whom are perennially insecure in their jobs.

For these reasons, inequities in the distribution of wealth will probably be an ever more potent political issue. Because the nature of the problem is not well understood, the temptation is strong to deal with it *symbolically* by imposing high, progressive income tax rates and by nationalizing large enterprises. However, political realities ensure that "loopholes" will always be retained that continue to allow the truly asset-rich to escape crippling taxation. The more notorious loopholes are eventually closed gradually, but in such a way that those with visibly high *earned* incomes are penalized first, whereas those with large *inherited* estates still have many means of avoiding the taxes. The consequence, as in the United Kingdom, is that it is increasingly difficult for anyone to penetrate the charmed circle of inherited wealth. Those who are already rich have some means of protecting what they own, but it is essentially impossible for an outsider to join the club. Social mobility slowly vanishes—like the grin on the face of the Cheshire Cat—in the name of illusory egalitarianism.

This does not necessarily lead to any kind of crisis of poverty within a developed society. In fact, a crisis seems most unlikely. The poorest people in the United States, United Kingdom, or Scandinavia are mostly not poor at all by the standards of neighboring less developed countries. Housing, food, appliances, furnishings, and cars are as plentiful to the bottom third of the people in the richest countries as they are among the prosperous upper-middle class of the LDCs.

*In terms of price-earnings ratios.

Of course, there is another kind of crisis of poverty that has been postulated, namely, one in which the prosperous advanced industrial countries of the Northern Hemisphere are overwhelmed (in some unspecified fashion) by the dissatisfied poor of the Southern Hemisphere. To quote the ubiquitous C. P. Snow again,[22]

> This disparity between the rich and the poor has been noticed. It has been noticed, most acutely and not unnaturally, by the poor. Just because they have noticed it, it won't last for long. Whatever else in the world we know survives to the year 2000, that won't. Once the trick of getting rich is known, as it now is, the world can't survive half rich and half poor. It's just not on.

Snow believed when he wrote these words twenty years ago that the "trick" of getting rich is to have an organized science/technology and that the major problem is to train enough technologists. I emphatically disagree with that conclusion for reasons that are discussed in a later chapter. Why can't the world continue to exist "half rich, half poor"? Or can it? This is a serious question.

There is no doubt that the discrepancy in wealth between North and South will continue to generate political antagonism and confrontations in the United Nations (if that forum survives) or in other arenas. However, the notion of a horde of impoverished Indian or Indonesian peasants physically arriving in New York or Paris is more than a trifle fanciful. The basic reason for poverty in the poorest countries is not that the wealthy countries refuse to share, but that the peasants in question refuse to change their ancient ways of living — which includes subdivision of cultivated land into uneconomic units, deforestation and overgrazing of common land, overfishing, preservation of useless animals for religious reasons, the use of animal manure as fuel instead of fertilizer, the use of child labor (in lieu of schooling), and simply having too many children.

I think these trends in the less developed countries will lead to very real and deadly crises of poverty for them. The impact on the developed world is another matter. However, to say the very least, I can see no simple "trick" for getting rich quickly, and, just as rich and poor individuals have long coexisted in the same city, I am afraid that rich and poor countries will long co-inhabit this Earth.

The rich will probably take certain measures to protect themselves against "get rich quick" schemes of an intolerable kind, such as piracy, hijacking, kidnapping for ransom, effective confiscation of foreigners' property by imposing retroactive "excess profit" taxes, and so on. Some countermeasures to poverty itself will be undertaken, no doubt. One such measure may be an expanded program of voluntary technical or financial assistance to the less developed world. Some will argue passionately that that would be the cheapest as well as the most humanitarian solution. This is unproven, of course. It may well be true that developing countries will do better if they learn to depend only on their own resources, as has China. It is neither inhumane nor silly to point out that "no strings" financial assistance is quite likely to be spent on projects of dubious value to the country* or, worse, used to import luxury goods for the elite or simply siphoned off into their private Swiss bank accounts.

On the other hand, "strings" are generally scorned by the recipient country as an affront to national dignity and an insidious form of neocolonialism. There is some truth in this proposition, since politicians are always sensitive to the interests of their constituents, which include firms anxious to increase their export business with the help of government subsidies. Some evidence exists – admittedly not conclusive – that the whole process of giving and receiving subsidies or grants-in-aid by governments or international agencies is counterproductive in the long run. However, that, too, is a subject for another discussion.

REFERENCES

1. F. Meyer and J. Vallee, "The Dynamics of Long-Term Growth," *Technological Forecasting and Social Change 7*, 285–300 (1975).
2. United Nations World Population Prospects 1970–2000, 1973 estimates.
3. United Nations, "Growth of the Worlds Urban and Rural Population, 1920 –2000," 1969.
4. United Nations Yearbook of National Accounts Statistics, 1975.
5. I. B. Kravis, A.W. Heston, R. Summers "Real GDP per capita for more than one hundred countries" *The Economic Journal,* June, 1978.
6. H. Kahn and W. Brown, "A World Turning Point and a Better Prospect for the Future," *Futurist,* December 1975.
7. Robert L. Stivers, *The Sustainable Society: Ethics and Economic Growth,* Westminister Press, Philadelphia, 1976, p. 60.

*A typical prestige project is a national airline (using Boeing, Lockheed, or Douglas jetliners, of course) to connect the national capital city to London, Paris, New York, or Moscow. It will be used primarily by diplomats, World Bank economists, senior government bureaucrats traveling to international meetings, and the like. Such an airline creates immediate and heavy requirements for advanced electronic navigational equipment, foreign-trained pilots, aviation fuel, trained aviation mechanics, tires, and spare parts, none of which are domestically available.

8. J. B. Schuman and D. Rosenan, *The Kondratieff Wave,* World Publishing Company, New York, 1972.
9. Edward Dennison, *Sources of Economic Growth & the Alternatives Before Us,* Committee for Economic Development, New York, 1962.
10. N. MacRae, "The Coming Entrepreneurial Revolution: A Survey," *The Economist,* December 25, 1976. Quoted with permission.
11. E. F. Schumacher, *Small Is Beautiful,* Harper and Row, New York, 1973, p. 13. Quoted with permission.
12. U.S. Department of Commerce Pocket Data Book, USA, 1973.
13. U.S. Department of Labor, BLS Bull. 1809, 1974.
14. N. MacRae, "America's Third Century," *The Economist,* Oct 25, 1975.
15. Daniel Bell, *The Coming of Post Industrial Society: A Venture in Social Forecasting,* Basic Books, New York, 1973.
16. *Statistical Abstract of the United States,* 1976.
17. *Business Week,* February 28, 1977.
18. U.S. Department of Commerce, *Business Statistics,* 1975.
19. Robert Lampman, *The Share of the Top Wealth Holders in National Wealth, 1922–1956,* NBER Princeton University Press, Princeton, N.J., 1962.
20. Ferdinand Lundberg, *The Rich and the Super Rich,* Lyle Stuart, New York, 1968, p. 11.
21. Hedrick Smith, *The Russians,* Ballantine Books, New York, 1976.
22. C.P. Snow, "The Two Cultures and the Scientific Revolution," Godkin Lectures, Harvard University Press, Cambridge, 1960. Quoted with permission.

CHAPTER FIVE

MEASURES OF MAN – MICROECONOMIC

INTRODUCTORY REMARKS

The previous chapter was quite long enough, but it did not touch on all the subjects of importance under the general heading of economics. The natural division is between *macroeconomics* – the study of the behavior of the economy as a whole – and *microeconomics* which concerns itself with the breakdown of that whole into its component parts. There is a wide range of topics that could be explored, of course, but in the interests of limiting the length of the book I focus primarily on a few trends of particular interest. There are two categories: commodities and services. The commodities I have chosen to examine explicitly are food, major metals, and major forms of energy. I also consider four service categories; namely, transportation, communications, health, and education. Omitted are wholesale and retail trade business and financial services, repair and maintenance services, insurance, entertainment, tourism, hotels and restaurants, and housing (even privately owned housing can usually be regarded as a service). I offer no detailed justification for the omissions – it is simply not possible to consider everything important in a book of modest dimensions.

It is hardly disputable that the levels of consumption of food, wood, metals, fuel, and electricity in various countries are important measures of the state of Man. It is helpful to bear in mind, however, that such statistics are often presented as indications of the magnitude of an impending *resource problem* such as a possible world food shortage or energy crisis. This is not my present purpose, inasmuch as technological aspects of the supply side are taken up in Chapter 7, and resource constraints are considered explicitly in Chapter 8.

FOOD CONSUMPTION

The usual unit by which food consumption is measured is Calories per capita per day. This is actually a measure of food energy.* It is, however, a poor indicator of dietary quality. People living on a diet consisting largely of starchy roots, such as yams or cassava, are likely to be malnourished due to protein deficiency despite an adequate caloric intake. Even cereal grains such as rice, millet, or maize (corn) are generally inadequate unless supplemented by beans or peanuts (i.e., pulses) or animal products such as milk, eggs, fish, or meat. A somewhat better unit of measurement of how well or badly people are fed is per capita protein intake (measured in grams per day). Again, proteins differ in their amino acid composition, and not all forms of protein are equally satisfactory. For instance, either maize or field beans would constitute incomplete sources of protein; fortunately, the combination — a dietary staple of Mexico — is reasonably satisfactory, since the deficiencies of maize protein are made up by the bean protein, and vice versa. Generally speaking, however, animal protein is dietarily superior to vegetable protein unless the latter is derived from a balanced variety of different sources. Thus a third commonly used measure of dietary quality is the fraction of protein from animal sources.

So-called dietary requirements are actually not very rigid, and a diet that would be inadequate for Americans may still be satisfactory for Chinese or Indians for the simple reason that they are, on the average, physically smaller.† In energy terms, as shown in Table 5.1, the EEC countries of Western Europe, North America, and the USSR all consumed an average of 3200–3300 Calories per day per capita in the late 1960s.[1] This is probably at least 10% too high for optimum health. On the other hand, the slighter but now highly prosperous Japanese consumed only slightly more than 2500 Calories per capita, doubtless an adequate amount. Yet the people of India survive on 2000 Calories per day, and the Indonesians are reckoned to be living below the adequate range on about 1750 Calories per day. Thus, even if their incomes were increased fiftyfold (to the Japanese level), the chances are that Indonesians would increase their daily Calorie consumption by no more than 40%. It would appear, on this basis, that food consumption is relatively inelastic to increasing income levels.

*1 Calorie = 1000 calories.
†Americans are probably at least 3 inches taller and 20–25% heavier than present day Asians. Exact figures are not available, of course.

Table 5.1   Direct Consumption of Food, 1970

Country (year)	1970 Consumption			
	Calories/Capita (day)	% Animal	Protein (g)/Capita (day)	% Animal
North America (1970)	3300	40	96	75
EEC (1968–1970)	3200	35	90	65
Japan (1969)	2550	15	72	40
USSR (1964–1966)	3200	20	90	40
Brazil (1966–1968)	2600	15	62	35
China (1964–1966)	2100	10	55	15
India (1968–1969)	2000	10	48	15
Nigeria	No data		No data	
World (1970)	2361	—	64	29

However, there are two caveats which must be noted. First, the average Japanese diet has been improving rapidly. In 1950 the Japanese probably ate little, if any, better than the Chinese do today. As their food intake has increased both in quantity and quality, Japanese children have started to grow significantly (as Europeans and Americans, too, have done in the last two centuries). This physical growth will eventually increase the minimum per capita Calorie and protein requirements in rough proportion as people gain in size. In the next fifty years it is likely that the well-fed Japanese will grow by an average of 2–4 inches in height and 20–40 pounds in weight, thus automatically adding significantly to their daily per capita food requirements.

The second caveat concerns the implications of increasing dietary quality by substituting animal products for vegetable products. Such a substitution has occurred in the United States since the nineteenth century. For instance, annual per capita consumption of wheat flour and cornmeal in the United States dropped by more than 50% in the half-century from 1910 to 1960.[2] Almost all this was replaced by meat and dairy products. More recently, similar shifts have been occurring in Western Europe, Japan, and the USSR. Thus overall demand for meat and dairy products in the more prosperous countries has risen dramatically.

The significant point is that to produce 1 Calorie of any animal product requires a number of Calories of primary production of whatever vegetable substance the animal has consumed. Feed/food conversion ratios vary from product to product (and from country to country), but in the United States, EEC, and Japan the ratios are roughly as follows:

Milk	2 : 1
Eggs	2.5 : 1
Chicken and turkey	3 : 1
Pork	6 : 1
Beef	10 : 1
Lamb and mutton	12 : 1

These figures reflect highly efficient and scientific methods of animal husbandry. In the USSR the ratios are certainly higher, although supporting data is lacking. In a country like India or Nigeria, cattle and chickens in rural areas are simply encouraged to forage as best they can. Ironically, although cows in India are skinny, such a cow foraging for itself probably consumes more than ten times as many Calories *per unit of milk produced* than a purebred dairy animal in Europe or America.

The apparent inefficiency of consuming animal products is somewhat less than the table implies in the case of ruminants (e.g., sheep and cattle), since these animals, with their specialized stomachs, are capable of digesting and utilizing cellulosic material such as grass and cornstalks—or even sawdust—that humans cannot utilize directly. Fairly large quantities of such material are generated as by-products of the cultivation of most agricultural or forest crops. To feed cellulosic wastes to ruminants entails no direct cost at all in terms of human food, but for optimum productivity even ruminants require high-protein supplements consisting of grain or (more often nowadays) cottonseed meal, soya bean meal, or fish meal. This could be used to feed humans directly without intermediate conversion by animals.

In terms of the number of people that could be fed, direct consumption by humans would be the most efficient use of vegetable protein: At least two or three times as many people could be fed on pure vegetarian diets as on Western-type diets that are high in animal products. To compare diets in different countries realistically, the indirect component (Calories fed to animals) should be taken into account. For instance, in the United States, about 1350 Calories per capita per day or about 40% of all dietary Calories comes from animal products. Let me suppose that 650 Calories, or about half of this, is from red meat (beef and pork) with a feed/food ratio of 8.* I assume that most of the remainder comes from dairy products with an average feed/food ratio of 2.5. Only the 50 Calories derived from fish have no indirect component (except, of course, from noncultivated sources). The current United States diet, then, is dominated by its indirect components as can be seen from the following:

North America

Product	Direct Calories	Total, Including Indirect Calories
Red meat	650	5200
Dairy and poultry	650	1625
Fish and seafood	50	50
Plant products	1950	1950
Total	3300	8825

Of this grand total of 8825 Calories per capita per day, 8775 ultimately were derived from plants — mainly agricultural crops — and 50 from the rivers, lakes, and oceans. The ratio of total Calories to direct Calories is 2.67 according to this calculation. Changes in this pattern will certainly occur during the next half century, but they will primarily arise from shifts in the method of production. For example, there will be less use of corn and greater use of protein supplements from single-cell organisms in the production of beef and pork. These changes are discussed in Chapter 7.

Although European diets have almost the same overall animal content as North American diets, the indirect Calorie component is considerably less, because more of the animal content is derived from

---

*About one-third of the indirect component for red meat (and probably less for dairy products) is derived from grass or other cellulosic feedstuffs not digestible by humans.

seafood and dairy products, and less is from red meat. The EEC pattern is something like this:

EEC

Product	Direct Calories	Total, Including Indirect Calories
Red meat	350	2800
Dairy and poultry	700	1750
Fish and seafood	150	150
Plant products	2000	2000
Total	3200	6700

$$\frac{\text{Total Calories}}{\text{Direct Calories}} = \frac{6700}{3200} = 2.1$$

For Japan, the overall diet is leaner, and a much higher fraction of the animal content is derived from seafood:

Japan

Product	Direct Calories	Total, Including Indirect Calories
Red meat	100	800
Dairy and poultry	50	125
Fish and seafood	250	250
Plant products	2150	2150
Total	2550	3325

$$\frac{\text{Total Calories}}{\text{Direct Calories}} = \frac{3325}{2550} = 1.3$$

For the USSR the pattern is intermediate between the Japanese and European, but the conversion ratios are higher due to less sophisticated animal-feeding practices. It is probably realistic to assume a feed/food ratio of 10 for red meat and 3.5 for dairy and poultry products. The Chinese diet is probably qualitatively similar to the Japanese, with a much smaller seafood component.

USSR

Product	Direct Calories	Total, Including Indirect Calories
Red meat	150	1500
Dairy and poultry	350	1225
Fish and seafood	150	150
Plant products	2550	2550
Total	3200	5425

$$\frac{\text{Total Calories}}{\text{Direct Calories}} = \frac{5425}{3200} = 1.7$$

Brazil really consists of a temperate, southern "developed" region, with a diet fairly high in dairy products and red meat — mainly range fed beef — and a tropical, northern "undeveloped" region, with a diet more comparable to that of other tropical LDCs. A breakdown would be based on guesswork, but an indirect component of 1000–1500 Calories per day and possibly more is indicated. The total/direct ratio is probably about 1.5.

The most interesting (and saddest) case is that of India, where 200 Calories per day per capita are derived from animal sources — virtually none from fish (!). Of this, an insignificant amount comes from red meat: animal protein is mostly obtained from milk and milk products, such as yogurt and some poultry and eggs. What of the feed/food conversion ratio? In India an estimated 100 million scrawny cows* roam freely, consuming whatever forage they can find, denuding the landscape, and yielding less milk than 10 million fenced-in and well-bred European or American dairy animals. Admittedly, they consume little or no grain, but the vegetation they do consume would — if better utilized — undoubtedly suffice for the needs of several times their number of humans. A conservative estimate of the feed/food ratio for India might be 5. I suspect that the truth is actually much worse (i.e., higher). On this basis, such animal protein as is consumed in India has an indirect component of *at least* 1000 Calories per day per capita — probably more — with a total ratio of 1.5 or so.

The ratio of indirect food (and feed) Calorie consumption to direct food Calorie consumption per capita is quite likely to decline for well-fed North America and Europe. This will be due partly to exploitation of possibilities for increased average efficiency of conversion of animal

*Not counting an equal number of nonmilk-producing bullocks (males).

feed to animal products and partly to a modest reduction in absolute per capita consumption. However, Japan will certainly increase its level of consumption of animal products, relying less on fish, which are becoming scarcer. The USSR and Brazil will do the same. As for the poorer countries, they will have little scope for dietary improvement. China may upgrade a little, perhaps reaching the present Japanese level by 2025. India and Nigeria will have to utilize animals much more efficiently than they do now to avoid mass starvation. Table 5.2 displays some plausible per capita projections, and Table 5.3 shows the implications in terms of overall food Caloric consumption based on population projections given in the preceding chapter.

To achieve the dietary outcomes postulated in Table 5.3, it is note-worthy that North America and the EEC countries increase their total Calorie consumption by a negligible factor (11% and 3%, respectively). Production in North America can undoubtedly be increased much more than that, yielding an increased surplus for export, mostly to Japan and the USSR where consumption will rise much more dramatically. (It is possible, but not certain, that the USSR can keep pace given its uncertain continental climate.) The real question is how the growing demands of the rest of the world can be met—if, indeed, they can.

Given the realities of the situation, outlined above, it seems idle for well-fed but guilt-ridden humanitarians in the West to recommend that Americans or Frenchmen or Germans should stop eating corn-fed beef so that the extra grain could be exported to feed the malnourished people of India. Indians may starve, but if they do it will be because

Table 5.2   Calorie per Capita and Total Direct Coefficients (estimated)

	1970		2000		2025	
Country	Cal/Cap	Total Direct	Cal/Cap	Total Direct	Cal/Cap	Total Direct
North America	3300	2.67	3200	2.4	3100	2.2
EEC	3200	2.10	3200	2.0	3100	1.9
Japan	2550	1.30	2900	1.6	3000	1.8
USSR	3200	1.70	3200	2.0	3200	2.2
Brazil	2600	1.50	2800	1.8	3000	2.0
China	2100	1.10	2300	1.2	2500	1.3
India	2000	1.50	2200	1.4	2300	1.3
Nigeria	2000 (est)	1.50	2200	1.4	2300	1.3

Table 5.3   Projected Total Food and Feed Calorie Consumption (Calories × 10⁹)

Country	1970	2000	2025	Ratio 2000/1970	Ratio 2025/1970
North America	1995	2219	2234	1.112	1.119
EEC	1626	1777	1682	1.092	1.034
Japan	346	645	782	1.864	2.260
USSR	1321	2010	2500	1.521	1.892
Brazil	371	1058	2180	2.851	5.876
China	1783	3244	4695	1.819	2.633
		3674	8118	2.255	4.983
India	1629	3181	4866	1.952	2.987
		2940	3577	1.804	2.195
Nigeria	165 (est)	395	869	2.4 (est)	5.3 (est)

they refuse to adopt serious birth control measures and choose, on religious grounds, to allow cattle to consume vegetation that would otherwise permit them to feed themselves more adequately. Even if Western consumers were altruistic enough to deny themselves meat for the sake of religious convictions or prejudices of Indians, United States or French farmers can hardly be expected to sell grain at a fraction of its production cost. Since the poorest less developed countries (LDCs) have no foreign exchange to purchase grain from the United States through normal commercial markets, the American taxpayer would have to make up the difference. In a period of straitened government budgets, slower economic growth, and increasingly acute inflationary pressures, this seems highly unlikely.

Let me summarize briefly the important points of the analysis. First, as countries develop economically and grow in prosperity they tend to improve their diets *quantitatively* (in terms of Calories) and *qualitatively* (in terms of protein, especially from animal sources). The advanced industrial societies (United States, Japan, EEC) have already done this, and the USSR and Eastern Europe are rapidly increasing the meat and dairy content of their national diets.* Recent sharp increases in the world price of cereal grains have occurred precisely because of this increased demand for animal products by the

*Large purchases of grain by the USSR from North America have resulted from setbacks in cereal grain production in 1963, 1965, 1972, and 1975. Nonetheless, food production per capita in the USSR did increase by over 50% from 1955 to 1973 — a faster rate of increase than in the United States, but from a lower base.

most prosperous countries. (Prices in terms of United States dollars have risen still faster due to the devaluations of 1972 and 1973.) Food consumption in the richer countries is and will continue to be related to their per capita incomes, which determines their ability to pay for imports, especially of animal feed.

Second, assuming that world output of grain and feedstuffs is relatively inelastic at any given time—which seems to be the case—what will be available for poor countries to consume in the future is, in effect, whatever is produced that the rich countries do not consume. (I do not actually expect India to export wheat to Europe or Japan, but it would happen if Punjabi farmers could obtain higher prices by selling in an export market than in their price-controlled domestic market.)

As a matter of practical necessity, food consumption by the less developed countries depends primarily on their ability to produce for themselves or to import at world market prices. Large-scale food aid on a continuing basis will certainly be advocated by well-intentioned individuals, and United Nations conferences dominated by potential beneficiaries will doubtless recommend it. However, in a world of independent self-governing countries, this will not happen on a large scale.

What, then, is the likely future for the poorer countries? Assuming a continuation of past trends of population growth and agricultural productivity, the recent Indicative World Plan (IWP) for Agricultural Development prepared in response to the FAO's 1963 Freedom From Hunger Campaign,[3] had this to say with regard to the most critical dietary element—protein from animal sources:

The prospects are for a hard battle. Animal production would have to grow very much faster, and *during the decade 1975–85 at over double that of the recent past* to reach parity with demand in terms of growth rates by 1985. If past trends (estimated to be 1.5 to 1.7 percent) were to continue, only a quarter of the extra demand for animal protein could be produced domestically in developing countries over the period of IWP. There would either be a drastic fall in per caput intakes of animal protein (for example from 14.4 gm/day in the Near East in 1962 to only 9.6 gm/day in 1985), or a massive rise in import requirements.

As already suggested, to increase food imports by such a large factor is only a theoretical alternative, since the necessary foreign exchange is and will be lacking. The United States—the only feasible global supplier—will be reluctant to undertake a burden that could only be expected to increase, decade by decade, without any limit.

The hard fact is that, although the poorest countries are badly malnourished at present, it is virtually a certainty that their situation will soon get much worse. There is no realistic prospect whatsoever for relief in the foreseeable future. This virtually guarantees increased malnutrition and even widespread starvation. In blunt terms, it is very difficult to see how the generation now growing to adulthood in the less developed countries will be able to feed its children.

ENERGY CONSUMPTION

Many people believe that energy is the most fundamental of all commodities and that energy consumption is the truest measure of economic development. I do not share this view, at least in its more extreme form. But there is no denying that the use of external sources of energy to supplement muscle power derived from food or animal feed is almost a defining characteristic of the industrial revolution.

Energy can be obtained in practice from various sources, including burning wood or dried animal dung, fossil hydrocarbons, wind power, water power, uranium fission, or direct sunlight. Following its initial "capture," it may be converted into one of several kinds of commercial fuel: solid, liquid, gas, or electricity. Subsequently it may be utilized as radiant heat, as steam, as kinetic energy, or in several other ways. Reflecting this diversity, a number of different and confusing units of energy and power have been established.* For simplicity, I follow United Nations practice and measure total energy consumption in metric tons of coal equivalent (or MTCE) in terms of contained heat value.

To fix a benchmark, the average person in the United States in 1972 consumed 11.6 MTCE directly and indirectly. By comparison, the average Englishman or German consumed 5.4 MTCE, and the average Japanese consumed 3.25 MTCE. The world average was about 2.1 MTCE per capita, but all the less developed countries — with about 65% of the world's population — currently consume only 14% of the energy, or less than 0.5 MTCE per capita. The average North American thus uses, directly and indirectly, more than twenty times as much energy as the average Indian, Nigerian, or Chinese.

Although many widely quoted energy consumption forecasts essen-

*For future reference, the major equivalent units are
MTCE = 44 bbl crude oil = 940 liters of gasoline
$\qquad$ = 27,800 cubic feet of natural gas
$\qquad$ = 27×10^6 BTU
$\qquad$ = 8×10^3 kWh (e)

tially extrapolate past growth rates, this procedure is tantamount to assuming that energy consumption is only a function of itself (i.e., its history). This proposition cannot be taken seriously for the long run. If it were true, an increasing trend could never stop increasing! To make sensible forecasts, it seems necessary to try to relate energy consumption to some primary cause. The obvious initial choice is the overall level of economic activity (GDP) in a country. The *correlation* between energy consumption and GDP is well established, although this should not be interpreted as a causal connection. If one expresses energy consumption per unit GDP, the discrepancies between countries seem to be greatly reduced and consequently more interpretable.

In these terms, the world average energy "intensivity" is 1.93 MTCE per thousand dollars of GDP.* North America is only slightly above this level, but the USSR and China are considerably higher (partly, no doubt, because of their cold winters), whereas Europe and Japan are lower, as are the tropical countries. Note that countries as far apart in terms of per capita wealth as the United States and India have very similar energy usage per unit of GDP. However, the similarities may be misleading. Traced over time as a function of GDP per capita, it becomes clear that there is a tendency for energy intensivity to rise during the early stages of economic development, reach a peak, and subsequently fall. All the developed countries are now in the declining range, whereas the LDCs are still increasing. The faster-growing LDCs (Brazil, China) should peak within the next twenty to thirty years if this view is correct.

United Nations data, presented in Table 5.4,[4] confirm that North America consumes significantly more energy than the other highly industrialized nations (EEC, Japan) in relation to its overall level of economic activity. One reason is that Americans are more addicted to private cars and detached houses than Europeans, and American cars and houses are bigger and consume more energy to run. Actually the average United States car in service gets about 13.5 miles per gallon of fuel (1974), whereas the average European or Japanese car is almost twice as efficient,† mostly (but not entirely) by virtue of being smaller. This is not because Europeans or Japanese do not "like" to drive large powerful vehicles—they do—but because motor fuels costs have for

*Or 1.93 kg of coal per dollar.

† In most countries the measure is fuel *consumption* in liters of fuel per 100 km of driving, rather than the familiar United States measure of fuel *economy* (mpg). The average United States car consumed 17 liters per 100 km, the average European car consumed about 9 liters per 100 km, and the average Japanese car consumed less than 7 liters, in 1975[5]. The discrepancy is decreasing, however.

many years been much higher in those countries than in the United States; thus cars on the average are much smaller and more efficient.

When gasoline costs were $0.35–0.40 per gallon in the United States, they were typically around $1.00 per gallon in most European countries (with slight variations from one to another). As United States prices drifted up to $0.55 or $0.60 per gallon after the OPEC price rise in 1973–1974, prices in Europe and Japan went up to $1.40–1.60 per gallon or more. The difference in prices is almost entirely accounted for by excise taxes. These are kept high in most oil-importing countries—except the United States—for the purpose of discouraging unnecessary uses of petroleum products which require foreign exchange.

In the United States—once self-sufficient in petroleum and still a major producer—the opposite policy has prevailed, and prices have been kept low explicitly to encourage consumption. Both policies have achieved their objectives. *It is ironic to note that if the United States were as efficient in utilizing fossil energy as Sweden or Japan, it would still have had an exportable surplus of oil into the 1980s instead of having to import as much as 50% of its supply from abroad.**

The availability of cheap energy in the United States and Canada has also encouraged other lavish and wasteful land-use patterns. The most obvious is the proliferation of low-density suburban housing, built of cheap materials without regard to operating costs—often with electric heating—and spread over the landscape in such a way as to virtually guarantee dependence on private cars for all transportation purposes. This has caused public transport systems patronage to shrink, initiating a cycle of declining revenues, followed by reduced maintenance and service cutbacks, followed by still further loss of patronage.

The spreading of urban population has also caused a wasteful duplication of urban services (water and sewer systems, electricity, telephone, schools, police, and fire protection). Many of these services can not be delivered efficiently on a small scale of operation; for example, in a small suburban town, or even over a wide area where the population density is low. Thus it is more costly and requires more energy to provide utilities and government services in "spread" cities than in compact ones of the European type.

---

*Crude comparisons between energy consumption per capita and GDP per capita in different countries can be quite misleading for a variety of reasons, since countries produce different "mixes" of industrial products, have different heating requirements, and so forth. However, when such factors are taken into account, significant differences in efficiency of energy consumption still remain.[6]

Table 5.4 Energy Consumption

Country	Intensivity MTCE per thousand dollars (GDP)			Calculated MTCE per capita			Calculated Consumption in Millions of Metric Tons Coal Equivalent (MTCE)		
	1972	2000	2025	1972	2000	2025	1972	2000	2025
North America	1.4	2.048	0.9	11.390	15.4	18.0	2625	4460	5600TR
EEC	1.578	1.1	0.7	4.607	6.6	6.9	1126	1831	1970
Japan	1.482	0.8	0.5	3.535	6.1	6.6	378	850	956
USSR	3.181	2.1	1.2	4.85	10.0	9.4	1202	3154	3350
Brazil	1.05	1.0	0.6	0.53	2.0	3.2	54	417	1154
China	3.078	1.9	1.2	0.56	1.6	3.3	449	1836	4815
India	1.826	2.4	3.5	0.19	0.45	1.25	107	477	1873
Nigeria	0.44	0.8	1.2	0.07	0.3	0.8	4.2	36	208
Subtotal of above							5945	13,161	19,826
World	1.93			2.00			7477		

Even within the United States it is interesting to note that, according to a recent study,[7] energy consumption per capita in the New York metropolitan area, *including suburbs,* is well below the national average, although incomes in the area are above the national average. Thus the densely populated New York area is more similar to the European pattern in terms of energy consumption than to the rest of the United States.*

Another consequence of cheap energy in North America has been a tendency to construct buildings without consideration for their later operating costs (i.e., heating and airconditioning). Insulation has been inadequate, and designs have tended to disregard technical efficiency in terms of heat retention or loss, ventilation, and so on. Recent studies have shown that large buildings can easily be designed to use very much less energy than they now do utilizing strictly conventional material and equipment. It is now known that savings of up to 80% can be achieved by proper design, without any new technology whatsoever![8] This is an indication of just how wasteful the recent United States consumption pattern has been.

A question of great interest in recent years has been whether continued GDP growth *requires* a parallel increase in energy consumption. A good many people have argued, in effect, that it does. This is tantamount to saying that energy consumption per unit of GDP is relatively fixed. Of course, the fact that other countries use less energy per unit GDP tends to contradict this notion. Indeed, the use of energy, even in the United States, is more efficient than it once was. Historically, the highest intensity of energy consumption per unit GDP for the United States occurred in 1929, at a level some 60% above the recent level.

Clearly, the intensity of energy use can change. Yet, it is not a question of substituting some other input for energy. (One can, of course, substitute one kind of energy-containing fuel for another, but that is a different matter.) In this sense, energy is indeed fundamental. What are the possible mechanisms, then, for changing energy consumption per unit of GDP? There are three which are significant and deserve attention. Before explaining them, it is important to bear in mind that GDP is a surrogate measure of "wealth" which is itself only imprecisely defined. What one would really like to measure is "welfare," but that is too abstract a concept for comfort. We compare GDPs when what we really mean to compare is how "well off" a society

---

*Admittedly, the New York area is not a center of energy-intensive heavy industry, which would affect the figures somewhat.

is compared to its neighbors or compared to its antecedent or subsequent state.

The first mechanism for changing energy consumption per unit GDP is a shift in the mix of "final" goods and services that a society consumes to satisfy its needs and its discretionary wants so as to put less (or greater) stress on energy-intensive products or services, such as transportation. For instance, if the notion of people "communicating to work"* were widely adopted in lieu of using physical means of transportation, there would be less need for cars and more need for wide-band high-resolution communications channels. However, the latter would require less energy to operate.

A second possible mechanism for changing energy consumption per unit GDP is for society to become more (or less) *efficient* in converting basic resources into "final" goods and services. In industrialized countries technological improvements should, in general, result in a steady increase in output per unit of material/energy input, which is a measure of efficiency of conversion. (This is discussed in the next chapter.) However, technological changes in developing countries are most likely to be undertaken to reduce labor inputs per unit output by substituting mechanical energy for human labor. In this case energy consumption per unit of output is likely to go up, not down. Even in the advanced countries such substitutions continue, particularly in households. Thus the use of labor-saving appliances may tend to increase energy consumption per unit of GDP, other factors remaining the same.

The third possible reason for a change in energy consumption per unit GDP is that the quality of the resource base being utilized may be shifting. It will decline on the average. But a major discovery (e.g., of natural gas) can actually improve the efficiency of resource utilization. This would occur, for instance, if gas replaced coal for home heating, since a gas heater can be much more efficient than a coal stove. Conversely, as the natural gas wells are exhausted—which is pretty sure to happen, sooner or later—natural gas may have to be replaced by *synthetic* gas from coal, where the conversion process is only about 50% efficient! In both cases the final output of the economy would remain the same, but the total energy required to produce it would increase considerably from one case to the other.

Thus a forecast of future energy consumption per unit GDP for any country should be based on an evaluation of the three mechanisms of change described in the foregoing paragraphs. In summary, these are

*A phrase first used in 1962 by John Pierce of Bell Telephone Laboratories.

1. Composition of goods and services in "final demand."
2. Changing technology of "conversion" and changing mix of energy types in final consumption.
3. Changing quality of the resource base.

If none of these factors is changing, energy consumption per unit GDP should remain constant. However, it is much more likely that all of them will change in the next half century. How? Let us consider the three factors, in order, over the past half century.

It is almost a truism that the introduction of new consumer products (especially labor-saving appliances) have been responsible for increased consumption of energy, notably electricity. So have central heating, air conditioning, household hot water, and automobiles. These things have also resulted in large increases in economic output, which contributes to GDP. It is not instantly clear that they have increased the energy consumed *per unit* of GDP. It seems prudent to withhold judgment for a moment and consider the magnitude of changes in "conversion" efficiency during the same time span.

Conversion technology has undoubtedly improved, at least in major industries such as petroleum refining, electricity generation, steel, and railroads. The improvement over the past fifty years seems to have been modest — on the order of 10–30% savings per unit of physical output. More important, many changes in industry have effectively substituted machines for human or animal labor; for example, in mining, agriculture, manufacturing, and construction. The machines use more energy than human workers but save on labor costs. In industries where this kind of substitution is actively under way, energy consumption per unit of output tends to rise, as can be easily documented. Finally, as noted earlier, the quality of the resource base tends to decrease with time on the average in all countries, as the best and cheapest deposits of minerals and fossil fuels are exploited first.

In summary, factors 2 and 3 taken singly or together should probably have caused the energy consumed per unit of GDP to *increase*. But since the late 1920s, the energy intensivity of economic activity, overall, has actually *decreased* (by 60%) in the United States. This can only mean that the introduction of new consumer products and services since the 1920s has added much more to GDP than it has to energy consumption — and more than the other change mechanisms have added, too. However, since the early 1950s, when the rapid "suburbanization" process (commented on earlier) began in earnest, increases in energy consumption have kept pace with increases in GDP.

On the other hand, the United States economy has only recently entered into the postindustrial phase in which services are quantitatively more important than manufactured products. Moreover, the post-World War II migration to the suburbs seems to have slowed down at last. The recent sharp increases in energy prices will also undoubtedly tend to encourage less wasteful patterns of living in the future. All in all, I think the downtrend in energy consumption per unit of GDP has already resumed and will continue, as indicated by Table 5.4. Electricity will continue to increase as a fraction of total energy consumed, but it too will grow less rapidly than GDP in the future (Table 5.5). These saturation phenomena may be temporarily embarrassing to some of the electric utility and oil industry executives who believe that twenty years of exponentially increasing demand (1950–1970) constituted a mandate from Mt. Sinai. Saturation will be very helpful indeed if the industrial countries are to avoid a real energy crisis in the next generation.

The other developed countries are slightly less postindustrial than the United States and, in most cases, will probably remain so. I noted previously that the United States, in the future, is likely to be a net exporter of services (and agricultural products) and a net importer of energy-intensive manufactured goods; Japan will reverse this pattern. Europe and Japan are more dependent on imported energy and have denser populations. They are and will remain more economical in their use of energy. The USSR, however, will be less efficient as a user of energy because its economy will remain more geared to heavy manufacturing, because it is more nearly self-sufficient, and because central planning is a much less efficient method of resource allocation than a market-price system. It will, in any case, use more energy per capita than countries with temperate or tropical climates.

As for the less developed countries, Brazil and China should be industralizing rapidly for most of the period, and (assuming the price of energy is not too excessive) they can be expected to substitute mechanical energy for human labor in many sectors. Energy consumption per unit GDP is thus likely to increase. This will happen in India and Nigeria, too, if the process of economic development in those countries does not falter for other reasons.

NONFUEL MATERIALS CONSUMPTION

There are so many different materials used by man that no simple aggregate measure such as tonnage would provide a meaningful description. At least three categories must be considered separately. As a

Table 5.5 Electricity Consumption

Country	Intensity (kWh per/$ GDP)			Intensity (kWh per capita)			Total Consumption (billion kWh)		
	1972	2000	2025	1972	2000	2025	1972	2000	2025
North America	1.633	2.0	1.6	9085	22049	30391	2094	6370	9953
EEC	1.335	2.0	1.9	3897	11986	18681	953	3328	5335
Japan	1.624	1.8	1.4	3874	13765	18446	414	1912	2673
USSR	2.269	2.4	2.0	3462	11477	15692	857	3605	5572
Brazil	1.103	1.4	1.9	559	2780	10056	56	584	3654
China	0.699	2.5	2.0	129	2056	5569	102	2416	8045
India	1.198	3.0	3.5	124	578	1251	71	597	1873
Nigeria	0.225	0.8	2.0	37	280	1299	2.1	36	347
World	1.36			1500			5639		

benchmark it is worth noting that in 1972 the average person in the United States consumed (directly or indirectly) the quantities of nonfuel materials shown in Table 5.6.[9]

Water is another material that is consumed in vast quantities, although it is often overlooked. In the United States in 1972 total direct and indirect use of water was about 1900 gallons per day per capita or 420 billion gallons per day for the nation as a whole. Major uses were roughly as follows:

Irrigation	39%
Electric utilities	34%
Other industrial	21%
Public utilities (urban)	5%
Rural domestic	1%

The direct use of water by an average urban dweller (in 1966) was 63 gallons per day per capita, of which toilet flushing accounted for 20.5 gallons and personal washing and bathing 18.5 gallons.[10]

It would be convenient for purposes of forecasting if similar patterns of use held for all countries and all periods. But of course they do not. Industrially undeveloped countries utilize less materials altogether than do highly developed countries. They also use more natural materials such as adobe or palm thatch in place of metal, plastic, wood, brick, or concrete. The availability of local resources is a major factor: in North America, Japan, Siberia, Brazil, and Southern Nigeria wood is still the major construction material because it is readily available in most locations. In Europe, including Western Russia, India, and China, however, wood is becoming scarce, and brick, stone, concrete, or adobe are now used almost exclusively for house construction.

Steel production has often been regarded as a *sine qua non* of industrial development and power. As a matter of fact, iron and steel are being gradually replaced by other materials in many applications. For instance, cast iron water pipe is being rapidly phased out in favor of cast concrete or plastic. Cast iron automobile engines are likely to be replaced fairly soon by aluminum; tinplated steel cans have largely been replaced by aluminum or plastic containers; steel rails will probably be replaced by cast concrete; and so on.

On examining detailed consumption data for the United States and a number of other countries, one pattern that does emerge unmistakably is the fact that the demand for iron and steel per unit of GDP* rises with increasing GDP per capita to a peak level and then drops.[11] For

*Whenever I speak of one unit of GDP I mean 1 million dollars.

**Table 5.6 U.S. Consumption of Primary Materials (1972)
(kg per capita)**

Sand and gravel	4000	Wood and pulp	1225
Stone	3800	Natural fibers, oils	22
Cement	360	Natural rubber	4.5
Clays	270	Plastics	51
Salt	200	Synthetic fibers	16
Other nonmetals	535		
		Iron and steel	535
		Aluminum	22.3
		Copper	11.2
		Lead	6.7
		Zinc	6.7
		Other metals	15.6
Subtotal nonmetallic	9250	Subtotal metals	600
		Subtotal organics	1320

the United States this peak occurred at about $3000 per capita (1972 prices), a level of steel consumption the United States reached in the late 1920s and again just before World War II. In 1940 United States steel production was over 200 tons per unit of GDP—almost twice the recent level.

Since the United States economy is becoming more service intensive and since iron and steel will continue to be used less lavishly or to be replaced entirely by lighter materials, I would expect the level of consumption per unit of GDP to continue to decline, dropping to about 75 tons per million dollars by 2000 and perhaps 35 tons per million dollars by 2025. I may be exaggerating the rate somewhat, but there is little doubt that steel is a declining industry. Nevertheless, total steel consumption per capita will not drop below the current level in the next fifty years in the United States. It will sharply increase in the developing countries, of course.

It is to be expected that the other highly developed countries will continue to consume more iron and steel per unit GDP than the United States for some time to come. Japan, being heavily export oriented and less service intensive, now consumes steel at two and a half times the United States level (per unit of GDP), but economic growth and technological substitution in that country may also proceed faster and tend to narrow the gap by the year 2000. The EEC falls in between the United States and Japan. The USSR will soon produce more steel than it can consume (except for armaments), but will shift only reluctantly to other materials like aluminum and plastic. The inertia imposed by centralized planning is partly responsible for this conservatism. The less developed countries will generally have increasing ratios of steel consumption per unit of GDP for most of the next half century, except for Brazil, which should reach its peak around the year 2000, and China, which will reach its peak between 2010 and 2015.

The situation with regard to aluminum and copper—the next two most important metals—is quite similar. Here, too, there is apparently a saturation effect, with a peak at some characteristic level of GDP per capita. In the case of copper, the United States peaked at a consumption level of about 2.5 tons per million dollars GDP in 1941 just before World War II. By 1971 the level was about 1.2 tons per million dollars GDP and still dropping slowly. In view of the increasing service intensity of the United States economy and a number of pending substitutions of other materials for copper—notably plastic and aluminum—the decline in intensity of use can be expected to continue. By the year 2000, I would expect United States copper consumption to be less than 0.6 ton per unit GDP and by 2025 to be down to 0.25 or less.

In the case of aluminum, the peak level of use has not yet been reached. There are some major new uses of aluminum—notably in automobiles—that are now pending. I think the peak consumption level will occur at about 4.5 tons per unit GDP at $8500 per capita* in the 1980–1985 period. Thereafter a gradual decline will probably occur, with consumption dropping to 3 tons per unit GDP by the year 2000 and 2.3 tons per unit by 2025. As with iron and steel, the consumption levels expressed per unit GDP in the other industrialized countries are likely to be a bit higher than the United States level due to somewhat greater emphasis on manufacturing and exports as compared to services in their economies.

As for the less developed countries, assuming that they are successful in their efforts to industrialize and energy availability is not a constraint, all of them will be at the stage of substituting machines for human labor as rapidly as possible. A moment's thought makes it clear that ipso facto this means utilizing more metals per unit of output of the economy. In contrast, the more developed countries have already eliminated about as much labor as they can by using conventional machines. (Future labor savings will come primarily from the use of computers.) Hence the amount of metal required to produce a unit of GDP will tend to rise for the slower-growing LDCs. In the case of fast-growing Brazil and China, intensity of use should peak within the next twenty to thirty years and begin to decline.

The foregoing results are summarized in Tables 5.7 and 5.8 with 1972 figures, based on United Nations data.[4] It must be obvious by now that the projections are essentially self-consistent "educated guesses" based on recent history and the considerations that I have cited. Consistent estimates of total consumption for each country may be obtained by multiplying the consumption intensity factors by projected GDP/capita figures given in Chapter 4, times population. The totals for future years are substantially less in most cases than one obtains by simple extrapolation of the historical consumption trends, as several influential forecasting studies have done.[12-14] For instance, if United States GDP by the end of the twentieth century is $3 trillion (in 1972 dollars), corresponding to about $11,000 per capita—a fairly optimistic assumption—then iron and steel consumption would probably be close to 200 million tons, copper consumption 1.8 million tons, and aluminum consumption 9 million tons. These figures are substantially below the Bureau of Mines forecasts for copper (4.4–7.2 million tons) and aluminum (15.7–31.2 million tons). They are closer to, but still well

*1972 dollars.

below, the most recent forecasts by Resources For the Future, Inc. (RFF) for copper (2.6–3.6 million tons) and aluminum (11.9–16.9 million tons). The latter studies, which I would characterize generally as alpha in approach, tend to assume less long-run elasticity in basic economic relationships—particularly technological substitutability—than I do.*

There are, of course, many other materials that are now used in large—or even very large—quantities. I cannot attempt to discuss most of them, even briefly. A few additional comments concerning wood, paper, fiber, and plastic must suffice at this stage.

As already noted, wood is only used as a construction material in countries in which it is readily available (North America, Japan, Brazil, etc.). Where it is not available or very costly, other materials are used in its place. The pattern is not likely to change in the next half century. Modestly increased demand for wood products can be met by modest improvements in sustained-yield forestry, but those countries not now utilizing much wood will not be able to do so in the future.

The demand for paper is more volatile. It has been rising fast in most countries—mainly due to increased use of packaging materials—and threatens to exceed the available annual output of pulpwood from northern coniferous forests of Canada, Scandinavia, and the USSR. Fortunately, other types of material can be used to make paper, including tropical hardwoods, which are still available in enormous quantities in a number of tropical countries that have significant forests, and the stalks of sugarcane plants (bagasse). Both wood and paper products, however, can only be consumed up to the limit of annual production, or by "mining" existing resources of full-grown trees—as is being done already throughout the tropics. Brazil is one of the few countries with large exploitable forest resources. (The forests of northern Siberia, although immense in extent, are very slow growing and somewhat inaccessible.) Total world consumption of wood and wood products can grow only modestly, and most of it will continue to be consumed by the most developed group of countries, plus Brazil.

For practical purposes, natural fibers can be limited to cotton and jute. The latter is a crude material of little intrinsic value and is easily replaced. Despite its importance to the economy of Bangladesh, demand will probably decline. Cotton is more intrinsically valuable and

*A 1972 study by Resources For the Future, Inc. utilized an input-output table of the United States economy with some explicit adjustments for clearly evident technological changes but no allowance for the impact of sharply higher energy prices. (The embargo occurred in 1973, remember.)

Table 5.7 Primary Iron and Steel Consumption

Country	Intensity (metric tons per million dollars GDP)			Intensity (kg per capita)			Total, Annual Average (thousands of metric tons)		
	1972	2000	2025	1972	2000	2025	1972	2000	2025
North America	118	60	35	656	660	665	151200	191000	218000
EEC	163	100	65	477	600	650	116500	165000	186000
Japan	270	80	50	644	610	667	68900	86000	95000
USSR	321	250	90	490	980	850	121200	300000	300000
Brazil	149.7	180	150	76	360	504	7642	75000	204000
China	180	200	125	33	164	348	26100	193000	500000
India[a]	157	200	200	16	39	72	9227	39800	108000
Nigeria	59.4	150	200	9.8	52.5	130	571	6700	35000
Subtotal							500000	1056000	1646000
World (=subtotal x 1.3)							650000	1370000	2140000

[a]Case 2 (median).

Table 5.8 Primary Aluminum and Copper Consumption

Country		Intensity (metric tons per million dollars GDP)			Intensity (kg per capita)			Total, Annual Average (thousands of metric tons)		
		1972	2000	2025	1972	2000	2025	1972	2000	2025
North America	Al	3.58	3.0	2.3	19.9	33.1	43.7	4586	9555	14300
	Cu	1.76	0.6	0.25	9.8	6.6	4.7	2253	1910	1550
EEC	Al	2.96	3.8	3.0	8.65	22.8	29.5	2114	6324	8420
	Cu	2.89	0.85	0.35	8.4	5.1	3.4	2060	1415	980
Japan	Al	4.77	3.9	3.6	11.4	29.8	54.3	1216	4145	7870
	Cu	3.68	0.7	0.3	8.8	5.4	3.9	938	744	570
USSR	Al	3.44	4.0	3.6	5.25	19.1	23.5	1300	6000	10000
	Cu	2.73	1.0	0.4	4.2	4.8	3.14	1030	1500	1140
Brazil	Al	2.80	3.6	3.6	1.4	7.1	18.2	143	1500	6920
	Cu	2.17	1.5	0.6	1.1	3.0	3.2	111	625	1160
China	Al	1.37	2.5	3.0	0.25	2.05	8.3	200	2415	12060
	Cu	1.85	1.5	0.75	0.3	1.2	2.1	270	1450	3000
India[a]	Al	3.11	4.5	5.0	0.32	0.87	1.8	183	895	2,675
	Cu	1.07	1.5	1.2	0.11	0.29	0.42	63	300	645
Nigeria	Al		No data available							
	Cu									

[a]Case 2 (median).

its unique properties of strength, softness, and absorbency have proven difficult for synthetic materials to duplicate—so far. However, notwithstanding its economic importance to the Southwestern United States and Egypt, cotton's long day as a major commodity will probably come to an end during the next half century. It cannot be produced truly economically in a world in which the same irrigated land could be used to grow rice or some other food crop to sustain a still-increasing human population. In addition, cotton is subject to attack by some extremely stubborn pests, such as the boll weevil, which have required the increasingly intensive use of sophisticated chemical pesticides* to control. Synthetic fibers—in a multitude of types and varieties—seem likely to be in use throughout the world by 2025, despite the objections of "simplifiers" like Schumacher and Commoner, who would prefer, instead, a return to greater dependence on natural materials and simpler processes.

Synthetic polymers and elastomers, such as synthetic rubber, have been the great materials breakthrough of the twentieth century. In tonnage terms, 1975 consumption of synthetics in the United States is at least 1000-fold greater than it was in 1930. The petrochemical industry has consistently been one of the fastest growing and shows no sign of reaching a saturation point. As of 1970, the amount of synthetic material used in the United States was roughly equal in bulk to the amount of steel, although its weight was very much less (about $1/8$). The day can be foreseen when plastic use might approach the use of steel even by weight. The major growth of plastics—apart from synthetic fibers—to date has been in containers, housewares, packaging materials, upholstery materials, and surfacing materials for walls, floors, and furniture. Molded or sheet plastics have successfully competed against hardwood flooring and veneer facings, ceramic tiles and crockery, glass and metal containers, and zinc or brass metal handles, knobs, and other small bits of hardware. Plastic film has made major inroads against paper and foil for packaging and has also created new uses for itself. Plastic foam has penetrated markets for insulation and lightweight structural materials; it too has created new uses. Recently plastics have begun to break into new and larger traditional markets: pipe, larger heavy-duty containers, and structural elements in motor vehicles, appliances, and houses. These uses will probably increase

---

*DDT is by far the cheapest pesticide. For this reason it is the one still mainly used in the less developed countries, where it inflicts a mounting toll on other forms of insect, bird, fish, and mammalian life. In the United States, DDT has been banned, and more expensive biodegradable organic phosphate pesticides are used instead.

dramatically over time—if raw material availability permits—in virtually all countries, eliminating many traditional uses of materials such as paper, wood, glass, ceramics, zinc, and brass. Although petrochemicals and plastics currently account for only a negligible fraction of petroleum and natural gas usage, this is not likely to be true by the year 2000.

TRANSPORTATION SERVICES*

One transportation statistic immediately commends itself as a possibly appropriate aggregate measure of human mobility, namely, total passenger miles traveled, or PMT. It is clear, however, that this statistic, even if it were easily measured and readily available, is "opaque" in the sense that it subsumes very different modes of transportation, with different characteristics. In reality, bicycles seldom compete with passenger cars, nor do passenger cars compete with aircraft. To make matters worse, there is no satisfactory means of measuring PMT by nonpublic modes.

More important, however, base statistics on passenger miles traveled do not reflect the truly salient fact about transportation today, which is the importance of the motor vehicle. This is not to say that automobiles are now the principle mode of travel in all countries. This is clearly not (yet) the case. However, the major differences between countries as regards transportation have to do largely with the extent that motor vehicles have replaced older modes (horses, mules, bullock carts, bicycles, trams, or railroad trains).

The differences are indeed qualitative as well as quantitative. This point does not really need much elaboration here, inasmuch as the revolutionary character of the motor vehicle and its potential for stimulating ancillary changes in urban form, personal lifestyles—even family structure—have been more than sufficiently applauded and lamented by hundreds of authors. Although even one more footnote to this vast literature may be excessive, it seems to me worthwhile to display some quantitative evidence of a kind with which most people are not familiar.

Figure 5.1 displays an interesting pattern. In brief, although significant differences exist between countries, there is clear evidence of an elongated S-shaped curve, with ownership increasing slowly for

*Because I cannot discuss everything, I also omit explicit consideration of freight transportation. To include it would add more length without much more light.

Figure 5.9 Automobile ownership as a function of average personal consumption expenditures (PCE) by country.

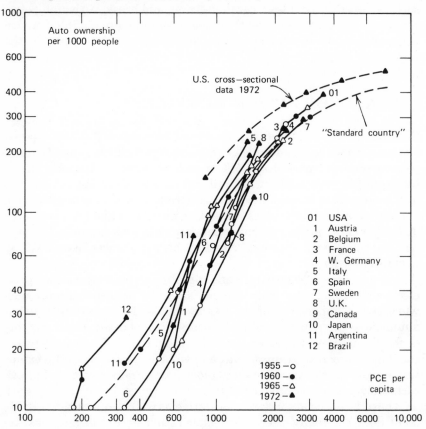

very low average income levels (mostly off the graph), speeding up for intermediate levels, and tapering off at higher incomes. Passenger car ownership seems to increase most rapidly between about $600 and $1500 per capita, where the curves are steepest.

The historical trends for individual countries (plotted from 1955 to 1972) always rise more steeply than the cross-sectional curve that one obtains by plotting points for different countries in any given year. This means that the cross-sectional curve for the world has been rising over the past several decades. The United States is the most auto-oriented country of all, and, not surprisingly, auto ownership for any given income group is highest in the United States. The reasons for this are obvious after a moment's reflection: (1) even the poorest people in the United States can easily own cars (second-hand, if not new); (2) driving is taught in public schools; (3) obtaining a license is easy and cheap (compared to a number of countries which actively discourage private ownership of cars); (4) public roads are excellent, while public mass transportation is poor; (5) gasoline is cheaper than anywhere else except the major petroleum-exporting countries of the Middle East. Thus the dashed line on Figure 5.1 labeled "U.S. Cross-Section Data 1972" is very probably an upper limit, which the rest of the world will not exceed.

The lowest curve, on the other hand, represents Japan, which is a crowded country with no domestic energy resources and excellent public transportation. Japan also imposes very heavy excise taxes on autos and fuel and further limits the number of drivers by requiring an elaborate and time-consuming driver training course. Except for the communist world, Japan probably represents a kind of lower limit on auto dependence.

In between the United States and Japan, I have drawn a compromise curve labeled "Standard Country," which is a useful basis for forecasting future car ownership as a function of increasing national wealth, as measured by Personal Consumption Expenditure (PCE) per capita.

Table 5.9 presents some key ratios for the benchmark year 1972.[4] Based on the observed "saturation" effects noted previously, but assuming other factors remain more or less equal, projections for the years 2000 and 2025 are also given. These are expressed in terms of vehicles per expenditure unit (PCE), vehicles per capita, and overall numbers of passenger vehicles for each country using assumed GDP and population growth rates discussed in Chapter 4.

The vehicles per capita estimates are probably the most meaningful to most people. To say that a country has 500 cars per 1000 persons means that there is one car for every two individuals. Since a significant number of people are either too young or too old* or otherwise incapacitated to drive, this is nearly one car for every possible driver. If the average household has two adults and two children, it means essentially two cars per household. This is obviously not a physical limitation, but it is likely that most households already having two cars would have better things to do with any surplus discretionary

---

*The percentage of the population that is under sixteen years and older than seventy years of age would be a rough measure. This depends strongly on the population growth rate: a quickly increasing population is mostly young, whereas a stabilized one has a much higher percentage of elderly people.

Table 5.9 Passenger Auto Ownership

Country	Ownership per million dollars (PCE)			Ownership per 1000			Total Passenger Car Stock (millions)		
	1972	2000	2025	1972	2000	2025	1972	2000	2025
North America	132	80	50	435	503	541	99.7	145.2	177.3
EEC	147	110	70	245	267	292	39.5	95.5	102.5
Japan	87	70	45	100	284	318	10.6	39.4	42.5
USSR	24	50	70	22	141	324	5.4	29.1	115.1
Brazil	83	120	100	28	139	317	2.64	35.0	115.4
China	neg.	15	30	neg.	6.3	42.6	0.03	7.4	61.6
India [a]	14	30	30	1.1	3.5	6.4	0.62	3.6	9.6
Nigeria	10	40	50	1.2			0.07		

[a] Case 2 (median)

income than buy a third car. Thus the saturation phenomenon reveals itself.

The USSR is a special case, since official policy has strongly discouraged the use of private passenger cars, both for economic reasons (to divert resources into more "essential" sectors) and ideological ones. However, this era appears to be ending now that the USSR has a large heavy industrial base and an enormous, long-pent-up demand for consumer goods, especially cars. This should be the world's biggest growth market for passenger cars in the next two or three decades, with saturation effects only beginning to appear around the year 2000.

Brazil, although much poorer, is comparable to the USSR as a producer of motor vehicles. It, too, is likely to be a major growth market for the next two decades, with a slowdown beginning some time after the year 2000.

The last three countries on the standard list of eight are not likely to begin to adopt passenger cars on a large scale before the year 2025, if then. If China's recent economic growth continues uninterrupted, it might be in a position to begin to permit a modestly increased amount of private consumption in thirty years or so,* but that seems too soon to me. Only by permitting (or perpetuating) blatantly inequitable income distributions between the urban and rural areas could India or Nigeria become significantly motorized in the next half century—notwithstanding Nigeria's undoubted oil wealth.

It is understood, course, that the increasing dependence of the industrialized countries on a few remaining petroleum exporters is not unlikely to result in further price escalation.† There will also be important technological changes in the auto industry (see Chapter 7). The passenger car of 2025 will be quite unlike the 1975 version in many details, especially with regard to the method of propulsion. It is even conceivable that cars of that era will no longer be privately owned. On the whole, I suspect that the changes will not be quite so radical. A passenger car will still be recognizable as such: it will neither fly nor run on tracks, nor will it operate automatically under centralized computer control.

---

*Assuming an average rate of increase of GDP of 7% per annum and a population increase of 2% per annum from 1975 to 2003. China would only quadruple its GDP per capita to $600, which is significantly lower than the level of Mexico in 1975. Also, Communist China will certainly resist the use of passenger cars on ideological grounds.
† There is, of course, disagreement on this. Hence my careful wording. The point is that sharply increased fuel prices would reduce the projections in Table 5.9. By the same token, a break in prices—due, for instance, to splits in OPEC—would increase the projections.

Personal expenditures on cars will tend toward a peak of between 10% and 20% of total PCE at a level of PCE per capita ranging from $4000 to $8000 or so, depending on the country. The United States and Canada will peak at a higher expenditure fraction than, say, Japan. On the other hand, the United States peak will probably occur at a lower income level due to the combination of circumstances mentioned above that conspire to make car ownership relatively easy in the United States — and alternative means of transportation relatively difficult — compared to other countries.

As a country moves from extreme poverty through the various stages of industrial development, accompanied by rising incomes, at first a continuously increasing fraction of PCE goes toward the purchase of an increasing number of passenger cars. During this stage, the average price paid per car may tend to fall as domestic manufacturers are able to exploit economies of scale. Later, further increments of income are used more and more to upgrade the quality of the motor vehicles in use. People "trade up" to more expensive cars. As disposable incomes* rise further still — beyond the $4000–8000 per capita range — people tend to spend their extra money preferentially on other goods and services, such as restaurant meals, airplane travel, pleasure boats, and so on.

This sequence implies, among other things, that auto manufacturers located in the most industrial (OECD) countries and geared for that market will tend to develop more and more luxurious, premium quality, expensive cars — which cannot satisfy the growing mass market in Eastern Europe, Africa, or Latin America. This trend is clearly visible: the manufacturers of quality cars such as Peugeot, Volvo, Mercedes-Benz, and BMW have thrived in recent years, whereas firms like VW, Fiat, and Renault, which once specialized in cheap cars for the masses, are busy redesigning their product lines to upgrade style and performance in addition to economy of operation. The higher-priced models manufactured by GM (Cadillac, Oldsmobile) or British Leyland (Jaguar, Triumph) have similarly outperformed the lower-priced models. It would not surprise me, therefore, if the demand for a "people's" car (and truck) in the developing countries were eventually fulfilled from sources other than the traditional manufacturers. Brazil, Mexico, Korea, or Taiwan could become major exporters of "Model T" vehicles suitable for the developing countries.[†]

*PCE is equal to disposable income less personal savings.

[†]As a matter of fact, in 1978 Mexico will start to export VW Beetles back to Germany, where they are no longer produced.

About 4.5% of the U.S. family's budget, or 30% of its transportation and communications budget, goes for purchasing new or used cars. Only about 1% of the total family budget goes to purchasing public transportation services of all kinds, including bus, tram, rail, and commercial aircraft. The remaining 8% of the family budget that goes to transportation and communications expenditures divides more or less equally between purchasing fuel for automobiles and miscellaneous licensing, maintenance, repair, insurance, and garaging costs associated with car ownership. Thus, in the United States passenger cars account for about 93% of all private expenditures on transportation. Spending on car ownership alone exceeds the level of spending on all kinds of communications by a ratio of more than eight to one.

These figures, although perhaps a bit dull, tell several important stories. First, I think they explain more clearly than words why rising motor fuel prices are likely to have a permanent impact on vehicle sizes and fuel economy. A 50% rise in fuel prices would raise the level of expenditure for motor fuel from 4% to 6% of the family budget. Not so bad? If people are truly reluctant to spend more than a fixed fraction of their disposable income on transportation and communication, 2% more for fuel means 2% less for something else.

For people contemplating the purchase of a new car, the obvious compromise is to delay the purchase or to purchase a smaller (presumably cheaper) car, or both. However, since only 4.5% of the consumers budget (on the average) went to vehicle purchases, a downward shift of 2% would translate into a 40% initial drop in new car sales.[†] Later on, of course, deferred purchases may be superimposed on "normal" ones, resulting in an exceptionally good sales year, such as 1976. However, in the long run it seems likely that fuel economy will have to be improved by one-third or so before the industry can reasonably expect to regain and hold its pre-1974 4.5% share of the consumer dollar.

The preceding paragraphs also indicate quite clearly that *the automobile manufacturers are not permanently in league with the petroleum producers,* as many environmentalists and consumerists have tended to assume. On the contrary, these giant industries have directly contrary interests, insofar as they are effectively competing for the same segment of the consumer budget. As this conflict is more clearly realized, the automotive industry—for decades quite uninterested in technological innovations that would conserve on the use of fuel

---

[†] This is almost exactly what happened in the United States in 1974.

energy — will become one of the major sources of new technology in the next twenty years or so.

Notwithstanding the obvious dominance of automobiles, some qualitative forecasters (the omega type) have asserted the inevitability of a great revival and expansion of public transportation in the coming decades. Technological writers have contributed to this notion by elaborating the possibilities of conceptual wonders like high-speed "gravity-vacuum" trains running in evacuated tunnels or "tracked hovercraft" utilizing linear induction motors or magnetic suspension systems. Supersonic, hypersonic, and VTOL aircraft have also had more than their appropriate share of attention. The emphasis on high-technology transport systems seems quite misplaced in view of the reality, which is that public transportation is nearly everywhere declining in importance (including the Communist countries of Eastern Europe and the USSR).

India and China already possess excellent rail networks, and with their dense populations they will undoubtedly concentrate on further developing this mode of travel as an alternative to motor vehicles. It is quite likely that, by the year 2025, China will have an efficient network of ultra-high-speed rail lines linking its major cities and utilizing the most advanced possible technology (see Chapter 7).* This will be supplemented by a "feeder" system of buses or trams penetrating to the remotest collective farms and provincial towns.

Notwithstanding the predominant importance of road and rail transportation for most of the world, I cannot leave this topic without discussing air travel — a newer and more dynamic mode. As already pointed out, automobile use is now approaching a state of saturation in the most developed countries. Not so air travel. From 1950 to 1970 the number of airline passenger trips in the United States increased over ten-fold (from 19 million to 204 million), which corresponds to an annual growth rate of about 12%. In other countries the rate of growth has been even more dramatic.

The 1969 recession and the sharp increase in petroleum costs beginning in 1973 raised costs and sharply curtailed growth for a time. This left many airlines burdened with overcapacity, and some (notably Pan Am) were in deep trouble. These events initiated a temporary phase of consolidation and slower growth — which was inevitable anyhow — but

*I say this without any specific knowledge of Chinese plans or programs. It is simply the logical course for a country with China's dimensions and resources, and the Chinese are supremely logical people.

the air transport industry has recovered and is beginning to command a larger share of the consumer transportation dollar.

In particular, unless the availability of fuel becomes a serious constraint, I suspect that as GDP per capita (in any country) approaches $8000–10,000 per year, the amount that is expended on passenger cars per capita will begin to level off, whereas expenditures on air travel will continue to increase, taking up a growing share of the consumer transportation budget. At a GDP of $20,000 per year per capita, air travel would probably begin to compete with car travel in terms of personal expenditures. The most advanced countries are likely to reach this point before 2025. It means a very significant expansion, not only in commercial airlines but also in the use of private aircraft.

Where weather conditions are conducive to flying and population densities are not excessive—as in Midwestern and Southwestern United States—most families are likely to own a plane (assuming, as noted, the continued availability of suitable aviation fuel*). Private flying will not be so widely practiced in Japan or Europe, because of congestion, mountainous terrain, and relatively unfavorable flying weather. Private flying will probably not be significant in the USSR for several decades, but public air transportation will continue to take a greater fraction of personal transportation expenditures than in the Western countries. Distances are enormous, roads are poor, railroads are slow, and air travel is comparatively efficient. The same pattern is likely in Brazil.

Supersonic flight at substantially lower rates than the initial commercial Concorde service (British Airways and Air France, beginning in 1976) could have a tremendous impact on the demand for air travel, especially to the Far East and the Southern Hemisphere. It would be a tremendous economic boon for Siberia, Australia, Japan, and Brazil, among other countries. Although supersonic planes consume considerably more fuel per seat-mile than subsonic planes, the more rapid turnaround also enables the costly capital equipment to be utilized more intensively and efficiently. Despite the objections—very possibly valid—of environmentalists and conservationists, I believe that most intercontinental air travel will eventually be supersonic, although another generation of technological development may well be required to bring costs down to attractive levels.

---

*"Fuel" need not be gasoline (see Chapter 7).

COMMUNICATIONS AND
INFORMATION SERVICES

In the preceding section on transportation I mentioned that consumer expenditure on communications is only about 1.5% of total household expenditures (in the United States) and only 10% of household expenditure on transportation. This is a somewhat narrow definition of communication, however, comprising telephone, telegraph, and postal services. More broadly, communication can be construed to include all means of transferring information from one place to another. This would include not only voice and written messages, but also radio and video transmissions and data transmissions (e.g., between computers). Needless to say, many of the users of data communications are not "final" consumers, but businesses.

In discussing transportation, I focused particularly on one mode (automobiles) because of its great predominance in the developed countries. Telephones are perhaps equally predominant in the transmission of messages. However, whereas automobiles are the active element in the automotive transportation system (roads being essentially passive conduits), this is emphatically not the case for telephones. On the contrary, telephones are relatively simple, inexpensive, and nearly passive instruments, representing a small fraction of the invested capital or the technological complexity of the telephone *system.* To compare countries' communication capabilities in terms of the number of telephones in service is easy and tempting. But any validity to such a comparison would be accidental; the measure itself is irrelevant. One certainly cannot equate telephones *per se* in different countries. Quality of service differs significantly. To give only one example, virtually any telephone in the United States has long been capable of being directly linked to a teleprinter, telecopier, or a computer terminal. This statement was not true fifteen years ago for the United Kingdom and France, although service in Europe and Japan is being upgraded. It is emphatically not true for telephones in most of the rest of the world today.

What matters, evidently, is capability to transmit information. Taking the broader viewpoint that communications means transferring information, it is clear that a variety of sharply different and somewhat incomparable technologies are involved. By somewhat incomparable I mean essentially that the types of information being transmitted are very different and that the technology appropriate for one may not be directly applicable to another.

Nevertheless, there is one technical measure applicable to all modes and which enables one to compare them; namely, "information content." Ultimately, all kinds of information, from handwriting to pictures, can be reduced to a simple sequence of code elements such as the "dash" and the "dot" (interspersed with "spaces") from which the so-called Morse code was built, or a set of musical tones may be introduced corresponding to all numbers from 0 to 9 as in touch-tone dialing.

Any type of information whatever can be broken down to, or reconstructed from these simple elements. For instance, a TV picture or a photograph can be transmitted over a telephone line and reproduced 10,000 miles away. The picture is reduced first to a sequence of intensity levels, corresponding to digital numbers, which corresponds to a complex wave form. The familiar digital numbers based on ten elements (zero through nine) can all be rewritten in terms of binary numbers based on only two elements (zero and one). This is the most convenient form for computers to operate on internally. Any piece of information whatsoever can be expressed ultimately in terms of a sequence of binary numbers, or "bits."

The quantity of information contained can be measured by actually counting the number of bits needed to express it. For instance, there are about 3.3 bits of information* "contained" in any one digit decimal number (because there are ten possibilities, but three bits can specify only $2^3 = 8$, whereas four bits can specify $2^4 = 16$ possibilities. Actually $2^{3.3} = 10$). Similarly, there are a little less than 5 bits of information in any single letter of the English alphabet (because there are only 26 possibilities, while 5 bits can specify 2^5 or 32 possibilities). And so forth.

I think it may be interesting to compare some of the different modes of information transfer in terms of current information volume measured in quadrillion bits per year. A set of projections to 1990 made a few years ago by Stanford Research Institute[15] is worth citing, even though the detailed assumptions on which the projections are based are probably obsolete and, in any case, far too complex to describe here. The methodology is uncompromisingly alpha. It is an easy exercise with numbers to extend the projections in Table 5.10 to later years (2000, 2025) using the same methodology. (All the Stanford projections are essentially exponential, with the exception of video transmission where hyperexponential growth has been assumed.[†]) The results are eye-opening.

*Actually, the exact figure is $\log_e 10/\log_e 2 = 2.30250/0.69315$.
[†] The SRI projections for video transmission (made in 1970) were rather too optimistic, having been based on the assumption that "picture phones" would soon begin a rapid penetration of the office communications market. This has not happened and is no longer considered to be likely.

Table 5.10   SRI Projections of Information Transfer Volume, United States, 1970–1990

	Local Volume (10^{15} bits)		Long Distance Volume (10^{15} bits)		Total Volume (10^{15} bits)	
Mode	1970	1990	1970	1990	1970	1990
Written[a]	5	9	10	21	15	30
Voice[b]	1900	9000	100	1000	2000	10,000
Video[c]	2.3	2050	3.3	250	5.6	2300
Data and private wire[d]	0.04	3	0.34	27	0.38	30

[a] Books and magazines, newspapers, mail.
[b] Telephone, radio-telephone, and radio transmission.
[c] Video telephone, cable TV, TV transmission.
[d] Public message telegraph, teletype (TWX, Telex), digital data transmission, and private wire.

Extrapolating to 2000, the volume of video information (in quadrillion bits) would exceed the volume of voice information by nearly a factor of three (80,000 to 30,000), whereas data and private wire transmissions would far exceed the volume of written messages (300 against forty or so). By 2025, however, video transmission would exceed voice by three orders of magnitude (600 million vs. 600,000), whereas data and private wire transmissions would be up to the 100,000 mark; written transmissions would meanwhile have risen to a "mere" 100.

In the fifty-five years from 1970 to 2025 the implied multipliers and rates of increase are shown below:

	Multiplier	Implied Annual Growth Rate (%)*
Video	100,000,000	37.1
Dalta and private wire	250,000	22.6
Voice	300	10.4
Written	6	3.25

(This little table shows, again, how deeply misleading a comparison of percentage growth rates can be.) Before discussing what these fantastic numbers might mean, if anything, it should be emphasized that,

*If the factor of increase is F over a number of N years, then *equivalent* annual growth rate a can be computed by solving the equation $\exp(aN) = F$ whence $a = 1/N \log_e F$. In this case N is 55, and F is given in the first column.

although I do not have comparable statistics for other countries, the recent rates of increase for Europe and Japan (at least) almost surely exceed the United States figures.

An important initial question here is this: Is it physically *possible* to provide sufficient communications channel capacity for the indicated growth in demand for information transfer to be satisfied? Without prematurely introducing difficult technological issues, I think it is safe to simply say that the answer appears to be "yes", more or less, although major technological changes would obviously be required.

Assuming technical feasibility, then, does the picture thus presented "make sense"? It is plausible? Indeed, what kind of society could conceivably demand video and data transmissions on such a scale? On reflection, such a level of demand implies a network of video links comparable to but substantially more elaborate than our present telephone system. Let me pursue this comparison in a little more detail.

If every existing telephone were replaced by a picture phone with a 250-line TV picture—sufficient to show a human face in recognizable detail—the required channel "bandwidth" is 1 MegaHertz, or equivalent to roughly 100 ordinary telephone circuits. Thus to convert the existing telephone system to picture phones would increase the demand for information transfer roughly 100-fold.

However, one reason picture phones have not been successfully introduced is that the video capability is much too limited to be of real value to potential users. To send only a standard commercial TV program one would need 625 lines, which requires a bandwidth of $(625/250)^2 = (2.5)^2 = 6.25 \text{ MH}_z$. Although this would permit the camera to show more than a single face, the resolution is insufficient for transmitting pictures of documents or drawings, for instance. To provide that capability, at least 1000 lines and preferably 2000 lines would be needed, implying a bandwidth of between 16 and 64 MH_z per circuit, or the equivalent of 1600–6400 ordinary telephone lines.

To convey a realistic three-dimensional (holographic) picture, probably the minimal requirement for a true "office-at-home," a much larger bandwidth would be needed. The minimum requirement is not known exactly, but Dennis Gabor, the Nobel prize winning inventor of holography, estimates the minimal requirement at 1000 MH_z.[16]

To summarize, if each existing telephone were replaced by a holographic video screen (with an audio channel, of course) and the entire system were utilized at roughly current levels of intensity, the information transfer demand would rise by a factor of $1000 \times 100 = 100,000$ over the present level. Greater intensity of use might conceivably add a further factor of ten or so, although it is doubtful. This would appear to define an upper limit of sorts. Actually, demand should begin to saturate at a substantially lower level than that, since many transactions simply do not require such tremendous capacity. Thus my simple-minded fifty-five-year extrapolation of demand would seem to have overshot the mark by a large margin (e.g., a factor of 1000).

In light of the foregoing considerations, two points emerge. Evidently, exponential (or hyperexponential) extrapolations of high growth rates cannot be extended very far—certainly not as far as 2025. Saturation effects would have to begin to slow down growth considerably sooner. This will probably happen soon after the year 2000, when video volume begins to significantly exceed voice volume. A second, related point arises: although video transmissions are currently quite separate, it would appear that the major ultimate market for video transmissions will arise from the *substitution* of video for voice links. This means that the growth of voice transmissions should actually begin to saturate much sooner, in the 1980s or 1990s. In fact, it should eventually reach a plateau and even begin to fall, slowly perhaps, around the year 1990 or soon after. I think that voice transmissions in the United States will peak at a level between two and three times the present level, or around 5000 quadrillion bits.

What about the demand for data and private wire transmissions? Here I think one can neglect the telegraph, teletype, telephoto, and long-distance Xerox components, although some of these will certainly grow. The big demand will come from links between electronic computers and data terminals of various kinds. Here the historical growth rate has, if anything, been even more phenomenal. Starting with the first commercial UNIVAC in 1952, the number of electronic computer installations passed 100 before 1955, reached 1000 in 1956, passed 10,000 by 1962, and hit 100,000 by 1970. With the new generations of minicomputers (already followed by "micro-computers-on-a-chip") the number in service by 1980 will certainly be in the ballpark of 10 million, mostly of the micro variety. The definition of an "installation" will meanwhile have become obscured to the point of near meaninglessness. By that time computers-on-a-chip will be routinely incorporated in watches, locks, automobile ignition systems, automobile brakes, all kinds of kitchen appliances, cash registers, typewriters, telephones, and industrial robots.

The biggest new use of large computers in the current decade is the automation of retail sales and financial transactions. This is a natural extension of the time-sharing concept introduced a few years ago, except that general-purpose input-output data terminals are being supplemented (or replaced, in some cases) by specialized point-of-sale terminals or information appliances that record a sales or credit transaction and automatically instruct a central computer to make a reservation, prepare a bill, check credit, and/or arrange a funds transfer. Such terminals are already being used extensively by banks, hotels, airlines, retail stores, and even supermarkets. Their use in the United States will probably quadruple in the half decade (1975–1980). The role of the retail clerk is not eliminated, but the preparation of input data for the computer no longer requires a separate punchcard or similar operation. It is done automatically by the cash register. Within a decade or two, the use of credit-card-initiated "autotransaction" devices, coupled with electronic funds transfer, should dramatically reduce the use of checks, just as credit cards have already substantially cut into the direct use of cash. All these trends, of course, imply substantially expanded use of electronic computers and telecommunications links between them.

It is already clear that larger computers will begin to be used extensively to coordinate and link the activities of smaller ones. For example, in every plant there will be a production-line minicomputer to supervise the microprocessors on individual machine tools. There will eventually be a "kitchen computer" to regulate the activities of the various individual appliances (e.g., to minimize electricity consumption). There will be a minicomputer in the car to help the driver control the various interacting subsystems (fuel, electrical, exhaust, steering, brakes), each with its own internal microprocessor. And so on. Ultimately, still larger computers will regulate and coordinate at the next level of organization, for example, the factory. When this happens in factories, true "automation" will occur, as humans are no longer needed to actually operate most kinds of machines.

A very few such automatic factories have been built in the world so far. But the technology is being developed rapidly. Many more automatic factories will be constructed in the 1980s and 1990s. By the year 2000 hierarchies of linked computers should also achieve the level of sophistication needed to operate most kinds of vehicles, including cars and aircraft, although human drivers would probably be retained in most cases as a backup. Here the big unsolved technological problem is to develop a suitable, high channel capacity information terminal onboard the vehicle. This is a very difficult technical challenge (except when the vehicle is confined to a track), and I think it is likely to delay the introduction of central computerized control of large fleets of cars and aircraft for at least another decade or two, to 2010 or 2020. By then most new cars at least are likely to be electric, which would suggest an integrated power supply and communication system to provide both energy and guidance to the vehicle.

The foregoing comments substantially overlap the subject matter of Chapter 7, but they are included here as an indication of some of the sources of potentially massive new demand for information transfer systems.

So far I have mainly discussed the United States, where the level of demand for information transfer is the highest and the relevant technology most advanced. Japan is only slightly behind at this point, however, and may soon take the lead in some applications. Europe is a little further back, mainly due to an inadequate telephone network, but is closing the gap. The USSR, at present, is far behind. Its computer industry has hitherto focused more on scientific and industrial than commercial applications. It will probably adopt automated factories more or less at the same time as the advanced Western nations, but it is not yet ready for the autotransaction concept. Nor will the USSR follow close behind the West in the wide use of high-quality video links in place of conventional telephone voice links.

In the less developed world, the developments just described will be limited to a few major cities (e.g., Rio, Sao Paulo) and to high-level government or military purposes. In China, for instance, I would expect that by the end of the century all significant towns and collective farms will be interconnected by high-quality wide-band voice links, most likely using coaxial cables. This may well be justified on national security grounds. However, individual telephones are not likely to be available to most ordinary Chinese for another decade or two, that is, until 2010 or so. Individual TV receivers will probably come sooner, initially as incentives to especially valuable workers or managerial personnel.

HEALTH SERVICES

It is relatively easy to find quantifiable measures of the consumption of some kinds of health-related activities. Certainly the numbers of practicing doctors, hospitals, hospital beds, and various kinds of procedures carried out (e.g., vaccinations or tonsillectomies) are frequently recorded, as is total expenditure on health services. However, none of these comes close to being an adequate measure of the service actually rendered to consumers.

Life expectancy at birth might commend itself as an alternate measure of output, but on a moment's reflection it is clear that this is largely a measure of the efficacy of *public* health services only, that is, control of communicable diseases and infant mortality. Apart from childbirth and pediatric care, health services in advanced countries are consumed by the chronically ill, those with degenerative diseases, and the elderly. A disproportionate amount is spent on sustaining or extending the lives of a small fraction of the population, with little real benefit accruing to the rest of society as a result. The benefits of health care are thus so unevenly distributed that I cannot find a reasonable aggregate measure of the output of health services that could be quantified.

It may be illuminating to review briefly the nature of the health care services as they are now provided in the United States. What exactly does the system *per se* achieve — in contrast to the permanent benefits accrued by the historical advance of medical scientific knowledge? I think it can be argued that the biggest single step in health care was the discovery of the role of microbes and the use of germicides and other means of ensuring sterility (e.g., of open wounds). These techniques were later adapted to the treatment of water supplies, with dramatic impact on the spread of diseases like typhoid, dysentery, and diphtheria. The next most important breakthrough was the discovery of effective anesthetics in the early nineteenth century. This permitted the development of surgery for practical purposes. Vaccination as a means of controlling communicable virus diseases was the third great leap forward, beginning with Louis Pasteur. Alexander Fleming's discovery of penicillin, followed by scores of other antibiotics, was probably the last really big breakthrough, although the synthesis of steroid hormones might also qualify for this encomium.

With those basic tools, plus some diagnostic devices and pharmaceuticals of lesser importance, I cannot escape the feeling that *most* of the results of present-day health care — despite its elaborateness — could be achieved by a modest "nineteenth century" type of health delivery service consisting of well-trained general practitioners assisted by medical technicians or orderlies. These would be supplemented by a reasonable number of trained midwives and district nurses, plus a small number of hospitals for surgery and other emergencies.

The major beneficiaries of the immense medical superstructure of specialists, hospitals, space-age diagnostic equipment, clinical laboratories, and so on that has been added on top of the "nineteenth century" system are those employed in it. The other beneficiaries include survivors of open heart or other radical surgery, large skin grafts, organ transplants, radiation or chemotherapy for cancer, kidney malfunction, serious accidents with multiple fractures and other complications, or rare tropical diseases.

Where, then, does all the money that is being spent on health care go? Although direct confirming evidence would require a rather deep study, the answer seems to be, essentially, to support hospitals and doctors associated therewith. Literally enormous sums of money are expended routinely on custody, monitoring, testing, and palliative "therapy" for degenerative diseases and functional disorders that are seldom actually cured and for which the nineteenth century type of health care system based on GPs and very few hospitals would provide *almost* equally effective relief.*

*This statement will seem outrageous to some. For the skeptics, I offer the following more detailed justification. The degenerative illnesses and functional disorders I chiefly refer to are

Heart disease	Arthritis
Hypertension	Emphysema
Cancer	Asthma
Diabetes	Schizophrenia

Consider them one by one:

- The only effective "treatment" for heart disease is diet, exercise, rest and a sensible lifestyle. Hospitals are of no help except during the initial stages of a coronary and in the few cases in which radical surgery is helpful.

- The basic treatment for hypertension is strictly dietary. There is no cure for a stroke, although rest and physical therapy may enable a patient to recover from temporary paralysis.

- Early cancers, once detected, can often be removed by simple surgery of a type not requiring elaborate facilities. There are no good treatments for advanced cancer. Radical surgery, chemotherapy, and radiological therapy all require extensive hospitalization, but taken together these procedures essentially add a few months up to a year or two to life expectancy — at staggering cost. The detection of most cancers is mostly a matter of superficial examination, X-rays, and public awareness of the symptoms. (However, confirmation involves laboratory tests in most cases.) For most cancer patients, hospitals are essentially custodial.

- The only treatment for acute arthritis is palliative: another hormone (cortisone) which can be administered by a nurse. For chronic mild cases aspirin is the treatment. Hospitals are essentially useless.

- There is no known cure or treatment for emphysema. It can, at best, be arrested if the causal agents — usually cigarette smoke — are removed.

- There is no medical cure for asthma. Some cases can be cured by psychiatric treatment, change of diet, a change of climate, or removal of persistent irritants such as air pollution in the environment. Acute asthma attacks can be abated by the use of self-administered drugs that are essentially based on a hormone (adrenalin).

- There is no reliable medical cure for schizophrenia, although a few patients have improved with the use of shock treatment or drugs. Hospitals would be necessary for this. Most treatment is essentially the use of tranquilizers, however. Hospital care is basically custodial.

Why, then, are hospitals so popular? The answer seems to be compounded of two factors. First, United States hospitalization insurance — especially under the so-called Blue Cross system — offers more complete coverage to many patients if the treatment is pro-

A forecast of the future demand for health care necessarily involves some kind of forecast of the nature of the future health care system. It would be simple, at first glance, to assume a continuation of recent trends. But such an assumption leads to a radical and implausible conclusion. Based on the astonishing rate of growth of expenditure in this area in the United States in the past two decades, it would appear that a very large fraction of the whole United States GDP would be devoted to health care—doctors, hospitals, paramedical personnel, clinical laboratories, medical instruments, pharmaceuticals, and so on—by the year 2000 (never mind the year 2025!). I find it difficult to believe that this will actually occur.

In the recent past, the "demand" for health care has been virtually controlled by the medical profession, rather than by the recipients of the care. A person with a serious medical problem is almost never told what the costs of this or that "option" are likely to be in relation to the likely benefits (or risks).

More commonly—if the patient has financial resources such as insurance—the doctor simply prescribes a course of treatment which "maximizes" the prognosis (and also the doctor's income), even if the difference between a "best" and an "average" outcome are slight. This is most evident in the case of near-terminal illnesses, where costly, humiliating, and painful treatments may be recommended even if they add only a few days or weeks to an extremely short life expectancy.* (The reader may recall—with a shudder—the last grisly days of President Harry Truman or Generalissimo Francisco Franco.)

The question at issue, then, is whether the medical profession will be permitted by the public to continue to manipulate demand for its services in this self-serving fashion. Frankly, I do not think that it will. A crisis is approaching inexorably, as the costs of health care continue to rise without comparably increased benefits to the taxpayers and citizens. Household budgets are tight and relatively inelastic,

---

vided in a hospital than if it is provided in a doctor's office or at home. Second, and more insidious, it is much more convenient and profitable for the doctors to have all their nonambulatory patients collected together in a single place with a "controlled" environment than to leave them in their homes. The controlled environment of hospitals is not necessarily a beneficial one, by the way. A great many patients have actually become ill (i.e., from staphylococcus infection) as a direct consequence of remaining in a hospital. In fact, infections picked up as a result of hospitalization are so common that their treatment and prevention is becoming a recognized distinct branch of medicine.

*Indeed, the medical profession currently regards it as "unethical" to proceed otherwise. It is curious that medical ethics stop short of providing these costly frills to patients whose savings are exhausted.

and people are—for good reason—becoming skeptical of the propaganda of the medical fraternity.

The health care delivery systems of most other advanced industrial countries seem to operate better for the majority of citizens than that of the United States. (Let us not confuse the operation of the health care system with the quality of personnel and facilities available. As regards the latter, the United States is probably supreme, precisely because the system has been so excessively "gold plated".) The gap between promise and performance cannot be ignored indefinitely.

Does the future lie with a National Health scheme, as in the United Kingdom? Its faults are almost the opposite of those of the United States system. National Health delivers uniformly low-grade care to all, at a low price to the patient, but at a staggering overhead cost to society. National Health rewards quantity far above quality in treatment. The incentives are such that the best doctors work outside the system or leave the United Kingdom altogether. As British doctors depart for North America or South Africa, they are being replaced by doctors from Pakistan or Nigeria (who are needed more in their own countries). It seems unlikely, therefore, that the United Kingdom system will be closely imitated by the United States.

I cannot foresee when or how the ultimate crisis will occur, except that it will probably be within a decade. In any case, a more detailed analysis of institutional or legislative possibilities seems beyond the scope of this chapter.

EDUCATION AND CULTURAL SERVICES

One of the critical ways in which the State of Man in 1978 is notably different from a century earlier is in terms of educational achievement, as measured especially in terms of people's ability to read and write (literacy). Since literacy is normally achieved by attendance at a school, the latter is a possible surrogate measure. Obviously some children pass through several years of schooling without learning much of anything, but on the average it is probably safe to assume that the more years of schooling a child receives, the higher his or her educational attainments will be.

As noted earlier, it is also not unreasonable to assume that the quality and productivity of a labor force is closely related to the amount of education it has received. A literate worker is capable of reading written instructions, for example, whereas an illiterate one must be taught verbally or by example. (The ability to read signs and labels is a great advantage, for example, in operating a motor vehicle or a machine tool. It is probably an absolute prerequisite for repairing either one.)

Table 5.11 summarizes the available data on school enrollment as it relates to the eight standard exemplary countries.[17] The historical figures are not very exact due to unreliable statistics, variations in definition of "enrollment," and other differences. The EEC figures are approximate weighted averages of the countries represented, all of which are quite closely grouped except for Italy, which lags about twenty-five points behind the other EEC countries and drags down the average slightly. Discrepancies between the countries in Europe in 1850 were much larger. At that time Italy had a 15% school enrollment rate compared to 40% for the United Kingdom and France and 52% for Germany. In the nineteenth century Canada also lagged considerably behind the United States.

Table 5.11   School Enrollment
(percentage of Population in age group 5–19)

Country	1860	1900	1960	2000	2025
EEC	35	55	70	85	90
North America	45	65	85	88	90
Japan	10[a]	33	73	90	95
USSR	5[a]	17	57	80	90
Brazil	Neg.	10[a]	37	50	70
India	Neg.	5[a]	29	40	60
Nigeria	Neg.	Neg.	26	34	50
China (PRC)	Neg.	Neg.	46	80	95

[a]Estimated by rough backward extension of available historical data.

The correspondence between school enrollment and economic development in the nineteenth century is too obvious to require much comment. Most of the sharp rise in school enrollment in the less developed world has occurred since World War II, and it is clear that economic development has not followed in proportion. One reason for the lack of correspondence is that there is a lag of fifteen years or so between first attendance in school and entry into the labor force. Thus an increase in school enrollment between 1950 and 1960 would only begin to significantly affect the quality of the labor force after 1965. A second and more cogent reason is that education is not the only factor needed to raise productivity, and it must be provided in conjunction with the other factors, particularly capital investment. In India, for instance, education is most urgently needed in the agricultural sector, which is precisely where it is most difficult to deliver. In the urban areas of India there is, if anything, a surplus of highly educated people. In China, on the other hand, the large agricultural communes—which are, in effect, towns with populations as high as 100,000—are able to provide schooling of the type and in the place where it can do the most good.

My tentative projections for the years 2000 and 2025 are consistent with recent historical trends, but the period since World War II is not necessarily a representative one. A more specific rationale is needed. I think the developed countries will keep most of their children in school through age 19 (or later) for several important reasons. First, they will not be needed (or employable) as workers, especially without advanced training. Second, the output of the economy will be increasingly service oriented, which means many more people will be involved in *producing* information-intensive, educational, and cultural services, and, quite important, many more years of education will be required to develop the understanding and appreciation required to induce people to *consume* such service.

The last statement deserves a bit of amplification. A functionally illiterate population cannot support a significant number of journalists, poets, novelists, or publishers. The more time people spend looking at TV, movies, or live theatrical performances, the more playwrights, screenwriters, photographers, directors, dancers, actors, and producers are needed. Similarly, the more people know about music the more they will listen to it, and the more songwriters, singers, guitarists, orchestras, and conductors—not to mention recording engineers, and hi-fi salesmen—will be needed. One could also mention sports events—spectator or participatory—tourism, recreational activities, and so on. In each case, learning of some kind is involved.

The point I am making is that education is a prerequisite not only for the high level skills of the creators, performers, and technicians involved on the production side; *it is also an essential element in developing a public demand for such services.*

It is perfectly true and relevant, by the way, that each of these services also serves an educational function and tends to increase the demand for itself. The more people go to concerts, as a rule, the more they learn about music and the more concerts they want to attend. The more they travel, the more they learn about the world and the more countries they want to visit. The same generally applies to theater, ballet, sports events, recreational activities, and art museums. The only limitations on aggregate demand for such services are discretionary income and discretionary time.

Unquestionably, as these activities become more and more important from an overall economic standpoint, there will be an increasing need to provide elementary training for them in the schools. The large amount of time now devoted to games and sports in United States schools and colleges is somewhat unconvincingly defended in terms of developing "character" and "sportsmanship" and improving physical conditioning. These are valid arguments (to some extent), but a more realistic one is that *a future audience for professional sports events is being created.** Similarly, participation in school plays or orchestras helps create appreciative audiences for professional actors and musicians. In the same way, driving classes help create potential consumers for automobiles. In coming decades schools are quite likely to increase their coverage of other types of entertainment, recreational, and cultural activities, such as fishing, sailing, skiing, chess, contract bridge, or Yoga.

For that matter, one may well ask, why shouldn't the schools also teach poker, blackjack, computer games, how to "trip" on pot (marijuana), or advanced sexual practices? Clearly, gambling, the use of consciousness-expanding drugs, and sex are already major—although illicit—industries, which are likely to grow in the future. The activities just noted are also relatively harmless in themselves. (Although taking pot cannot be certified absolutely safe, neither is smoking tobacco or driving a car.) It is clear that the American public of 1978 is not ready to accept any of these as legitimate or appropriate subjects for teaching in school. However, it must be recognized that students do learn much in school that is not officially taught (sex and smoking, for instance). It is also worth noting that mores can change quite rapidly. The new attitudes towards sex are clearly much more liberal than those of any earlier generation. Sex education, of sorts, is already a part of the curriculum of many schools, and it would not be altogether surprising if the contents of such courses were expanded in scope. Indeed, I would be surprised if they were not expanded.

I have commented so far only on the *quantity* of education, as measured by school enrollment. What about its *quality?* A major controversy erupted in 1975 when it was publicly revealed that Standard Achievement Test (SAT) scores for United States' college entrants have been declining since 1963 and that the rate of decline has recently begun to accelerate. Many groups have undertaken to investi-

---

*Lest anyone think that education is not required to watch an American football game, I suggest the experiment of watching a game of English cricket. For anyone not familiar with its subtle nuances, the game is a colossal bore. But afficionados attend matches lasting two or three days!

gate this ominous phenomenon and to determine whether it is real and, if so, what are the causes. Numerous hypotheses have been put forward, of which four appear particularly plausible to me.*

First, the beginning of the decline in SAT scores coincides roughly with the first generation of school graduates who had television as a principal source of entertainment and a competitor for their attention throughout their school careers. It has been verified that each child in the United States, on the average, spends several *hours* watching TV each day. There is no reasonable doubt in my mind that this competing demand for time and attention must have reduced the time available for study and reading—and that the results would show up on SAT scores.

Second, the last decade has been a period of rising militancy and unionization of public school teachers. Again, there can be no reasonable doubt—notwithstanding teachers' propaganda to the contrary—that the organization of effective teachers' unions has tended to reduce the average level of performance by the teachers (just as unions have reduced productivity in almost every other trade or craft where they have successfully penetrated).

Third, the 1960s was a decade of widespread experimentation in curricula and teaching methods. At the beginning of the decade many influential voices in the education world were raised against such long-established practices as learning by rote, objective tests, letter grades, and undue emphasis on academic skills (the so-called "three Rs"). It was widely alleged that these practices tended to discriminate against culturally deprived minorities and "slow starters," to suppress creativity, and to enforce conformity. As a consequence, in many schools objective standards were deemphasized or eliminated, and many new "creative" courses were added to the curriculum at the expense of "skill" courses, such as grammar and mathematics. During this period, too, traditional mathematics was largely supplanted by "new math," which was supposed to teach the subject in a more fundamental axiomatic way than traditional arithmetic, algebra, geometry, and trigonometry. Unfortunately, in retrospect it appears that many of these reforms were either unwise to begin with or they were badly carried out. In any case, the United States educational establishment currently appears to be backtracking on most of the innovations of the 1960s.

Fourth, the 1960s was also a decade of significant change in the nature of family relationships in the United States (as well as other

*This is not to suggest that other factors may not be equally or more important. I do not know.

countries). In brief, families were decreasing in size, many more mothers took jobs, and the divorce rate rose sharply. These social factors must have had a negative impact on the structure of many families and on the motivation of some children. With school also becoming less structured, and traditional forms of discipline being relaxed, it is likely that many children simply drifted through school, rather than applying themselves.

These four factors are particularly significant in, but not exclusive to, the United States. For instance, TV is much less widespread in Europe, where most broadcasting is government controlled. It is virtually nonexistent in the USSR, India, Nigeria, and China. Educational quality has not deteriorated notably in any of these countries.

A new factor has appeared on the world scene in the past two years which may also conceivably have an adverse future impact on education, namely, the hand-held minicalculator. It is too early to predict the broader consequences, but it seems highly likely that many students will not develop as much facility with ordinary arithmetic as they previously did. This development may *not* actually be a great impediment to learning technical subjects if the availability of cheap little calculators removes one of the major sources of fear which now induces people to avoid studying subjects involving the use of basic arithmetical skills. There is simply no basis for a guess either way.

Considering all the factors, however, I believe that educational quality in public schools is likely to continue to decline at a modest rate for a time in the United States and probably to a lesser degree in the other advanced countries, but, quantitatively speaking, the decline should not be too severe. There are some compensating factors to be considered. These include minor but cumulatively significant improvements in curricula and teaching methods, better texts, better equipment, and higher standards of education for teachers. In addition, slower economic growth will mean fiercer competition for jobs, which will probably increase the motivation of some students and teachers relative to the situation in the past decade. Furthermore, if public schools become too ineffective, citizens put pressure on school boards to upgrade standards. People also vote with dollars. Students from affluent families transfer to private schools. This creates political pressures that can be a stimulus to the public school teachers and administrators.* In the longer run, the compensating factors already mentioned, plus other innovations (such as the explicit use of cable TV as a supple-

---

*In response, teacher's unions can be expected to (1) try to organize private school teachers and (2) support legislation to make it harder for private schools to stay in business. In this, however, they are not likely to be very effective.

mentary part of the education system), could bring about a reversal of the current downtrend.

I have discussed mainly the advanced industrialized countries. In the less developed world the social motivation for raising the general educational level is somewhat different. First, elementary education is an essential prerequisite for "traditional" peasants or primitive tribesmen to learn better methods of producing things—from planting and harvesting to operating machines. Second, education is an essential prerequisite to effective family planning. Only with the help of schools can people be taught the importance of limiting family size and the available methods of doing so. These reasons do not necessarily justify children remaining in school for as many years as in the postindustrial societies, however. Although it is vitally important to increase the *breadth* of primary educational coverage, the *depth* is not critical, at least for the immediate future. Thus the long-term forecasts of school attendance for the less developed countries remains lower than in the developed ones. Although the quality of education is not proportional to the quantity of schooling, I expect the advanced countries to continue to dominate in quality as well as quantity over the next half century.

REFERENCES

1. *United Nations, FAO Production Yearbook, 1970.*
2. U.S. Department of Agriculture, *Agricultural Statistics, 1961.*
3. United Nations FAO, Indicative World Plan for Agricultural Development.
4. United Nations, *Statistical Yearbook,* 1975.
5. See, for instance, World Road Federation, *Transport Statistics* (Geneva, 1975) for comparative data on cars in service, fuel consumption, and fuel prices.
6. J. Darmstader, J. Dunkerley, and J. Alterman, *How Industrial Societies Use Energy: A Comparative Analysis,* Resources for the Future, Inc., Johns Hopkins University Press, Baltimore, 1977.
7. J. Darmstader *Conserving Energy: Prospects and Opportunities in the New York Region.* Johns Hopkins University Press, Baltimore, 1975.
8. D. Gazis, "The Role of Computers in Materials Procurement and Conservation," in A. G. Chynoweth and W.M. Walsh, Jr., eds., *Materials Technology —1976,* AIP Conference Proceedings No. 32, New York, 1977.
9. *Materials Needs and the Environment, Today and Tomorrow,* Final Report of the National Commission on Materials Policy, June, 1973.
10. Gordon Fair et al., *Water and Waste Water Engineering,* Wiley, New York, 1966.

11. Committee on Economic Studies, *Projection 85: World Steel Demand,* International Iron and Steel Institute, Brussels, Belgium, March 1972.

12. J. Fisher, L. Fischman, and H. Landsberg, *Resources in America's Future,* Resources For the Future, Inc., Johns Hopkins University Press, Baltimore, 1960.

13. U.S. Bureau of Mines, *Mineral Facts and Problems,* 1975.

14. L. L. Fischman and H. H. Landsberg, "Adequacy of Non-Fuel Minerals and Forest Resources," (R. Ridker ed.), for the Commission on Pop. Growth and America's Future, U.S. Government Printing Office, Washington, D.C., 1972.

15. "A Study of Trends in the Demand for Information Transfer," Stanford Research Institute, Menlo Park, Ca., February, 1970.

16. Dennis Gabor, *Innovations—Scientific, Technological and Social,* Oxford Press, 1970.

17. UNESCO data compiled by Hudson Institute, 1970.

CHAPTER SIX

MEASURES OF MAN —TECHNOLOGY (I)

INTRODUCTION

Technology is too often regarded as an uncaused cause capable of inducing all sorts of good or bad changes in other spheres. In this chapter I want to focus on the question of technology as *deus ex machina*. In brief: To what degree should technology be feared as a threat or relied on as a panacea? As a means of penetrating the superficial truth of appearances, the method of confrontation between pro and con arguments often commends itself. I use it very explicitly in this chapter, letting advocates of several different views speak for their respective positions in their own words. My personal conclusions are clearly labeled as such.

THE "SCIENTIFIC REVOLUTION":— IS TECHNOLOGY THE PANACEA?

A few short years ago in the early 1960s scientists and engineers were riding very high indeed, both in their own and public estimation. Their euphoria was marred, it is true, by their exaggerated guilt feelings (concerning the discovery and military applications of nuclear fission) and by the noncomprehending disdain of some social philosophers and nonscientific intellectuals. Such was the intellectual atmosphere in the late 1950s and early 1960s when C. P. Snow—a former physicist turned novelist—delivered his celebrated Godkin Lectures at Harvard University, entitled "The Two Cultures and the Scientific Revolution."[1] Snow's principal message was conveyed in the second half of his title; namely, that twentieth century organized science and technology constitute a kind of secret weapon capable of creating a revolutionary change in man's economic and social prospects. He was critical of the failure of the nonscientists—who did and still do control the world's affairs—for failing to appreciate the potential of science as a creator of wealth. Letting Snow speak for himself:

> For the task of totally industrializing a major country, as in China today, *it only takes will to train enough scientists and engineers and technicians.** Will, and quite a small number of years. There is no evidence that any country or race is better than any other in scientific teachability: there is a good deal of evidence that all are much alike. Tradition and technical background seem to count for surprisingly little. . . .

> There is no getting away from it. *It is technically possible to carry out the scientific revolution in India, Africa, Southeast Asia, Latin America, the Middle East, within fifty years.* There is no excuse for Western man not to know this. . . .

Snow states further that "technology is rather easy." He heaps scorn on people, such as " old Asia and Africa hands," who believe that other factors might be involved—such as the attitudes and values discussed in Chapter 2. To Snow these views were "technologically illiterate."

Perhaps it is unfair to pick on C. P. Snow, but life is unfair. In this assessment he was surely sadly mistaken. Life in the next century would indeed be easier for all of us if technology truly had the power and potency Snow and Mumford (and many others) have attributed to it from their very different perspectives. The "industrialization of China" was Snow's great example. To be sure, China has certainly progressed significantly from its miserable state of anarchy and apathy after World War II. But it has not, by any stretch of the imagination, succeeded in industrializing itself in a mere twenty years, as Snow claimed. Communist China today is perhaps 50% more prosperous per capita than noncommunist India, but in 1975 its GDP per capita was less than one-tenth that of the USSR and only one-fortieth of the United States level, despite incredible sacrifices and the severe rigors of a harsh totalitarian regime.

The case of India is perhaps even more relevant, and, of course, we know much more about what happens in that country. After the United States and the USSR, India had the third largest pool of trained scientists and engineers in the world in 1975 (not larger than Europe as a whole, but more than any single European country or Japan.) It has an advanced nuclear research program, including home-

*My italics.

234 Measures of Man—Technology (I)

made nuclear weapons. It produces its own jet aircraft.* It has built and orbited a scientific research satellite (launched on a Soviet rocket). However, all this scientific talent and investment has proved inadequate—indeed, irrelevant—to the mundane tasks of persuading people to agree to limit family size, to reforest the barren eroding hills, or to rid the country of the plague of half-starved cattle that consume every unprotected leaf of grass or tree sapling.

Snow's excessive optimism stems from the traditional scientists' disdain for practical engineering and elementary economics. He simply assumed that because the Chinese were able to produce a hydrogen bomb, China must be "industrialized." He was not alone in this misconception, but it is really inexcusable; no ordinary nonscientific observer would have been fooled for a moment. It is a splendid example of what Herman Kahn calls "trained incapacity."

Another writer who neither doubts the existence of a "scientific revolution" or that it is essentially a good thing is Robert Prehoda, author of *Designing the Future*. One or two samples will suffice to convey the flavor.[2]

Science may be on the threshold of greatly extending your life span to 100 years, 200 years, or more. If all causes of biological aging are discovered and cured, man eventually may have an indefinite life span extending for many centuries.

Some of you may bypass the immediate future, finding a door through and via human hibernation. Total suspended animation at very low temperatures is a more distant possibility. The winter of your lives may be spent as cold slumber, allowing the sleeper to awaken in a golden age of perpetual spring; then this metamorphosis may include further biological transformations, curing past ills and restoring the vigor and the appearance of youth. . . .

Many will be disturbed because longer life implies learning new skills and working in an unfamiliar environment. But you will not learn as you did in the past. Computer-controlled teaching machines will quickly and painlessly impart new knowledge. Chemicals will improve your memory retention, actually raising your basic intelligence.

Your children may start school when they are only 3 years old. . . .

Injections of hormones given to women during pregnancy may cause their children to be born with slightly larger and much more

*But so do Sweden and Israel.

efficient brains. Genius may be imparted through the hypodermic syringe, rather than the rare gene. . . .

All forms of communication will be improved. Color television will be coupled to the telephone, allowing instantaneous conferences between several individuals thousands of miles apart. Drawings and written material will be reproduced instantaneously by electrostatic attachments to the videophone consoles. Letters and important documents will be sent electronically, speeding up the tempo and the efficiency of commerce and the exchange of all other human information.

We will soon begin to communicate directly with machines, advanced computers which will answer questions with words and images on a cathode-ray tube. These supercomputers will evolve into "intelligence-amplifiers," allowing a man-machine partnership that will greatly increase the productivity of people in every profession. The intelligence-amplifier will take the drudgery out of science. Data from a world library will be summarized quickly. The machine will inform scientists which specialist to contact for information that may not yet be recorded.

In the 21st century, we may even decipher the complex programing sequence of our brains. Such knowledge might allow a man-computer symbiosis—a direct electronic hookup of the computer into the living brain. This would permit a vast amount of information to be transferred instantly from machine-to-man, and man-to-machine. The man-computer symbiosis is an exotic possibility, but basic research is under way which may show us how it can be accomplished.

Evidently Prehoda—omega forecaster par excellence—perceives no inherent danger in these stupendous developments. He urges us to embrace the future and its wonders as ardently as children in Disneyland. We are assured that, through applied science, all earthly problems can be solved.

Still another rampant optimist of the 1960 era is the Nobel prize-winning geneticist Hermann Muller, who wrote enthusiastically of the potential for using artificial insemination to breed a superior race of humans. The method he describes involves the use of[3]

sperm and ovum . . . having been taken from persons representing the masculine ideal and the feminine ideal, respectively. The reproductive cells in question will preferably be those of persons dead long enough that a true perspective of their lives and works, free of all personal prejudice, can be seen. Such cells will be taken from cell banks and will represent the most precious genetic heritage of humanity . . . The method will have to be applied universally. If the people of a single country were to apply it intelligently and intensively . . . they would quickly attain a practically invincible level of superiority. . . .

For a scientist of German extraction to publish such notions with serious intent so soon after Hitler's ghastly attempt to create a "master race" boggles the mind. Still, the words speak for themselves. Muller simply does not concern himself with the means whereby his utopian ends might be achieved. This is another vintage example of omega thinking.

Dennis Gabor is another savant who argues, persuasively, that the scientific revolution is a reality.[4] Gabor goes beyond speculative forecasting for its own sake and discusses where and how the cumulative processes of technological change can (and should) be regarded as truly revolutionary.

It would be highly misleading to consider the change from the individual inventor in his garret, who took his little knowledge out of old textbooks of physics and chemistry, to the modern superteam, with all grades of men, from the mathematician to the mechanic, the compression of time from a generation or two to a few years, merely as a change in quantity. A change on such a scale means a *change in quality,** a change in the intrinsic nature, aims, and consequences of the process of invention and innovation. . . .

There are three factors in this: the change of the *time-scale,*† the change in the *magnitude,*† and the *social consequences*† of the innovation, and the change in scope or aim. . . .

These three revolutionary factors—time compression, qualitative changes in magnitudes, and social impact—are important and worth further examination. The compression in time scale of technological change is the most widely accepted of three factors noted by Gabor. This has been elaborated by the guru of *Future Shock*, Alvin Toffler;[5]

Whether we examine distances traveled, altitudes reached, minerals mined, or explosive power harnassed, the same accelerative trend is obvious. The pattern, here and in a thousand other statistical series, is absolutely clear and unmistakable. Millennia or centuries go by, and then, in our own times, a sudden bursting of the limits, a fantastic spurt forward. . . .

*Italics by Gabor.
†Italics by Ayres.

Thus it is not merely true, as frequently noted, that 90 percent of all the scientists who ever lived are now alive, and that new scientific discoveries are being made every day. These new ideas are put to work much more quickly than ever before. The time between original concept and practical use has been radically reduced. This is a striking difference between ourselves and our ancestors. Appollonius of Perga discovered conic sections, but it was 2000 years before they were applied to engineering problems. It was literally centuries between the time Paracelsus discovered that ether could be used as an anaesthetic and the time it began to be used for that purpose.

Even in more recent times the same pattern of delay was present. In 1836 a machine was invented that mowed, threshed, tied straw into sheaves and poured grain into sacks. This machine was itself based on technology at least twenty years old at the time. Yet it was not until a century later, in the 1930s, that such a combine was actually marketed. The first English patent for a typewriter was issued in 1714. But a century and a half elapsed before typewriters became commercially available. A full century passed between the time Nicholas Appert discovered how to can food and the time canning became important in the food industry.

Today such delays between idea and application are almost unthinkable.

There is no arguing with the self-evident fact that science has been more closely wedded to technology in our own times than in the nineteenth century or earlier. Not infrequently, long delays in the past occurred because some necessary component of an invention was missing. Toffler cited the cases of the aeroplane, which was invented on paper long before 1900, but could not lift itself off the ground without an internal combustion engine. The earliest gas turbines failed for lack of an adequate compressor and high-temperature alloys. Holography—invented by Dennis Gabor in 1948—became practical only with the advent of the laser in 1963. Thus the apparent time compression phenomenon is probably due in large part to the larger common base of scientific knowledge, materials, and components that are now available. As Toffler says, "Technology feeds on itself." This is true, up to a point.

The time span for reduction of scientific theory to an engineering prototype has indeed decreased. On the other side of the coin, evidence is accumulating that the time required for taking an engineering prototype from laboratory into production and its establishment in the marketplace has lengthened considerably in the past century. For instance, the first successful demonstration of the telephone by Alexander Graham Bell in 1876 was followed in a matter of months by the organization of a company to exploit it and by the rapid growth of that company into an industrial giant. The first private telephone exchange in Hartford was already in operation by mid 1877, and the first commercial telephone system (in New Haven) began service January 1878. There were 70,000 phones in service in the United States by 1880, a mere thirty months later.

Or consider the early days of the automobile industry. Ford Motor Company was founded in June 1903 with 125 employees. Its first cars were on the market in October (and the company made a profit from that moment on). Today it is generally admitted that a major change in body style requires three years, and an engine redesign would require five years. To substitute a completely new *type* of engine such as a gas turbine or Stirling cycle engine would take closer to fifteen years from laboratory to mass production.

To bring nuclear power from the first working uranium reactor under the grandstand of the University of Chicago football stadium to the first commercial (but heavily subsidized) generation of electricity for commercial purposes required close to twenty years. Nuclear power was not generally recognized as a cost-competitive option for the electric utility industry until the late 1960s, nearly thirty years after the first "pile"—notwithstanding very heavy government research and development spending throughout this period. Nuclear power is by no means out of the woods, even yet.

Is the overall compression in time scales since the nineteenth century really so great? I think the answer is no. At any rate, if there was a compression, it has probably stopped.

The second revolutionary factor cited by Gabor as evidence of a true scientific revolution was that *magnitudes* have changed radically and *qualitatively*: "Gunpowder, the Maxim gun, even the bomber plane with high explosive could kill only a fraction of a population; the hydrogen bomb and perhaps also some devilish viruses bred in biological warfare establishments, could kill as good as the whole of it . . ." Or he might equally well have pointed out that Gutenberg's first press runs could reach only a few hundred people, whereas the modern electronic media saturates the waking hours of men and women all over the world with news and entertainment disseminated from a very few sources. In McLuhan's words[6]: "Ours is a brand-new world of allatoneness. 'Time' has ceased. 'Space' has vanished. We now live in a Global Village. . . ."

I find this argument more persuasive—indeed, very persuasive. Again, there are separable aspects of magnitude, which qualify the conclusions. One can distinguish magnitude increments that arise strictly from the potency of the technology *per se* from magnitude increments that arise from the fact that the world was once a collection of more or less independent communities or cells and is now (or is in the process of becoming) a highly interconnected and interdependent "organism" in which a change in any part affects and is affected by every other part. The existence of giant transnational marketing organizations guarantees that Nestle instant coffee, Kentucky Fried Chicken, Coca Cola, Arrid deodorant, Gillette razor blades, and Pepsodent toothpaste are available in virtually every corner of the globe. Nor is the large-scale marketing organization dependent in any way on the technologies involved in manufacturing these products, which are relatively simple.

The nuclear fission bomb certainly represented a very large increment in explosive power. At Hiroshima in 1945 a single plane could do as much damage (more or less) as several hundred or a thousand conventional bombers over Tokyo or Dresden a year earlier. This is a horrifying increase in killing power, without doubt. But to say that the hydrogen bomb can kill "as good as the whole" of a population is confusing and misleading. It is also possible to kill a whole population with hydrogen cyanide, as the Nazis did to the Jews of Europe, or even with fire and sword, as the Romans killed the Carthaginians. On the other hand, for all its power, a single hydrogen bomb will *not* destroy a modern nation larger than Monaco. Indeed, even several thousand of them would be inadequate to destroy either the whole population or the military power of a large country such as the United States or the USSR.*

Or consider the question of scale in disseminating the printed word. Remember that the printing press burst on a world in which copies of books were made individually, by hand. With the invention of movable type, this limitation on reproduction quantity was completely removed. From Gutenberg to Hearst was a matter less of engineering sophistication than of large-scale organization. The importance of technological innovations in the spread of "wireless" communications has been greater. Marconi's early radio apparatus was rather a primi-

*This point was quite carefully documented by Herman Kahn in his well-known book *On Thermonuclear War* (1959).[7] It has been confirmed by numerous strategic studies in many countries since then. Many laymen have believed (or wanted to believe) that a large-scale nuclear war would be equivalent to Armageddon—the end of the world. Nevil Shute's novel *On the Beach* exemplifies this popular but technically unjustified view. Of course, to point out that nuclear war would not necessarily be the end of the world is not an argument in favor of it.

tive device, useful in special circumstances (mainly to communicate with ships at sea) but hardly earth shaking. It has taken several generations of successive scientific breakthroughs to harness the wayward electron to the degree necessary to permit modern television broadcasting. Even so, it takes more than television broadcasters and receivers to create a "Global Village." Clearly, this phemonenon—to the extent that it is real—is again due rather to global organization of the technology than to globe-girdling technological capabilities *per se*.

Gabor's third revolutionary factor in support of the idea of a qualitative change in the nature of science and technology is that the *scope* of inventions has changed. However, the change he is talking about is really a transition from the revolutionary to the evolutionary. Gabor believes, and I concur, that most of the "archetypal" inventions—like the airplane and the telephone—are now behind us in the past. Most hardware invention in the future will probably be improvements of existing technologies. Many of the capabilities that appear in science fiction novels—"hyperspace drives," anti-gravity, radiation shields, time-reversal, arrest of the aging process (immortality), exchange of bodies, and so on—are probably nothing more than dreams.

Major new discoveries in physics are certainly possible, but with each passing decade they become more expensive and less relevant to the needs of our society. It has been said that microbiology and biochemistry are the new frontiers of science. This seems very plausible. But the difficulty of formulating sharp alternative hypotheses and devising unambiguous experimental tests by which the number of possibilities can be reduced has been seriously underestimated. Biological research is, in many ways, far more difficult than physics research because of the tremendous complexity of the systems being studied and the large number of variables that must be controlled. Spectacular results in applied biology cannot be expected in a few years, as we are beginning to realize as we see the slow progress of the much touted "war" against cancer.

Gabor asserts that "the most important and urgent problems of the technology of today are no longer the satisfactions of primary needs or archetypal wishes, but the reparation of the evils and damages wrought by the technology of yesterday. . . . We cannot stop inventing because we are riding a tiger." This sobering thought has been amplified by Herman Kahn and his colleagues:[8]

Civilization has made a commitment to science, technology and industry—one that might indeed be called a "Faustian bargain." For, as we remember, Faust (in Goethe's play) bought magical (that is, secular) knowledge and powers that he was compelled to use and then perforce he had to proceed to the next experience, the next project — or be forever damned. And that illustration provides a good analogy with some formulations (not ours) of the current predicament. We do agree that mankind is involved in a process that probably cannot voluntarily and safely be stopped, or prematurely slowed down significantly, even if there are good arguments for doing so. But we maintain that on balance and with some exceptions (for example, nuclear proliferation), the arguments are heavily against deliberate policies to halt or slow down the basic long-term technological trend, even if it could be done with safety. Indeed, we would prefer to accelerate some aspects of this trend, while being prudent and generally watchful in order to prevent or reduce the impact of the baneful possibilities.

TECHNOLOGICAL THREATS — IS TECHNOLOGY OUT OF CONTROL?

Up to this point, I have focused mainly on the positive role of technology. That it has been changing rapidly cannot be questioned. That the changes are pervasive is equally indisputable. That it offers the key to solving all man's social and economic problems can and will be disputed. Many people believe, deeply, that technology is basically dehumanizing, threatening, immoral, or even absolutely evil. Surprisingly, most scientists and technological optimists have never really encountered this view of the world, still less come to grips with it. Scientists talk mainly to each other; so do novelists, humanists, and social philosophers. This is the "two culture" gap which C. P. Snow so perceptively discussed in his famous Godkin Lectures. How, then, does the non-scientific culture view the accomplishments of science? And why?

A good enough starting point is at the very beginning of the Scientific Revolution. It was Galileo Galilei (1564–1642) who confirmed by observation Copernicus' conjecture that the Earth rotates around the Sun, rather than vice versa, as established doctrine held. Galileo naturally wished to publicize his discoveries and the scientific method of analysis which he used to arrive at them. He wrote a book, sought the official *imprimatur* of the Church for publication, and apparently received a qualified approval. Galileo had, after all, once been on personal friendly terms with the Pope. He was sure in his own mind that there was no irreconcilable conflict between science and faith. He was mistaken. On deeper consideration of the matter, the Vatican authorities decided that Galileo was a dangerous heretic. He was turned over to the Office of the Inquisition for trial, notwithstanding his age, fame, and personal piety. He finally escaped with his life, but only by recanting his opinions and permanently giving up all his scientific activities.

Rationalists like Galileo typically see no reason why scientific truth based on observation and deduction should not be perfectly compatible with the revealed truth of religion. Many individual scientists, to this day, are perfectly well able to combine faith in God and His teachings with an active, skeptical pursuit of scientific knowledge. The ecclesiastic hierarchy, however, saw the conflict clearly and foresaw its adverse impact on the power of the Church.

Indeed, the fundamental hostility of organized religion to science – and its stepchild, technology – has never abated much, although it has gone "underground" in the last century. One of the last open challenges to science arose from the discoveries of Darwin. After Galileo, the Roman Catholic Church ungraciously learned to coexist with scientific discoveries in the realm of astronomy, physics, and chemistry. Darwin's theory of evolution aimed a shaft directly at the Biblical interpretation of the Creation itself.

It has been explicit Christian doctrine that man is descended from Adam and Eve, who were created by God in his own image. In the eighteenth and nineteenth centuries scientific evidence began to accumulate suggesting that the Earth was much more than a few thousand years old, that it had gone through several "ages," and that it had once been inhabited by creatures – such as the dinosaurs – that no longer exist. All this was very hard to reconcile with the Bible. Darwin went even further and showed that existing species have evolved from ancestral forms (often extinct). It was natural to conclude that man also has biological ancestors in common with the present-day anthropoid apes.

Darwin was immediately supported by some reputable scientists such as Thomas Huxley, although he was attacked by others who were joined by a covey of influential Victorian churchmen including the eminent Bishop Wilberforce. The controversy raged for decades in England – and elsewhere – with the Darwinists very gradually gaining the upper hand as teachers; they increasingly began teaching the scientific, rather than the Biblical, version of biology in schools. One famous episode in this long battle occurred in 1925 when one John T. Scopes, a biology teacher, was tried and convicted (in the "great monkey trial") of teaching Darwin's theory of evolution in Tennessee public schools, contrary to the law of the State. The matter was finally resolved in 1970 when the last law prohibiting the teaching of evolution in public schools was ruled unconstitutional by the United States Supreme Court.

Many scientists appear to believe that this type of issue has been settled permanently in their favor, and that religion, in future, will be forever satisfied to leave objective truth to secular science, restricting itself to the subjective (or spiritual) domain. I do not think this is a realistic view. Fundamentalist religion is currently experiencing something of a revival, and I think its natural hostility to secular science is also on the increase, although it is too early to predict just where and how this will manifest itself.*

Whereas organized religion is fundamentally antiscience (although most Jews and many liberal Protestants have arrived at a formula for coexistence), many humanists are simply antitechnology because they do not like the external attributes of a secular, technologically oriented society. Lewis Mumford, for instance, complains that instead of offering[9]

a wide margin of choice at every point, with greater respect for human needs and preferences, (technology) instead, limits its offerings to those for which a mass demand can be created. . . . In short, megatechnics, so far from having solved the problem of scarcity, has only presented it in a new form. Results: a serious deficiency of life, directly stemming from *unusable and unendurable abundance.*

According to Victor Ferkiss, another leading social philosopher,[10]

Unbridled technological dominion over nature is also incompatible with the preservation of human cultural and biological identity; the uncontrolled development of the technology of genetic engineering and the technologies which kill off other species and put an end to the last vestiges of wilderness can destroy the identity and purpose of the human race. As one sociologist put it, we must change the Marxian formulation and recognize that "the devaluation of the human world increases in direct relation to the decrease in value of the world of things."

Or, consider the words of Gordon Rattray Taylor, a popularizer of science,[11]

The industrialized nations have now managed, broadly speaking, to provide their citizens with food, shelter and clothing. As a result, those citizens are becoming more aware of other and subtler needs. But a society geared to the production of goods is precisely a

*For instance, the "Right to Life" (anti-abortion) movement in the United States is certainly drawing much of its strength from the Fundamentalist constituency.

244 Measures of Man—Technology (I)

society which is poorly adapted to satisfying psychological needs. The very processes by which we manufacture goods so effectively actually *reduce* psychological satisfaction.

In another place Taylor adds:

> In addition, as I have already related, social change disrupts the social machine in ways which make the attainment of goals more difficult.
>
> Technology is the ultimate author of these ills and especially too much technology too fast. We need a breathing-space to find ways of handling the technological novelties we have, before we are presented with any more. Violence, insecurity, suicide, loneliness, these, and more, are the price we pay for living in a mass society, and for the "wider horizons" and the "freedom" which it provides. When we come to understand the conception, we may begin to wonder whether the price is too high.
>
> To sum up then, to restore community and cure anomia, we should have to *reduce the rate of social and technological change, reduce the mobility of the individual and perhaps even discourage communications;* we should have to limit the inflow of new members to communities and we should have to preserve the "uniques" in each cultural sub-unit, accepting cultural diversity rather than standardization and a common culture as a social aim.

One of the harshest indictments of science and scientists comes from the French sociologist, Jacques Ellul.[12] Here is a sample:

> When we reflect on the serious although relatively minor problems that were provoked by the industrial exploitation of coal and electricity, when we reflect that after a hundred and fifty years these problems are still not satisfactorily resolved, we are entitled to ask whether there are any solutions to the infinitely more complex "hows" of the next forty years. In fact, there is one and only one means to their solution, a world-wide totalitarian dictatorship which will allow technique its full scope and at the same time resolve the concomitant difficulties. It is not difficult to understand why the scientists and worshippers of technology prefer not to dwell on this solution, but rather to leap nimbly across the dull and uninteresting intermediary period and land squarely in the golden age. We might indeed ask ourselves if we will succeed in getting through the transition period at all, or if the blood and the suffering required are not perhaps too high a price to pay for this golden age.

If we take a hard, unromantic look at the golden age itself, we are struck with the incredible naïveté of these scientists. They say, for example, that they will be able to shape and reshape at will human emotions, desires, and thoughts and arrive scientifically at certain efficient, pre-established collective decisions. They claim they will be in a position to develop certain collective desires, to constitute certain homogeneous social units out of aggregates of individuals, to forbid men to raise their children, and even to persuade them to renounce having any. At the same time, they speak of assuring the triumph of freedom and of the necessity of avoiding dictatorship at any price. They seem incapable of grasping the contradiction involved, or of understanding that what they are proposing, even after the intermediary period, is in fact the harshest of dictatorships. In comparison, Hitler's was a trifling affair. That it is to be a dictatorship of test tubes rather than of hobnailed boots will not make it any less a dictatorship.

Novelists have been among the deepest pessimists. Aldous Huxley contributed an unforgettable nightmare in *Brave New World,* written in the 1930s, which propounded the thesis that technology is the natural ally of totalitarianism. Arthur Koestler in *Darkness at Noon* (1940) argued also that every new invention is a threat to popular democracy because it adds to the unfathomable complexity of the human environment and makes it that much more incomprehensible to the ordinary citizen. George Orwell's famous book, *1984* (written in 1948), reiterated Huxley's theme, with an earlier timetable and some additional horrors, notably, nuclear weapons, perpetual surveillance ("Big Brother is watching you"), and total manipulation of all channels of information to produce total propaganda in the interests of the State ("Peace is War," etc.).

I have no pat answer to the social critics who blame technology for virtually everything they dislike about contemporary society. Some of them use rhetoric that suggests a wish that the world were other than it really is. Most, however, are sensible enough to realize that the future can only be reached from the past via the present — with all its problems. As Gabor says, "we are riding a tiger." The best that can be hoped for is to learn to tame the beast (if that is what it is) to a greater degree. The degree to which this is possible is discussed later in this chapter and in the next.

In addition to the generalized indictments of technology, there are many more pointed criticisms. Some of the threats have been named and described in reasonably precise detail. Let me now review some of them.

The generalized threat of total surveillance described so vividly by Orwell in *1984* has been described very precisely in nonfictional terms. Harry Kalven, Jr. wrote the following for *Daedelus* in 1967,[13]

It is becoming increasingly possible to invade privacy without trespassing — that is, to invade it by remote control. Many can now photograph from afar, conceal microphones in tiepins, observe by closed-circuit television, tap telephone lines, pick up conversations in another room by the use of electronic devices, and determine the content of mail without opening it. There is no reason to doubt that the technology will continue to improve — probably at a geometric rate — and that by the year 2000 it will be possible to place a man under constant surveillance without his ever becoming aware of it. . . .

The intrusions will not be limited to government measures in aid of law enforcement or national security. The technology may become a commonplace in the hands of private parties — employers interested in the off-hours activities of employees, competitors interested in one another's integrity and trade secrets, estranged spouses interested in perfecting grounds for divorce, insurance companies interested in claimants they have paid, and the idly curious who are just interested. Thus, by 2000, man's technical inventiveness may, in terms of privacy, have turned the whole community into the equivalent of an army barracks. . . .

A third kind of threat turns on the prospect of a great improvement in the process of record-keeping and of collating information about individuals. When, as is likely, this technological efficiency is coupled with the government's ever increasing demands for special information, the prospect is one of a formidable dossier on every member of the society. . . .

Another threat is the problem of being constantly exposed to communications one does not wish to receive, whether by billboard, sound truck, mass protest, second-class mail, unsolicited telephone calls, Jehovah's Witnesses, or more imaginative and less familiar methods. The threat here is that the society may, from one quarter or another, largely become a captive audience.

I need add nothing to Kalven's remarks. The technological capabilities he describes are real and constantly increasing. It seems likely that various legislative means of controlling abuses will be attempted. It also seems likely that legislation will be ineffective on the whole. On the other hand, in the tradition of a Faustian bargain, there may well be effective *technological* countermeasures — such as shields. scramblers, bug detectors, and the like — that will continue to make it possible for citizens to enjoy some degree of privacy and security, at a price.

Regarding the extreme form of electronic surveillance postulated by Orwell — two-directional TV screens used as permanent surveillance devices, permitting Big Brother to tune in, at will, on the activities of any citizen — this seems technically infeasible. In the preceding chapter, I touched on the prospects of linking computers and substituting high-quality holographic video projection-transmission devices for telephones within the next half century (not by 1984, however). There is a superficial similarity to the scheme postulated by Orwell. But it is hard to see how such a system could be designed to override the desires of sophisticated individual users or, if it could be, imposed on them.

The very complexity of the telephone system — and its high degree of automation make it vulnerable to unauthorized use and manipulation by criminals or mere pranksters. It is an established fact that people who understand the operation of the system and take a little trouble can make long-distance calls and have them billed to nonexistent numbers or to innocent people. This is already a nontrivial financial loss to the telephone industry. One well-known movie star was recently accused of defrauding the Bell System of $5,000 in unpaid long-distance telephone calls by such means. Since many computers are already operated by phone and activated by coded account numbers, it is also possible for those sufficiently skilled and unscrupulous to enter false data or to extract confidential data from computerized files.

Thus the real problem may well turn out to be the growth of computer crime rather than the accumulation of dossiers about citizens. Indeed, if the many anonymous dossiers that now exist (and are available to official agencies or individuals with the "right" credentials) were coordinated and combined into a single one, *to which the citizen has access and rights of challenge,* the present chaotic situation might even be improved on balance.

The possible breakdown of large, interdependent systems — such as the electric power network — is another oft-cited threat. The famous Northeast blackout of November 9, 1965, which covered the 80,000 square mile area of the Ontario (Canada), New York, and New England electric power pool, serving 30 million persons, seems to be an example of this kind of problem. One author who has examined a number of such scenarios is Roberto Vacca, in *The Coming Dark Age.*[14] Vacca's thesis is that progressive deterioration, heralding future catastrophic breakdown, is already underway in systems for electric power generation and distribution, transportation, water supply, sewage disposal, communication, and information processing. It is asserted that as much as half of the population of the most advanced countries may be at risk.

Frankly, I am not impressed by the credibility of this particular doomsday forecast. For instance, although 800,000 people in New York were trapped in subways when the blackout occurred, there was only one known fatality directly attributable to the incident—a man who fell down an elevator shaft. Also, it is worth noting that in the years since 1965 the electric power industry has introduced a number of new protective measures to prevent a recurrence. Curiously, a recurrence did occur in New York City in 1977, although a smaller number of people were affected.

The major potential cause of system breakdowns, in my view, would arise from strikes or sabotage, not from mechanical failures. For instance, New York City has experienced devastating subway and sanitation strikes in the past few years. Japan had its first national railway strike in 1975. France, Italy, and Canada have recently had lengthy postal strikes which eliminated mail service for up to several months. The United Kingdom suffered a paralyzing midwinter strike of the electric power utility workers a few years ago. Firemen struck for several months in the United Kingdom in the winter of 1977.

None of these shutdowns has led to major fatalities, except perhaps a few accidents. More significantly, perhaps, even extended strikes by unionized telephone workers in the United States have not seriously affected current telephone service, due to the high degree of automation. (The major impact of a strike is on maintenance and new installations. Supervisory employees handle day-to-day operations at such times.) For the same reason, there have been few, if any, strike-related shutdowns of electric power, water, or sewage service in the United States.

At present, transportation and sanitation (i.e., refuse collection) are the most vulnerable to strikes, because of their high labor content. Precisely for this reason, unions representing these workers have fought bitterly against automation. Yet automation of rail rapid transit is state of the art today, and its introduction to major cities like New York that depend on transit for their survival cannot be indefinitely delayed. Like the dock workers, printers, typesetters, and elevator operators, subway motormen are obsolete and will soon be totally anachronistic. By the year 2000 this job classification should have disappeared in the advanced countries. (Bus and truck drivers cannot be eliminated as quickly because the substitute technology is not yet available, but they too may be out of the picture except in a backup capacity by 2025.)

The foregoing comments lead directly to another technological threat that has received great attention in the past. This is the prospect that large numbers of workers will be displaced and made unemployable by automation. Ever since machines first began replacing human hands in specific job categories, the workers' initial response has been to blame the machines and resist their introduction to "preserve" jobs. Extremists, on occasion, have actually attempted to destroy the machines that have replaced them. For instance, in 1811 a group of British weavers, unemployed as a result of the introduction of the mechanical loom, demanded that

> The House of Commons passes an Act to put down all Machinery hurtful to Commonality, and repeal that to hang Frame Breakers ... We petition no more – that won't do – fighting must. Signed by the General of the Army of Redressers, Ned Ludd, Clerk.

Since then, those who threaten or practice violence to delay (or reverse) technological progress have been named Luddites, but the original Luddites were naive in their straightforward attempt to stop the wheels of technological progress. The Luddites were imprisoned or hanged for their pains. Labor unions have since become more sophisticated, more indirect, and more effective in their continuing guerilla war against changing technology. Now they insist on slowing down the pace of work or limiting its span to preserve "health" and doubling the required manpower for operating a machine or vehicle for the sake of "public safety." Teachers insist on smaller classes and shorter hours "for the benefit of the students." And so on.

Despite the resistance, machines have continued to replace human hands, to the point at which physical strength is now virtually irrelevant as an attribute for a worker. Today's industrial workers largely control machines; the machines actually do most of the work. However, a new and major development is on the way: the combination of sensitive electronic sensory devices, plus computers, is beginning to make the human machine operator obsolete. Of course, this process does not occur overnight. The least skilled, most repetitious functions, such as operating elevators, were replaced first. Some of the most difficult functions, such as piloting aircraft, or driving motor vehicles in traffic, cannot be entrusted entirely to electronic controls for many decades to come – if ever.

To say that jobs will not be replaced particularly quickly is not to deny that a threat to some kinds of jobs may exist. Certainly, it is perceived as such by organized workers. The issue is widely misunderstood, however. From an economic standpoint, job replacement is part and parcel of increasing productivity – which is an absolute prerequisite to economic growth. If jobs are preserved, whether needed or not, economic growth will stop. This is probably the greater threat, but it cannot be laid on the doorstep of technology. (Rather, it may be the ultimate weapon of the anti-technology movement.)

The most horrifying extrapolations of technology out of control can be found in the field of biology. A number of possible biological nightmares have achieved literary notoriety, beginning with Mary Shelley's *Frankenstein.* Several such themes have been explored by successive generations of novelists. One of the most persistent is the notion of external manipulation or control of the human mind through the use of esoteric techniques such as hypnosis, truth drugs, brainwashing, and so on. Aldous Huxley explored this theme in *Brave New World.* The well-known thriller, *The Manchurian Candidate,* is a modern example of the same basic scenario.

A variant is the idea – fearlessly advocated by Prehoda, it may be recalled – of linking the human brain directly to an electronic computer, using biofeedback, and perhaps controlling the body also (see *Terminal Man* by Michael Crichton). An even more shocking and bizarre notion – eliminating the body entirely, and preserving the brain in an artificial environment – has been explored by Lawrence Sanders in *The Tomorrow File.* These chilling books are worth mentioning because they are based on relatively modest and very plausible extrapolations of existing technology.

Recent progress in surgical transplants of vital organs, such as kidneys and hearts, has resulted in some interesting literary speculations regarding long-range implications. For example, it is reasonable to expect that if biologists overcome the problem of rejection, which currently limits the applicability of transplants, there would be a soaring demand for replacement organs. If the demand for spare human parts exceeds the supply, why not increase the supply by vastly extending the grounds for capital punishment? Is it unreasonable to expect a black market to be supplied by criminals or "organleggers"? (See Larry Niven's science fiction detective stories, published as *The Long Arm of Gil Hamilton.*)

Government control over human procreation through eugenics has been possible in principle for a long time. It was – in a crude form – part of the program of Nazi Germany. Some reputable scientists, such as Nobel prize-winning geneticist Hermann Muller, have been frank advocates. (Muller was quoted earlier in this chapter.)

Of course, Muller's naïveté makes him an easy target. Social critic Jacques Ellul's scathing commentary is summed up by an obvious question:

How shall we force humanity to refrain from begetting children naturally? When (scientists) speak of preserving the seed of outstanding men, whom, pray, do they mean to be the judges? It is clear alas, that they propose to sit in judgment themselves. It is hardly likely that they will deem a Rimbaud or a Nietzsche worthy of posterity.

Evidently Muller's utopia is very nearly indistinguishable from Aldous Huxley's *Brave New World* and George Orwell's *1984*. Luckily this nightmare seems unlikely to come to pass in the foreseeable future.

Doubtless in the next fifty years, man's ability to manipulate his gene stock will increase. One favorable prospect, amidst many possibilities for abuse, is progress in conquering degenerative disease. Fortunately for society, this will probably *not* greatly increase human life expectancy. Even if virtually all cancers are controlled—which would be optimistic indeed—most people are still likely to die before the age of 80 or 85. The process of aging, as such, has not yet been slowed down in the slightest by any medical or public health procedure yet adopted.*

Norman MacRae of *The Economist* has suggested that geriatric research will in fact produce a serious problem by keeping older people alive[15] (and consuming, but not producing) longer. My own belief is that people will not live much longer, but that some small added life expectancy will be achieved at outrageously high cost to the rest of society. Either way, meddling with the aging process is a significant threat to economic growth and political stability.

Before passing on to other issues, it might be as well to point out that modern civilization also has some lethal social diseases which could tend to counteract any tendency toward longer life expectancy. Automobile accidents are a case in point. There are 50,000 fatalities per year in the United States from this cause alone, concentrated heavily among younger adult males. Pollution of the environment certainly increases death rates in certain areas at certain times. Smoking cigarettes is probably more deadly than anybody has yet admitted. The mortality from lung cancer in the United States was 2 per 100,000 in 1900. By 1934 it had risen to 5.3. The sequence thereafter is appalling. It was 9.4 in 1940, 19.5 in 1950, 36 in 1960, and 63 per 100,000 in 1969. Most of the recent increase is from women, who took up smoking after

---

*Recent headline publicity about research advances in this area are quite misleading, since the studies done to date on aging (of animals) tend to suggest that the main available "levers" for affecting the aging process are diet—mainly in infancy and adolescence—and metabolic rate. These are not easily changed for adult humans. Drugs do not appear very promising to date.

World War II as a part of the "liberation" of women. Based on the present mortality rate, 500,000 people now alive will die from lung cancer. Based on other evidence, many of those who could stop smoking already have. If so, most of those still smoking cannot quit, although 80–90% say they would like to do so.

The potential of mind-altering drugs, also foreseen by Aldous Huxley, has already been partially realized in practice. Although his hypothetical "soma" — offering instant escape without bad side-effects of any kind — does not (yet) exist, various tranquilizers and consciousness-expanding drugs like marijuana, mescaline, psilobycin, and LSD are now in widespread use, both licit and otherwise. The use of such drugs by young people, without adequate safeguards or preparation constitutes a significant danger to health and perhaps to social order. The long-term impact of such drugs on motivation, as expressed in the work ethic, is difficult to assess. But the range of possibilities seems to be from neutral (no impact) to rather negative.

Another biochemical threat of completely unknown magnitude (at present) arises from the widespread and indiscriminate use of coloring agents, flavoring agents, preservatives, antioxidants, growth hormones, and other chemicals — not including pollutants — in the environment. The thalidomide disaster of a few years ago is one example. Recently, several chemicals have come under strong suspicion, including "red dye #2," a popular coloring agent, saccharine, the major artificial sweetener, and sodium nitrite, a commonly used preservative for ham, bacon, and sausage. Effects possibly attributable in some cases to the ubiquitous chemical additives range from cancers to ulcers, allergies, "hyperactivity" in children, and premature degeneration of liver, kidney, or other organs. None of this is proven, but the growing body of indirect evidence is disturbing, to say the least.

Perhaps the most serious biological threat facing the world is the creation (or importation from space) of new and potentially dangerous forms of life. This theme, too, has been expanded in literature — for example, *The Andromeda Strain* by Michael Crichton. The potential for doing this kind of thing has been vastly increased in the past few years as a result of the (accidental) discovery of an unsuspected class of bacterial enzymes capable of breaking and splicing genetic materials — DNA — to form new genetic combinations with specifically desired properties. A large number of experiments using the "recombinant" DNA technique have been proposed to the National Institutes of Health, the major United States funding agency for biomedical research. Displaying a surprising degree of scientific restraint, concerned scientists observed a two-year voluntary moratorium on experiments until NIH had an opportunity to formulate a set of safety guidelines in mid-1976. The restraints since published are not as restrictive as some had hoped they might be, although they do, for instance, prohibit DNA experiments with cancer cells and dangerous pathogens.

Nicholas Wade, a reporter for *Science Magazine*, writing for *The Washington Post* (1976), summarized the dangers eloquently:

First, the new forms of life can be expected to escape quite regularly, particularly from the less meticulous laboratories. Even the most careful scientists become exposed to the organisms they work with, and the best available containment methods used in the Army's biological warfare laboratories at Fort Dietrich, for example, did not prevent 423 cases of infection and 3 deaths over a period of 25 years.

Escape is made more certain by the circumstance that the bacterium to be used as host for many of the new life forms is Escherichia coli, a common inhabitant of the human gut and nose. If a human pandemic or some other "worst case" accident occurs, future historians will never be able to understand why of all the bacterial species at our disposal, we made the most reckless possible choice. They will not credit the reason, that the human gut bacterium was simply the most convenient organism available at the time.

Most of the new life forms will perish outside the laboratory, unless deliberately designed to survive. But some may find suitable niches, in our crop plants, in our domestic animals, or in human populations. At worst, the consequences could range from mass infection to the virtual eradication of a species.

People worry about the proliferation of nuclear technology to more than a handful of countries. The "recombinant DNA" technique puts what will one day become an almost equally awesome technology into the hands of every biological researcher with access to a modern laboratory. Sooner or later, one of these researchers may try to put the technology to evil use. But more to be feared is the do-gooder who attempts to take some unilateral action for what he conceives to be the benefit of mankind.

Many of the projected experiments involve the insertion of genes from higher cells into bacteria. Bacterial and the higher forms of life interact intensely with each other as organisms. But they ceased to interact on the genetic level hundreds of millions of years ago. To transgress the genetic apartheid that nature appears to have set up is to risk endowing bacterial with the genetic control signals of higher cells — a kind of molecular-level betrayal of state secrets that could equip bacteria with a whole new weaponry for attacking plants and animals.

The technique and its immediate uses now being discussed are only the prelude to a more fundamental intervention in the process of evolution. Do we really want to assume responsibility for life on this planet?

I have not yet mentioned the category of technological threats that is most widely perceived. This is summed up in the phrase "the atomic age" and comprises anything from a limited accidental escape of radioactive materials from a nuclear power plant to an exchange of hydrogen bombs. This set of topics has been given far more public exposure than the others I have mentioned. I do not ignore these problems, although I defer discussion of them to the next chapter. I think enough has already been said here to establish that technology is *not* the panacea that many scientists hoped a few short years ago, and there are many specific dangers associated with the exploitation of particular technologies.

SYNTHESIS – THE DYNAMICS OF TECHNOLOGICAL CHANGE

In Chapter 1 of this book I interjected a quotation from Mumford exemplifying a widely held view of technology, namely, that technology is a "self-generating" force, progressing by its own internal dynamics. The same view was expressed more simply by Alvin Toffler's phrase "Technology feeds on itself."

One further illustration will suffice to make it clear that the view of technology as an uncaused cause is not rare. Here are the words of E. F. Schumacher from his eloquent book, *Small Is Beautiful — Economics As If People Mattered:*

... Strange to say, technology, although of course the product of man, tends to develop by its own laws and principles, and these are very different from those of human nature or living nature in general. Nature always, so to speak, knows where and when to stop ... Not so with technology. ... Technology recognizes no self-limiting principles — in terms, for instance, of size, speed, or violence. It therefore does not possess the virtues of being self-balancing, self-adjusting and self-cleansing. In the subtle system of nature, technology, and in particular the super-technology of the modern world, acts like a foreign body, and there are now numerous signs of rejection.

Even if one grants the validity of many of the antitechnology arguments cited in the preceding section, it must be recognized that it is a central issue whether technology is a self-generating entity like a cancer — "uncaused" so to speak — or whether it is really a response to other deeper, but understandable forces. I personally think that much of the virulence of the antitechnologists would abate if it could be shown clearly that technology is not an independent "agent," subject only to its own "laws," but simply the basic operating mechanism of any social system that is organized to create and accumulate wealth. The central role of innovation in this process has been stressed by Joseph Schumpeter, one of the towering figures of twentieth century economics:[16]

> The fundamental impulse that sets the capitalist engine in motion comes from the new consumer's goods, the new methods of production or transportation, the new markets, the new forms of industrial organization that capitalist enterprise creates.

Technology is nothing more than science applied to the solution of practical problems. Technological change is, indeed, an absolute prerequisite to innovation in the productive sphere. Thus the socialist countries, which have shut off the private entrepreneurial channel for linking technical possibilities to social needs, have had to put even more emphasis than the capitalist democracies on the scientific research which creates new technological possibilities in the first place. This emphasis is clearly evident in the hierarchical importance of science in the USSR — and the favored treatment of leading Soviet scientists.

Clearly, the voices against technology do not come from either the right or the left of the conventional capitalist/socialist political spectrum. These are more or less equally dedicated to economic growth. Rather, the objections are largely to growth (and wealth) itself. Schumacher, at least, is consistent: His approach has been labeled "Buddhist" economics. He regards relative poverty in the material sense as inevitable (if not morally uplifting) and focuses on the achievement of other social values.

The Roman Catholic Church, too, officially scorns the accumulation of material wealth and advocates that those nations which have wealth should share with those that do not.* Yet its position is logically inconsistent, insofar as it also advocates large families, rejects most measures for population control, and explicitly puts the onus for providing for the needs of the worlds growing population on "technology."* Once again one sees that technology has been elevated—by nontechnologists—into the status of *deus ex machina*.

This reflects a deep misunderstanding of the nature of technology. The error is simple but subtle: it is the notion that technological changes are direct *consequences* of inventions and scientific discoveries, and that the latter occur automatically, without social causation, guidance, or control. This also implies a curious and interesting economic hypothesis that, as far as science and technology are concerned, *supply creates demand.*

It is clear that this hypothesis is open to both theoretical analysis and empirical test. In recent decades a number of academic studies have been conducted to elucidate the true supply-demand relationship, starting in the 1930s with the work of University of Chicago sociologist, S. Colum Gilfillan.[17] More recently, economists such as Jacob Schmookler[18] and Edwin Mansfield[19] have added much to our understanding of the subject. There have also been many case studies of specific inventions and industries. An unmistakable consensus conclusion has emerged from this research, and it is quite contrary to the idea of self-generation. In the vast majority of cases that have been studied, *invention was only called forth by clearly articulated need.*[+] Contrary to popular impression, most inventors do not work in basements or garages, stimulated only by their own fancies. If society is not ready and waiting for their output, they do not invent. They find other occupations which are demanded by society.

An example due to Gilfillan makes the point clearer. In the mid-1930s navigational devices for aircraft were clearly inadequate and better means were needed, in particular for flying and landing in bad weather. Gilfillan, writing before the discovery of radar, pointed out the seriousness of the problem and listed a number of *possible* inventions for dealing with it. He did not attempt to guess which of them would provide the best answer. (He would almost certainly have guessed wrong, in any case.) He did, however, accurately predict that many researchers would be working on the problem and that several candidate solutions would probably be forthcoming in the near future. He was absolutely correct. These inventions did not come earlier, be-

---

*See Chapter 2 and the discussion of Pope Paul VI's Encyclical *Populorum Progressio*.

[+]Exceptions do crop up occasionally, as I have already noted. The laser seems to be the latest major one, but its importance does not make it less exceptional.

cause there was no market for them until commercial aviation had reached a certain minimal level of development.

It is important to emphasize that the "need" noted by Gilfillan was a purely functional one: better means of speed and position determination and identification for aircraft. The need was not specified in terms of particular technological solutions. That is, of course, the province of the inventor. If the forecaster could describe the solution exactly, he would automatically *be* the inventor.

Another example may be helpful. Consider the invention of the telephone, which I have referred to several times. What was the stimulus for its invention? There is no doubt on this point, since it has been extensively documented. The telephone was invented by Alexander Graham Bell in the course of a development project that was initially directed toward the improvement of the telegraph — a very successful product in a rapidly growing market. The capacity of the telegraph system was severely limited, however, by the fact that only one message at a time could be sent over a given circuit (i.e., wire). As the demand for telegraphic communications grew, it rapidly began to outstrip the physical capacity of the telegraph system. Bell's job was to learn how to send more information without proportionally increasing the number of wires in use, that is, to use the existing wires more efficiently.

In response to this need, Bell's first major contribution was the harmonic telegraph. This was the first application of the principle of multiplexing which is now widely utilized in radio and telecommunications. In effect, by using different wave bands Bell learned how to send a number of telegraph messages simultaneously, thus multiplying the capacity of the telegraph network many-fold. At this point serendipity played a part: in the process of developing this significant invention, Bell realized that the principles of the harmonic telegraph opened up the possibility of sending messages that utilized the full acoustic frequency spectrum, namely, the human voice. Thus the telephone was conceived.

It could be argued that no "need" for voice-band communications had been precisely articulated up to that time. Bell's financial backers tried to discourage him at first, but the functional demand for telecommunications was growing very rapidly indeed, and the marketplace was more than ready to accept the invention, as already noted.

The fact that inventions are stimulated by perceived needs is one plausible explanation for the otherwise mysterious phenomenon of *simultaneous invention* or discovery of the same thing at almost the same time in different places. Gilfillan has listed many such cases.

The telephone was one of the most spectacular illustrations of this phenomenon. Although Bell is known to history as "the" inventor, a telephone was also developed virtually simultaneously and independently by another inventor, Elisha Gray. Bell and Gray became aware of each others' work and both applied for patents almost simultaneously. There was a protracted and fairly bitter personal and legal dispute over priority and ownership. The coincidence of simultaneous independent invention often seems so incredible (as in this case) that each inventor tends to suspect theft or piracy on the part of the other. Yet in retrospect it appears that there was nothing of the kind. Rather, both men were responding at the same time to the same functional need for better means of communication by wire.

The same dynamics are applicable in other cases. To take an obvious one: given the existence of an intense political-military rivalry — as the United States was competing with the USSR in the Sputnik era — there will be a perceived need for newer and more potent weapon systems. The atmosphere becomes favorable to the acceptance of major innovations. Industry will respond by supporting the necessary scientific and engineering work, as the United States aerospace industry did in the late 1950s and early 1960s.

If or when, for some reason, the rivalry becomes less intense, or one of the parties loses faith in itself or in its military establishment and ceases to compete in this area, the pace of technological innovation will also slow down on both sides. This, too, has happened. A few years ago (circa 1970) the United States aerospace industry began releasing large numbers of unneeded engineers. Many could not find other engineering jobs. Some became teachers, some went back to school to study law or medicine, some went to work for government agencies, some even drove taxis or became salesmen. There has been no rapid push forward in other areas of technology because science and technology were being cut back, across the board, by the Nixon administration.

A new area of societal interest in technological progress seems to be developing now; the production and conversion of energy. If the interest is sufficiently real to create a situation in which new technology is accepted and applied, the rate of technological progress is likely to accelerate in this field. Invention will be rewarded, and inventors will be attracted. If the need has been exaggerated, the technological response will be correspondingly muted.

In short, technology is not some kind of mysterious self-energized engine that drives society where society does not want to go. Quite the contrary, technologists merely produce what society wants and will put to use. Like educators, doctors, lawyers, or insurance agents, scientists and engineers provide a professional service. If there is an increased societal demand for the services in question, the supply of such services will grow as new people are attracted into the field, and conversely.

Earlier I discussed "parasitism" in the economy and pointed out that a number of economic activities do have — in varying degrees — the ability to ensure the demand for their own products or services. The legal profession is an outstanding example: by means of its control over the process of making and enforcing laws, it has artificially expanded the need for legal services to the point at which most lawyers are engaged (very profitably) in solving problems created by the law itself.

Some other activities are also parasitic in the same sense of being able to create demand for themselves, although generally to a lesser extent than lawyers. Advertising is an example: In addition to selling the products of other industries, it also sells itself. Medicine is another case in point. Doctors have successfully exploited their unique position as consultants on sickness and health to generate an artificial demand for therapies and hospital services that are of dubious real value to patients or their families. Education is still another case: Educators are in an ideal position to indoctrinate future taxpayers on the value of education.

It is fair to ask whether scientists and technologists also have any similar built-in ability to guarantee future demand for their own services. Insofar as they are also educators, they may have some influence on the future taxpayers and voters. Insofar as they contribute to the economic well-being of an industry, they are likely to be pampered to some degree. But do inventions *per se* create a need for more new inventions? In some narrow areas the answer might be yes. For instance, the invention of a more accurate guided missile might stimulate the development of more sensitive radar missile detection systems. In general, more powerful offensive weapons seem to encourage better defensive systems, and vice versa.

However, outside of the military area, the need for new technology seems to be determined by the state of the *industry* — whether it is growing or declining, for instance — and independent of the state of the technology as such. That is, technology does not seem to create a direct need for more technology through the marketplace.

Technological progress does generate new needs indirectly, however, through so-called external effects. Thus the invention of the internal combustion engine led to the development of the worldwide motor vehicle industry. The use of cars in vast numbers has generated problems of congestion, pollution, noise, and excessive dependence on liquid hydrocarbon fuels that will eventually be exhausted. Indeed, most of the technological "threats" discussed in the preceding section can probably be controlled only by utilizing other countervailing technologies. This is the sense in which technological progress can perhaps be said to be irreversibly "addictive." Or, in Dennis Gabor's words: "We are riding a tiger." The next chapter considers the prospects in a more systematic sector-by-sector fashion.

REFERENCES

1. C. P. Snow, *The Two Cultures and the Scientific Revolution*, Godkin Lectures, Harvard University Press, Cambridge, 1960.
2. Robert W. Prehoda, *Designing the Future: The Role of Technological Forecasting*, Chilton Book Company, Philadelphia, 1967, p. 5.
3. Quoted by Jacques Ellul, *The Technological Society*, Vintage Books, New York, 1967 (translated from French).
4. Dennis Gabor, *Innovations*, Oxford University Press, New York, 1970.
5. Alvin Toffler, *Future Shock*, Bantam Books, Random House, Inc. New York, 1970.
6. Marshall McLuhan and Quentin Fiore, *The Medium is the Message*, New York, Bantam Books. 1967.
7. H. Kahn, *On Thermonuclear War*, Princeton University Press, Princeton, N.J., 1959.
8   H. Kahn et al., *The Next 200 Years*, William Morrow and Company, New York, 1976, P. 164.
9. Lewis Mumford, *The Myth of the Machine: The Pentagon of Power*, Harcourt, Brace, Jovanovich, Inc., New York, 1964, p. 337.
10. Victor Ferkiss, *The Future of Technological Civilization*, Braziller, New York, 1974.
11. Gordon Rattray Taylor, *Rethink: A Paraprimitive Solution*, E. D. Dutton & Co., Inc., New York, 1973.
12. Jacques Ellul, *The Technological Society*, Vintage Books, New York, 1967 (translated from French).
13. Harry Kalven, Jr., "Problems of Privacy in the Year 2000," in *Daedelus*, "Toward the Year 2000," 1967.
14. R. Vacca, *The Coming Dark Age*, Doubleday, New York, 1973.
15. Norman MacRae, "America's Third Century," *The Economist*, Oct 25, 1975.
16. Joseph A. Schumpeter, *Capitalism, Socialism and Democracy*, 3rd ed., Harper Brothers, New York, 1950.
17. S. C. Gilfillan, *Sociology of Invention*, M. I. T. Press, Cambridge, 1970,
18. J. Schmookler, *Invention and Economic Growth*, Harvard University Press, Cambridge, 1966.
19. E. Mansfield, *Economics of Technological Change*, W. W. Norton & Co., Inc., New York, 1968.

CHAPTER SEVEN

MEASURES OF MAN
—TECHNOLOGY (II)

TECHNOLOGICAL PROSPECTS IN DEPTH

In this chapter I review systematically, but for the most part nonquan-titatively, the prospects for technological change in the next fifty years. Unlike most technological forecasts, this will *not* be a catalog of possible inventions. It seems to me that to compile such a shopping list —as has been done a number of times by various writers, but most competently by Dennis Gabor[1]—is to help compound the erroneous view of technology as a self-generating force. Rather, I approach the question from the direction which provides the proper perspective on causality; starting with apparent societal needs, described in func-tional terms, and working back toward possible technological solutions.

The order of the survey is as follows. It begins with *extraction* (of mineral and ocean resources) then goes on to *agriculture, finished ma-terials, energy,* and finally *new products and services.* This systematic procedure puts the emphasis where it should be and guards against important omissions. It also may help me avoid the common author's pitfall of discussing glamour technologies at unreasonable length while ignoring the mundane but important things. For instance, many technological forecasters have been extreme enthusiasts of space travel. I give this topic very little attention for the simple reason that there is no visible societal need (or political demand) for it in the next half century.

EXTRACTION AND PROCESSING OF
MINERAL AND FUEL RESOURCES

The consumption of mineral products, as such, was discussed in Chap-ter 5. Their continued availability and discoverability in the Earth's crust and their subsequent disposition to the environment as wastes are discussed in Chapter 8. Here only the technology of extraction is considered. The mineral resources of chief interest are fossil fuels, nuclear fuels, metals — both ferrous and nonferrous — and a few miscellaneous nonmetallic minerals such as sulfur, phosphorus, halogens (fluorine, chlorine, bromine), potassium, silicon, the atmospheric gases, and the aggregate materials.

Petroleum and gas are currently obtained by drilling wells, which are increasingly deep and expensive. The major breakthrough in drilling technology took place in Texas in 1908. It was the invention of self-lubricating, multiple-edged "roller bits" by Howard Hughes, Sr., founder of the Hughes Tool Company of Houston (now Toolco) and father of the recently deceased billionaire recluse, Howard Hughes, Jr. Drilling from offshore platforms on the continental shelves is a more recent and spectacular accomplishment, although it is difficult to pinpoint any single critical invention. The most important advances have come in the area of theoretical geology and methods of geophysical surveillance enabling drillers to select promising sites efficiently.

In the past the scientific and engineering aspects of the extraction business were subordinated to the subsequent production process (which is technologically trivial). In the future, however, most producing wells will be owned and operated by nationalized oil production companies, not by the international oil marketing firms. Increasingly, the latter firms will have to concentrate on selling their "know-how" and advanced technology for oil discovery and ultradeep, arctic, and offshore drilling. Firms that do not possess such technology will find themselves excluded entirely from the extraction side of the oil business.*

What new extraction technologies may become available in the next half century? As far as drilling is concerned, no major breakthroughs seem to be imminent. Mechanical rock drills will certainly dominate for some time to come. Other conceivable methods of breaking up rock tend to use too much energy or leave awkward residues. When mechanical drills are eventually replaced, they may be followed by nuclear-heated "lithocrackers" which melt their way through solid rock, leaving a glassy, impervious lining. However, this remains a distant prospect.

More rapid progress will take place in the field of geophysical mapping. The "breakthrough" here is in large-scale data-processing capability. Using the latest computers, it is now possible to process and

---

*Although they may specialize in refinery operations or marketing.

interpret data from large arrays of sensors and develop fairly exact three-dimensional pictures of what strata lie under the ground or under the oceans to a considerable depth. In the next twenty or thirty years most of the world will probably be mapped in this way.

A matter of considerable current interest is the possibility of extracting crude oil from tar sands (e.g., in the Athabasca River Basin of Canada or the Orinoco Basin of Venezuela), or from oil-shale (e.g., the Green River formation of Colorado and Utah). One of the first consequences of the 1973–1974 oil embargo was a sharp renewal of interest in these resources. The interest quickly abated, however, when it turned out that the price at which crude oil could be economically extracted from either source was far above the level it had been supposed to be.

In both cases the first stage of extraction is superficially similar to strip mining for coal. But that is only the beginning, since the organic material adheres tightly to inorganic particles or rock. In the case of tar sands, it can be loosened by pulverizing the "ore" and washing it with high-pressure steam. This yields a poor quality but refinable crude oil and a large quantity of very dirty (and hence largely useless) sand. In the case of shale the problem is even more difficult: After being pulverized the shale must be "cooked" and hydrogenated to convert the insoluble organic stuff (called kerogen) into a form that can be mechanically separated from the inorganic component and subsequently refined. Waste pulverized shale is very dry and powdery (as well as dirty) and much bulkier than the original ore. To keep it from blowing away it must be fixed by planting grass (or something) over it, which requires a substantial quantity of water. Unfortunately, the shale reserves are located in one of the driest parts of the Western United States.

Engineering improvements can be expected to reduce the costs of these extraction processes to some extent, but similar improvements can be expected in the case of competing technologies such as coal gasification and coal liquefaction. Also, although rehabilitation of areas that have been strip-mined for coal will add significantly to the cost, especially in dry areas such as Wyoming and Montana, it will not be nearly such a formidable undertaking as rehabilitating an area that has been strip-mined for shale. The ultimate use of oil shale may depend on the success of an underground "retorting" process now being developed by Occidental Oil Company. If this process works, it will solve the problem of surface disposal of the wastes and bring shale oil from "possible" to "probable" status, where exploitation is merely a matter of time.

Regarding solid minerals — coal, metal ores, and aggregates — exploration is relatively less important, and the biggest problem is extraction. There are basically three methods now in use: underground mining, open-pit mining (or quarrying), and underwater dredging. A fourth method, *leaching*, using steam or chemical reagent, is used in some special situations.* Conventional underground mining (e.g., of coal) is decreasing in importance in the major industrial countries for the simple reason that the work is unpleasant and dangerous and workers do not like to do it. Where unions exist, they tend to force up wage levels to the point at which domestic resources become uneconomic to recover by this means. Automated mining machinery and programmable robots (such as UNIMATES†) may eventually come to replace human workers in some underground mines, for example, for scarce, high-value metals or diamonds, where the supply of willing human labor dries up. Underground retorting (already mentioned) also remains a possibility for coal, but thus far an unattractive one due to the difficulty of controlling the process and preventing destructive fires. In many cases, underground mines will simply be closed.

The trend in extraction of bulk materials is unquestionably toward open-pit mining, quarrying, or dredging. These methods are amenable to the use of extremely large (and economical) machines. Inevitably, a great deal of waste material is mixed with the ore; thus efficient methods of grinding followed by preliminary separation or "beneficiation" by screening, flotation, filtration, or special devices such as magnets must be integrated into any viable system. The major technological "gap" here seems to be the development of more efficient grinding and mechanical means of separation of particles by density or size — especially means that do not require such large quantities of energy and/or fresh water. Water is scarce in many areas that have otherwise exploitable minerals. The problem of mechanical separation is also fundamental in a number of other vital processes, notably sulfur and ash removal from coal and separation of useful materials from wastes in many industries.

That dramatic progress should be possible in the presently primitive technology of reducing inhomogeneous solids to powder form and then separating the various components is suggested by the fact that

---

*The major one is the so-called Frasch process for recovering native sulfur by liquefying it with steam. Leaching with sulfuric acid or ammonia is increasingly seen as an alternative to the present method of mining and smelting copper, among other metals. Placer mining (using a water jet) can be regarded as a varient of leaching.

†Trade name of Consolidated Controls Corporation, Bethel, Connecticut.

existing methods of grinding require about 100 times more energy than should theoretically be required. (That is, ball mills and rod mills, now in use, are only about 1% efficient!) Experimental processes show promise of reducing the wasted energy by five- or tenfold. It would be idle to speculate on which methods will be adopted, but I freely predict that rapid progress will take place in this backwater of technology, because it is both technically feasible and very badly needed. When this problem is eventually resolved, a subsequent difficulty will reveal itself: the disposal of finely powdered waste materials (wet or dry) by reaggregation into some more convenient form without undue energy consumption.

Dredging is a minor variant of open-pit surface mining, as applied to extraction aggregates such as sand and gravel. It requires great sophistication, of course, to dredge for manganese-nickel-copper nodules at a depth of 10,000 feet in the ocean! However, adequate technology appears to be available already, and several industrial consortia are actively developing proprietary ocean mining systems.* It is widely expected that nodules will be mined commercially within a decade or two at most and will constitute a large fraction of total production for the metals in question before the year 2000.

The potential of acid leaching, especially for surface copper mining, deserves comment. The basic method has been known for some time: The idea is to "dissolve" the copper from a granulated low grade (e.g., 0.5%) ore by means of sulfuric or hydrochloric acid. The copper sulfate or chloride can then be extracted by evaporation or precipitation as a reasonably pure salt, which is subsequently reduced by electrolysis. The very dirty process of smelting can thus be avoided. However, the copper industry has had little incentive to convert from a successful known technology to an untried one until recently. The imposition of tough new environmental standards on the existing smelters may be exactly the needed stimulus, since low-grade sulfuric acid will actually be produced as a by-product of the air pollution controls. Thus it would be natural to evolve a kind of hybrid process combining both acid leaching and conventional smelting on the same site.

Two other major extraction techniques of the future should be mentioned. One involves the separation of various salts from seawater or brine lakes. Sodium, potassium, magnesium chloride, carbonates, lithium carbonate, boric acid, and bromine are currently recovered in this way. The other involves separation of atmospheric gases — oxygen, nitrogen, and argon — from the air. Regarding the latter, two basic meth-

*Of which the Hughes' "Glomar Explorer" (of CIA fame) is only one.

ods are possible. The most important is to consume the oxygen in an oxidation reaction (i.e., combustion), leaving the nitrogen, which can then be reacted with hydrogen at high temperatures and pressures to yield ammonia, the basic chemical for fertilizer, or for further chemical synthesis. The usual synthetic ammonia process utilizes natural gas (mainly methane) to supply the necessary hydrogen, as well as energy. However, all new ammonia plants will probably be based on an alternative process using coal and steam to generate hydrogen in place of natural gas.

To obtain liquid air, liquid nitrogen (for cryogenic purposes*), or pure oxygen (e.g., for the "basic oxygen process" of steel making), a different method is normally used: The air is cooled by a cryogenic refrigerator until the various components begin to liquefy. Since oxygen and nitrogen boil at slightly different temperatures, they can be separated by a method akin to distillation. This is quite energy intensive.

An alternate future process for manufacturing oxygen which also yields pure hydrogen is to decompose water by electrolysis, using a nuclear power plant as a source of energy.[†] Here an interesting realm for speculation opens up, since the world will sooner or later (and possibly within our fifty-year time frame) largely run out of natural gas. Disregarding the problems of finding alternative sources *as such* (discussed in the next chapter), there is a secondary but related problem of distribution. The cities and factories of the developed countries are currently linked by a system of gas pipelines. What will flow in them? The two obvious possibilities are (1) synthetic methane derived from coal and (2) pure hydrogen. Synthetic methane would, in any case, require large quantities of hydrogen in its manufacture. Thus hydrogen is almost certain to be an important material in the future.

It might be noted in passing that pure hydrogen is not now produced in large quantities, and most of what is produced is derived from the methane in natural gas. Thus the present basic relationship of industry (natural gas → hydrogen) is likely to undergo a reversal (hydrogen → synthetic gas) within four or five decades, assuming that nuclear electric power is generated on a significant scale.

The separation of alkali-halide salts from sea water is carried out, at present, in only a few places and for the sake of the salts them-

---

*Literally, "cold-generating."
[†] Recently, several thermochemical processes have been suggested for the same purpose. In principle, such a method might utilize heat instead of electricity, although it would come ultimately from the same source.

selves. However, long before the year 2025, pure fresh water—for irrigation and drinking—may be the most important product of desalination plants, with other elements being recovered mainly as by-products. In addition, large extraction plants will probably be needed eventually to extract either uranium or deuterium ("heavy hydrogen") from sea water for use as fuel for nuclear power production—based either on uranium fission (as at present) or on the fusion reaction between deuterium and tritium.

At present it is impossible to predict the principles on which the sea water processing plants of the future will operate. Desalination research is now primarily directed toward perfecting distillation-type processes, although refrigeration plants are receiving some attention. The use of molecular "sieves" or ion-exchange membranes of various kinds is a third, but generally disregarded, possibility. Chemical methods—analogous to the Dow process for extracting magnesium from sea water—constitute a fourth possible route. It is not unlikely that some combination of all these techniques will be used and that large-scale nuclear-powered plants will produce a range of chemical products including pure water, hydrogen deuterium, oxygen, chlorine, bromine, hydrochloric acid, sodium hydroxide, sodium metal, magnesium metal, and uranium.

The location of such plants is likely to be a matter of major international concern and controversy, in view of their enormous scale. The most obvious locations from an economic viewpoint would be offshore but close to large irrigable arid areas with nearby industrial consumers such as Western Australia, Spain, or Southern California, or close to urban agglomerations that have outstripped their natural fresh water supplies; for example, the Northeastern United States.

AGRICULTURE AND FORESTRY

Although high technology methods for producing food and fiber have received much attention in the press, the important innovations in agriculture and forestry over the last century have been

- Mechanization by elimination of draft animals and substitution of tractors and other machines powered by internal combustion engines
- Selective breeding of plants and animals for greater productivity and resistance to disease (e.g., the "green revolution")
- Synthetic fertilizers
- Synthetic chemical pesticides such as DDT

These innovations, in addition to earlier ones such as irrigation and crop rotation, have only been exploited widely in the temperate United States and Europe in recent decades. They have not yet been fully utilized, by any means, in the tropical countries. Specifically, the use of hybrid seed and synthetic fertilizer is still at a relatively low level in the tropics. Mechanization lags even further, and very damaging practices, such as overgrazing in areas with arid or monsoon climates, are still widely practiced in Africa and South Asia. Such practices have only recently been stopped in China.

A number of breakthrough possibilities for agricultural technology have been suggested, especially in the realm of biological engineering:

- Increasing photosynthetic efficiency in plants; for example, by utilizing special light sources, light filters, and so on in a controlled "greenhouse" environment
- Improved control over plant growth using hormones
- Biological control over insect pests; for example, by utilizing "custom-made" test-tube grown bacteria or spreading artificially bred insect predators (such as wasps, spiders, lady beetles, praying mantises, etc.)
- New hybrid crop species to develop useful new characteristics such as salt tolerance, drought tolerance, and nitrogen fixation ability*

Many of these developments will doubtless occur, but I think none will be revolutionary. In the advanced countries the prospect for the next half century is, essentially, for a series of minor improvements in present techniques. For instance, water will be used more efficiently (because it is becoming scarce), and a variety of methods of preventing unnecessary evaporation or surface runoff will be perfected. The latter will also conserve on the use of nitrogen fertilizers, which are water soluble.

Animal feeding in the advanced industrial countries will be developed further, with progressively greater use of "waste" forms of cellulose such as sawdust, finely chopped forestry wastes (branches, leaves, bark), corn stalks, water hyacinth, seaweed, sugarcane bagasse, dried sewage sludge, manure, and so on. Protein supplements to animal feed are now mainly derived from soybeans, cottonseed meal, and other

---

*Nitrogen fixation will be one of the primary targets of recombinant DNA research. I suspect that within a decade the nitrogen fixation capability will be successfully induced in nonleguminous plants and that within two decades hybrid seed with this capability will be commercially available.

plant products. Over the next fifty years an increasing proportion will come from single-cell organisms such as algae and yeast, produced under industrial conditions.* In tropical countries there should be greater use of dried fish meal, produced as a by-product of domestic fish ponds.

Synthetic foods or food additives made from soybeans and other vegetable protein will gain importance in the advanced countries. They will be used most extensively in bread, ready-to-eat cereals, snack foods, and as meat or pasta extenders. In sophisticated developing countries like Mexico, protein extenders might also be added to commercial corn meal (for tortillas) and beans (frijoles). However, "vegetarian steaks" and the like seem unlikely to achieve significant acceptance.

Protein deficiency—manifested by the diseases Kwashiorkor and Marasinus—are one of the major causes of infant and childhood mortality in the underdeveloped countries. This has prompted nutritionists to suggest that synthetic amino acids could be manufactured and added to the diet. In the words of one such expert,[2]

> The first step in improving the Asiatic diet by the use of synthetic materials would be to supplement the inadequate protein of the grains and legumes by the addition of small percentages of two amino acids: lysine and methionine. Since production methods for both lysine and methionine are already available, *it would be necessary only to build the facilities and to develop methods for incorporating the amino acids in the diet.* †

Doubtless the author is absolutely right. However, "developing methods for incorporating the amino acids in the diet" is quite a challenge in a country like India where 80% of the population are rural peasants who seldom, if ever, consume any commercial foodstuffs. Children are normally suckled by the mother until the next child comes along. Quite apart from this problem, it is horrifying to contemplate the likely impact on India's already excessive population growth

---

*Cultivation of microorganisms on crude petroleum has been investigated for a number of years by several oil companies. The problem is not to get the organisms to grow, but to separate them from the growth medium. Unfortunately, petroleum is not a uniform or homogeneous material. It is a variable mixture of hydrocarbons, some of which are toxic and carcinogenetic. An acceptable process would have to eliminate all the unwanted chemicals from the product. This is a problem that has proved insuperable, to date.
† Italics added.

rate if up to half of all the children who now die before the age of ten were to grow up and have children of their own.[†]

In the less developed countries the best chance of increasing outputs will come from improved methods of cultivation and the development of hybrid species of grains and pulses that are suited for tropical climates. However, the experience of the introduction of hybrid wheat into India and Pakistan and hybrid rice in a number of countries of South Asia should not be forgotten. The new strains increased yield per acre but also dramatically increased consumption of synthetic fertilizer and made all the countries in question more dependent on imported petroleum.

As it happens, the major sources of high-quality plant protein in South Asia (and elsewhere) are not grains but pulses, such as peanuts, soybeans, field beans, chick peas, and lentils. So far, despite considerable effort, there has been no significant progress in the United States or anywhere else in the world in raising output per acre of this category of crops. Plant breeders remain hopeful, but skepticism is naturally growing. It seems distinctly possible that some sort of natural limit is involved here, although I personally doubt it. In any case, the agricultural breakthrough that the world truly needs is a collection of new and more productive hybrids of the bean-pea family.

Trees are a major world crop, and techniques that have long been utilized to increase the output of food and fiber crops can also be used to grow trees faster, straighter, and taller. Such methods are now widely used in the United States and will doubtless be employed extensively elsewhere. There is substantial room for increased productivity. China is involved in extensive reforestation projects. Much of India and Java are now on the verge of losing their last vestige of forest cover as the growing population continues to cut trees for building material and fuel. Massive reforestation is already needed in India, although it cannot succeed as long as the cattle are free to graze where they will, as at present. I return to this topic later in connection with the discussion of energy.

Two peripheral possibilities that have received considerable attention deserve brief mention. One is the use of desalinated sea water for large-scale agriculture in desert areas such as the Sahara. This is technically feasible, but it makes sense economically only if nuclear

---

[†] Some population experts believe that reducing infant mortality will (eventually) reduce birth rates by reducing people's incentives to keep on having children. This would be more convincing if public health progress in the past had not led to a population explosion.

energy is very cheap. Schemes to combine large nuclear power plants with desalination — the so-called Nu-plex concept — were proposed optimistically a few years ago by Oak Ridge National Laboratory. However, the future of nuclear power itself is clouded (to say the least). Also, suitable sites for such a facility are not as common as might be imagined, since an unpopulated desert area must be located reasonably close to an urban area that can utilize the electric power. The most plausible possibilities would seem to be in Spain, Egypt, Israel, Western Australia, the Rajasthan coast of India north of Bombay, the Persian Gulf, or possibly along the Pacific coast of Mexico or Chile. The chances that this would have a major impact on world food production seem fairly negligible, although a joint Egyptian-Israeli project in the Sinai (for instance) could have an enormous impact on the Middle East.

The other possibility that has been heavily touted is "ocean farming." It is clear that conventional fishing in most oceans has already approached the natural limits on output. A few underexploited species of fish may remain, but some fisheries (such as the North Atlantic) are already being overfished to the point of declining output. This situation should be ameliorated in part by the forthcoming general adaptation of a 200-mile offshore "economic zone"* by most countries. Under this new arrangement the Japanese and Soviet trawlers, which have been the main cause of overfishing, would be forced to pay substantial licensing fees for fishing rights in such zones, and they would probably be excluded altogether from other overfished places such as the North Sea, the ocean around Iceland, and the Grand Banks off Nova Scotia.

Effective national control over the waters of the continental shelves is a basic prerequisite for mariculture,† since no private entrepreneur (or country) will make any investment in improving the productivity of an area if others are free to harvest the output. However, a 200-mile limit, in itself, does not achieve anything useful. The simplest way of increasing fish output — already being adopted in a few locations — is to implant suitable shelters for smaller fish on the ocean floor (analogous to coral reefs). Old tires have proved surprisingly useful in this regard. Oysters and mussels are now grown commercially, mainly in Italy and France, on artificial frames to which the shells affix themselves. These can be pulled out of the water for easy harvest. Hatcheries are also feasible for fish (like salmon) that habitually return to their point of

---

*Whether or not formally incorporated into a "law of the sea."

† Or, indeed, any meaningful conservation measures whatever. Given the present state of the UN, international control is not a viable possibility.

origin. Occasionally it is even possible to introduce a new species into an area, with good results—as in the case of the Cohoe salmon, recently implanted in the Great Lakes.[‡]

However, mariculture has far to go before it can be anywhere near as efficient as agriculture on land. Most commercial fish (except shellfish) are several steps up the marine food chain, which starts with single-celled photosynthetic plants called phytoplankton that are consumed by (mainly) microscopic animals (zooplankton), and so on to higher and higher trophic levels. Each such stage involves a substantial loss of food energy. Thus it is far more efficient to produce oysters, mussels, or shrimp than cod or tuna.

On land the farmer can decide what he will grow; he can also exclude unwanted species by physical removal, that is, weeding. The farmer on land can also use carefully selected hybrid seed which he can fertilize to maximize its rate of growth. In the ocean the techniques corresponding to weeding, seeding, and feeding are almost totally undeveloped. In the absence of a massive crash program to perfect such methods, progress in ocean farming will be very slow in the next half century.

The countries that have done the most to increase the productivity of the oceans are Italy, France, and Japan. Japan, in particular, is likely to invest heavily in this area, especially since its long-distance fishing activities are likely to be curtailed and the Japanese have a highly developed taste for seafood. They also now have the wealth to indulge it. Unfortunately, the "Inland Sea" of Japan—the obvious place to cultivate for harvest—is now heavily polluted. It will require decades for the Japanese to restore this area to a biologically healthy state, but the odds are quite good that Japan will undertake the task. In the meantime the Japanese may find other suitable sites for mariculture among the large coral atolls of the South Pacific. However, insofar as most of the world is concerned, the ocean offers no immediate potential for vastly increased output.

MATERIALS

There are, of course, an enormous number of different materials, used for a wide variety of purposes. To simplify the discussion without

---

[‡]Actually, this was a countermeasure to the accidental introduction of the sea lamprey and later the alewife which got into the lakes from the St. Lawrence River and disrupted the fisheries. The salmon has restored a balance of desirable species in the lakes.

going into endless (and uninteresting) detail, it is helpful to focus attention on the functions that are served by materials. As a starting point, let me distinguish between *durable* materials and *consumable* materials.

In the durable category are all the materials that are used to make things (machines, clothes, furniture, structures) that can be used many times through a period of years. Obviously, stone, brick, and metals are durables by this criterion, as are paper (in books), fabrics (in clothing), carpets, and wood in furniture. On the other hand, paper napkins and bags, magazines, tissues, wrappings, plastic bags, cups, and trays, bottles, cans, aluminum foil, and so on are *not* durables.

Consumable Materials

What I really mean by a consumable is a physical material that is transformed by use into some other material, or contaminated, or converted into a waste that must be discarded. Thus liquid paint is a consumable. (It is transformed into a solid impervious protective coating). Motor oil and axle grease are slowly converted by engine heat into a useless, contaminated waste material. (They can be re-refined however.) Soaps and detergents combine, in use, with particles of dirt, which are discharged in waste water. Acid, bleach, or lye react chemically with contaminants and are themselves destroyed in the process. Food is literally consumed and is converted by the body into tissue and metabolic wastes.

Some consumables other than food can be termed labor-saving materials in the sense that they are more or less direct substitutes for human labor. Soap or detergent are clearly substitutes in exactly this sense for the labor of scrubbing. In primitive societies clothes are cleaned (more or less) by beating them on rocks to dislodge the dirt. Pesticides and herbicides are obviously substitutes for hand picking insect pests and removing weeds. Engine oil and grease are used to reduce the resistance (and wear) of friction. An axle can be made to turn without grease, but it requires more energy. Throw-away containers, paper napkins, and so forth are perhaps the most blatant examples of using materials in place of labor. Some consumables are partly substitutes or "extenders" for durables. Thus the soap or detergent used in washing also lengthens the life of the clothes. Similarly, motor oil and axle grease extend the life of the machine. Paint is primarily a life extender for other durable materials. The same can be said of preservatives, fire retardants, and so on.

A rough generalization already suggests itself: Purely labor-saving materials, such as packaging or cleaning agents, are demanded primarily in advanced economies where wages are high and human labor is expensive. But durable material extenders, like lubricants, detergents, paints, and preservatives, may be even more valuable in poor countries than in wealthy ones, since they effectively reduce the need for new materials.

A further point arises with regard to consumables. Some of the substitutions in question — for instance, between the labor of collecting and sorting returnable bottles and the material consumed in nonreturnable bottles — are clearly functions of the cost of energy. (Returnable bottles require much less energy than nonreturnables.) As energy prices go up — as I expect — some of these substitutions will no longer be economically attractive.

Similarly, as environmental protection requirements inevitably become tighter (see Chapter 8), discharging waste materials will gradually become more costly.* This trend, too, will tend to encourage greater use of materials that extend the life of durable goods, like paint, but the rising cost of waste discharge will discourage the use of valuable materials as direct substitutes for human labor. This will particularly affect the types of packaging materials that are used in the future.

Thus far I have ignored the durable materials. How and for what are these used? There is, unfortunately, no simple answer. Uses depend on physical properties, which occur in a wide variety of combinations. A particularly simple example is road ballast, which need only be incompressible and weather resistant. In the remainder of this section I consider just three (of many possible) subcategories of durables: structural materials, "skin" materials, and electrical conductors.

Structural Materials

Load-bearing beams and frame elements for fixed structures like buildings must be rigid, strong, and weather resistant. Materials with these characteristics in various degrees include concrete, brick, stone, wood, and steel. The choice is a function of local costs (and availability), climate, and, of course, building design and height. Wood is weather resistant in dry climates, but not in damp ones. High-rise

---

*Historically the environment has been used freely — without cost to the user — as a place to discharge wastes. Increasingly, however, there will be direct costs attached (e.g., for dumping permits) or requirements for waste treatment of various sorts prior to discharge.

structures are virtually limited to steel and/or reinforced concrete. To serve as a frame or body for a moving vehicle or a suspension bridge carrying heavy vehicular traffic, a further pair of attributes are needed: light weight and toughness to resist shock and vibration. This combination tends to rule out masonry and wood and reduce the effective choice to metals like steel or aluminum or metal-reinforced concrete.*

The moving parts of machines such as axles and engines, which are obviously vital to an advanced industrial society, have even stiffer requirements: They must be dimensionally stable (rigid), strong, hard, tough, and wear (or heat) resistant. Until the twentieth century only a few metals could serve — mainly heat-treated cast iron or forged steel. A few decades ago aluminum alloys finally reached a stage of development at which they could be used in place of iron or steel, particularly in aircraft engines. Aluminum will soon be more widely used in automobile engines to reduce weight. Another light metal, titanium, is likely to find specialized uses within a couple of decades.

A rather exciting breakthrough appears to be imminent: the use of cast ceramics† in place of metals for the critical high-performance parts of machines and engines. The initial application will most likely be in gas turbines. Later, ceramics may be used in other types of aircraft or auto engines, either piston or rotary (Wankel) type. The advantages are, potentially, higher-temperature operation and consequently lighter weight for a given level of performance. The major problem remaining at this time seems to be to develop suitable methods of mass production. (This is not, by any means, a simple matter, but I think it will probably be solved.)

For extremely demanding structural applications, there are also exciting new high-strength materials becoming available, consisting of very fine filaments or fibers of carbon, beryllium, quartz, or boron embedded in a plastic or ceramic. Developments of this kind dominate the forward thinking of the frontier researchers in the field. However, the potential applications are mostly in the aircraft industry — for example, to fabricate large turbine compressor blades, engine mounts, or wheel struts. Such materials apparently offer a significant step forward to centrifuge technology. The obvious application is to replace the gaseous diffusion method of separating the scarce fissionable uran-

*I am aware that suspension bridges using cables woven from natural fibers have been used successfully for centuries in Peru, Tibet, and elsewhere, but these are barely adequate for pedestrians and a few animals.
† Such as aluminum oxide or "alumina."

ium isotope U^{235} from the relatively inert U^{238}. West Germany and Holland have already developed this method to the near-commercial stage. China also apparently has a centrifuge plant.*

A few consumer applications of the super-strength materials have already appeared—notably lightweight golf clubs and tennis rackets, but these will not set the world on fire. One outside possibility is worthy of notice, however. With the advent of very light, high-tensile composite materials there may conceivably be a revival of the use of flywheels as energy storage devices; for example, for vehicles. On the basis of preliminary data, such a flywheel would appear to be comparable in energy and power storage capacity to the high-energy electrochemical cells that are now being developed. Some exploratory studies along this line have already been initiated. (I mention this again in connection with transportation technology.)

"Skin" Materials

For the outer "skin" (as opposed to the load-bearing frame) of a rigid structure—such as the roof, walls, or floors of a house, the body of a car or airplane, the hull of a ship, the casing of a household appliance, or the surface of a piece of furniture—different properties are needed. Sometimes the rigid shell is designed to carry all the load stresses (as in a fiberglass speedboat or missile), but normally it must simply be stiff enough to retain its dimensions, weatherproof, fireproof, and resistant to penetration by air, water, and accidental encounters with rough or sharp objects. It must also have a reasonable lifetime and a pleasant appearance. A coating (e.g., of paint) often suffices to provide weather resistance and pleasant appearance for a rigid structure. The desired degree of impenetrability can be obtained in many ways, but all are incompatible with low breaking or tearing strength or brittleness. Thus glass—which shatters easily—is not a very suitable skin material unless it has been laminated or tempered. Similarly, paper is a poor skin material unless it has been chemically waterproofed, fireproofed and strengthened by the addition of fibers to make it tear resistant.

Many simple materials have some of the minimally necessary prop-

*The gas centrifuge technology sharply reduces the cost of uranium enrichment and was therefore highly classified by the United States on the grounds that it would hasten proliferation of nuclear technology. However, gas centrifuges are no longer the cheapest method. The West German nozzle process appears to have superseded it. A still cheaper separation technique using lasers has been unmistakably hinted at in unclassified publications.

erties, but few—except concrete, aluminum, and stainless steel—have virtually all of them. The best materials for most applications are composites of some sort, generally pairing an adhesive binder with a granular or fibrous material that adds strength. Either may be synthetic. Since synthetic organic materials are almost infinitely variable in their properties, most skin materials tend to be composities with a synthetic component, usually a binder or strengthener. For cost reasons it is a safe prediction that most composites will contain a cheap and bulky natural aggregate of some sort. Plastic-impregnated wood and fiber-strengthened plaster (for instance) will expand their domain at the expense of solid or homogeneous natural materials. They will also displace metals from some applications where the greater strength of the metal is not needed. Waste materials will be used increasingly as aggregates in place of natural sand, gravel, gypsum, or groundwood.

There is another category of skin application for which flexibility rather than stiffness is needed and weatherproofness is less important. Clothing, household linens, upholstery, drapes, printed material, and some packaging materials constitute the main examples. Historically, woven fabrics and paper have competed for these uses, with synthetic fibers gradually gaining ground against all natural fibers, including wool and cotton. Cotton has been the last holdout, but cotton-synthetic blends are now commonplace, and a synthetic substitute for cotton itself will be commercially available within the decade.

Paper has had little effective synthetic competition for most of its uses except in the area of wrapping and packaging, where plastic film has become dominant. On the other hand, paper has gradually nibbled away at some traditional fabric uses; for example, paper napkins, paper towels, paper handkerchiefs ("Kleenex"), and so on. In recent years, chemically impregnated and strengthened paper has begun to compete with cotton fabrics for underwear and bedsheets. Even light summer dresses and swimwear are now available in paper. (The advantage of "throwaway" clothes, of course, is that they need not be laundered. This is another, rather extreme, example of a labor-saving material.)

The big question mark is whether synthetic polymers (plastics) can replace bleached paper as a medium for printed matter. Bleached coated paper is rising sharply in price because of the need for more stringent pollution abatement in the paper industry. (Unbleached paper is cheaper, but it is yellowish in color and turns brown and brittle in a few years.) There have been suggestions that synthetics might eventually take over this market, but I doubt it. Basically, it is hard to see how it could ever be economical for a synthetic polymer "reconstructed" from fossil hydrocarbons to replace nature's basic original structural material (cellulose) in its simplest form.* Although there are losses in separating the cellulose fibers from other components of wood (lignin), the long-run answer seems to be to find means of utilizing the lignin, either as a chemical or biological "feedstock."

One peripheral possibility should be mentioned here. Most structures designed for human use are rigid, but there have always been applications for flexible structures. The archetype is a simple tent, consisting of a woven cloth fabric skin supported by ropes and poles. In recent years the advent of high-strength plastics and plastic-impregnated fabrics has opened an entirely new structural concept: the air-supported tent or bubble dome, which dispenses with the need for any rigid frame elements at all. Only the airtight skin itself and some lightweight anchor cables are needed, along with an efficient, reliable air pump capable of maintaining a pressure slightly higher than atmospheric against leakage through the entrance flap. Such bubble domes are now routinely used in the advanced countries for enclosing tennis courts and swimming pools in winter, providing "instant" exhibition space, and other moderately exotic uses.

The obvious question is whether the bubble concept has potential application to housing, factories, offices, or other major enclosure needs of society. Although there is little external confirmation at present, I think the answer is probably yes. Two major possibilities come to mind. The simplest is an air-supported bubble that is designed as an instant expansion room for a compact motor home. This would require an electrically operated compressor not much different from that in a refrigerator. It could be produced and marketed today by an imaginative manufacturer. It would greatly expand the effective interior space available and thus the extent to which motor homes could compete effectively with small conventional homes or permanent vacation cottages. A more advanced (later) application would be the instant office or instant workshop, also linked to a motor home or trailer, for a military base, construction site, or some other temporary occasion involving a life of up to a few years.

Electrical Conductors

Along with machines, electricity is perhaps the *sine qua non* of any industrial society. There are, of course, a vast number of devices based

---

*Cotton is cellulose, also, but in a much more refined (essentially pure) long fiber form that is a very small part of the biomass of the plant. Wood, on the other hand, constitutes almost all the biomass of a tree.

on special electrical, magnetic, or electronic properties of materials. Some of these properties may not, at first glance, seem to be electro-magnetic in nature.* In any case, I cannot begin to discuss them all in a few pages. I limit myself to the most important single property: the ability to conduct electricity.

Conductors are obviously required for the transmission and distribution of electricity, from the generating plants where it is produced to the electric lights, appliances, and machines where it is put to work. Conductors of various kinds are also an essential element in most of the electrical devices with which we are surrounded.

For instance, electric lights utilize a special conducting element — the tungsten filament — that resists the flow of current and converts electric energy into heat. It then becomes white hot (incandescent) and radiates in the visible part of the electromagnetic spectrum. Electric heaters operate in a similar manner, but at a lower temperature, to radiate in the infrared wavelengths.

Electric motors and generators are both based on the fundamental discoveries of Michael Faraday (1791–1867) that if a conductor such as a wire moves "through" a magnetic field (or, equivalently, if a magnet is physically moved past a conducting element) an electric current will be excited in the conductor. Moreover, if a current is passed through a conducting wire or coil of wire, a magnetic field is produced. Interestingly enough, the magnetic field that is required by an electric generator can be produced *internally* by an electromagnet utilizing part of the electricity output of the generator itself. Thus electrical conductors are the only basic elements actually needed to make a motor, generator, or magnet.†

Until recently copper was almost exclusively used for all electric purposes. Silver and gold are as good or better in terms of intrinsic conductivity, but the two precious metals are much scarcer. However, aluminum is also a fairly good conductor, and it can replace copper in most applications; wires must be slightly thicker, and resistance losses are a bit higher. Since it is significantly cheaper, aluminum has recently begun to replace copper for a number of applications, starting some time ago with high-voltage transmission lines. Aluminum wiring is a little less satisfactory than copper for household use, because it tends to heat up more in case of an overload. This would also inhibit the use of pure aluminum in motors and generators (copper cladding

---

*For instance, visible light is one type of electromagnetic wave. Thus optical transparency is actually an electromagnetic property.
† Other elements, such as iron cores, may be added to enhance the magnetic field, but this is peripheral.

reduces the problem but adds to the cost). Thus aluminum is not likely to replace all copper wire in the foreseeable future.

But several new competitors for both aluminum and copper are coming on the scene. One rather surprising alternative is metallic sodium, which is an excellent conductor at room temperature but even better than copper for carrying large currents at ultra-low temperatures because of its unusually low intrinsic magneto-resistance.[†] Of course, the metallic sodium must not be exposed directly to air or water (it reacts violently to moisture), but this can be accomplished by encasing a sodium conductor in a plastic sheath and then armoring the whole cable.

Superconductors are another old scientific dream, that is gradually approaching realization and commercial viability. A superconductor is a material which when cooled to a low enough temperature loses *all* its electrical resistance. A superconducting loop can literally carry a current for an indefinite period with no dissipation. It has long been hoped that it may be possible to synthesize an organic superconductor that will operate at room temperature, but no significant progress in this direction has occurred for several years. To date, the best superconductors are alloys of metals: niobium, zirconium, vanadium, titanium, and various rare earths. All these become superconducting at a temperature in the range of 18–20°K, which is about −350F. To maintain this temperature requires the use of liquid helium as a refrigerant — nothing else will do — plus very high-quality vacuum insulation. Yet the savings for a major electric transmission line in energy not lost as heat can probably justify the cost of such an elaborate conductor. At this point, all that seems to remain in the way of practical application is a manufacturing capability and a customer. As energy costs continue to soar, these will probably be found within a decade, although the large-scale use of superconductors may not occur until after 2000.

The last substitute for copper is the most interesting of all. A great deal of copper wire is presently used in telephone cable. It must be remembered, however, that, although the signals are electric in nature, it is *information* not *energy* that is basically being conveyed. The wire is merely a channel along which an electromagnetic (EM) wave may propagate freely within a certain limited frequency range. In effect, copper wire is transparent to EM signals with a frequency up to several thousand cycles per second. Beyond that frequency range, the

---

[†] Magneto-resistance is a special type of electrical resistance that is proportional to magnetic field strength. It is important for large current-carrying applications because (1) the current itself generates a strong magnetic field, and (2) if the amount of electricity involved is large, *any* loss is costly and worth reducing as far as possible.

resistance increases gradually and the signal is attenuated so that an impracticable number of amplifiers and repeaters would be required to transmit over any distance.

Since the information that can be conveyed by a signal is roughly proportional to its frequency bandwidth, it is clear that higher frequencies are theoretically desirable. Thus microwave-based systems developed since the 1940s are already in use as a supplement to the standard coaxial cables. However, the big communications breakthrough of the past decade is the use of light as a direct signal carrier. Just as copper is transparent to low-frequency EM signals in the kiloHertz range, glass is transparent to EM signals in the optical (megamega Hertz) range. The major technological gap for a long time was a means of generating and amplifying *coherent* signal in this frequency band. This gap was filled dramatically by the invention of the laser in 1962. Two other major problems remained: a means of modulating the carrier (i.e., impressing a meaningful message on it) and a waveguide with a suitable low attenuation. A variety of modulation schemes are under investigation, and several of them show promise. Meanwhile research in the United States and Japan has produced a coated glass fiber that virtually eliminates the major cause of attenuation — imperfect internal reflection — and which can be mass produced.

The wide use of optical waveguides may be two decades in the future because of the tremendous existing investment in wire-based communications. But it is interesting that when the demand for information transmission justifies the necessary investment — as the discussion in Chapter 5 suggests may occur before the year 2000 — the requisite technology is already available.

ENERGY

I noted that one of the most pervasive elements of modern industrial society is the use of electricity. To an engineer or economist electricity is merely one of many forms of energy, although admittedly a very useful one. From a more fundamental thermodynamic viewpoint, electricity is the ideal form of energy: It is the only form that can accomplish "useful work" (in principle) without loss.*

Machines are another *sine qua non* of the Industrial Revolution. Machines are simply devices to convert nonmuscular forms of energy into mechanical work. They do what human or animal muscles do, but

---

*As noted earlier, it can also be stored indefinitely, without loss, in a superconducting current loop. This is a feasible (but inordinately expensive) possibility.

they utilize some kind of energy-containing fuel—such as coal or gasoline—or they utilize electricity as a source of energy.

Thus the topic I now discuss is really the conversion of nonhuman forms of energy into finished fuels (such as gasoline) or electricity. There are many technological questions of interest, but given limited space I can only discuss those which are relevant to the largest issues which now face our industrial society, notably the forthcoming transition from dependence on fossil hydrocarbon fuels to other basic sources of energy.

It is noteworthy that even the United States, which is the most lavish energy-consuming country on Earth, did not use fossil fuels for more than half its total needs until after 1885. Yet the (first) "age of coal" had already reached its peak by World War I when coal accounted for 75% of total energy used. Since then coal has declined in relative importance as petroleum and natural gas have increased tremendously. But what of the next fifty years?

There are really two separate and distinct questions to be addressed. One question is the amount of additional oil and gas that actually remains in the surface of the Earth and how long it can be made to last by various means of conservation. The reserves yet to be discovered are highly uncertain, but I hazard some comments in the next chapter.

The technology of recovery of already known reserves, particularly those which occur in nonliquid forms such as shale and tar sands, was discussed briefly under "extraction." To repeat the conclusion of that discussion: Undoubtedly a modest amount of oil from tar sands can be exploited at a price not too far above the current price of liquid oil. However, the price at which oil from the deeper sands and shale will be economically recoverable is probably well above the price at which coal can be gasified and probably also above the price at which coal can be liquefied. Thus shale and tar sands should probably be regarded as marginal reserves at best, and, after the year 2000, the best remaining source of fossil fuels will be coal.

The potential for energy conservation is only peripherally a question of technology. To the extent that it is, I discuss it further in the concluding section of this chapter. However, it is primarily a policy question and, as such, outside the scope of this book.

The second key question is, given the forthcoming exhaustion of petroleum and natural gas—whether it occurs nearer to 2000 or 2100—what sources of energy will our descendents have to depend on, and when will they be available? Here the choices are relatively circumscribed: Coal? Nuclear power? Other sources? Or must we endure sharply reduced consumption?

The third possibility (other sources) is the easiest to deal with, and to get it out of the way will simplify the argument. Under other sources of energy I include solar energy collected on Earth or in orbit, geothermal energy from "hot rock," wind power, wave power, ocean thermal gradient power, "energy plantations," and a few other bright ideas that scientists have been proposing for a decade.* One of the problems with such schemes is that there are too many of them and not enough research and development money to support them all. The first three on the list are receiving serious attention at a moderate level of funding in the United States. The last three are only ideas at present.

Solar energy is the most advanced and is getting the lion's share of available research and development funding apart from coal and nuclear power. The most elaborate scheme is the orbital solar collector concept. This requires that the Sun's energy be collected by solar cells or some other device in orbit, converted into microwaves, beamed to the surface of the Earth, re-collected by a large phased-array microwave antenna system, and then rectified to DC or 60-cycle AC. In my view, this scheme is not much more than a hobby-horse of the space lobby. Its chief attraction seems to be its grandiosity. None of the requisite hardware exists, except perhaps launching rockets. The hardware development alone would cost billions. The giant orbiting collector would also be uniquely vulnerable to attack (or even sabotage) by any country with access to suitable missiles. In addition, there are grave worries about the side-effects of the interaction of high microwave fluxes on the Earth's upper atmosphere, particularly the ionosphere. Potential biological side-effects of microwave radiation are also becoming known. For these and other reasons, I do not think this project will ever get off the ground.

Solar collectors on the surface of the Earth fall in two very different categories. One encompasses photovoltaic solar cells which convert sunlight directly into electricity. After two decades of intensive development by Bell Laboratories and other research groups, the best existing solar cell utilizes ultrapure silicon crystals, grown in a vacuum. It has a theoretical maximum conversion efficiency of 18%. The solar cells manufactured by Western Electric† cost anywhere from 100 to

---

*I omit tidal power, since there are only a few natural tidal funnels (or amplifiers) — like the Bay of Fundy — where the daily rise and fall is sufficient to make power generation feasible on a realistic scale.

† Western Electric Corporation is the manufacturing subsidiary of AT&T (The Bell System). Solar cells have been used mainly for energizing satellites; they account for as much as one-third of the net cost of such an object. However, the current price is a matter of some conjecture, since production is strictly "custom."

1000 times too much for practical electric power generation. Recently Bell Laboratories has reported several alternative photovoltaic materials which, although less efficient (15%), are much less sensitive to the presence of minor impurities and consequently potentially easier and cheaper to manufacture. Nevertheless, to reduce production cost by a factor of 100 (or more) is bound to be a formidable undertaking.

It is perfectly true that such cost gaps have been overcome before in the electronics industry. But it would be excessively optimistic to suppose that this will be done again and in less than two decades.* Even after that, it would require another couple of decades before a significant number of installations could be put in place.

The other type of possible solar collector is far more modest: It simply uses solar energy for low-temperature heat (air or water) in place of gas- or oil-burning furnaces. Or, it may be combined with a conventional heat pump which acts like a refrigerator operating in reverse. The technology is not especially complex or difficult—indeed, it may be too simple for any except the largest enterprises to develop.† The problems are essentially related to design, compatibility of materials, durability, repairability, and manufacturing cost. Technically adequate solar heating systems for homes or office buildings are commercially available now (1976) but at a "Cadillac" price—around $10,000–20,000 for a rooftop solar collector for a medium-sized house, depending on climate and location, of course.

There is already a small market. However a mass market will not develop until the price drops to one-third or one-quarter of its present level. This should occur in a few years largely as a consequence of marginal design improvements, large-scale production, and more convenient installation. By 1980 I think solar heating will be a standard option for new construction in the central and southern part of the United States and probably in Southern Europe and the main islands of Japan. The rate at which it displaces conventional heating methods depends largely on the cost of fuel and on government policy.

However, it is important to realize that even assuming the most optimistic rate of market penetration, solar space heating is unlikely —by itself—to replace more than half the fuel requirements of newly constructed buildings by 1990 and perhaps two-thirds by 2000. In the

---

*If Bell Laboratories is a casualty of the current antitrust action against its parent organizations (AT&T and Western Electric Corporation), this technology could be delayed another decade or more!

† Why should a small firm do the pioneering work if it has no effective protection against a larger firm that can manufacture cheaply and distribute more efficiently?

advanced countries, I suspect that something like half the buildings that will exist by 2000 have already been built.* Except in Japan, hardly one-third and probably less than one-quarter of the total could conceivably incorporate solar heating.

Assuming that space heat accounts for 25% of all domestic energy consumption, it is clear that in twenty-five years, the maximum impact of solar space heat in the United States and Europe is in the range of 7% or so. (For Japan, admittedly, it might be somewhat more than 10%.) This is worthwhile, but hardly revolutionary. It is the same order of magnitude of saving, incidentally, that could be achieved by other improvements in building design and construction, especially the greater use of insulation.

The potential significance of solar heat would be much greater, as it happens, if solar collectors could also be used in industry, especially to provide low-temperature process steam (120°C). This seems technologically feasible, but it is certainly further down the road. It would probably involve the use of high-performance electric heat pumps in place of (or as a supplement to) conventional boilers. Once the technology exists, it could be widely implemented in a couple of decades, since industrial steam-generating facilities depreciate faster than housing and commercial or public structures. Existing boilers could be retained to provide necessary reserve capacity. However, heat pumps capable of operating reliably and efficiently in this range are not yet available, and active development has barely begun.

Geothermal energy from natural steam geysers, hot springs, and the like is significant in Iceland but in few other places. However, Los Alamos Scientific Laboratory is actively investigating the possibility that artificial geysers may be created by drilling deep wells several miles into the Earth's crust, fracturing a certain volume of hot rock, and pumping water through the fractured region. It would come back as steam, hopefully at a temperature and pressure suitable for operating a steam-electric generator.

Preliminary calculations seemed promising, and a test well is now being dug. But numerous questions—both geological and technical—remain to be answered before this scheme can be taken very seriously. In any case, it can be applied only where underlying rock strata are suitable. These questions will require some years of basic research to

---

*Probably more than half in Europe, where masonry construction is virtually universal. Perhaps rather less than half in the United States. Japan and the USSR will replace most of their present structures, but because of the climate, solar heating is signficantly less attractive in the USSR.

resolve. If the answers are entirely favorable, an engineering program could presumably be initiated by the late 1970s and a pilot plant constructed by 1983 or so. An expanded program might conceivably be underway by 1990, but hardly sooner. Thus this technology is probably twenty to thirty years behind that of conventional nuclear power. Its potential extent of applicability is unknown. However, it might come on-stream in time to constitute a viable alternative to the breeder-reactor.

With regard to wind power, it is clear that on a small scale the technology already exists. Small windmills are moderately common-place on the windy high plains of the Western United States. A revival of windmills in Holland and elsewhere around the North Sea would also seem to make a good deal of sense. For a few thousand dollars a small farm can have a useful source of energy for pumping water, operating grinding machinery, or generating electricity—except that if the wind dies down, so does the power.

Scaling up to a nationwide network of giant wind power generating plants linked to the national electric grid is another proposition. Even exploiting the most advanced known aerodynamic technology, such plants would be quite costly in relation to their average power output. (Average power output rises roughly as the square of average wind velocity.) Occasional windy days would not justify investment in wind-powered electric generators unless the demand for power is also extremely elastic. The most feasible proposition would seem to be to locate a few such large plants in especially good locations where the winds are reliably brisk. However we cannot depend on wind power for more than a minor fraction of total electrical output in the foreseeable future.

As for the three purely theoretical schemes (wave power, ocean thermal gradient power, and energy plantations), costs can only be guessed at. The first two involve the exploitation of essentially untried mechanisms for energy conversion. Both would require some years of laboratory experimentation, followed by a major program of hardware development. It must be borne in mind that the ocean is a very difficult and unforgiving environment in which to operate. In both cases the projected economics seem very questionable, even if one allows the proponents the benefit of most of the doubts. I would say they start at least a decade behind the Los Alamos hot rock geothermal scheme and with rather less attractive long-term prospects.

The energy plantation scheme is deceptively simple. The idea is to grow trees (or some other cellulose-producing vegetation) very intensively, harvesting the product and using "clean" fuel in a conventional steam-electric power plant located on the same site. This is technically feasible. However, the cellulose harvested would not be suitable for burning until it had been pressure- (or otherwise) dried and pulverized. Even then, oxygen enrichment would probably be required to get the flame temperature high enough to operate a power plant efficiently. A major industrial fuel-processing plant is evidently required, and this would involve a significant amount of development. Also, the economics are highly dependent on the assumed value of land and alternate uses of the products. Unless water can be recycled quite efficiently, only sites with substantial water availability could be considered. My own hunch is that cellulose will always have higher value uses for food production or structural materials than as fuel for an electric power plant, almost regardless of what assumptions one makes about the price of electricity. However, this is still an open question, and I may be wrong to be so skeptical.

To summarize the other possibilities briefly, none of them can realistically be expected to have a major impact on the energy supply picture within twenty-five years. However, solar electricity, space heating, and low-temperature steam generation—combined—may well become a major factor after that. The other proposed schemes will be applied only where special opportunities exist (suitable geothermal strata, wind funnels, tide funnels, etc.) or not at all.

Having indicated the limited potential of other sources, the energy argument boils down to coal versus nuclear energy versus "use less." The latter has its strong advocates—the "no growth" school, as exemplified by Schumacher—but frankly I cannot take them seriously as a political force. If economic growth stops in the next two or three decades, it will not be as a result of deliberate choice by the citizens of industrialized countries, but because of the cumulative consequences of many policy blunders.

Actually there is no immediate alternative to coal as a substitute for petroleum and natural gas, except insofar as the latter have been used to generate electricity. For the latter purpose there *is* a choice to be made between reverting to coal-fired steam-electric plants or building many more nuclear plants. Coal-fired plants are not ideal neighbors. Even with the best available electrostatic precipitators, they produce some smoke, and the problem of eliminating sulfur dioxide from the stack gas is still vexatious.* Moreover, coal must be dug from mines, with their well-known environmental, health, and safety problems. Underground mining is dangerous, and strip mining is devastat-

---

*Some critics, like Edward Cook, Former Chairman of Americal Electric Power, Inc. (the biggest utility in the United States), argue vociferously that the Environmental Protection Agency's proposed solutions are worse than the problem. This is going much too far, in my opinion.

ing to the land (unless a costly land restoration program is undertaken afterwards).

Still, coal is the "Devil we know" and nuclear power is the "Devil we don't know." A major commitment to nuclear power now means that our descendants for many generations will have to live with a legacy of hazards that are truly frightening, at least in terms of their potential. One of these is the need for permanent storage of the dangerous waste products, many of which have an effective half-life of thousands of years. Most scientists now agree that, because of geological and seismological changes in the Earth's crust, there is no such thing as a permanently safe method of disposal by burial or dumping in the oceans. According to biologist-writer Barry Commoner, it would require a kind of "nuclear priesthood" to watch over permanently and prevent the escape of these wastes. Such a priesthood is not *ipso facto* out of the question, but it is no light commitment to impose on our descendants.

Another hazard is the possibility of a serious accident of the type known as a "meltdown," which could lead to large-scale release of radioactivity in escaping steam. Although none has yet occurred in the United States—the nuclear industry brags about its safety record— there have been close calls. The closest occurred at Brown's Ferry (Alabama) in March 1975, when human error caused simultaneous failures in several of the safety systems. Several other plants have had to be shut down for more or less extended periods because of fires, condenser ruptures, or other failures. In 1976 the Vermont Yankee 540 megawatt plant was ordered closed because computer analysis of the safety system (conducted by GE, the designer of the plant) showed that a sudden release of pressure in the so-called suppression chamber —a large tank at the base of the reactor containing 500,000 gallons of water to shield the reactor—might cause the entire chamber to shift by as much as 5 inches. It is a moot question whether the chamber could remain intact after such a jolt. If the reactor containment vessel were to be ruptured, radioactive materials might be widely dispersed over the surrounding landscape in a matter of hours.

Unfortunately, the physicists and engineers themselves are deeply divided on the probability of such an accident and the likely consequences. A three-year study for the AEC* released in 1975, directed by MIT physicist Norman Rasmussen, put the odds of a fatality resulting from a nuclear reactor accident at one chance in 5 billion per year. According to Rasmussen, this makes nuclear reactors "thousands of

*Now the Energy Research and Development Agency (ERDA).

times" safer than fires, nonnuclear explosions, toxic chemical releases, dam failures, and earthquakes. If Rasmussen is correct, worry over reactor accidents is badly misplaced and is probably costing the nation billions of dollars by slowing down a vital program.

Nevertheless, doubts remain among the experts. Many physicists dispute Rasmussen's figures. The American Physical Society sponsored a study of its own, which concluded that the nuclear power establishment had underestimated the consequences of an accident and overestimated the effectiveness of the much vaunted safety systems.

As for the consequences of an accident, another MIT physicist, Henry Kendall, stated in an interview that if the accident suggested by the computer analysis of the Vermont Yankee plant had happened in reality, it would have caused immediate death for most of the 55,000 people living within a 20-mile radius of the plant and radiation sickness, leukemia, and other lingering effects for thousands of others over an even wider area. In short, it would be "an accident on a scale unknown to a peacetime nation." In answer to this, an official for the utility merely said the likelihood of all this was "extremely remote."

As for the effectiveness of the safety systems themselves, the GE engineer who directed the Vermont Yankee computer test, Dale Bridenbaugh, later resigned from his job, along with two others from the Reactor Division, Richard Hubbard and Gregory Minor. All three have testified to the inadequacy of safety standards and test procedures before the Joint Committee on Atomic Energy and the Nuclear Regulatory Commission. A member of the commission's own staff, Robert Pollard, also resigned within a few months to call attention to "inadequate" safety standards at Consolidated Edison Company's Indian Point (New York) plant. The three GE nuclear engineers said in their joint statement to the press[3]: "nuclear generation is a technological monster that threatens all future generations." Minor added in his letter of resignation[4]: "My reason for leaving is a deep conviction that nuclear reactors . . . now present serious danger to the future of all life on this planet."

The danger is not only from reactor accidents or leakages of stored nuclear wastes. Perhaps the most worrisome problem of all is the possibility that has been raised repeatedly by Dr. Theodore Taylor, a nuclear weapon designer at Los Alamos in the 1950s and mid-1960s, Deputy Director (Scientific) of the Defense Atomic Support Agency, which is the official nuclear weapons department of the Pentagon. From 1967 onward Dr. Taylor has pointed out to anyone who would listen at the AEC, the Joint Committee, and the Pentagon itself that it was never particularly difficult to build a small workable nuclear explosive device, and, since the basic principles have long been available in declassified documents, it is now relatively simple.*

Dr. Taylor claimed that, given the necessary quantity of plutonium, a small group of technicians, including one physicist and possibly a chemist, could construct a workable, if somewhat inefficient (i.e., "dirty"), bomb in a few months.[5] He pointed out, moreover, that plutonium, the fissile material, has been transported in *unguarded* trucks from nuclear fuel reprocessing plants to other locations. (Why unguarded? Apparently because the powerful Teamsters Union objected to either guards or AEC clearance procedures. The AEC did not care to insist!) For years the AEC official reaction was to dismiss Dr. Taylor's statements as "unfounded" or "exaggerated." He was regarded as a near-crank until, in 1974, the regulatory staff of the AEC was finally goaded into asking an independent group of experts for their assessment. All had been previously skeptical, but after reviewing the evidence, the group essentially confirmed Taylor's conclusions. Subsequently, an MIT graduate student was asked by producers of the Public Broadcasting System's Nova television series to submit a design for a homemade bomb. After a few weeks of library research, he did so. The professionals were forced to agree, reluctantly, that it would not have been very "efficient," but it would have worked.

What does this matter? In the first place, even a relatively undeveloped country can extract plutonium from the wastes of an enriched uranium reactor—as China and India have proved. Second, the advanced countries are busily competing to sell such reactors to the LDCs. Apart from the United States, Japan, Canada, Britain, France, and West Germany are all anxious to export. Brazil has negotiated to purchase a complete fuel-reprocessing system from West Germany, and France is selling such a system to Iran. The United States has been negotiating to sell reactors to both Egypt and Israel,* evidently for short-term political reasons. France even agreed to sell reactors to Libya, although that deal was later canceled under pressure from the United States. Dozens of other countries are now or soon will be in the market to buy nuclear power plants. Third, all these countries, plus the USSR, are trying to develop plutonium "breeders" to extend the natural uranium supply. Fourth, and worst, nuclear materials have

---

*The tremendous cost and complexity of the original Manhattan Project were mainly attributable to the problem of separating the fissionable isotope U_{235} from U_{238}; since nobody knew the best way to do it in a hurry, a number of different approaches were tried simultaneously. Later, much effort was devoted to testing and designing "fail-safe" remote-control trigger mechanisms, shielding, miniaturization, and so on. The basic bomb design was never much of a problem.

been so sloppily protected, in the United States at least, that any competent criminal or terrorist organization could probably obtain enough plutonium for several bombs with a determined commando attack on a fuel-reprocessing plant or (still easier) a truck carrying reprocessed fuel. Groups like the Palestine Liberation Organization, the Irish Republican Army, the Japanese Red Army, and the Mafia have all demonstrated both the competence and ruthlessness to hijack the ingredients, hire or kidnap the scientific talent, and explode a nuclear bomb somewhere in a city. The motivation hardly matters. It could be a simple holdup for ransom, a political gesture, or an egomaniacal act by a twisted personality.

Threats of this sort have already been received by several cities, including Orlando, Florida and Paris, France. They have been consistently discounted by the authorities, and no attempts have ever been made to inform or evacuate the populations affected. (Fortunately, all the threats to date have been phony.) Nor have the governments of the world yet instituted effective measures to prevent the diversion of fissile materials into illicit channels, or even—despite repeated outrages—to suppress the terrorists.

Despite all the disquieting evidence, industry and official reaction everywhere has been to deny the existence of any problem. For example, Mr. John H. MacMillan, Vice President of Babcock and Wilcox, a major reactor builder, said in a March 1976 press conference[6]:

> Plutonium is no more dangerous than other radioactive materials. The notion that some criminal nation or group could steal or buy plutonium and make a hydrogen bomb out of it is *fantastically absurd*. It would still take the thieves years and the expenditure of a billion dollars on technology to make the bomb.

MacMillan's remark about plutonium is irresponsible nonsense. Not only is plutonium uniquely suitable for making bombs, but it is one of the most carcinogenic substances known to man. I do not know whether his reference to a "hydrogen bomb" is a deliberate red herring or a simple mistake on his part. Dr. Theodore Taylor, who has principally raised the alarm on the possible misuse of nuclear materials by criminals or terrorists, has never suggested that such a group could build a hydrogen bomb. Why should they, when a Hiroshima-type (or even cruder) fission bomb can easily kill 50,000 or 100,000 people?

*According to published *Time Magazine* stories, Israel already possesses at least thirteen nuclear bombs that can be carried by jet fighter aircraft. All the nuclear material must have been obtained from a research reactor in the Negev Desert.

MacMillan's evident intention was to reassure the public on a sensitive issue so that his company can get on with its profitable business. Even if he is only guilty of carelessness and not deliberate deception, it would seem that he has not read any of the serious studies on the subject — which are not concerned with hydrogen bombs.

MacMillan's attitude is fairly typical of the nuclear establishment, however. I find myself most concerned with the evidence of extreme casualness with which responsible officials — both in and out of government — persistently deal with such weighty issues. The public's evident reluctance to believe the official spokesmen who keep saying there is nothing to worry about is increasingly justified by evidence that these same spokesmen do not know, or choose to ignore, the elementary facts.

At the moment the nuclear establishment is almost exclusively interested in the plutonium breeder cycle, in which the isotope uranium 238 is converted by neutron irradiation to plutonium 239 in a reactor that is simultaneously generating power by "burning" plutonium. All uranium reactors produce at least a little bit of plutonium as a waste product, but the amount can be increased by adjusting the parameters of the reactor design.

There are at least five types of possible breeders. The United States has concentrated on the liquid metal (sodium)-cooled "fast breeder" concept, which has the largest plutonium yield, although it is the most complex and expensive to develop. The first United States prototype breeder reactor was the Enrico Fermi reactor of the Detroit Edison Company. It developed many problems (and political enemies) and was shut down. There are several other breeder projects in the United States but as I write, it appears that France is now leading the field with its Phenix breeder — a less efficient but less difficult type — and there is scare talk in the United States about a uranium gap to justify a "no-holds barred" crash program in breeder development.

Curiously, despite the mounting evidence that plutonium is simply too dangerous to depend on, means to have nuclear power without plutonium have scarcely been explored. One such possibility would be to concentrate on developing a fuel cycle based on thorium 232. This can be converted by neutron irradiation into uranium 233, which is about as fissionable as plutonium or U^{235}. Instead of using pure plutonium 239, the reactor would use uranium 238 enriched by U^{233}. This diluted material *cannot* be used to manufacture an explosive device, for instance, without an isotope separation and enrichment stage which is probably beyond the means of a terrorist or criminal gang. I do not know why the thorium-U^{233} cycle has received so little attention.

Of course the ultimate source of nuclear power would be fusion, similar to the type of nuclear reaction that energizes the Sun and stars. For application on Earth, the most attractive possibility seems to be based on the heavy isotopes of hydrogen, deuterium, and tritium. Deuterium occurs naturally; approximately one hydrogen atom in each thousand is the heavy isotope. Tritium is manufactured by artificially irradiating an isotope of lithium (Li^6).

The United States and the USSR are actively (and collaboratively) trying to develop the technology for fusion power. There are two basic approaches. The first is continuous containment. An ionized gas (or "plasma") of deuterium plus tritium contained by a magnetic "bottle"* is suddenly brought to a very high pressure and temperature — sufficient to initiate the fusion reaction — by pulsing the magnetic fields that contain the plasma. A number of different magnetic configurations have been tried, but the most successful so far is the Soviet TOKOMAK device, which is a toroidal cavity with both axial and longitudinal magnetic fields. Similar devices have been built in the United States. The best results yet obtained are less than an order of magnitude , and perhaps as little as a factor of two, away from the fusion threshold in terms of density, temperature, and containment time. According to recent announcements, the next generation of experimental models to be built (late 1970s) should determine whether this class of device has a future.

The other basic approach to fusion is, essentially, to "tame" the hydrogen bomb. One variant is to actually explode a series of small "clean"* bombs in underground caverns or salt domes, capturing the energy as steam. (The cavity can also be used as a source of contained neutrons for "breeding" either plutonium 239 or uranium 233.) Los Alamos is presently investigating such a project.

A second variant is the extreme miniaturization of the hydrogen bomb principle: a tiny pellet of deuterium-tritium "fuel" † can be simultaneously irradiated on all sides by powerful pulsed laser beams.[7] The energy absorbed by the pellet causes the outer surface to vaporize and blow off explosively. To conserve momentum, the remainder of the pellet "implodes" to a very tiny sphere of material with a density 10,000 times normal. At such high compressions, the fusion process is

*The plasma must be kept away from any solid surface or it loses most of its heat almost instantaneously.

*"Clean" simply means that no heavy fissionable materials are used at all, even to initiate the fusion reaction. The original bombs did use fission bombs as a first stage.

† Actually, the pellet would be a hollow spheroid. Experimental versions are made of deuterated plastics for ease of fabrication.

easily initiated and the fuel "burns" before the pellet can fly apart again. Thus the containment problem that has plagued fusion researchers for years is apparently bypassed. However, the laser fusion scheme is of relatively recent origin, and a tremendous amount of development is needed on lasers, pellet manufacturing, and other related technologies.

Only a specialist could possibly be qualified to give a judgment as to the prospects of the various possibilities I have noted, and even the most eminent authorities are deeply divided. I can only state my view as an interested ex-scientist: I think there are reasonable technical prospects for dealing with nuclear wastes, safely designing nuclear power plants that are virtually fail-safe against any type of credible accident, and locating them in such a way that the risks of even an incredible accident would be tolerable. However, I do not believe there is any safe way of utilizing plutonium for purposes of generating electric power on a large scale. If the nuclear establishment persists in this route, there will eventually be a catastrophe. I think this outcome is avoidable. There are enough attractive technological alternatives — including fusion — to make the use of plutonium unnecessary.

There appears to be ample justification for Alvin Weinberg's[8] oft-quoted description of the nuclear energy program as a "Faustian bargain" with a devilish technology. Whether, like Marlowe's Faust, Man will be the ultimate victim of his own arrogance or, like Goethe's Faust, he will repent at the eleventh hour and escape damnation, remains to be seen. The bargain itself seems to be already sealed and struck. In the industrialized countries that have no good alternative energy sources, especially Western Europe and Japan, a powerful industry-government coalition appears to be gaining momentum and riding roughshod over all opposition. Objections are simply being ignored or dismissed. Short of a major nuclear accident or terrorist bombing in the next few years, only one thing seems likely to slow down the nuclear bandwagon, although it will not be stopped altogether. That is rapidly escalating costs. Virtually all the reactors now in existence took longer to build and turned out to be much more expensive than expected. The problem of high front end capital costs and long delays between project commitment and delivery have caused many recent cancellations of planned nuclear plants. Rapidly escalating uranium prices and uncertain availability have compounded the problem. The nuclear power industry has, to say the least, suffered a considerable economic setback in the last few years.

Unfortunately, coal is the only other feasible source of energy to replace petroleum and natural gas as the latter are depleted. In the case of large fixed installations such as power plants and industrial boilers, the substitution of coal for oil or gas is quite straightforward. (In many cases, the substitution was in the reverse direction only a few short years ago.) The problem is that coal is, and burns, dirtier. This problem can be ameliorated—at a price—through the use of electrostatic precipitators and one or another of a class of processes now being developed under sponsorship of the Environmental Protection Agency (EPA) to remove sulfur dioxide from the stack gases.

For smaller fixed installations such as domestic space heating, hot water, cooking and—above all—motor vehicles, the problem of replacing oil or gas is much more acute. In the case of new structures, as discussed previously, solar heat is, or soon will be, a feasible alternative.* For existing buildings, a liquid or gas fuel is still required if existing pipelines, burners, and boilers are to be retained. For future motor vehicles, after some delay—perhaps a decade—for research and development, alternative fuels or even electricity could be accommodated. For existing motor vehicles powered by internal combustion engines, only gasoline or diesel fuel, specifically, will do.

Fortunately, there is still enough petroleum and natural gas to supply the needs of the heating plants and vehicles now in existence throughout their projected lifetimes, with some left over. This statement will probably remain true for another decade. It may *conceivably* be true for two more decades if demand does not grow too rapidly. It will almost certainly *not* be true after the year 2000. (A more extended justification is found in Chapter 8.)

The constraints are tight. Sometime in the next decade we must stop building houses and offices and cars that utilize liquid or gaseous hydrocarbon fuels. Some alternative must be found. What can it be?

The answer which was uniformly given by all the energy experts as recently as the early 1970s was that cars must be built to run on *electricity* from presumably cheap nuclear power plants. However, the nuclear development program has hit economic and environmental snags, and the El Dorado of nuclear power seems little closer in 1978 than it did in 1965. Now there is serious doubt about the ability of the electrical generating industry to expand its capacity fast enough—as well as deeper doubts about the wisdom of permitting it to do so.

What other technological possibilities are there? The two that now receive the most attention and a significant share of research and

---

*Solar heat would not replace *all* conventional fuel in a typical space-heating or industrial steam-generating installation. A conventional backup capacity capable of using gas or electricity would normally be retained to deal with extended periods of bad weather.

development funds are *coal gasification* to substitute synthetic gas from coal for natural gas and *coal liquefaction* to substitute synthetic crude oil made from coal for natural crude oil. The "syngas" would be distributed by existing gas utilities through existing pipelines and used in existing gas furnaces, water heaters, stoves, and so on. The "syncrude" would be refined like natural petroleum and used as a basis for all the manufactured products, including gasoline, that are now derived from petroleum.

There are many possible processes for manufacturing "syngas," but they can be divided into two groups, depending on the nature of the output. One possible product would be a low BTU gas, which is mainly carbon monoxide, similar to the kind of "coal gas" that was once widely produced and sold in all the industrialized countries. An alternative possibility is a high BTU gas consisting mainly of methane and chemically similar to the natural gas that is now widely used. The latter would be vastly preferable to most consumers, since it is both less toxic and has a greater heating value.

The basic chemistry of these processes has long been known, and the development process is primarily concerned with increasing efficiency and output while reducing unit costs. The best large-scale coal gasification processes available to date are still several times more expensive per unit of output than natural gas at current United States prices. As long as price controls persist and supplies are reasonably assured, industry will not invest significantly in the more expensive alternative technology. Why should it? However, supplies are dwindling, and gas pipeline companies are beginning to renege on some contracts. It is not even certain that lifting price controls at this point would preclude a really severe gas shortage. Thus a reasonably well-funded research and development program for several years should bear some fruit. By 1985 I would conjecture that "syngas" will start to look like a reasonable alternative to natural gas. Some gas utilities are already planning plants, although construction is not yet underway.

The problem then remains: Can "syngas" facilities be built fast enough in the 1980s and 1990s to take up the slack as natural gas production drops? This is a moot question, but not the most difficult one we face. For argument's sake, I assume that the answer to this one is yes.

In the case of "syncrude," things are much less rosy. The processes are much less well developed, and some serious technical problems have yet to be solved—notably, separation of the major product from various wastes or secondary by-products. It must be remembered that the product is a very viscous liquid from which various entrained solids must be removed somehow. Costs have not yet been nailed down. Optimists believe the process will be commercially viable, but equally knowledgeable pessimists do not think it will ever be competitive.

Actually there are some other alternatives, although they have been largely ignored. One is to convert coal into a finely pulverized fuel of pure carbon. This involves developing suitable processes to remove the ash, sulfur, tars, and volatile components. The technology is qualitatively similar to coke manufacturing, which has been known for a century, but the product would have to be cleaner. Methods of grinding coal to the requisite degree of fineness also remain to be developed.

The use of powdered carbon involves some hazards (mixed with air in the right proportions it is explosive—but no more so than gas or gasoline), and suitable methods of handling, transportation, and storage would be needed. A carbon-water slurry might be the answer. In any case, the carbon fuel would require no further refinement and could be burned *as such* by both stationary furnaces or boilers and by engines of the external combustion type. Although some costs would be associated with replacing the existing type of motor vehicle power plant—gasoline or diesel engines—powdered carbon fuel might actually be *cheaper* than present liquid fuels. (This is one of the few areas in which one can foresee at least an outside possibility of lower prices.) It might, in particular, be cheaper than liquid hydrocarbons refined from syncrude.

Another possibility is the use of coal to manufacture methanol, which could be burned as a fuel in place of heating oil, gasoline, or diesel oil. The chemistry is known, and the process is already fully developed. However, it would be expensive: Methanol is now produced commercially from petroleum, even though coal is substantially cheaper per BTU. Methanol could be used today in place of gasoline at roughly the same cost per gallon, but only half the energy value. Thus methanol from coal would probably cost somewhat more than twice as much as gasoline from petroleum (pre-tax, of course), in terms of vehicle miles per dollar of fuel expenditure.

Of course, methanol can also be obtained from wood or other natural sources of cellulose. This has repeatedly been suggested as a nonpolluting alternative to fossil hydrocarbon fuels. (Actually, it is a variant of the energy plantation idea mentioned earlier.) The fundamental problem with this solution is that it involves the use of land to grow fuel instead of food. At present, as it happens, United States agriculture already requires several calories of (fossil) fuels to produce a single calorie of edible food. The idea of using land to grow cellulosic fuel (to replace fossil fuels) to drive tractors to grow grain is rather mind boggling.* It would make more sense, all around, to go back to mules. As noted before, I think agricultural or forest products will always be too valuable to use in this way.

PRODUCTS, SERVICES, AND MISCELLANEOUS

In the course of discussing various other issues, I have touched on a number of "downstream" technological possibilities including new uses of computers, new forms of communication (video phone), and new forms of shelter (bubble domes). To minimize wordiness I do not review these topics again. In any case, I have no intention of attempting a systematic survey of all the interesting possibilities that have been put forward by various inventors. There is no particular need to go into detail about different kinds of space hardware or exotic medical/biological capabilities, for example. The fact that a large number of such possibilities are within our collective grasp has been well enough established for my purposes.

What is more important to understand and has received less critical attention, it seems to me, is the significance of these "gee whiz" possibilities for broader social concerns: Does it matter greatly if dreams can be programmed? Or if 3-D holographic movies are made commercially? Or if truly nonfattening foods are developed? Or if shaped charges or superconducting magnets or fluid amplifiers or lasers or fluorocarbon plastics are widely used? To all these the answer seems to be "not much," except, of course, to a few affected individuals or industrial enterprises.

In this last section, therefore, I try to limit myself to a few topics where inventions really might matter a good deal to society as a whole. I also touch on some topics that have received disproportionate public attention for various reasons. I focus here on motor vehicle power plants and other forms of transportation, biological engineering, and military technology.

Automotive Power

To discuss this subject sensibly, we must distinguish two periods of

---

*The use of fossil fuels to grow food also raises other significant issues, but I am not trying to discuss everything at once. Some other points come up in Chapter 8, however.

time. First, the coming span of two or three decades during which fossil hydrocarbon fuels will still be generally available, and second, the period which follows the "age of oil."

During the initial period there may or may not be a shift away from the present type of vehicular power plant, based on the internal combustion engine. The decision, of course, rests with the motor vehicle manufacturers. They all prefer to stay with the existing technology as long as possible. If the industry does change, it will be because of a possibility of significant fuel savings and superior performance (including, but not limited to, lower emissions), plus multifuel capability.

No change has been decided on as of 1978, but if it occurs, the substitution will probably take place over the time span 1985–2000, and the successor to the internal combustion engine will either be a gas turbine of very advanced design or a Stirling cycle* engine (Rankine cycle* engines are a very dark horse at this point.) Either engine would probably utilize cast ceramic components (see section on materials) in place of costly "superalloys" used in existing prototypes. Although gas turbines have received much more development, I would personally bet on the Stirling cycle engine, which does not involve pushing so many technologies to their extreme limits.

Either of these engines has an important theoretical advantage: Unlike gasoline or Diesel engines they can burn *any* fuel (liquid or gas). Stirling or Rankine engines could also burn pulverized solid or slurries, such as powdered carbon. Refining the fuel is helpful, especially to reduce emissions of sulfur or ash, but it is not essential for operation of the power plant *per se.*

If the internal combustion engine is replaced by an "external combustion engine"—which seems to me to be a 50–50 possibility at the moment—it will probably still be the dominant power source by 2025. Major changes in the auto industry simply cannot be accomplished much quicker. Preliminary engineering and tooling up would require five to ten years. During any manufacturing changeover period there will be at least ten years during which both kinds of engine are produced simultaneously. For at least fifteen years subsequently, both old and new types would still be in service.

Many futurists unfamiliar with the auto industry (or any industry) are rather contemptuous of such mundane interim possibilities and project—or prefer—a direct shift to electric cars. Numerous advantages are casually claimed for electric propulsion, including

Stirling cycle and Rankine cycle engines are classified as external combustion engines.

Low operating cost (using "cheap" nuclear power)
Ease of operation
Low maintenance
Long life

Apparently, the last three advantages are based on analogy with simple electrical household appliances, compounded by widespread misinformation about just how long conventional automobiles do last.* The sad fact is that all the claimed benefits are totally hypothetical and, at best, remain to be proved. More than one may be illusory.

More important, the electric car cannot be a practical reality without a substantial improvement in electric storage batteries or fuel cells. (The latter would be of no interest without fossil fuels, however.) Since 1960 or so the familiar old lead-acid storage battery has been upgraded by about 50% in terms of performance, but this is nowhere near enough to power an electric car for everyday use in city or highway traffic. At least a tenfold improvement in lead-acid storage battery performance is required, and this has proved very difficult to achieve despite several decades of research.

So-called "advanced" storage batteries using exotic electrochemical combinations such as lithium and sulfur are still laboratory projects. If they ever emerge into production, there is little doubt that the cost of the combined motor-control-storage system would be at least three times — and possibly as much as ten times — as much as a comparable gasoline engine and transmission combination. For the same weight, they will provide less power and less range.

Will there be a dramatic breakthrough? Before 1990 or 2000 it seems to me most unlikely. There will probably be a future for electric cars later, however, because the electronics industry will eventually solve a very difficult technical problem: how to provide *external* power to a moving vehicle without unacceptably high losses or awkward mechanical contacts. Only by this means can transportation be truly systematized and begin to get away from the pattern of individually driven and powered machines competing with each other for space on the road and dissipating most of their energy in useless and wasteful stops and starts.

Almost certainly the best method will be to provide energy in fairly

---

*Most people guess about seven years. The truth is that the *median* age of automobile scrappage in the United States has consistently ranged between eleven and twelve years. Trucks are about the same. Buses last twenty years or more.

large increments or "pulses" and not on a steady continuous basis. The old overhead wire or third-rail devices used by trolleys and subway trains are inadequate for obvious reasons (aesthetics, cost, inflexibility, risk of accident). The science fiction idea of picking up power from a microwave broadcast beam covering a wide area can also be discarded at once: the efficiency of transmission would be too low, and intensity levels that would be safe for humans would be inadequate to operate a vehicle.

I do not attempt to "invent" a complete conceptual system here and now. There are far too many variant possibilities, and I would surely fail to think of some of the better ones. Merely to demonstrate that such a scheme makes a certain amount of sense is sufficient for my present purpose. What I envision is a small, lightweight vehicle driven by air-cooled electric motors, probably in the wheels. It would have a fairly sophisticated (but after 2000, cheap) solid-state electronic power control system and a high-capacity energy pickup unit under the car. It would also have an intermediate storage capability good for distances of 30–50 miles.

The storage system could be either an electrochemical cell (e.g., lithium-sulfur) or a high-tensile ceramic flywheel. In the latter case, the flywheel would actually be the rotor of a specially designed motor-generator unit capable of converting pulses of current from the external pickup into kinetic energy of rotation and also capable of converting rotational kinetic energy into electric power for the wheel motors. The wheel motors would also operate, in reverse, as regenerative brakes, converting the kinetic energy of the car itself back into electricity and storing it.

Recharge would have to take place automatically as the car passed over special recharge units in the road. Since fairly close tolerances are likely, I would expect the car to synchronize with and temporarily "lock onto" a moving cable in the roadway. This would trigger the charging device. A single pass might require 60 seconds or so and provide enough energy for 2 miles of driving. For densely traveled routes the vehicle would remain permanently locked on the external guide cable, except for turns. Within cities, a certain number of off-street "full" recharge locations would also be likely, probably at parking facilities.* The cost of each refill would be by credit card (and probably electronic funds transfer). Computers could also check the

---

*Such a unit would obviously have to be located where pedestrians would not be using the roadway.

registration of passing vehicles, automatically checking for cars reported stolen or in violation of traffic regulations, thus discouraging car theft and irresponsible driving.

Obviously, such a vehicle would be of marginal utility away from a network or grid where it could readily obtain power. Since the charging facilities would be costly, they would be limited to major arteries and points at which heavy vehicular traffic could be expected. Thus the system is, of necessity, urban in orientation.

Such a system would still be far short of a fully automatic (driverless) transportation system. In contrast, here is Arthur C. Clarke's 1958 vision[9]:

> The auto-mobile of the future will really live up to the first half of its name; you need merely tell it your destination—by dialing a code, or perhaps even verbally—and it will travel there by the most efficient route, after first checking with the highway information system for blockages and traffic jams. As a mere incidental, this would virtually solve the parking problem. Once your car had delivered you at the office, you could instruct it to head out of town again. It would then report for duty in the evening when summoned by radio, or at a prearranged time. This is only one of the advantages of having a built-in chauffeur.

Unfortunately, the notion of electronically controlled vehicles acting like chauffered limousines is probably fanciful. It would be intolerably lavish in use of both energy and capital—and very possibly technically infeasible—to have individually owned units utilizing a common network; a private vehicle being shuttled empty from a drop-off or pickup point to a remote storage location would be excessively wasteful.

On the contrary, it seems to me that if passenger cars ever become fully automatic, they will also inevitably become part of a public transportation system. When that happens—scarcely before 2025, I suspect—the distinction between taxis, limousines, jitneys, and buses will be one of size and route only. Small vehicles will provide individualized service at a higher price; larger vehicles will provide cheaper group service on limited routes and/or times. The customer will call for individual service by utilizing automatic special purpose telephones located on all street corners, inserting his magnetically coded credit identification card for personal identification and specifying by number code the size and type of vehicle desired. The nearest empty car of the appropriate type will make its way automatically to the point at which the call originated, ready to be activated by the *same* credit card (and no other). The customer will then specify his destination (and route, if desired) to the car itself.

A system of the kind described would require only a fraction of the number of cars now in service in advanced countries, since each car would be much more fully utilized. The vehicles would individually cost more — being complex and designed for ultralong life — but overall capital outlay for cars would be comparable to the present investment. Maintenance would be centralized. Electronic controls and automatic electric power distribution would also be comparable in magnitude and cost to the present traffic control and fuel refining and distribution system.

There would, however, be a dramatic saving in terms of energy *vis-à-vis* the present arrangement. The vehicles themselves would be more efficient. Most cars would be small and utilitarian in design, light in weight, and not especially powerful. (High speeds would only be possible on intercity highways, requiring special long-range cars, of which there would not need to be many). Average payload to weight ratio would be two or three times higher than that of present-day autos, and average "load factor" — the fraction of a twenty-four-hour day during which the vehicle is actually in use — should also be at least three times higher than at present. Congestion would be reduced, since on-street parking would be absolutely eliminated. Out-of-service vehicles would simply go to queues — like taxi ranks — in prespecified locations. Automatic traffic control would guarantee much smoother flow and many fewer stops and starts (and fewer accidents).

All factors taken together, plus electric drive, could raise the overall efficiency of the vehicular ground transportation system, in terms of energy use, by a factor of 5 or even 10.* Putting it another way, it appears technologically feasible, within fifty years, to transport people and goods on the ground for an energy consumption per passenger mile or per ton mile of 20%, if not 10%, of the present outlay.

Other Transportation Technologies

Before leaving the subject of ground transportation, a few comments may be appropriate in regard to the future of high-speed long-range

---

*My estimate of the *present* efficiency of motor vehicles for moving "payload" is no more than 3 or 4% of what could be achieved in principle. This seems like a very low figure, at first, but it can be defended with detailed calculations.

(intercity) transport. Recently the trend has been away from rail and toward air transportation. The inherent advantages of air travel over fixed rail are essentially the advantages of the automobile over the trolley or subway: flexibility and speed. However, major airports are now becoming congested, and interface time for airline passengers— the time required to travel from home or office to or from the terminal, check or reclaim baggage, pass through official formalities including security search, load and unload, taxi, circle, wait for clearance to takeoff or to approach the unloading ramp, and so on—is now *comparable to or greater than* actual travel time for most trips of less than transcontinental length. As planes become larger to conserve energy and labor, these interface times also tend to increase.

The supersonic airliner is an attempt to cash in on a large presumed market for still greater speed. For transoceanic flights this does make some sense and, as I commented earlier, if the cost of a supersonic airline seat mile can be cut somewhat, the demand for travel across the Pacific and to and from Latin America, in particular, can be expected to grow. The world can still shrink in some dimensions.

However, the big market for air travel is intra- (rather than inter-) continental, and commercial airlines are already being replaced by private or corporate aircraft for the most affluent people who want maximum speed and convenience regardless of cost. Airlines are now mass transportation and very definitely subject to the economics of mass markets. As energy costs rise—inevitably—so will air travel costs. Compensating advantages of scale have probably been largely exhausted by the jumbo jets. The larger the planes the less flexible the system. Short- and medium-range air transportation appears to have reached a technological plateau.

It was once thought that the next logical step was the short takeoff or landing (STOL) plane or even the vertical takeoff or landing (VTOL) plane, which would be capable of utilizing small local fields, perhaps close to downtown areas. In the past few years the VTOL has been revealed as a technological abortion. Whether a practical individual flying platform will ever become available—as conjectured by Kahn and Wiener[10]—is anybody's guess. If so, it would probably involve some combination of known principles, if not a new and unsuspected one. Its practicality as a transportation method would still ultimately depend on its energy requirements, which would probably be prohibitive.

The STOL is more practical and has already found a market in short-haul feeder routes, for example, between small regional airports and large metropolitan ones. However, since an extra interface stage is required, there are only a few routes where this method would offer significant advantages over ground transportation (primarily where ground vehicles cannot go, as between islands of an archepelago).

A few years ago there was a great flurry of interest in new forms of high-speed ground transportation systems. Some concepts involved creating new, totally enclosed, and possibly evacuated underground guideways. The advantages were thought to be protection from all possibility of external interference and theoretical elimination of all curves, so that extremely high speeds could be achieved. Unfortunately, the cost of digging thousands of miles of tunnels would negate these hypothetical advantages. Another, probably prohibitive, problem is seismic instability: Even a minor earth tremor could destroy the integrity of an arrow-straight, evacuated underground tunnel. Only a technological breakthrough out of left field could alter this pessimistic conclusion.

The more practical answer to high-speed ground transportation (200 plus miles per hour) appeared to involve surface routes. Now the topography must be considered, rights of way secured, and the impact of, and on, neighboring land uses must be taken into account. A truly straight, smooth ground-level right-of-way between major cities would be a colossal—and probably politically impossible—undertaking. To avoid unreasonably expensive underground tunnels, an elevated route would be necessary, but, again, a train traveling at 200 miles per hour along an elevated right-of-way would be a dangerous and probably intolerably noisy neighbor for a densely populated area.

The possibility remains of moving at relatively low speeds in the urbanized area and speeding up for the intercity gaps. In effect, this is what railroads now do, and performance can certainly be improved in a variety of ways—as the famous Japanese "bullet train" exemplifies. For speeds up to 125–150 mph, the most that seems likely to be attainable given the other constraints, steel wheels running on steel rails still appear to be superior to any alternative suspension system, especially for efficient acceleration and braking.

Thus the air-suspension system ground effect machine (GEM) can be disregarded as a serious contender for fixed-route systems. Although several experimental units have been built in different countries, they cannot be justified economically except at speeds higher than can be attained on realistic routes. They consume too much energy for too little benefit. Like the VTOL, the GEM is a technological abortion.

What about GEM's over nonfixed routes? Arthur C. Clarke, writing in the late 1950s, was extremely enthusiastic[11]:

> Because they have no physical contact with the surface beneath them, G.E.M.'s can travel with equal ease over ice, snow, sand, plowed fields, swamps, molten lava — you name it, the G.E.M. can cross it. All other transport vehicles are specialized beasts, able to tackle only one or two kinds of terrain; and nothing has yet been invented that can travel swiftly and smoothly over a single one of the surfaces just mentioned. But to the G.E.M. they are all alike — *and a superhighway is no better.*

> It takes some time to grasp this idea, and to realize that the immense networks of roads upon which two generations of mankind have spent a substantial fraction of their wealth may soon become obsolete. Traffic lanes of a sort would still be needed, of course, to keep vehicles out of residential areas, and to avoid the chaos that would result if every driver took the straightest line to his destination that geography allowed. But they need no longer be paved — they would merely be graded, so that they were clear of obstacles more than, say, six inches high. They would not even have to be laid on good foundations, for the weight of a G.E.M. is spread over several square yards, not concentrated at a few points of contact.

> Today's turnpikes might well last for generations without any further maintenance if they had to carry only air-supported vehicles; the concrete could crack and become covered with moss — it would not matter in the least. There will clearly be enormous savings in road costs — amounting to billions a year — once we have abolished the wheel. But there will be a very difficult transition period before the characteristic road sign of the 1990's becomes universal: NO WHEELED VEHICLES ON THIS HIGHWAY.

From the perspective of 1978 this was evidently a pipe dream. The only real advantages cited for GEM is the elimination of highways costing "billions a year" and freedom to travel over all kinds of terrain. (Well, not quite — hedges, rocks, trees, walls, or ditches would still be impassable.) But at what cost?

Energy is the key. A GEM is actually a specialized form of aircraft — more economical than a helicopter because of the cushion effect of compressed air under the vehicle, but much less economical than a car. The GEM requires a separate system (usually a shrouded turbo-fan) for propulsion and braking, which is very inefficient as compared to a wheel in contact with the road.

Because of these technical limitations, GEMs can only be justified

—if at all—in very large sizes and across a water barrier. The only ones in commercial service today are the experimental hovercraft ferries operating across the English Channel. Because there are so few opportunities that would justify a GEM in place of an ordinary boat, mass production cannot realistically be expected. I rather expect this technology to wind up in a museum.

Other Energy Conservation Technology

It is arguable whether this discussion should be included under "energy." I put it here because it cuts across several classifications.

The major point is that opportunities for conservation are not merely marginal. Many studies have concluded that it is "easy" to save 15% or so from current consumption by means of measures such as lowering speed limits and thermostats, using computers to ration the use of fuel in industrial processes, repairing leaky valves, insulating steam pipes, and so on. The implication is that further improvements are much harder, if not impossible, to achieve. This is nonsense.

I already mentioned that optimal design of office or commercial buildings can save as much as 75–80% of the energy now consumed for space heating, ventilation, and air conditioning. Even existing buildings could save a lot of energy by upgrading insulation, improving temperature regulation and heat distribution (to prevent overheating one part of the building to achieve a minimal level of comfort elsewhere), adding storm windows, entrance vestibules, and so on. Heat exchangers to use waste heat from air conditions to heat swimming pools could save a significant amount of energy. In factories, there are vast opportunities for increased use of heat exchangers or recuperators to recapture waste heat from boiler smokestacks, hot metal castings or ingots, slag heaps or incinerators. Local on-site electric power generation is economic in many locations because of the possibilities for utilizing both the heat and the electric power. Much of this low-grade waste heat could be put to economic use in winter; for example, in adjacent greenhouses or fish hatcheries.

There are numerous other possible energy-saving devices ranging from microwave ovens to superconducting power transmission to solid-state photoluminescent lighting systems. One of the most potent— although seldom considered—means of conserving energy is high-rise cluster housing, linked by pedestrian walkways, shuttle-buses, or moving sidewalks to nearby commercial or office buildings or factories.

Reflecting on the range of possibilities, it seems evident that there are no fixed lower limits on energy consumption per capita or per dollar of GDP. It is perfectly true that economic activity requires energy, and increased industrial and agricultural productivity in the past two centuries is largely, but not entirely, due to increased use of nonhuman energy in place of human labor. Hasty generalizations about this subject — often to support an ill-considered short-term political position — often disregard glaringly obvious facts. One of these facts is that Swedes, living in the far north with long, cold winters, have achieved an average standard of living equal to the United States, with barely over half the average United States energy consumption per capita. Most Swedes would admit that Sweden, too, has many unexploited opportunities to conserve energy. Much more could be said in this vein.

Although there is no visible ultimate limit, there is a limit to what can be done in a year or in five or ten years. Some changes can be achieved overnight (e.g., drive slower and lower the thermostat). Better insulation or storm windows can be installed in a year. However, it takes fifteen years or more to replace the automobile fleet. Even before that can be done, it takes a number of years to retool the factories. It takes generations to rebuild cities to a more (or less) efficient pattern. These are the limits that really matter. However, I am straying into the realm of policy, which is beyond the scope of this book.

Biological "Engineering"

I commented at some length on some of the favorite themes of the technological forecasters of the 1950s and early 1960s. There is no need to repeat what has been said. I do wish to comment here, however, on some possible inventions or discoveries that might have a rather more beneficial impact.

One such invention is advance sex determination for children (at the time of conception), which is widely regarded as a likely development in the next few years. In the advanced Westernized countries this would probably not matter much, since preferences between boys and girls are roughly equal. (The commonest preference is for one child of each sex.) There might be a temporary increase in the ratio of males to females, but I think it would soon correct itself. There would also be some reduction in the number of births, however, since the case of the family that has three or four girls in the vain attempt to get a boy (or conversely) would be eliminated. This could have a measurable, but not dramatic, effect.

In the Muslim and Indic cultures, however, the impact could be revolutionary. Based on existing cultural patterns, many families would choose, if they could, to have *only* boy babies—until after a decade or so the growing shortage of girls would begin to increase their social value (and standing). Meanwhile a substantial reduction in total births would occur, with an even sharper impact on future family formation.

It takes little imagination to see some of the potential ramifications of this. It might be one of the most potent population control methods that could possibly be devised for the countries of North Africa and South Asia, especially India, Pakistan, and Indonesia. The real problem, needless to say, is to make the necessary procedures known and available to the rural people in these countries. Here another breakthrough—which I cannot easily imagine—might be needed. Undoubtedly it would involve the use of the electronic media to spread the information.

Another notion that has often been suggested in the context of birth control deserves brief comment here. This is the idea of regulating fertility by means of some (otherwise harmless) substance that could be added to municipal water supplies. I doubt if any substance exists that would be both uniformly effective and harmless, but even if it did it would probably affect much less than 20% of the combined population of India, Pakistan, and Indonesia (the fraction living in urbanized areas). Moreover, the urban population would inevitably be aware of the presence of the inhibitory substance and would find ways to neutralize or avoid it when they wished to have children. Thus this particular hope appears to me to be misplaced.

Speaking of India, still another interesting notion has been put forward. (In this case the technology almost certainly exists.) It is, in effect, to wage biological warfare against the hundred million (or so) cattle that are, in reality, the greatest scourge of the land. Obviously, the simplest and most economic method would be to round up the (relatively) unproductive females* and slaughter them, utilizing the meat as food. Since this is now impractical for religious reasons, however, an indirect method could be utilized, namely, to deliberately introduce a virulent strain of some disease (like rinderpest) that affects cattle but not humans. This could be done by releasing the appropriate disease vectors (fleas, ticks, flies, etc.) more or less simulta-

---

*The castrated males (bullocks) are the major source of motive power in rural India. They could only be replaced gradually as alternative motive power sources become available.

neously in a number of locations. Valuable pure-bred cattle could, of course, be innoculated in advance. The operation could be carried out by a relatively small number of technicians and veterinarians.

Of course there would be unfortunate side-effects, most notably a shortage of milk and the sudden creation of a large number of putrescent and disease-breeding carcasses. An immediate increase in malnutrition — already serious — followed by a secondary epidemic of diseases of humans would be the likely consequence.[†] For these reasons I find it difficult to imagine any reasonably humane government embarking on such a program. On the other hand, a communist government in the ruthless Stalinist tradition might conceivably do so as a means of simultaneously "solving" an acute ecological problem, reducing the pressure of human population, and quelling dissent and resistance among the villagers.

In conclusion, it might be worthwhile to pose the question: are there any possible new "wonder drugs" that would really yield great benefits for Mankind? A few possibilities occur to me:

1. A non-addictive drug that can "replace" hard narcotics such as heroin, and which will — after a period of use — provide immunity to its physiological effects. (Methadone has sone of these characteristics, but is itself physiologically addictive.) The difficulty here is that the phenomenon of addiction is seldom purely physiological. There is a psychological component that no drug can eliminate.[*]

2. Ditto for alcohol, smoking, and eating. That is, "painless" pharmaceutical methods of eliminating the physical craving for alcohol, cigarettes, and food would be valuable. Again, the addictions in question are usually at least partly psychological. How can a mere pill replace the positive feelings of comfort, sensory gratification, satisfaction — the "filling" of an inner emptiness? Evidently this is too much to expect, which puts a limit on the value of such inventions.

3. A drug capable of actually dissolving and eliminating arterial depositions of cholesterol would be quite beneficial. This would not eliminate heart attacks, but it would improve blood circulation and allow many older people to maintain a beneficially higher level of

---

[†] Note that this same sequence of events would also follow a major epidemic of natural origin. Such an epidemic could well prove to be "nature's" ruthless but effective resolution of the present impasse.

[*] That is to say, there are addictive personalities. These people will probably find something else to get "hooked" on. However, almost anything would be less dangerous than heroin.

physical activity. Fewer elderly people would vegetate unproductively. Working life might be extended.

4. The most significant (but, I suspect, the least likely) would be a true broad-spectrum antivirus and/or cancer drug, namely, a chemical substance harmless to ordinary cells but lethal to viruses or cancer cells. This would probably extend average life expectancy by several years. But its real benefit would be in reducing the number of painful, long drawn out, terminal cases that clog hospitals and drain the financial resources of relatives and communities. It would also alleviate one of the greatest fears that prey on people as they get older. (Most people, if they could, would choose almost any means of death other than cancer.)

Unfortunately, real progress in the past few decades has been remarkably slow in all four of these areas. One would have to be quite optimistic—more so than I am, at least—to expect great breakthroughs during the next few decades, although some advances will certainly take place.

New Frontiers for Human Settlement

The most persistent theme of technological forecasting in the 1950s and early 1960s was the conquest of space and the undersea environment. From Sputnik I onward, most physical scientists and science fiction writers regarded the continuation of the United States/Soviet space program of the 1960s and its extension into the oceans as a foregone conclusion. Orbiting bases and scientific laboratories, colonies on the moon, even colonies on the ocean floor, were taken for granted.

I do not regard any of this as inevitable, or even likely, in the next fifty years. The reason is, simply, that there is no economic or political demand for this kind of program. The satisfaction of scientific curiosity might be a sufficient motivation for the few scientists among the population, but very different, and certainly more tangible, benefits would be needed to justify more adventuring in space to the rest of the taxpayers. (Military "advantages" will not suffice.)

Efforts to find convincing economic justification for lunar or orbiting colonies have utterly failed so far. There are, admittedly, some industrial processes that could be carried out more efficiently in a high-quality vacuum.* But the immense capital investment in recoverable

*The growing of ultrapure silicon crystals for making solar cells is perhaps the most interesting of these. Another distant possibility is the processing of nuclear fuels and the disposal of wastes.

nuclear rockets — not to mention the needs of a totally self-contained community designed for permanent habitation — appears to overwhelm any conceivable benefits. The even more bizarre scheme for permanently orbiting colonies in space, recently put forward by Princeton physicist, Gerard O'Neill can be even less justified for a world with many more straightforward practical uses for its limited resources.

Undersea colonies are equally unrealistic: In shallow water (up to a few hundred feet in depth) where visibility is reasonable, they offer no significant economic advantage over operations from fixed platforms or ships. In deep water they would be virtually useless — even if they could be constructed — since there is no known optical or acoustical means of conducting any detailed surveillance of the surrounding ocean floor. Only actual samples of water and the ocean bottom itself offer any real assistance in determining what is there.

The exploration of outer space and under the oceans will continue, of course, but only to the extent that economic (or military) needs justify it. Unmanned satellites have found a number of important uses — most notably for communications, weather forecasting, and military surveillance. The dredging of manganese-nickel-copper nodules from the ocean bottom is almost certain to begin fairly soon, as already mentioned. Oil drilling will also extend further offshore. Beyond these limited activities, other possibilities will gradually evolve. The Moon is likely to remain uninhabited for at least several more decades — and perhaps permanently.

Defense

I have not focused much attention on strictly military matters, for the simple reason that it is perfectly obvious to everyone that a major nuclear war would be a calamity. The kinds of sequences of events (or scenarios) that could lead to a massive exchange of ICBMs have been explored elsewhere.[12] The *likelihood* of such an event was once widely perceived as very high. C.P. Snow stated some years ago that nuclear war "within a decade" was "a statistical certainty." Luckily he was wrong about the timing at least. I personally think that a nuclear war between the United States and the USSR (or China) is very unlikely indeed, given the present political situation in the world. However, that is another topic.

The question I want to explore briefly before ending this very long discussion of technology is, simply, is there any real prospect of a *defense* against a hypothetical nuclear attack?

Such a defense could theoretically be either passive or active. A passive defense would essentially consist of warning devices, evacuation capability, deep underground shelters, reserve supplies of food and water, air filtration equipment, medical facilities, and so on. Sweden, the USSR, and China have invested heavily in civil defense measures of this kind. There is no reasonable doubt that these countries would be able to survive a nuclear exchange as functioning entities, in better shape than most of the rest of the world.

An active defense would consist of systems designed to detect and intercept enemy missiles (or bombers) before they could penetrate to vital regions. The so-called antiballistic missile (ABM) program of a few years ago was a half-hearted attempt to achieve this. It was taken seriously by some of the military brass, but primarily as an element of an overall strategic posture and a potential bargaining tool. The original crude ABM was rendered obsolete rather quickly by an advance in offensive weaponry, the MIRV (or multiple independent reentry vehicle). This is an ICBM capable of carrying several small warheads (rather than a single large one), to be released after reentry. Each warhead is capable of being guided precisely to a different target, and the defense has no way of determining the ultimate targets from the trajectory of the carrier. Nor can an interception path be computed in advance, since the incoming rockets are capable of evasive action.

What possibilities are left to the defense? The ABM seems to be a deadend. It was trumped by MIRV. The main future hope of a defensive antimissile breakthrough is the high-energy laser, virtually a death ray, based on an orbiting satellite powered by solar cells. A modest level of research and development is going on in this field — $200 million a year according to the *Wall Street Journal*[13] — mainly to increase the power output and efficiency of lasers. This research is also important for the laser-fusion program. Steady progress can probably be expected, and, if funding is not discontinued, I would expect some significant technical successes to be achieved by the early 1980s. However, even a partially effective laser ABM system could hardly be deployed before 1985 and most likely not until after that.

The proliferation of nuclear weapons among politically unstable countries has already begun to accelerate, and this trend could provide incentives to increase the emphasis on purely defensive weapons. As long as "the enemy" is assumed to be the USSR, it is obvious that no active defense now envisioned could make much difference. However, if the problem is to defend Europe or the United States (or the USSR) against an international renegade or a twenty-first century military pirate organization using stolen or captured armaments left over from "brush fire" wars in Africa or South Asia, such a defensive capability would be invaluable.

REFERENCES

1. Dennis Gabor, *Innovations—Scientific, Technological, Social,* Oxford University Press, New York, 1970.
2. Archibald T. McPherson, "Synthetic Food for Tomorrow's Billions," *Bulletin of the Atomic Scientists,* September 1965.
3. UPI, February 4, 1976, *Mexico City News.*
4. Marquis Childs, February 26, 1976, *Mexico City News.*
5. John McPhee, *The Curve of Binding Energy,* Farrar, Straus, & Giroux, Inc., New York, 1974. or, Mason Willrich and Theodore B. Taylor, *Nuclear Theft: Risks and Safeguards,* Ballinger Publishing Company, Cambridge, April, 1974.
6. UPI, March 10, 1976, *Mexico City News.*
7. See, for example, "Laser Fusion," *Science News,* Vol. 106, August 17, 1974.
8. Alvin Weinberg cited by A.V. Kneese, "The Faustian Bargain," *Resources,* Number 44, September, 1973.
9. Arthur C. Clarke, *Profiles of the Future,* Harper and Row, New York, 1958, p. 30.
10. Kahn and Wiener, *op. cit.*
11. Arthur C. Clarke, pp. 39–40, *op. cit.*
12. The best-known references are Herman Kahn's books *On Thermonuclear War* (1959), *Thinking About the Unthinkable* (1962), and *On Escalation* (1963).
13. *Wall Street Journal,* April 15, 1976.

CHAPTER EIGHT

MEASURES OF THE ENVIRONMENT — NATURAL RESOURCES

INTRODUCTORY COMMENTS

The environment of man is both man-made and natural. The man-made part of the environment — man himself — has been, in effect, the subject of six chapters. In this short chapter I want to discuss the problem of resources from a general and long-term point of view. In this context, it should be understood from the outset that resources include, but are *not* limited to, industrial raw materials. A resource is anything that can provide a service to Man.

Air, soil, sunshine, and water are environmental resources. The millions of other species of plants and animals with which man shares the Earth also constitute an environmental resource. Man relies on other species not only for food and fiber, but to recycle his metabolic waste products and the metabolic wastes of other animals, to regulate temperature and humidity, to control pests, to condition the soil, to regulate the carbon, oxygen, and nitrogen cycles, and to gratify the senses. The gene pool, analogous to a vast library of genetic information that has been accumulated by eons of evolutionary development, constitutes an important environmental resource. Finally, scenery, landscapes, beaches, mountains, forests, even deserts, may be resources because of their ability to provide recreation or sensory pleasure. In this chapter I examine these resources as degradable and/or exhaustible assets.

That natural resources are capital assets of a sort is undeniable, although often forgotten. That degradation or exhaustion of these assets is tantamount to "living on capital" — the greatest Victorian economic sin — can hardly be disputed. Since the beginning of the Industrial Revolution, the natural capital assets of the Earth have been gradually converted into or, in effect, replaced by man-made capital assets, ranging from physical structures and machines to technical knowledge and educated people. The unanswered and very difficult question is whether the *total* stock of productive* capital on the Earth is increasing or whether it is being depleted by lavish and wasteful consumption of exhaustible resources, especially fossil fuels.

Although this question is clearly of great importance for Mankind's future, I have never seen it clearly posed, much less answered. The prevailing view among conventional modern economists and technologists in the western countries *seems* to be that technological knowledge is the major long-term form of capital asset. It is implicity assumed that losses due to degradation or exhaustion of natural resources can and will be overcome or made up by the application of technology. This school of thought essentially believes that the natural capital stock can and will be enhanced by the discoveries of modern science and their application. The Marxists do not agree as to the overwhelming importance of technology (interpreted as knowledge), since Marxist theory attributes all accumulated asset value to surplus profits withheld by owners of capital from payments to labor. The Marxists still deny any significant importance to the availability of natural resources as such. They, too, believe, in effect, that man is the sole and independent arbiter of his own destiny.

There is another radical school which, as one might expect, takes the opposite view entirely. E. F. Schumacher (whom I also quoted in Chapter 4), for instance, asserts that technological knowledge and physical infrastructure constitute "but a small part of the total capital we are using. Far larger is the capital provided by nature, and not by Man—and we do not even recognize it as such. This larger part is being used up at an alarming rate. . . ."[1] The two views are contrasted in Figure 8.1.[2]

Schumacher is not alone in his perception. This view is substantially shared by many others of the "no growth" persuasion who have formulated the proposition in other ways. It might be as well to point out here that the growing clamor among the world's poorer nations for "sharing the wealth" more equitably is based essentially on the notion that wealth is actually based on possession of, or access to, exploitable natural resources. Logical inconsistencies in the underlying economic

---

*Conventional housing, private automobiles, and major appliances are counted as consumer durables, not producer durables. This distinction is actually rather arbitrary, since consumer durables produce services, and some economists prefer to include household labor, for instance, as (unpaid but) productive work. To be on the safe side, I conceptually include all kinds of durable goods as productive capital. However, since the discussion is strictly qualitative, it does not matter much.

Figure 8.1 Two contrasting views of the relationship between natural and man-made capital overtime.

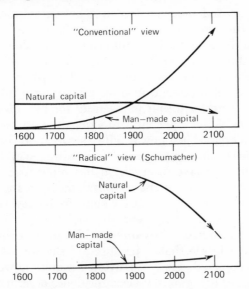

theory need not concern us at this point, nor does it matter that self-interest plays an obvious role in framing the arguments. The point is simply that a growing number of Third World intellectuals do assert and defend this position. They are receiving some support from respected Western intellectuals.

It may be that logic and analysis do not matter here (since the "truth" can never be rigorously established in any event). Perhaps this is an issue destined to be argued for the next few decades in terms of political idealism, national self-interest, or – God forbid – "class struggle". Insofar are possible, I would like to explore the matter in less technicolor terms. The key questions are: to what extent is natural productive capital being degraded or exhausted by the activities of Man? Is there a real danger that this degradation will overwhelm our efforts to enhance and improve our natural endowment by technological means? Are we unwittingly "living on capital"?

MECHANISMS FOR DEGRADATION OR EXHAUSTION OF NATURAL RESOURCES

Some few natural resources, like sunshine, rainfall, or scenery, are not depleted by any use. The underlying assets are untouchable – in trust, so to speak – and the service output is perpetually available.

Unfortunately, there are many other resources which cannot be utilized as such — only the "income" can actually be consumed — but which can be degraded and even destroyed by contamination or abuse. This is true of the atmosphere, the land surface, the lakes, streams, and oceans, and the biological environment.* Man, along with all animals, breathes the air every minute of his life. Plants also require air, from which they derive carbon dioxide and moisture. Some plants, with the help of soil bacteria, also fix atmospheric nitrogen into a water-soluble nitrate form that is essential for life. Most people are only dimly aware of the other vital functions the atmosphere serves. Nor is it well understood just how fragile a structure it really is.

Regarding its role in oxygen, carbon, and nitrogen cycles, the atmosphere is merely a passive reservoir. It has other more active roles, however. The atmosphere is the essential medium for filtering the Sun's rays. It permits light in the visible frequency range to pass through, but excludes the dangerous ultraviolet frequencies. This protective function is carried out by ozone, which is a special three-atom form of oxygen molecule that is produced in the stratosphere. If the ozone layer is depleted, more ultraviolet radiation will reach the Earth's surface, resulting in increased incidence of skin cancer to humans (especially people with light skin) and damage to crops such as cotton and soybeans.

The atmosphere is also an insulating heat blanket for the Earth. It prevents the surface from cooling off too much at night and in the winter by trapping and re-reflecting the Earth's thermal (heat) radiation back to the surface. This insulating function is carried out by the carbon dioxide and water vapor in the air. As the carbon dioxide level rises, as it has been doing for several decades,[3] the "greenhouse" effect of the atmosphere will become more pronounced. If carbon dioxide alone were increasing, the effect would be to raise the mean temperature of the Earth's surface. A rise of a few degrees, in turn, would cause the jet streams to move several hundred miles to the north, shifting the temperate zone rainfall pattern significantly.[4] Eventually, a warmer climate would cause the polar ice caps to shrink and raise the level of the world's oceans.

*What is casually and inaccurately termed "the ecology." Ecology is actually the science of interspecies relationships in natural communities, or "ecosystems." The Earth as a whole is an ecosystem, of course.

† A small temperature difference can make an enormous difference in how much water is trapped as snow and ice. During the "ice ages," when glaciers covered most of Europe and North America, the mean air temperature was probably less than 7.5°C below its present level. However glacial accumulations melt slowly.

As it happens, there is another atmospheric phenomenon which seems to be acting in the reverse direction; that is, to *cool* the surface of the Earth.[5] The amount of dust that is suspended for long periods in the stratosphere determines how much of the incident solar radiation is transmitted downward to the ground level and how much is reflected (or scattered) into outer space. The more sunlight that is reflected, the less heat reaches the surface. Only very small particles of dust—less than about 10^{-4} cm or 1 micron in diameter—are truly effective light scatterers.

Such particles can be swept up by dust storms or thrown up by forest fires or volcanoes. More recently, man-made industrial pollution has been a factor. Small particles of dust or smoke are quickly removed by wind and rain in the lower atmosphere. However, above 50,000 feet or so, in the calm, stable stratosphere, tiny particles (less than 10 microns in diameter) can remain suspended for years. Nobody knows how important man-made dust clouds are in comparison to natural ones. But many industrial processes certainly contribute a share. Cement plants, coke ovens, blast furnaces, electric arc furnaces, and large thermal power plants are particularly potent smoke producers,* as are automobiles and aircraft.

It is possible that the contrary effects of increasing carbon dioxide from fossil fuel combustion and small dust or smoke particles in the upper atmosphere—also largely from combustion—may simply cancel each other out. It is also quite possible that the balance is only temporary and that the cooling or warming effect will eventually predominate.

The atmosphere plays another vital role in the regulation of heat and cold. It is one of the two chief agencies by which excess heat from the tropical regions is transmitted into the polar regions. (Ocean currents are the other.) The heat is actually carried by water vapor, which is evaporated mostly from the surface of tropical oceans—thus cooling them—and thence carried into the temperate zones where it falls as rain. The heat of condensation, released again into the atmosphere, warms the region that receives the rainfall.

When ordinary global heat transfer mechanisms do not operate rapidly enough and temperature differentials between the tropics and the temperate zones exceed some threshold level, nature has another

*It must be emphasized that *visible* smoke, which comes from particles larger than 30 or 40 microns in diameter, is irrelevant here. These particles are much too large to be good scatterers or to stay for any significant length of time in the stratosphere. Electrostatic precipitators are effective at trapping the large particles, but not at catching the tiny ones.

faster mechanism to dissipate the excess heat energy. This mechanism is the tropical storm. It is called a hurricane or typhoon, depending on which ocean one is in. One such storm contains as much energy as 1000 *megatons* of TNT (or several dozen large hydrogen bombs), all of which is dissipated in the temperate latitudes within a few days as wind and heat of condensation.

It is clear that immense natural forces are involved in this thermal regulatory system. Hence anything that disturbs it *might* cause staggering (if unknown) consequences for life on the Earth. I return to this topic at the end of this chapter (the energy-climate dilemma). Apart from the question of climatic change, there are several other ways in which activities of Man may adversely interfere with the atmosphere or the oceans. (I freely acknowledge that some of these may also turn out to be quite harmless.) They include (1) oil spills, (2) dust, (3) water vapor and other pollution from high-flying jet aircraft (or rockets), (4) aerosol propellants, (5) massive irrigation and water engineering schemes, (6) deforestation, and (7) cities. I discuss them in order.

In the case of oil spills, the oil floats in a very thin layer, gradually spreading over a wider and wider region. Until the oil layer is removed by some means or other, it covers the water and inhibits evaporation. Under the oil, the water warms up. (It also becomes oxygen deficient.) Meanwhile, less water vapor reaches the atmosphere, and there is less rainfall on some land surface.*

Regarding dust in the lower atmosphere, there is evidence that it plays a role in providing nuclei for condensation. If there are too many nuclei present, the water droplets may remain in the air as haze or mist and never come down as rain. Thus it is conceivable (but unproven) that the water vapor content of the atmosphere in the temperate zone could build up to a higher equilibrium level as a result of excessive dustiness. This might result in changing precipitation patterns. For instance, there might be more orographic precipitation over mountains, less "warm" rain over the plains, and greater overall cloudiness. The combined impact on agriculture could be quite adverse.

High-flying aircraft burn large quantities of fuel producing massive quantities of water vapor and CO_2 plus sulfur oxides from contaminants and oxides of nitrogen from the high temperature of combustion characteristic of a jet engine. The water vapor tends to condense into clouds (known as contrails) which may remain for quite a long time in the stratosphere before dissipating. This reduces the amount of solar

---

*About half of all the world's oil spills occur off the coast of South Africa—for reasons having to do with tanker routes and the storminess of those seas. Simultaneously, sub-Sahara Africa is suffering a prolonged drought. This is probably coincidence, but . . . ?

radiation reaching the Earth beneath. The detailed interaction of SOx and NOx pollutants in the upper atmosphere is not completely known, but there are two possible mechanisms that may be important. First, nitrogen oxides can apparently catalyze the recombination of ozone (O_3) and monatomic oxygen (O) to form ordinary oxygen (O_2). As noted above, ozone plays an important role in protecting the Earth from destructive ultraviolet radiation. Second, both sulfur oxides and nitrogen oxides can form acid radicals which combine with ammonia — present in the air in trace quantities due to the decay of organic material — to form tiny ammonium sulfate or ammonium nitrate particles. These particles, being extremely small, can scatter light effectively and may also contribute to a cooling of the Earth's surface.

The use of aerosol propellants (and refrigerants) based on certain long-lived fluorocarbon compounds (known as F-11 and F-12) can result in a build-up of these compounds in the stratosphere. There they are dissociated by ionizing ultraviolet radiation, releasing some chlorine atoms. These, in turn, combine with atmospheric oxygen yielding chlorine oxides, which are even more effective than nitrogen oxides in terms of reducing ozone. This mechanism has only recently been discovered, but the risk is so great that the United States National Academy of Sciences has already proposed a ban on the two chemicals in question for use as aerosol propellants.[6] The two cognizant agencies (FDA and EPA) have announced that the ban will be implemented.

Major irrigation and water engineering projects, deforestation, and urbanization can all have an immediate impact on climate and rainfall patterns in some locations by increasing evaporation and ground surface temperature by removing vegetative cover in other areas. These effects are immediate and distinct from any long-term effects on the land itself.

As I said, the ultimate consequences of all these mechanisms are speculative. They may not be adverse at all, or they may be negligible in magnitude. I mention them to stress the fact that human activities are already on a scale potentially sufficient to interfere significantly with vital atmospheric processes, in particular.

Land can become unproductive through various mechanisms, but the usual sequence involves some combination of deforestation, overgrazing, overcultivation, erosion, salination, and desertification. A permanent change of climate sometimes follows. The degradation of land through surface contamination — as, for example, by mining residues — is also increasingly important. North Africa, the Middle East, India, and China were certainly much more fertile and productive 2000 years ago than they are today. The now barren mountains were forested and the valleys were green. As the tree cover is removed, the soil surface heats up, loses water faster, and retains less moisture than formerly. The humus (organic detritus) oxidizes. Without surface vegetation and organic humus to anchor it, the top soil becomes dry and powdery. It blows easily; every rainfall carries a load of dust into the sky and silt into the rivers. Eventually soil fertility is lost. Irrigation is required to grow crops. Only deep-rooted, water-conserving species can grow in nonirrigated areas. Thus the arid deserts grow at the expense of surrounding semi-arid lands.

Lakes and rivers too can be degraded and destroyed by abuse. Silt from eroding land is one of the mechanisms. A heavy load of silt makes water turbid and impenetrable to light. Green water plants and algae cannot grow, thus cutting off the natural food chain for fish and water birds. Only anaerobic decay organisms can survive in heavily silt-laden streams.

Pollution is another environment-damaging mechanism of more recent origin. Organic or inorganic poisons such as pesticides (e.g., DDT) or heavy metal compounds found in certain kinds of mining or industrial wastes can damage a stream. One common form of pollution is acid mine drainage from old abandoned coal mines. What happens is that coal itself and heaps of sulfur-containing trash are exposed to the air. The sulfur oxidizes to SO_2 and SO_3 which readily dissolve in water, forming sulfuric acid. The acid kills the fish.

Organic wastes such as sewage or animal manure that would normally be recycled in a perfectly natural way can also damage a stream or lake if the quantity being dumped is excessive. Organic material normally decays by an oxidation process via the agency of aerobic (air breathing) microorganisms. This uses up the oxygen in the stream. If the amount of waste is too great, all the oxygen dissolved in the water will be exhausted, thus killing the aerobic bacteria and all fish or other air-breathing animals. At this point the waste begins to accumulate on the bottom of the stream or lake where it continues to decay slowly, with the help of anaerobic bacteria. The decay products consist mainly of carbon, tars, and hydrocarbons, such as methane. If left long enough, the result is peat or, ultimately, coal, petroleum, or natural gas.

Sewage can cause a stream to become anaerobic even if it is given primary bio-treatment before it is dumped. The reason is that the residual waste contains nitrogen and phosphorus,* which are plant nu-

---

*Some nitrogen and phosphorus are contained directly in the human metabolic wastes or in other food wastes (garbage). But quite a bit formerly reached the surface waters via detergents, which used the chemical sodium tripolyphosphate as chelating (water-softening) agent. Recently, the amount of phosphorus used in detergents has been reduced.

trients. Thus the treated sewage is a kind of fertilizer, which causes green plants, especially algae, to grow. The process is known as eutrophication, which merely means enrichment, but is eventually lethal to the water body. A "bloom" of algae must end when the nutrients are all gone. It is typically followed by a sudden die-off. The dead algae must then decay, resulting in eventual exhaustion of oxygen and the death of the fish. When this repeatedly happens in a fresh water lake, the organic material settles to the bottom and fills it up. The lake gradually becomes a swamp or a bog. In nature this takes thousands of years, but with human intervention it can happen in a mere few decades.

Still another form of degradation applies to the biological assets of the Earth. I am talking about reduction in the number and diversity of species and the number of unique protected "niches" or communities in which different species can survive. One of the major continuing impacts of modern industrialized Man has been to reduce or eliminate barriers to travel. Where Man may go, plants, animals and microorganisms invariably follow. Thus in recent decades there have been scores—possibly hundreds or thousands—of cases in which a species was imported accidently to a location where it had no natural enemies and caused havoc.

I mentioned in another context the examples of the sea lamprey and the alewife, which invaded the Great Lakes and crowded out the trout, perch, and whitefish. As an "answer" to this, the Cohoe salmon was deliberately introduced to feed on the teeming alewives. This did not restore the lake fishery to its original form, of course. To these cases, even a casual survey would have to add a few more spectacular ones. The European rabbit was introduced to Australia in the nineteenth century as a domestic pet and source of food. A few decades later it was ravaging the continent—as it still does. An imported species of starfish has devastated the Great Barrier Reef of Australia. Marine biologists are seeking to control it by importing some of its natural enemies—wherever they may be found. The water hyacinth was introduced to the rivers and canals of Florida as an exotic flowering plant. Now it chokes the waterways (although it may have an interesting future as a "pollution eater"). Meanwhile, alligators, dugongs, and other native animals are rapidly being eliminated from the Everglades—although alligators originating in Florida may have established themselves in the sewer systems of some Northern cities. They probably escaped from households to which they were introduced originally as "pets." These are just a few cases in point.

A number of insects, pests, and plant diseases have crossed the oceans to find attractive havens. The Japanese beetle is one notorious, unwanted immigrant to the United States. The gypsy moth is another. The chestnut blight, from Europe, has utterly destroyed the American chestnut species which once dominated the vast hardwood forest east of the Mississippi. Another tree disease from Holland has decimated the American elms which once provided shade to the small towns of New England and the Midwest.

When a new species thrives in a new environment, the original inhabitants are sometimes crowded out. Man himself is a chief hunter and destroyer of many wild animals and birds. Eagles, falcons, and hawks, for instance, do not nest near human habitations. The "American eagle" and numerous other species of raptors are gradually being extinguished—with considerable assistance from blood-thirsty "sportsmen." Wild mountain sheep, timber wolves, mountain lions, lynx, otter, grizzly bears, and polar bears are all becoming scarce in North America. Thanks to hunters, the American bison, dominant natives of the Great Plains, were almost eliminated. The last wild elephants, tigers, bears, panthers, and leopards will surely disappear from India within a generation. Their forests are being cut down for fuel, and their skins or tusks are valuable trophies. Gorillas and orangutans are likely to vanish in a few decades along with smaller, less well-known anthropoid apes and monkeys. The rhinoceros is becoming rare even in African game reservations, because of persistent poachers who kill the beast for its "horn"—traditionally valued in India as a aphrodisiac. Some of the larger sea mammals, including blue whales, "killer whales," manatees, and dugongs are also near extinction—again, due to hunting.

What benefit does man sacrifice if there are no more wilderness areas or large wild animals to live in them? Even the hunters—who are most responsible—will surely miss the source of their destructive pleasure. The rest will lose something that is far more important, although I cannot begin to quantify or even describe it. Earth without dragons and unicorns seems a sadly diminished place. To lose virtually all the most interesting animal species which still share the planet with us—as seems inevitable within another century—will be an unspeakable, yet totally unnecessary, tragedy.

A third category of resources can be described as exhaustible. It consists primarily of concentrated deposits of fossil fuels and metal ores, which are dispersed and modified by use. They are not literally consumed, since an atom of copper or cobalt is never actually destroyed. But they may be so degraded or dispersed by use as to be, effectively, used up. The resources I call degradable can, in principle, be reused forever with proper care. This is not true of the metals and fossil fuel deposits.

Admittedly, the distinction between degradable and exhaustible is fuzzy. For fuels, normal use means combustion. Here the degradation is inevitable and essential to the process. No fuel can be burned twice. However, many metals, in some of their applications, can be used again. In fact, some items like gold jewelry, lead automobile batteries, steel rails, and copper tubing or cable are nearly 100% recycled. On the other hand, other uses of the same materials are seldom or never recovered for secondary uses. For instance, gold paint or gold plating for electrical switches, tetraethyl lead in gasoline, tungsten welding bars, incandescent light filaments, coatings for TV tubes or fluorescent lights, silver compounds used in photographic film, titanium, zinc, chrome or lead pigments, iron nails, copper sulfate fungicide, and scores of other metal or metal-containing products are virtually irrecoverable.

Since large fractions of every finished material are ultimately lost or dispersed as such, one can roughly relate the rate of consumption of scarce materials to the rate of approaching exhaustion. The time at which this final state of nonrecoverability will be reached depends on the size and distribution of the original stocks.

The importance of distribution is that some of the Earth's original stock of mineral wealth was in a form so concentrated and so accessible that it could be extracted by an extremely primitive technology. For example, nuggets of pure copper or silver were still being mined in the Western Hemisphere through the nineteenth century. On the other hand, some minerals are so dispersed—for instance, in sea water or in granite rock—that no conceivable price would justify their extraction and separation. For instance, gold *could* be recovered from seawater, but I cannot imagine any reason for doing so.*

To get to the key point, the total amount of a scarce mineral or fossil fuel that is actually in the ground does not matter. The effective stock at a given moment is the amount that is discoverable and recoverable, based on the current technology of exploration and extraction. As the technology improves, the recoverable fraction grows in relation to the total amount in the earth, but at a decreasing rate. Eventually it must approach some upper limit, which is the ultimate stock. I should add, however, that the ultimate stock (e.g., of a metal) can be defined to take into account the recyclable fraction of the scarce material. Recy-

*Uranium, too, can be recovered from seawater. In this case, the process might possibly be worthwhile if the price of uranium becomes high enough.

cling may extend the available stock considerably in some cases, but since there is always some loss in use, the ultimate stock is still finite unless there are natural biogeochemical cycles that are capable of renewing the supply indefinitely. I return to this later. For some materials, at least, the ultimate stock must eventually be exhausted.

I passed very quickly over another important topic that deserves clarification. I asserted without any explicit justification that technological improvements in exploration and extraction (including recycling) *cannot* increase the recoverable fraction of a resource stock without limit. Some technological optimists might deny this, judging from published statements. The justification for my skepticism comes from the economic axiom of "declining returns to scale" as applied in particular to investment in exploration, extraction, and recycling. In simple terms, each additional dollar of expenditure tends to buy less in the way of results than the dollar before. This phenomenon is a natural consequence of the fact that, in a world in which the social discount rate (or interest rate) is greater than zero, the easiest and cheapest improvements are undertaken first. Certainly every economist — even Marxists — accepts the general validity of this rule.

The impact of the law of declining returns can, unfortunately, be obscured for a time — even quite a long time — by other concurrent changes. The law implies that extractive resources will inevitably become more costly per unit of output as sources are progressively degraded and improvements in extractive technology eventually fail to compensate. How long does it take for this to happen? Will the economy as a whole ever "notice" the effect, *or can it be entirely masked by substitutions?*

Experience in the United States from 1900 to 1970 helps explain the optimism of those who foresee no resource crises. In Table 8.1 the costs of extracting key natural resources used in the United States are shown in GDP units.[7] Except for an increase (due to arming for World War I), the cost of the acquisition of mineral resources has consistently declined as a fraction of the overall United States GDP.

Table 8.1 shows a superficially reassuring, but not necessarily extrapolatable, trend. Deeper analysis (which I do not specifically cite here) does show, for instance, that real *costs* of petroleum production in the United States have declined consistently for several decades up to 1970 or so, even though wells were deeper, harder to drill, and less productive. Improved technology compensated for all these differentials and more.[8] However, the future in this case need *not* be an extension of the past. On the contrary, available evidence points to a sharp increase in future energy extraction costs coincident with the depletion of the large Middle East oil and gas reserves. The actions of OPEC

Table 8.1   Resource Acquisition Costs In GDP Units (United States)

	1900	1910	1918	1929	1940	1950	1960	1970
Metals	1.32	1.25	1.70	0.90	0.90	0.80	0.60	0.62
Nonmetals	0.48	0.45	0.36	0.42	0.31	0.27	0.33	0.27
Fossil fuels[a]	3.6	3.8	4.2	3.6	3.4	1.9	2.3	1.80
Total	5.3	5.5	6.26	4.92	4.61	3.97	3.23	2.69

[a]Plus fuel wood.

have merely advanced the date of the price increase that would have occurred sooner or later.

However, technology offers one "out" from the apparent dilemma of inevitable exhaustion, namely, the possibility of substitutions between materials or, more significant, between the uses of materials. Let me expand on this point. The slippery question is, what is a resource? On closer examination one can see that underlying the "limits to growth" argument is a belief that a resource is something fixed by nature both as to its availability and its uses. Geologists and industrialists tend to believe this with particular fervency. A resource is assumed to have certain unique and useful properties not exactly matched by any other material and therefore essential to human and industrial life. How do we know it is a resource? The implicit answer is: Because it is something we currently use! The underlying premise is that this material has been essential to industrial production in the past and will, *ipso facto,* continue to be essential in the future. This notion is, incidentally, clearly alpha in terms of the alpha/omega dichotomy introduced in Chapter 1.

Two illustrations suffice to show the questionable nature of the "fixed resource" notion. Copper is an example that quickly comes to mind. The red metal has valuable properties of electrical conductivity, malleability, resistance to corrosion, and so on which have made it a very convenient material for electrical and telephone cables, motors, generators, noncorroding household water pipes, noncorroding small pieces of hardware (brass), and various other purposes. Copper has long been regarded as a truly essential resource for an industrialized nation. The limits to growth hypothesis is based on the assumption that the uses to which a resource such as copper is put today *will always be the uses of that material* and that no other material can quite take its place.

As soon as the premise is made explicit, its falseness becomes evident. Copper was once used for roofing and sheathing the hulls of wooden ships. It no longer is. Aluminum, a much more abundant metal, has already replaced copper in many applications, including high-voltage electrical transmission lines. It is also gradually replacing copper for household wiring and is on the verge of doing so for automobile radiators. Brass, an alloy of copper, is rapidly being replaced by other materials, including aluminum, for all sorts of hardware applications. New technology is continuing to alter the nature of electrical transmission and communication. The telephone industry, for example, has worked out the technological problems of voice and data transmission by means of modulated light beams transmitted through tiny glass fibers and amplified by lasers—a system using virtually no copper at all. The fibers are made mostly of silica, a material in unlimited supply. This technology will almost certainly replace the huge quantities of copper now tied up in telephone lines and cables within two or three decades and release it for other uses.* Finally, plastics (notably PVC) developed by the chemical industry are already beginning to replace copper water pipes. As a consequence of these accumulated technological changes, the world copper industry is already facing the prospect of a long-term glut—not a shortage—with sagging prices and excess supplies.

A second illustration underlines the point. Natural rubber was once the sole basis of automotive (and other) tire production. It was thought to be a unique and irreplacable product on which a number of key industries depended absolutely. Rubber was derived from the sap of a tropical tree *(Hevea brasiliensis)* growing wild in West Africa and Brazil and was at first gathered by natives in the forests and brought to river towns, such as Manaus on the Amazon, thence shipped to processing plants in the United States and elsewhere. For a while the rubber barons enjoyed a monopoly, and Manaus was, briefly, the "fifth richest city in the world." But its wealth was ephemeral: The seeds of rubber trees were smuggled out, and raw material production was shifted to rubber plantations in such places as Malaya and Vietnam, where output could more easily be controlled. By 1940 most of the world's rubber supply came from plantations in Malaya and Indochina. When Japanese military expansion threatened Southeast Asia at the beginning of World War II, it appeared to many that this event would deprive the Western world of a unique and essential resource essential for rearmament! United States policy toward Japan prior to Pearl Harbor was strongly influenced by this misconception. As we now

---

*It will also probably release the large quantities of tantalum in electromechanical switching systems.

know, the consequences of Japanese takeover were minimal as far as rubber was concerned. Within two or three years natural rubber was largely replaced by synthetic rubber made from petroleum, and this substitution was not only swift but irreversible. There is still a small market for natural rubber, but the countries that once cultivated rubber plantations and grew rich are looking for other uses for the land and wondering how to replace their lost export markets.

A "material" resource, therefore, cannot be defined as something having a unique set of properties and a permanent function, but rather as a material that happens to be useful at a particular time because of a conjunction of historical circumstances. These circumstances tend to change. When they do, what was formerly an essential material may no longer be so. A factor that is very likely to trigger such a shift would be an impending scarcity and a rapid anticipatory price rise.

There is virtually no material in use at the present time that cannot, under imaginable circumstances, be replaced by another. Indeed, almost every material* we use in our everyday lives today is a candidate for substitution within the lifetimes of ourselves or our children. Of course, technological substitution is a gradual process, and for a major metal like copper there are many specific uses, each of which is a separate arena for competition between alternatives.

Quite apart from the possibilities of substitution for scarce materials, it must be pointed out that some materials are *not* scarce and will always be available and extractable. This is probably the case for some sixteen elements that are major constituents of air, seawater, crustal rock, and biological organisms, respectively:

From Air	*From Seawater*	*From Deep Sea Nodules*	*From Rock*	*From Plants*
Oxygen	Oxygen	Manganese	Silicon	Carbon
Nitrogen	Hydrogen		Aluminum	
	Sodium		Iron	
	Potassium		Calcium	
	Magnesium		Magnesium	
	Chlorine		Titanium	
			Manganese	
			Potassium	
			Phosphorus	

*Energy in "available" form (e.g., as electricity) is the exception, but energy *per se* is immaterial.

These elements are not all obtained right now from their "ultimate" sources, but all easily can be. There are also one or two marginal elements, such as sulfur, that are quite widely distributed on the Earth's crust and might conceivably be added to the list. One could add nickel and copper, which will be available in very large quantities from deep sea nodules as a by-product of manganese.

Note that basic components of plastics (carbon), glass (silica), and ceramics (silica, lime, alumina) are all abundant. Plastics need *not* be produced from fossil hydrocarbons, although it is convenient to do so; they can be manufactured from other organic materials. Nor will steel ever be in short supply. Most of the intrinsically scarce alloying elements such as nickel, chromium, molybdenum, and niobium are probably replaceable by combinations of other elements such as silicon, aluminum, titanium, and nitrogen. Even stainless steel can be made, in principle, without scarce constituents.*

A reader who has followed the above reasoning closely will realize at this point that the exhaustible resources we worry so much about are either replaceable or avoidable, without excessive difficulty. There are two provisos:

1. That approaching exhaustion should be perceived far enough (usually several decades) in advance to stimulate and allow time for the necessary substitutions.
2. That there be an adequate supply of energy for extraction of the nonscarce materials from their ultimate sources.

As to the problem of warning, any kind of free competitive market for commodities would virtually guarantee this: Approaching exhaustion will be signalled infallibly by rising prices. Only if supplies are controlled by a cartel or if prices are kept artificially low by some sort of nonmarket mechanism such as a subsidy or by indirect regulation is it possible that the price warning mechanism be by-passed. †

The availability of adequate energy on earth *in principle* (at least

---

*In fact, a type of stainless steel was manufactured over 2000 years ago in cities of Northern India before the time of Christ. A massive rust-free steel column attributed to King Asoka (273–232 B.C.) is a major tourist attraction in New Delhi today. The "secret" has been lost, regrettably, although metallurgists now understand the basic principles involved.

†Unfortunately, something rather like this has happened in the United States with both natural gas prices (regulated) and petroleum (subsidized by the depletion allowance). This is the fundamental reason the United States has been so unprepared for energy conservation.

for a few more millions of years) is not in doubt. The problems associated with extracting and converting much of it are immense, of course. During the next half century these problems will be especially awkward because finding a substitute for petroleum and natural gas is now rather urgent (as I discussed in some detail in Chapter 7), and much less wasteful patterns of energy consumption must simultaneously be adopted, especially by the United States. These are primarily issues of technology and policy, rather than resource availability. The latter is of importance primarily because of its influence on timing, which I take up in a later section.

TIME SCALES FOR DEGRADATION OF THE LAND AND OCEANS

It is almost impossible to estimate from direct evidence the worldwide rate of degradation of land lakes and seas as a productive resource. In the first place there are virtually no statistics before the twentieth century: Evidence of agricultural and fishery productivity of North Africa during Roman times, for instance, is anecdotal at best. In the second place, there have been several large-scale climatic fluctuations that we do know about in the past several thousand years, which are partly responsible for observed changes on the land surface. (To confuse matters further, at least some of the climatic variation is probably attributable to the changing vegetative cover on the land.) The obvious measures—agriculture or fishery output—mainly reflect changing technology and increases in land under cultivation, or fishing intensity rather than natural fertility.

There are suggestive indications, however. When colonization of the Western Hemisphere began in the early 1600s, some of the richest agricultural land in the world was in what is now the southeastern United States, especially the states of Georgia, Alabama, and Mississippi. The major commercial crops were cotton and corn (maize). The land was never overpopulated or overgrazed, but neither was it conserved. In 300 years of careless planting, erosion carried away most of the topsoil, leaving millions of acres of marginal land that is now primarily suited for growing yellow pine or slash pine rather than agricultural crops. Since the 1930s, heavy investment in land reclamation—especially in the Tennessee Valley (TVA) area—has slowed the erosion, healed some of the scars, and restored some of the fertility of the region. However, the conservation and reclamation process has been costly and slow. The heedless waste of natural capital has required a substantial infusion of man-made capital to compensate for it. For the United States as a whole, it was estimated twenty years ago by the Department of Agriculture that the annual loss of topsoil through erosion might still be as high as 0.5% per year. It was undoubtedly far higher at earlier periods, such as during the "dust bowl" episode of the 1930s. The growing need for synthetic fertilizers to replace lost natural soil fertility is understandable in light of numbers like this. Evidently, a large investment in synthetic fertilizer manufacturing plants *plus* the raw material feedstocks required to operate them is, at least in part, a form of capital replacement for lost topsoil.

Obviously, a further large investment in flood control dams and dikes and irrigation ditches is another element of the capital cost of land reclamation and waterway protection. The cost of planting trees or grass on eroded hillsides (often by hand) and their permanent withdrawal from any form of exploitation is another. Forest fire control in watersheds is still a third cost, since heavy erosion occurs immediately after a forest fire has denuded a hillside of soil-holding trees.

The magnitude of the capital investment required to reclaim a desert is immense. The effort expended by Jewish immigrants to Palestine since the late nineteenth century exemplifies it. Orange groves bloom near Jaffa today, but much of the land of Israel is still barren—a far cry from the fertile "land of milk and honey" into which Moses once led his people. The famous cedars of Lebanon, too, are long gone from the once-heavily-forested mountains to the north. They were cut to provide timber for the merchant ships of Tyre and Sidon and the war galleys of Rome. A single grove of patriarchs is all that now remains.

Despite a few scattered efforts at land reclamation, the deterioration continues. Indeed, it is certainly accelerating. The Sahara is creeping southward, a few miles every year, leaving devastation. West and Equatorial Africa are affected in the south; the Sudan, Ethiopia, and Somalia in East Africa are also under siege. The deforestation of mountain slopes from Morocco to Tibet and from Ceylon to Sumatra is accelerating.[10] Runaway population growth increases the pressure of overgrazing (particularly by sheep and goats), slash burning, and the cutting of timber for fuel. As of 1972 or so, only 8% of the land area of India was forested. The peasants of remote Nepal now must walk for miles up the steep hillsides from their villages to find wood for fuel. Even the limbs of the few remaining large mature shade trees are constantly threatened by midnight "wood-nappers." Reforestation in India today is little more than a gesture, frustrated equally by the depredations of wandering cattle and fuel-hungry peasants. To assure its survival, each pathetic sapling planted by the government along

major roads must be protected by an elaborate perforated metal device
like an inverted trash container—a shocking indication of the cost of
replacing ravaged forests!

Land use patterns shown in Table 8.2 are also somewhat suggestive
of the trends, if we compare different regions.[11]

Table 8.2 Land Use by Region (1968)

	Arable, cropped (%)	Pasture (%)	Forest (%)	Waste (%)
Europe	31	18	28	23
USSR	10	17	39	34
Oceania	4	54	9	33
North America	10	13	42	35
Latin America	5	20	48	27
Africa	9	21	25	45
South Asia	22	13	25	40
East Asia	10	15	12	63
World	11	19	30	40

Notice that South Asia as a whole was still 25% forested in 1968,
attributable to large remaining forest tracts in Ceylon (Sri Lanka),
Burma, Thailand, Indochina, and Indonesia.* In fifty years, following
present trends, the pattern for all South Asia would be like that of
India today.

In the developed countries of Europe, North America, and Japan
agriculture and forestry are now—after some sad experiences—mainly
practiced in a conservative manner that will not destroy what remains
of the productivity of the land. Regrettably, the advanced countries are
not yet conservationist in other areas, notably ocean fishing, mineral
extraction, and materials processing.

As I commented earlier, the major problem with ocean fishing is
that the capital asset—the ocean itself—is *common property*. It is
freely accessible to anyone with the means of exploration and owned
by none. Thus no one has any incentive to conserve it for future use.
Accordingly, it is not only the income—the annual production—that is
being harvested, but the breeding stock itself. The declining output of
ancient fisheries such as the Grand Banks and the North Sea is a

*Most of the population of Indonesia is located on the fertile volcanic island of Java. The
other large islands, Sumatra, Celebes, Borneo, and Western New Guinea, are much less
fertile and much less heavily populated. Even so, deforestation is proceeding very
rapidly.

matter of record. As the 200-mile "limit" becomes internationally accepted in place of the long-standing 3–12 mile limits, much of the overexploitation may be stopped, to the benefit of all nations (including those that are landlocked!)

The problem with mining is that the ancient method of underground mining is now rapidly being replaced by the open-pit or strip method, which facilitates the use of very large machines and is much less dangerous to the workers. However, the resulting scars to the Earth's surface are very damaging. In regions with heavy rainfall they can lead to serious erosion and acid drainage problems that affect all the downstream river valleys. In extremely arid regions only the scenery may be affected, but this too is a permanent loss to Man.

Techniques for restoring the land surface after open-pit mining have been perfected in Europe (mainly Germany). With care, the end result can, in some cases, actually be an improvement on the original. However, it is much harder to restore the land if the mining is not carried out with eventual restoration in mind. Thus old strip mines in most places tend to be permanent unhealing wounds in the Earth. Moreover, restoration requires ample water to establish a vegetative cover. This is a major impediment in the semi-arid areas where much of the mining is now done. Placer mining — mainly for gold — is another technique that is extremely damaging to the land. Whole mountainsides are deliberately washed away by high-pressure water jets to dislodge and capture a tiny metallic component. Yet long after the miners' fortunes have been made and spent, the fertile downstream river bottom lands lie buried under sterile gravel heaps.

The process of winning and smelting metals from their ores has also left extremely long-lasting scars, particularly in the neighborhood of copper, silver, lead, or zinc refineries. All these are mainly found in combination with sulfur and extracted by a process that typically includes roasting. This is a step in which the sulfur is recombined with atmospheric oxygen and driven off as gaseous sulfur oxides (SO_2 or SO_3). However, these gases are highly water soluble, and they quickly combine with any water droplets in the air to form sulfurous or sulfuric acid — which comes down as an acid rain or haze on the surrounding area. Mountain valleys where copper smelters have long been located tend to look like the surface of the Moon. Nothing green grows for miles around — nor will grow for decades, even long after the copper ore is exhausted and the smelting stops.

Lead and zinc smelters also tend to poison their surroundings with arsenic and/or cadmium-containing dust. These are highly toxic materials* that tend to be associated with lead and zinc ores and are produced as by-products. Silver smelters once saturated the neighboring area with mercury vapor. † Now they use a different process based on an equally toxic chemical, sodium cyanide.

Other industrial wastes can also result in contamination of, or damage to, the land surface or the coastal waters. However, nothing now known would touch the devastation of a major nuclear reactor melt-down (Chapter 7). This fortunately has not yet happened, but even the slight possibility causes many people to worry about the plutonium breeder concept. Conceivably, tens of thousands of square miles of land and water would be contaminated by highly radioactive and toxic materials, including plutonium. Any region thus contaminated would have to be totally evacuated and quarantined, lest the dangerous materials be spread even further by wind, flood, or wandering animals. If the ocean itself were contaminated by radioactive wastes, the consequences would be permanent: There would be no conceivable method of restoring it to purity.

TIME SCALES FOR EXHAUSTION OF MINERAL AND FUEL RESOURCES

As I said before, there are several factors that jointly determine the length of time an exhaustible resource will last. The rate of current consumption in relation to the total stock would be a helpful index — except for the fact that we do not (and never can) know the size of the latter with any precision. Hence most quantitative discussions use a more limited category; namely, reserves, or, more precisely, "known reserves recoverable at current prices." To this must be added several other less certain categories; namely,

---

*Arsenic is a well-known poison once used mainly as a rat killer and fungicide and featured in many murder mysteries. Cadmium poisoning is less well-known but equally bad. In Japan many people living near a smelter have been afflicted with the "Hai-Hai" (ouch-ouch) disease, so called because its victims constantly undergo excruciating pains.
† Mercury is highly toxic in almost any chemical combination. It has been discovered recently that even metallic mercury can be metabolized by anaerobic bacteria into a lethal organic compound: "methyl" mercury. It has been responsible for the so-called Minimata disease, which has claimed thousands of victims among fishermen and their families along the shores of a bay in Japan, into which a major chemical plant discharged mercury waste over a period of years.

- Identified reserves recoverable at higher prices (conditional resources)
- Undiscovered resources in known districts (hypothetical resources)
- Undiscovered resources in unknown districts (speculative resources)

The relationships between these four categories are shown in Figure 8.2.[12] What we actually know accurately is the magnitude of the known reserve category. The magnitude of the identified reserves depends on technological and economic forecasts. The magnitudes of the third and fourth categories can only be estimated indirectly, based on historical rates of discovery in various types of geological formations, and data on what areas have (and have not) been surveyed in detail.

As I said, many authors have used the known reserves data where a more general definition would have been more appropriate, for the

Figure 8.2 Classification of resources.

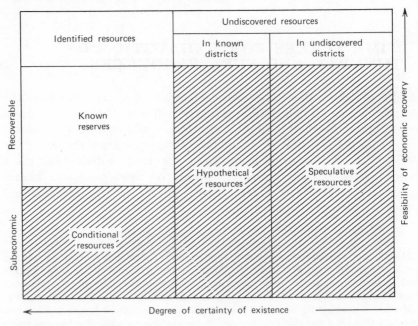

Table 8.3   Increases in Known Reserves (World)

	1956	1960	1970
Chromium, 10^6 short tons	200	—	775
Copper, 10^6 short tons	100	170	307.9
Lead, 10^6 short tons	40.5	48.8	95
Mercury, 10^6 flasks	0.6	2.0	3.2
Platinum 10^6 Troy ounces	25	25	424
Tin,[a] 10^6 long tons	5	5	6.5
Zinc[a] 10^6 short tons	Over 70	67	90

[a] Free world only.

understandable reason that solid data on the others are simply lacking. Combined with extrapolated consumption data, this practice gives rise to dramatic statements—often quoted in popular books or by the press—to the effect that platinum will be exhausted in twelve years, mercury in thirteen years, natural gas in fourteen years, zinc in sixteen years, and so on.[13] The calculations are perhaps arithmetically accurate, but the implications—interpreted as "facts"—are misleading.

The reason is that detailed surveys and evolving technology are continuously causing "conditional" and "hypothetical" resources (see Figure 8.2) to be reclassified as "known reserves," so that "known reserves" keep increasing. In recent decades this has generally been happening as fast as, or faster than, the old reserves are used up, as shown by Table 8.3.[14] (Meanwhile, the other categories are also being added to as a result of continuing exploratory work.)

In several cases, known reserves increased quite dramatically. In the case of platinum, for instance, this is certainly due to reclassification of conditional reserves because of increased demand for the metal. The latter resulted from newly developed uses as a catalyst for petroleum refineries and (more recently) for exhaust emission abatement in automobiles. Of course, reserves cannot continue to grow indefinitely. Exhaustion must occur, eventually, at some point, but comparing current consumption with published "known reserves" cannot tell us when that will happen.

Another weakness in the extrapolation of current rates of consumption is that, given sufficient motivation, consumption patterns for most materials can change dramatically in a short time. This obviously does not apply to the fossil fuels or the very large tonnage metals (iron, aluminum, copper), but it is demonstrably true for most others. I noted that demand for a minor material can rise very sharply as a new use is developed. This has happened in the past several decades for several metals other than platinum, including germanium (transistors), selenium (photosensitive plates used in xerography), uranium and zirconium (nuclear reactors), beryllium and titanium (aerospace applications), europium (phosphors for TV tubes), and niobium (alloying element for steel).

Other metals have experienced very sudden temporary or permanent declines due to substitutions. Tin has been slowly losing its chief market (tin-plate) for years. Cast zinc is losing out to plastics and aluminum. Aluminum is replacing copper for many electrical applications. Tungsten lost a major market as an alloying element for high-speed tool steel when molybdenum largely replaced it during the Korean War (1949–1953). The use of silver for coins was stopped almost overnight by the Coinage Act of 1965 which authorized cupronickel coins in place of silver coins for the United States. Lead lost a major market in the United States when new cars (after 1972) were designed for unleaded gasoline. Mercury is currently losing a major market as a catalyst for the chemical industry as a result of concern over mercury pollution of the environment in Japan and, more recently, the United States and Canada. Some of these substitutions took place in a very few years.

Taking into account our existing knowledge of reserves, rates of discovery, and rates of substitution, it is almost certain that one can rule out the possibility of a critical shortage of any mineral resource prior to 2025, with the exceptions already noted: natural gas, petroleum, and (unless a viable breeder system is developed) uranium. All are used for the production of energy – the latter being a partial substitute for fossil fuels.

During the nineteenth century, coal succeeded wood as the major fuel for the industrialized world. The age of coal, a century long, came to an end around the time of World War I, and coal was succeeded by petroleum as the chief source of inanimate energy for the world. Since World War II, natural gas has had an even more spectacular growth in popularity.

Sadly, the amount of liquid petroleum and natural gas available in concentrated form on the Earth's surface is much smaller in terms of energy content than the amount of coal that remains. Measured in billion (10^9) metric tons of coal, equivalent (BMTCE), the world *known reserves* in concentrated deposits, based on then current prices for energy fuels in the mid-1960s were[15]

Coal	700	@ $5/ton
Petroleum	60	@ $3/bbl (= 300 billion bbl)
Natural gas	70	@ $0.20/m.c.f. (= 2 trillion m.c.f.)
Shale oil (73%)	750	@ $25/kg, contained
U^{238}	3000	
U^{235}	20	

The rate of petroleum discovery was quite high during that period, and known reserves of petroleum, for instance, had more than doubled by 1975 to around 125 BMTCE (or 600 billion bbl).[16] However, natural gas reserves remained about as they were in 1965, which is moderately disturbing.

By comparison, world energy *consumption* in 1970 was about 8 BMTCE, of which about 6 BMTCE was derived from petroleum and natural gas. Thus, at 1970 prices and rates of consumption, the world had enough known reserves of coal to supply *all* its energy needs for nearly 100 years,* but only enough oil and gas for about fifteen years. The U^{235} recoverable at 1970 prices for uranium would have supplied the world's entire energy needs for only $2^{1}/_2$ years, whereas if the U^{238} were utilized via a breeder, it would last 350 years.

The first qualification of these numbers is that they must be interpreted in light of what I have already said about "known reserve" estimates. Moreover, they have all been rendered obsolete by recent sharp price increases for all energy fuels, not to mention new discoveries stimulated thereby. Because more of a known resource can be extracted economically at a higher price, it follows that known recoverable reserves have been substantially increased by the addition of formerly conditional and hypothetical resources.

No one except possibly the producers themselves knows exactly how sensitive the long-run supply of oil and gas is to the price. Some economic models have suggested that natural gas, for instance, should be quite price sensitive. (This argument was used recently by those senators who favor eliminating price controls.) Other evidence suggests that, for technical reasons, the natural gas supply may be unusually insensitive to price. As a general rule, however, the recoverable resource supply will continue to rise as prices go up in the future.

Estimates of world *ultimate* reserves of crude oil and gas are theo-

---

*Note that the coal would last much longer if it were only used at the *present* rate of consumption of coal. Ditto for oil and gas. On the other hand, increasing consumption levels obviously reduce the life expectancy of the reserves.

retically price independent in the sense that future price increases are presumably taken into account. In actuality, there is no consistent methodology for doing this, hence estimates vary widely. This is regrettable, but perhaps not surprising.[17] The National Academy of Sciences reports that remaining undiscovered but recoverable deposits of crude oil amount to a little less than twice the presently known reserves (1130 billion bbl = 235 BMTCE), and still-undiscovered reserves of gas may be slightly more than double the presently known reserves (4.9 trillion m.c.f. = 175 BMTCE).[18] These numbers are a bit lower than some other published numbers. For instance, the United States Geological Survey "midpoint" estimates (1973) are about a factor of 3 higher for both petroleum and gas.

On the other hand, world absolute consumption of energy has also been increasing rapidly and is likely to continue to do so. In the advanced industrial countries it is likely that higher energy prices will stimulate greater conservation. As wealthy societies move from the industrial to the postindustrial phase, energy consumption per dollar of GDP should begin to decline, as explained in Chapter 5.

However, in the developing countries like Brazil and Mexico that are still in the process of becoming more heavily industrialized, the trend would probably be in the other direction. That is, energy consumption per unit of GDP will tend to increase. For at least two more decades, I think that world energy consumption will continue to keep pace with world economic growth. It will probably increase on an absolute basis until well beyond the year 2000 – unless the world economy collapses utterly.

Somewhere in the neighborhood of 75% of the world's current energy consumption is derived from petroleum and natural gas. The exact percentage varies over time and from country to country, of course. But it must soon begin to decline, if it has not already. Within a few decades at most, the "age of oil and gas" must reach and pass its peak.

Unfortunately, there is no means of predicting exactly when this will occur, since it depends on several unknowable factors. The most important unknown is the amount of these resources that will be discovered in the next thirty years or so. This clearly depends somewhat on what happens to petroleum prices in the meantime. A second factor of great importance is the rate of increase of world energy consumption. A third key factor is the rate of introduction of substitute sources of energy, for example, coal, nuclear power, and solar power. Only by making specific assumptions about these uncertainties can one arrive at any definite estimate.

For purposes of argument, let me suppose that the ultimate recoverable supply of petroleum is five times greater than the known reserve as of 1970, or 300 MTCE. (This would be consistent with a slowly but steadily increasing price level.) And, let me be "optimistic" — from the energy conservation point of view — and assume a slow 2.5% per annum rate of increase of world demand for energy. Based on a realistic split between oil and other forms of energy, a plausible exhaustion schedule for oil would be[19]

25% of the ultimate supply used up by 1985
50% used up by 2000 (peak production year)
75% used up by 2025

For natural gas the situation is comparable. Obviously, if the ultimate supply is much larger than I have assumed, the peak production year can be later, but probably not much later. For instance, if the ultimate supply is twice as large as I have assumed, the day of peak oil output might be delayed by ten to twenty years, depending on other factors. Conversely, if the rate of discovery in the future is slower than it has been in the past, the ultimate supply may be smaller and the peak production year would come sooner. If energy consumption increases faster than I have assumed, the exhaustion milestones would also be pushed forward correspondingly.

It is very important to bear in mind that the schedule applies to the world as a whole. For the United States, which started exploiting its domestic petroleum and gas resources earlier, the peak production period has apparently occurred already, and the fraction of energy that must be imported is already rising rapidly.

NATURAL RESOURCES AND INTERNATIONAL COMPARATIVE ADVANTAGE

The existing comparative levels of the exploitation of various natural resources are often, but erroneously, regarded as a valid index of permanent advantage. This is quite unrealistic. School children of twenty or thirty years ago might have been imporessed by the fact that the United States was then the world's largest producer of the majority of the major mineral resources, including petroleum, natural gas, coal, iron ore, copper and lead, sulfur, and phosphate rock, as well as many lesser materials. It was a major exporter of several of these. As of the mid-1970s, the USSR has taken over first place for petroleum, gas, coal, manganese, iron ore, and potash, among others. Canada is now top in zinc and nickel production and second in sulfur and potash. The number one phosphate producer is now Morocco.

When known reserves are considered, the picture changes sharply once more. The major world petroleum reserves are in the Middle East, especially Saudia Arabia. The USSR, Algeria, and Iran are especially rich in natural gas. Morocco, Algeria, and Mexico have the best-known deposits of phosphate rock. Chile, Peru, and Kinshasa (Zambia) have the highest-quality copper ores. In the future nickel will come mainly from lateritic (oxide) ores in tropical countries. Manganese (plus some copper and nickel) will probably be taken from the deep ocean nodule deposits. Siberia, Brazil, and Venezuela still have mountains of high-grade iron ore. South Africa is dominant in chrome (with Rhodesia), platinum, gold, and diamonds. Australia is the major source of bauxite and uranium. China apparently has most of the world's tungsten.

Hypothetical and speculative resources are even more likely to be found in the less developed regions. Europe and North America have been thoroughly prospected. Siberia, China, Africa, Australia, and much of Latin America have not. It would be fairly surprising if any major new mineral discovery were made in the continental United States or Western Europe. It would be astounding, however, if major new discoveries are *not* made in China, Brazil, Afghanistan, New Guinea, and Ethiopia, among other places.

The point is that the countries that have been the first to exploit their natural resource assets will, in general, be the first to run short. They will become increasingly dependent on the countries that still have extractable resources available for use. Increasingly, the countries that still possess high-quality exploitable resources will choose not to export them in raw form. Rather, they will undertake increasingly more advanced forms of processing, at least up to the stage of refined metals and basic industrial chemicals.

Thus the center of gravity of the world petrochemical industry can be expected to shift gradually but inevitably to the Middle East. The political instability of the area may slow down the process, but cannot stop it. Saudia Arabia, Algeria, and Iran will doubtless use their natural gas to make ammonia and nitrogen fertilizers for export. Mexico will convert its fluorite into fluorine chemicals; Morocco, Algeria, and Mexico will manufacture and export phosphate fertilizers, not just phosphate rock. Increasingly, too, metal ore producers will build smelters and metallurgical industries, as Brazil and Venezuala are now doing.

With regard to so-called renewable (but degradable) resources, only moderate changes in comparative advantage between nations can be expected. These will arise in part from population growth and movements, partly from shifts in land-use patterns, and partly from the degradation processes discussed previously. In most cases, the combination of these factors will only increase the existing comparative disadvantages of Africa and South Asia in regard to food production.

Latin America is in a different situation, however. According to Table 8.2, only 5% of the land area is currently under permanent cultivation, as compared to 10% in North America (and, also, the world). Yet only 27% of the land in South America is waste, compared to 40% for the world average. Of course, the Amazon-Orinoco forest accounts for part of the difference: It is not waste land, but neither is it arable. Even so, there remains a significant potential for increased cultivation, especially in South Central Brazil, Uruguay, Paraguay, and Argentina. In principle, Latin America might even be able to outproduce North America and become a major food exporter. Whether this happens in practice depends on the governments in the region. However, in view of the obvious need, I would think there is quite a good chance that the temperate zone countries of Latin America will take advantage of their opportunity.

There are two renewable resources that are *not* degradable and that may confer significant economic benefits in a few more decades. One is uninterrupted sunshine—essential for large-scale industrial utilization of solar energy. The countries of North Africa and the Middle East will be permanently energy rich if they utilize their petroleum wealth to develop (or buy) technology capable of utilizing the Sun's energy directly. The other key resource is iceberg or glacier ice, which is potentially valuable both for its fresh water and for its energy content. (Natural ice can, obviously, substitute for electricity or other forms of high-quality energy in all applications where cooling or refrigeration is desired.) The only missing factor is an adequate technology for protecting and towing large masses of ice. When such technologies are ultimately developed, as now seems quite likely,[20] countries in a position to capture floating icebergs and tow them to specified destinations will also control a significant renewable resource.

THE ENERGY-CLIMATE DILEMMA

I have already touched on the roles of CO_2 and particulates as they may affect the vital thermal regulatory system of the Earth—which is, of course, the "engine" of climatic change. What I want to do here is bring several related aspects of the complex energy-climate problem into a clearer focus. To do so I must introduce some quantitative elements. It is important to acknowledge that some of the key numerical estimates were made very recently and may be quite uncertain. The subject is being reviewed at present by several scientific bodies, including the National Academy of Sciences, and it is possible that the concerns I raise here will turn out to be overstated. On the other hand, perhaps not.

Briefly, the undisputed facts are these: Combustion of fossil fuels has increased enormously in recent decades, and the concentration of CO_2 in the atmosphere has increased concurrently.* However, on comparing the actual quantities involved, not all the excess CO_2 produced by combustion has remained in the atmosphere. Moreover, combustion of fossil fuels is not the only source of "excess" CO_2. Deforestation and loss of humus due to plowing may account for an additional major input of comparable (but uncertain) magnitude. Thus anywhere from 50% to 75% of the excess CO_2 produced by combustion has apparently "disappeared." The obvious sink is the ocean. That is, it seems that a significant fraction of the excess CO_2 has been taken into solution in the surface waters. The only mechanism for removal (other than re-release to the atmosphere) is for the CO_2 to be taken up by single-celled plants (phytoplankton). Eventually some of this carbon is fixed as calcium carbonate ($CaCO_3$), mainly in the skeletons of tiny animals (zooplankton) such as radiolarians or coral. When these microscopic organisms die in the deep ocean, their bodies sometimes drift below the range of the various scavengers into the deeps, where some of the organic material and the calcium carbonate is incorporated into a carbonaceous ooze. This is gradually covered up, compressed, and eventually petrified to form shale or limestone.

It is generally agreed that the rate of CO_2 removal from the upper oceans via the mechanism noted above is normally quite slow (perhaps just enough to balance the natural rate of oxidation of geologically exposed hydrocarbons). It could only be speeded up by a significant increase in the biomass of phytoplankton in the surface waters of the deep oceans.[†] If all other nutrients (e.g., phosphorus and nitrogen)

*The preindustrial concentration of CO_2 in the atmosphere is thought to have been about 290 ppm. It has been increasing quite rapidly in recent years — by about 1 ppm/year of late — to about 330 ppm in 1976. (See Keeling and Bacastow, reference 3.)

[†] Note that over the continental shelves there are numerous species of bottom-dwelling organisms, such as molluscs and crustaceans, which consume organic detritus and are themselves eventually returned to the food web. Coral is the major exception.

Figure 8.3 Box model of CO$_2$ cycle.

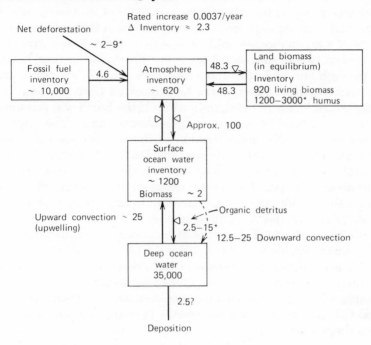

* Major disagreement between different authorities

△ Key points where flows may change in relatively short—run

Units: 10^9 tons of C

were freely available in these waters, increased CO$_2$ concentration in the water might result in more phytoplankton production, leading to faster CO$_2$ removal from the water to the ocean bottoms. However, it does not seem to work out that way, because in the open oceans CO$_2$ is not the limiting factor in phytoplankton production. A "box" model of the CO$_2$ cycle is shown in Figure 8.3.[21]

What this means is simply that higher atmospheric CO$_2$ levels tend to equilibrate fairly rapidly with the oceans, resulting in higher levels of dissolved CO$_2$ in the surface waters. Assuming that CO$_2$ cannot be removed to the ocean bottoms any faster than before, it follows that excess CO$_2$ simply accumulates in the water itself.

So far so good. An obvious question now arises: What will happen if the consumption of fossil fuels and production of CO$_2$ *continues to* increase following recent trends? Here it is necessary to enter more speculative areas. It has already been noted that, in theory, a higher concentration of atmospheric CO_2 will act like a thermal blanket for the Earth. Carbon dioxide tends to absorb and reradiate intrared (IR) radiation (that is to say, heat) back to the Earth, rather than letting it pass through and be lost to the outer space. This IR radiative loss to outer space is what balances the heat received from the Sun. If the radiative heat loss is reduced, the surface of the Earth will presumably heat up — as implied by the phrase "greenhouse effect." The exact relationship between CO_2 concentration in the atmosphere and equilibrium temperature on the surface of the Earth is not known, but the results of recent research with mathematical models seems to be that, in the absence of possible simultaneous countervailing effects (e.g., from greater cloudiness) a 200% increase in atmospheric CO_2 concentration (from 300 to 600 ppm) would lead to a 0.8% increase in the absolute temperature of the lower atmosphere. Translated into familiar units, this would amount to 4.5°F or 2.5°C.[22]

All this begins to look serious enough. However, it is possible that the climatic response may be much more nonlinear and unstable than the foregoing comments suggest, because the concentration of dissolved CO_2 in the water of the oceans is really dependent on three interacting factors:

1. The atmospheric concentration of CO_2
2. The concentration of dissolved carbonate ions in the water
3. The water temperature

The warmer the water, the less dissolved CO_2 it can retain.* An increase of 1° in the average temperature of the air in the lower atmosphere should be matched by a corresponding rise in surface water temperatures, but if the water warms up, other factors remaining the same, it would tend to cause the CO_2 concentration in the water to drop and increase the amount of CO_2 in the atmosphere correspondingly, thus reinforcing the "greenhouse effect." Of course, the rising atmospheric CO_2 concentration would inhibit the further release of dissolved CO_2 to some extent, but not enough to compensate. In effect, we have a self-reinforcing (or autocatalytic) process with a "positive feedback" loop as illustrated in Figure 8.4. Once the warming trend starts it must

*Specifically, at −1°C, seawater retains 6.724 moles of CO_2 per liter of seawater per atmosphere of CO_2 (partial) pressure at the surface. At 40°C, this absorbtion coefficient declines to 2.082, a drop of nearly 70%.[23]

Figure 8.4 Climatic warming mechanism, with positive feedback loop.

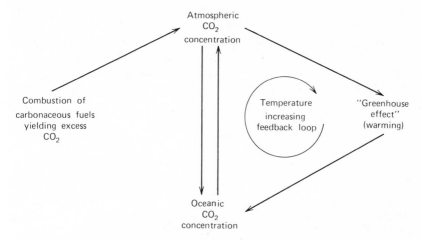

accelerate until some other factor comes into play to slow it down. One can be fairly sure, on the basis of physical laws alone, that such a self-propelling mechanism exists, although empirical evidence is another matter. There are complicating factors, to be sure.

Common sense also tells us that there must be other factors that eventually bring the CO_2 release cycle to an end. The mechanism(s) that eventually reverse the warming cycle cannot be assessed quantitatively without much more study. One stabilizing factor in the past must have been an accelerated growth of carbon-fixing photosynthetic plants on land (where nutrients other than CO_2 may be less limiting), resulting in vast lush rain forests. The roles of water vapor, cloud cover, and snow cover are also critical. It is clear that if the ocean became warmer, the rate of water evaporation would *also* increase, leading to an increase in the average amount of water vapor in the lower atmosphere (i.e., humidity and cloud cover) and an increase in precipitation over land.

To the extent that cloud cover increases, solar radiation is more effectively reflected, thus cooling the Earth.* To the extent that precipitation takes place over arid areas, where water is the limiting factor in plant growth, this will automatically trigger the photosynthetic

---

*It is *not* clear that greater lower atmosphere humidity and a faster hydrologic cycle necessarily result in increased overall cloudiness. Although lower atmosphere cloudiness would increase, upper atmosphere humidity would be expected to decrease, and the net change could be in either direction.

activity that tends to extract excess CO_2 from the atmosphere and fix it in the form of biomass. To the extent that precipitation occurs over dry areas such as Northern Canada or Siberia as snow, a different result occurs: The accumulation of winter snow over the land lasts longer in the spring and increases the reflectivity of the Earth's surface. (Snow is a very efficient reflector of sunlight.) Thus less of the heat of the Sun is captured by absorption, and a cooling trend begins automatically.

Here a *negative* feedback loop can be identified, as shown in Figure 8.5. It appears that these processes taken as a group are likely to be self-stabilizing, rather than the converse. That is, the warming trend caused by CO_2 release from the oceans would eventually trigger a set of changes that bring about a compensatory cooling trend, beginning in the polar regions. (This phenomenon could conceivably be related to the long glaciation cycles.) It is significant that the cooling mechanism is only triggered by a prior warming, which implies that fairly large-scale climatic fluctuations may be in prospect, depending of course on the rate of excess CO_2 production in the coming half century.

There are several possible approaches to this problem. Given that 97% of the world's energy consumption today is derived from burning fossil fuels, it is obviously not unreasonable to assume that the world

Figure 8.5 Climatic stabilization mechanisms, with negative feedback loops.

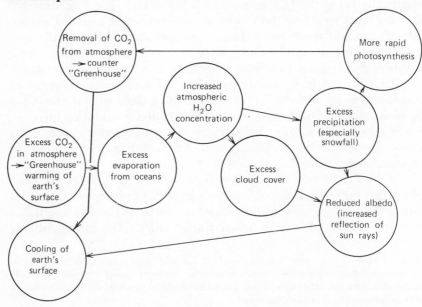

will continue to depend on fossil fuels as long as they constitute the cheapest energy source. This makes the problem conceptually simple: We need only project the total amount of fossil fuel that is recoverable from the Earth's surface. Based on a range of estimates of total reserves of oil, gas and coal, it appears that annual fossil fuel consumption ten or more times the current level may occur before impending exhaustion forces a decline. This could result in a drastic increase in atmospheric CO_2 to 375–400 ppm by the year 2000 and an ultimate peak concentration much higher than that. A model taking into account most of the known factors affecting the CO_2 cycle has been developed by Keeling and Bacastow. Depending on assumptions about the rate of energy demand growth, it suggests a factor of increase (from preindustrial levels) between about 6.75 and 7.75, depending on the sharpness of the consumption peak. Once having peaked there would be a slow decline, lasting as long as 1000 years. Climatic consequences cannot be predicted accurately, but the onset major climatic perturbations seems overwhelmingly likely.

Will it happen like this? Unless a major change in energy policy is simultaneously undertaken by all the nations of the Earth, there seems to be no escape. Nuclear power is a dangerous and probably inadequate alternative. Solar energy is far more expensive (at present) and not readily available, especially for such uses as personal transportation. We are unquestionably facing a technological and political challenge of immense proportions.

REFERENCES

1. E. F. Schumacher, *Small is Beautiful: Economics as Though People Mattered,* Harper Colophon Books, Harper and Row Publishers, Inc., New York, 1973.
2. R. U. Ayres, *Resources, Environment and Economics: Applications of the Materials/Energy Balance Principle,* Wiley-Interscience, New York, 1978.
3. C. D. Keeling and R. B. Bacastow, in *Energy and Climate: Outer Limits to Growth,* National Academy of Science, Report of Panel on Energy and Climate, Washington, D. C., 1977.
4. Dahlem Workshop on Global Chemical Cycles and Their Alteration by Man, Berlin, Germany, November 1976.
5. F. D. Robinson, in *Energy and Climate, op. cit.*
6. National Academy of Sciences, *Halocarbons: Environmental Effects of Chlorofluoromethane Release,* Report of Panel on Impact of Stratospheric Change, 1976.

7. Calculated by the author based on data compiled by Resources For the Future, Inc.
8. R. B. Nordgaard, "Resource Scarcity and New Technology in Petroleum Development," *Natural Resources Journal 15* (2), April 1975.
9. See M. Morgenstein, ed., "Papers on the Origin and Distribution of Manganese Nodules in the Pacific and Prospects for Exploration," International Symposium, Honolulu, Hawaii, July 23–25, 1973.
10. E. Ekholm, *Losing Ground: Environmental Stress and World Food Prospects,* W. W. Norton and Company, New York, 1976.
11. C. Ogburn, "Why the Global Income Gap Grows Wider," *Population Reference Bureau Bulletin # 26* (1970)
12. U.S. Bureau of Mines, *Mineral Facts and Problems,* Washington, D.C., 1970.
13. See Dennis Meadows et al., *Limits to Growth,* Universe Books, New York, 1972.
14. U.S. Bureau of Mines, *op. cit.*
15. "Energy R&D and National Progress," U.S. Government Printing Office, Washington, D.C., 1965.
16. National Academy of Science, "Mineral Resources and the Environment." A Report of the Committee on Mineral Resources and the Environment (COMRATE), 1975.
17. See Keeling and Bacastow, *Energy and Climate: Outer Limits to Growth,* for a number of recent estimates.
18. COMRATE, *op. cit.*
19. I am indebted to Jeffrey Marsh, formerly of Hudson Institute, for some of these calculations.
20. This topic has received a good deal of popular press coverage recently. A symposium of scientific papers on the subject was held at Iowa State University, Oct. 2–5, 1977.
21. R. U. Ayres, Proceedings of Dahlem Conference on Global Chemical Cycling, Appendix III, *op. cit.*
22. S. Manake and R. Wetherald, "The Effects of Doubling the CO_2 Concentration on the Climate of a General Circulation Model," *J. Atmos. Sci. 32:* 3–15 (1975).
23. R. W. Weiss, *Marine Chemistry,* Vol 2., p. 203, 1974.

CHAPTER NINE

THE SCENARIOS

INTRODUCTION

Any fool can describe a "future" and call it a prediction; many do. True foresight is another matter entirely. Oracles are out of style, crystal balls provide no light, and the time machine remains a figment of H. G. Wells' imagination.

A projection (as distinguished from a forecast) is a reasoned exploration of what *could* happen under a given set of circumstances, assuming certain actions are taken by key people. It takes into account broad trends that are already evident. There is always a range of possibilities, since events in the future depend on decisions by ordinary people as well as political leaders. There is no possibility of certain knowledge of what governments and individuals will do in any particular situation. Hence it is useful to examine several scenarios, each representing plausible internally consistent scenarios. Each scenario seems *possible*, but none is necessarily *likely*. I do not know which one (if any) will come closest to realization.

It makes no sense to waste time on extremely unlikely scenarios, such as all nations agreeing to give up their sovereignty to a world government or the invasion of the Earth by beings from another planet. It is useful to distinguish between scenarios that are unlikely to the point of being inconceivable and ones that, even though improbable, could come to pass under a particular set of possible circumstances. Examination of the latter is an essential element of contingency planning.

In exploring various alternative trajectories of future events, it is important to identify the kinds of *differences* between alternative futures that would be most significant to a planner or decision maker. Evidently, one of the major reasons for uncertainty about the future is that we do not have a clear enough intuitive (or empirical) understanding of political and economic processes. Although decisions undertaken by large numbers of individual humans can often be adequately "modeled" statistically—as in economic demand forecasting or traffic flow studies—this is not the case with decisions in highly structured political institutions subject to complex implicit, as well as explicit, constraints. It is extremely difficult to foresee when (if ever) a legislative body might enact certain kinds of legislation or an executive or administrator might make a certain kind of decision.

Human experience clearly confirms, however, that one's perceptions of what seems highly unlikely today may change very sharply tomorrow (or the day after). Who would have forecast, say, in 1967, that in a few years a hard-line anti-communist Republican president would travel to Communist China and reestablish political relationships with that country? (A forecaster might have classified it as "unlikely," although certainly not "inconceivable.") Who, even as late as 1972, would have forecast that a President of the United States, could, within less than three years, be impeached* for suppressing evidence of criminal actions by his immediate staff and abusing the powers of his office? (It would have seemed "highly unlikely" and close to "inconceivable.") Who would have predicted as late as the summer of 1977 that the President of Egypt would be seen by 100 million TV viewers warmly embracing the Prime Minister of Israel—himself a former terrorist—in Jerusalem, or that he would receive a hero's welcome on his return to Cairo? Yet it happened three short months later.

What must be emphasized is that even the "quite unlikely" scenarios must be periodically reexamined. Events may seem very unlikely at one moment, yet they may come to pass quite naturally a short time later as a result of altered circumstances. Some of the scenarios we are about to examine could be considered fairly unlikely today, but can we be sure that this will be so eight or ten years from now? Over the long term, tomorrow's actuality—whatever it turns out to be—would probably be regarded as "unlikely" from today's perspective. I have selected for detailed examination in this chapter three scenarios that cover a range of future possibilities. None could be called "likely" now. Yet none is inconceivable. All most be considered as real possibilities.

The three scenarios are, briefly:

1. A scenario of *world energy crisis* in the mid-1980s, for which no adequate preparations had been made, with skyrocketing energy prices in world markets and crippled industrial growth in both rich and poor countries. The scenario explores the possible technological

---

*Nixon was not actually impeached, of course, but he resigned from office because impeachment had become inevitable, otherwise.

and industrial adaptations to the crisis and the probable economic, political, social, legal, and international consequences.

2. A scenario of *world food crisis* in the mid-1980s, envisioning a series of eco-catastrophes leading to mass starvation in South Asia and Africa. The scenario explores the possible political repercussions and social upheavals ensuing.

3. A scenario of *United States withdrawal into isolationism, uncontrolled nuclear proliferation throughout the world, and political/ economic crisis in the communist countries.* The scenario traces the interrelationship of these possible events and their consequences.

SCENARIO 1 – WORLD ENERGY CRISIS

Why a Crisis?

Technology is not the malign force that some of its detractors fear, but neither is technology alone capable of solving every problem of man. In the discussion of energy technology in Chapter 7, I hope it was made clear that to develop new energy resources on a sufficiently massive scale to replace fossil fuels will take intensive research, a large amount of capital, and a fairly long time – several decades, at least. Whether the world has *enough* time depends, in part, on how fast the available petroleum in the ground or under the seas is used up. That, in turn, depends on how much petroleum remains to be discovered and how fast the demand for fossil fuel rises. If the world's economy grows substantially during the next decade or two, the world's petroleum resources will be used up very much faster than if recession conditions prevail. This is true regardless of short-term conservation measures. Thus the more prosperous the world becomes in the years immediately ahead, the sooner a really severe energy crisis is likely to develop.

The key assumption of this scenario is that a crisis develops in the mid-1980s, triggered by a second Arab oil embargo taking place in 1983. (The year does not particularly matter, of course.) Because the Western world has so greatly increased its dependence on imported oil by that time, the effect of the squeeze is far greater than was the case in the 1973 embargo. In fact, it awakens the whole world to the impending scarcity of oil and gas. Even the ordinary citizens become uncomfortably aware that production by the major producers has begun to decline. Producers, both foreign and domestic, deliberately reduce their rate of production to tighten the squeeze, in the expectation of higher prices later. World oil prices thus rise faster and farther than the economic structures of most nations can absorb, putting intolerable strains on the institutions on which nations and peoples depend. This scenario explores what might be expected to happen under such circumstances.

It is fairly clear to everyone familiar with the facts that government, industry, or people generally have not, up to now, given more than superficial attention to what will happen when oil and gas become scarce. In January and February of 1974 the effects of the 1973 embargo had people all over the United States lined up at half-empty gasoline pumps. That crisis passed quickly, fuels became easily available in a few weeks, and people resumed their high energy consumption habits, irrationally convinced that the shortage was just a maneuver by the oil companies to increase their profits. There remain a few permanent reminders: gasoline and heating oil prices are much higher, high speed limits have been permanently reduced, and the auto industry in the United States has mandatory fuel economy standards to meet in the next few years. However, the real lesson of that brief skirmish has not been learned: All industrial nations have become dangerously dependent on an uninterrupted supply of increasingly scarce fossil fuels and are becoming more so with every year that passes, despite the obvious fact that the supply will one day run out.

The crisis envisioned in this scenario disrupts the economies, lifestyles, and institutional structures of the principal industrial nations more severely than many major wars have done. An energy crisis, in fact, would be more difficult in some respects for a nation to adjust to than a war (except an all-out nuclear war) for reasons which it is worthwhile to examine.

In conventional wars (except the Vietnam War, which was unique in a number of ways), people in each of the warring nations know, or think they know, who the enemy is. Many are willing to subordinate their personal interests to help defeat the enemy. In an energy crisis, on the contrary, few people can clearly identify the enemy. Everyone, in such a case, seeks a villain. But the villain is elusive. Some people will blame the oil companies and want to punish them by eliminating their favorable tax status or even breaking them up. The oil companies, in turn, blame the price controls put into effect in the United States in 1972 (and still continuing on natural gas and so-called "old oil") for restricting fuel production. The politicians of each party will blame those of opposing parties. Great numbers of people may blame the politicians for failure to anticipate the crisis and head it off. Many people will blame the Arab nations for imposing the oil embargo. Others will blame Israel for the policies that goaded the Arab countries into doing so. The Arab nations will blame inflation in the West and the United States support of Israel. Many people will blame the environmentalists for delaying the Alaska pipeline, hindering offshore oil drilling, and slowing the development of nuclear power. There will be protracted, paralyzing disputes about what ought to be done (in contrast to the situation in a "hot" war), with the result that different agencies and groups will be working at cross purposes. Meanwhile, governmental and industrial officials are likely to issue soothing public statements: "Don't panic! There is plenty of fuel for all legitimate needs. Just wait your turn and bear with us." However, there is *not* plenty of fuel, and the situation gets worse day by day.

Another important difference between an energy crisis and a war crisis is in the time scale. A war is not expected to last longer than a few years at most. If it does, people's enthusiasm for it wanes, as the United States found in the Vietnam involvement. However, an energy crisis could easily last twenty or thirty years during which time lifestyles would be drastically and permanently altered. Imagine a change in the American style of life which eliminates the private automobile as the principal vehicle of family transportation! When in history has a democratic society successfully survived such a challenge to its established way of life? Would the society that emerged be considered "democratic?"

A third reason why an energy crisis may be more difficult to handle than many war crises have been is that modern mechanized war demands of a nation exactly what, in an energy crisis, it does not have: vast quantities of fuel reserves for its military machine. The ability of the United States, for example, to meet the war crises of 1942–1945 and 1949–1951 and to mobilize, equip, and ship abroad large fighting forces was, in part, a consequence of its huge domestic reserves of petroleum. How would a nation in a fuel crisis find the means to defend itself?

Assumptions Regarding the Genesis of the Crisis

It is assumed in this scenario that a world energy crisis arises in the mid-1980s as a result of a series of untoward circumstances and policy blunders.

First, it is assumed that the governments of major nations, especially the United States, have not taken *effective* steps to prepare their citizens or modify their institutions to meet a long-term energy shortage. Among the steps *not* taken are:

1. We have not developed a coherent long-term energy policy or strategy. (There has been no agreement on what such a policy should be,

and the responsibility for different aspects of energy are typically scattered among many different branches and levels of government.)

2. We have not developed comprehensive contingency plans for any such eventuality nor made preparations for putting such plans into effect.

3. Citizens are not convinced of the necessity of conserving energy, nor has any machinery been created for implementing significant conservation measures.

4. We have not provided strong incentives for public or private corporations, municipalities, and individuals to conserve fuel and electricity. Buildings continue to be erected with inadequate insulation and ventilation, requiring excessive heating in winter and/or air conditioning in summer. Solar energy is used only on a small scale. Automobiles are still unnecessarily wasteful of fuel; research on more efficient automotive engines has not been strongly supported. There are no meaningful programs, especially in the United States, to rebuild networks of public transportation. United States railroads have continued to deteriorate. City transportation systems, continuing to lose money, have become a severe financial drain. More, rather than fewer, people have become dependent on the automobile.

5. We have given too little attention to the implementation of programs to develop nonnuclear energy sources that might partially or wholly replace petroleum.

A second assumption of the scenario is that several actions actually taken by a number of governments have combined to make the crisis more severe. These actions include:

1. Legislative and regulatory attempts to hold down fuel and energy prices and to limit the profits of oil and power companies. These measures have discouraged investment and increased the nation's vulnerability to shortage.

2. Continued antitrust or legislative attacks on the international oil companies, based on the assumption that they have conspired to control markets, eliminate competition, and charge excessive prices.*

3. Slowed development of the United States coal industry by unre-

---

*This should not be construed to mean that I am opposed to antitrust regulation. On the contrary, I favor it when corporations are using their power to stifle competition. Nevertheless, antitrust regulation for its own sake, based on arbitrary definitions of market dominance (as, for example, in the attempt to separate Western Electric Company from AT&T), may well be counterproductive.

solved controversies over regulation of strip mining[†] and by environmentalists' opposition to increased use of coal in power plants and industry.

4. Historically one-sided allocation of available research funds in the United States where non-nuclear projects, such as developing means of utilizing solar energy for space heating and low-temperature industrial process heat, have received comparatively little support, whereas large funds have been devoted to a narrow and questionable concept of nuclear power development.

On the political side, the scenario assumes that the Israeli-Egyptian rapproachement of 1977–1978 continues, but that the Palestinian question remains unsettled and the hard-line Arab countries remain extremely hostile. Saudi Arabia and Kuwait occupy an uneasy middle ground between the two factions during the period 1977–1982.

The scenario further assumes that during the period 1976–1983 all the industrialized noncommunist countries have increased their dependence on imported fuels. This is especially true of the United States, which by 1983 imports 65% of its oil. Meanwhile, the petroleum industry throughout the world has expanded relatively little to meet the increased demand. Oil and natural gas reserves have turned out to be lower than expected, and the cost of drilling new wells much greater then expected (due to rising labor, materials, and capital costs). There have been no great new oil discoveries in the Western world during this period.

The scenario assumes that the OPEC cartel is still strong and is taking increasing advantage of the industrial nations' growing dependence on imported oil. The unfolding of the crisis is portrayed in the form of brief quasi-journalistic "news" items from various parts of the world, beginning in 1981 (with apologies to real reporters).

Unfolding of the Crisis

Atlantic City, New Jersey June 7, 1981

HUGE OIL SPILL FOULS NEW JERSEY BEACHES

Last Wednesday's collision between a Brazilian freighter, Pedro II, and the new 500,000 ton Aramco supertanker, Arpet, 60 miles

---

[†] Here, also, I must point out that I oppose unregulated strip mining because of its devastation of the Earth's surface and the erosion, flooding, and damage to adjoining lands it causes. It should be possible to permit strip mining provided it be promptly followed by systematic land reclamation.

off this coast is threatening all New Jersey beach resorts from Barnegat to Cape May, according to Walter Holliday, President of the New Jersey Resort Hotel Association. "We face catastrophe," he said. "Not even Hurricane Debra last year caused such havoc. Miles of beaches are covered with black gunk and littered with dead fish and birds. Both economically and ecologically, the loss is incalculable. Resort hotels are facing almost an entire season of lost income. On top of that, the oil companies are planning to drill wells offshore here. We have to stop that. It could ruin us."

Comment: There have been major oil spills ever since tankers, and tankers are getting bigger. In December 1977 a 250,000-ton supertanker collided with a 330,000-ton supertanker 22 miles off the coast of South Africa. Early in 1978 most of the coast of Brittany was fouled by the breakup of the Amoco Cadiz.

Sea Island, Georgia　September 11, 1981

SEARCH FOR NEW OIL DROPPING OFF

"There probably is oil under the oceans along both the Atlantic and Pacific Coasts, but we have cut back sharply on our drilling program. We can't justify the costs." The speaker was James Springer, President of Gulf Oil Corporation, at a conference on oil exploration held here. "Safety and environment-related costs — imposed by the government — have soared beyond the point where we can have reasonable assurance of a return from drilling new wells on the North American continental shelf. The law requires extremely costly equipment and procedures to safeguard against accidents and oil spills and, even so, we face constant harassment from private lawsuits. Altogether, the costs have gone beyond the limits of prudent investment." "Does this mean no new wells are being drilled by your company?" he was asked. "Yes, so far as this continent is concerned," he replied, "and from what I hear other oil companies are coming to a similar conclusion."

Comment: Major oil companies have started to diversify by putting their money into nonenergy types of businesses that appear to offer better returns. One notable example is the purchase of Marcor Corporation (Montgomery Ward Department Stores), by Mobil Oil Company in 1975.

Washington, D. C. November 30, 1981

RESIGNING OFFICIAL ATTACKS ENERGY POLICY

Albert Calhoun, who resigned last week as Assistant Secretary
for Research and Development of the Department of Energy
(DOE) attacked the one-sided allocation of research funds in the
energy field. "The priorities are upside down," he said in testimony before the House Interior Committee's Subcommittee on
Energy. "Sixty percent of our research funds are still being fun-
nelled into nuclear power, particularly the liquid metal-cooled
fast breeder reactor, which will probably never be used on a large
scale because it's too dangerous. Only 20% of our funds are going
into research on the production, processing and liquefaction of
coal — the fuel we possess in greatest abundance. Less than 8% is
going into solar energy research, and only 5% is being spent on
conservation."

"What do you propose in place of the breeder reactor, Mr.
Calhoun?" asked Mr. Hunt.

"A major program of conservation — now," Calhoun replied.

"No wonder the President fired you. A cutback on energy consumption means a slowdown in the economy and more unemployment. The American people won't stand for that," replied Con-
gressman Jenkins of New York.

Washington, D. C. June 8, 1982

RISING GASOLINE PRICES BLAMED ON
OIL COMPANIES

Witnesses testifying before the Senate Subcommittee on Economic Policy became embroiled in a sharp dispute on the cause of
the steady upward drift of retail gasoline prices which now average $.90 per gallon in the United States. After lengthy testimony
by Frederick Stockbridge, Chairman of Exxon, who attributed
the price rise largely in the interaction of supply and demand,
Raymond Dill, President of Associated Consumers of America,
leaped to his feet and said, "Mr. Stockbridge, your statement is
not true and you know it isn't true." When the ensuing uproar
quieted down, Dill launched into a bitter attack on oil company
policies which he claimed amounted to a "sweetheart" arrangement between the international oil companies and the OPEC
producers to keep prices high. He demanded vigorous antitrust
prosecution of the oil companies and separation of their produc-

ing, refining, and marketing facilities. "They have lined their pockets at the public's expense," he asserted. "It's time to make them cough up some of their loot."

Comment: It is regrettable, but true, that the public is vastly ill-informed on the subject of profits, especially by large oil companies. Public opinion polls have shown that the average American believes that industry profits range from 30 to 60% of sales. (He also believes that 15 or 20% would be reasonable.) The reality is quite otherwise: Industry profits actually average about 3% on sales.

Vienna, Austria August 11, 1982

PETROLEUM PRODUCERS ACCUSED OF HOLDING BACK PRODUCTION

A study of world petroleum production released today by the OPEC Statistical Commission shows a surprising 3% decline during the past three years in the total amount of oil produced despite a continuous growth in demand. "The causes are various and complex," according to the report. "Part of the decline is a result of the high cost of drilling new wells, resulting in a sharp drop in new production. Part of the decline reflects the normal depletion of existing oil fields. A disquieting element is an accumulation of evidence that, despite intensive exploratory activity, new discoveries are occurring at a sharply reduced rate. Consequently, producers are deliberately holding back on production, either to delay the exhaustion of their fields and spread production over a longer time period or in anticipation of higher prices later—or both. Some producers are very frank about it. "Why should we pump oil out of the ground at maximum capacity when we know our oil will run out in about twenty years?" asks Reza Zahavi, Iranian Oil Minister. "We'd be crazy to do that. We're going to spread it out, make it last twice as long. And we won't actually lose money because oil will command far higher prices a decade from now than it does today."

"What about the people who need your oil now?" he was asked.

He shrugged, "They will have to use less eventually. They might as well start now," was his answer.

Tel Aviv March 17, 1983

TERRORIST ATTACK IN DOWNTOWN TEL AVIV

Thirty terrorist infiltrators, armed to the teeth, barricaded themselves in a government office building in downtown Tel Aviv at 4
a.m. today, and held off the Israeli Army for four hours. All the
terrorists were killed in the ensuing battle, but the building was
demolished and more than twenty Israeli soldiers and 100 civilians, caught in withering crossfire, were killed. "This is the worst
terrorist attack in our history," said Defense Minister Moshe
Abram. "We believe we know who is responsible – we will verify
that soon. And make no mistake – we will make an appropriate
response."

Cairo March 18, 1983

WAR THREATENED IN NEAR EAST

The armies of Israel, Syria, Jordan, Libya, and Iraq were put on
emergency alert yesterday following the terrorist attack in Tel
Aviv. An Israeli communique reported the attack as the work of a
fanatical Arab group called Avengers for Allah with headquarters in Libya and warned Libya that Israel regarded the support
of this group by the Libyan government as an act of war. In
response, the several Arab governments informed Israel that an
attack on Libya would be considered an attack on the entire Arab
world. The Soviet Ambassador in Tripoli issued a statement of
support for the Libyans, warning that "our government will not
stand aside and allow Israel to invade Arab states." Soviet military equipment and supplies have been pouring into Libya and
Syria at increasing rates during the past six months.

Tripoli, Libya March 20, 1983

ISRAEL BOMBS LIBYA

Israeli planes bombed Tripoli this morning in a lightning thrust
that left the presidential palace and several government buildings in smoldering ruins. Civilian casualties are reported to be
high – in the hundreds. President Addoubi, in a television interview, called the attack "barbaric and unprovoked." He blamed
the United States as a "co-conspirator."

Cairo, Egypt March 21, 1983

NEW OIL EMBARGO AGAINST THE UNITED STATES

An emergency meeting of foreign ministers of the OPEC nations voted unanimously this morning to impose an embargo on the export of oil to the United States or to any other country that sells oil or oil products to the United States. "Why should we deal with those who attack us?" asked Ahmed Hassani, Algerian Oil Minister. "The time has come to distinguish friends from enemies. We will sell no more petroleum to the United States or any other nation that gives support to Israel." Asked about the possibility of military seizure of the oil fields, Mr. Hassani said, "Arabs will unite to defend their lands and what is theirs."

Comment: The Arabs are indeed quite well armed — mostly with United States weapons. More to the point: The United States has no Indian Ocean fleet and no airlift capability that would permit military intervention in the Persian Gulf on a significant scale. It is unlikely that the United States could secure landing rights anywhere in Europe in such a situation. During the 1973 Yom Kippur War, only Portugal, of all the NATO allies, permitted United States planes to land en route to Israel.

New York, New York March 22, 1983

PANIC ON STOCK EXCHANGE, TRADING SUSPENDED

There was turmoil on the stock exchange floor this morning as a result of the Arab oil embargo. "It's panic!" exclaimed Richard Gatsby, financial editor of the *Wall Street Journal*. "It's 1929 all over again, but worse." Asked why the stockmarket's reaction is so much more severe today than in the oil embargo of 1973, Gatsby pointed out that in 1973 the United States imported only 35% of the oil it consumed, mostly from Venezuela and Canada. Today we import 60% of our oil, and most of it comes from the Middle East. We no longer get any from Canada, as you know, and Venezuelan production has been declining. We get a little from Mexico, but an embargo, if long continued, would ruin us. "Face it!" said Gatsby. "The Arabs have us by the throat. If we have to choose between supporting them or Israel, the choice is clear. I can see no way for us to survive economically without petroleum from the Persian Gulf."

Comment: The figure of 60% is not out of the question. Canadian exports to the United States will phase out before 1980. Mexican production is unlikely to increase rapidly enough to make a significant difference.

Washington, D. C. March 25, 1983

CALL FOR MILITARY ACTION AGAINST ARAB STATES

In a fiery speech to a VFW Convention, Representative David Ashcan (D, Alabama), Chairman of the House Military Appropriations Committee, attacked the "sob sisters" who are helplessly wringing their hands over the oil embargo. "The answer is simple," he said. "Send the paratroops direct to the Persian Gulf and seize the oil fields. We could have all the important ones in our hands in twenty-four hours. Pay no attention to the Arabs' talk about blowing up their oil wells. That's a transparent bluff and we'd be imbeciles to be taken in by it. I'm not impressed by the noises from the Soviet Union, either. The Reds love to make trouble for us, if they can, but they're much too smart to get involved in a shooting war over this."

Comment: The possibility of United States military intervention was suggested — by inference — after the Yom Kippur War by no less a personage than United States Secretary of State, Henry Kissinger.

Washington, D.C. March 28, 1983

GENERAL REED CAUTIONS ABOUT MILITARY ACTION

General Alexander Reed, Chief of Staff of the United States Air Force, threw cold water today on talk of military intervention in the Persian Gulf. "We have information," said General Reed, "that the oil fields of Suadi Arabia, Kuwait, and Iraq were expertly mined by West German technicians two years ago. Apparently the Arabs are fully prepared to carry out their threat. The threat of Soviet intervention is no bluff. Their forces are based thousands of miles nearer the oil fields than ours. The Soviets could quite easily have their troops on the ground ahead of us to welcome our arrival. The Europeans and Japanese aren't with us on this, either. Militarily, it's a no-win proposition. We would also have a hostile population to contend with. I think we should look for other means of assuring access to oil." Asked for his comments, Representative Ashcan (D, Alabama) said, "We ought to begin by getting the blushing violets out of our armed forces. We could use a few Pattons right now."

Comment: Representative Ashcan's view would certainly have its advocates. It is not necessary to be specific about names. I assume they would not prevail, but their bellicose statements would doubtless inflame the Arabs even further.

Washington, D.C.　March 30, 1983

EMERGENCY GAS RATIONING AND PRICE CONTROLS INSTITUTED

President Garrison today declared a State of Emergency and imposed a federal system of gas rationing. Responding to pressure from Congress, the decree also rolls back gasoline prices to $1 a gallon from the $1.60 levels to which they had risen in some localities after the oil embargo. "This is an emergency situation," the President announced. "We must have rationing immediately, and I cannot allow further delay. I will submit legislation to Congress within a ⸀ ⸀ days to deal with the problem of price stabilization."

Comment: President Garrison is hoping the problem will go away. His reaction is a classic stall. Unfortunately, Lady Luck is out of town.

Detroit, Michigan　April 10, 1983

CHAOS ON THE HIGHWAYS

Gasoline prices are back down to $1 a gallon when you can get it, but buying gas has become a nightmare. Lines of cars waiting to buy gas are 2 miles long in many parts of the Detroit area, and service stations are generally out of gas by 9 a.m. The only way you can get your four gallons of gas is to wait in line all night. Fourteen hundred workers at the Ford plant at Dearborn were unable to get to work today, and the absence of key personnel forced the plant to shut down. Every industrial plant in the area seems to be having similar troubles. Trucks are unable to deliver supplies because of a shortage of diesel fuel. Trucks are stalled along the highways in many states, unable to continue their trips. Independent trucker Hans Zimmerman of 1410 South Street has three trucks of Florida oranges stalled on Route 75, out of fuel and unable to proceed to their destinations. "Guys like me are going broke. There will be food shortages," he warned. "The trucking business is breaking down."

Comment: I have understated the likely impact. It is worth remembering that the brief fuel shortage of 1973–1974, together with mild price controls and modestly reduced speed limits, was enough to create extreme turmoil and distress in the trucking industry.

Boston, Massachusetts April 11, 1983

HOMES OUT OF HEATING OIL. EPIDEMICS FEARED

Thousands of homes in the Boston area have run out of heating oil and cannot obtain deliveries. "My ration card says I'm entitled to 110 gallons of heating oil to see me through until next month," said James Eaton of 1995 Munster Street. "But just try to get it! I've been to every dealer in town. Each of them puts me on a waiting list. And I haven't had any heat in my home for seven days. Those politicians in Washington — they should be out in the cold!" Frances Friese, an elderly resident of Chelsea, has had no heat for six days and fears she is coming down with pneumonia. "I can't stand the cold," she said. "I never dreamed our country would come to this. Can't someone haul the oil companies into court? I hear they're holding back on production to make bigger profits."

Comment: The harsh winter of 1976–1977 caused widespread hardship in the Northeastern United States without a national fuel shortage. The high cost of heating oil was financially devastating to many low-income families, especially elderly and retired persons. Unpaid bills also caused many bankruptcies among heating oil distributors.

Bayonne, New Jersey April 12, 1983

OIL TANKERS REDIRECTED

Twenty-five oil tankers en route to the United States were diverted to other countries in the past two weeks, according to Frank Allison, General Manager of the EXXON refinery here. "We're getting no oil to refine, and if this continues we'll have to lay off workers and stop deliveries to local distributors," he told this reporter. "With the price controls recently imposed by Congress, producers of crude oil can get better prices in other countries, and the oil isn't coming here. In fact, some independent producers in the United States are shipping crude oil *out* of the country."

Comment: This, too, happened in 1973–1974. It is very difficult to prevent those with portable stocks from selling them to the highest bidder.

Cairo, Egypt August 19, 1983

ARAB FORCES PUSHING ISRAELIS BACK

Jubilant crowds in Damascus last night celebrated the advance of the Arab armies into the Jordan River Valley after yesterday's defeat of Israeli forces in the Golan Heights. "We will liberate every square meter of territory taken from us," proclaimed President Ahmad in a TV address. "The time of retribution has come." But among informed Syrians and military officers the jubilation was mixed with fear. The Israelis are known to have nuclear weapons, and no one knows how or when they will use them. This fear may explain the slowness with which Arab mechanized forces appear to be consolidating their gains. Meanwhile, the Israelis are digging in behind prepared fortifications.

Comment: For purposes of this scenario I assume that the United States does not abandon Israel, despite some domestic pressure to do so. Having failed to gain a quick decision, both sides settle down to a low-level war of attrition, each hoping to exhaust the other.

Washington, D.C. September 8, 1983

BREEDER REACTOR PUSHED

In hearings before the Senate Subcommittee on Energy, Dr. Charles Powers, Secretary of the Department of Energy, announced increased efforts to speed the development and construction of the liquid sodium breeder reactor. "We have no alternative," he said. "No other energy source can meet our needs quickly enough and free us from dependence on foreign fuel sources. This project has been inexcusably delayed by environmentalists who have grossly exaggerated possible future dangers. They make a big issue out of safety and the problems of storing radioactive wastes. Those problems will unquestionably be solved. But this is a program of the utmost urgency, and it can't wait for the ultimate resolution of endless niggling questions. I've told our engineers, 'Get it built and we'll deal with these other problems later'."

Washington, D.C. December 6, 1983

PROCLAMATION OF NATIONAL EMERGENCY

Yesterday Congress gave President Garrison powers equivalent to those of wartime. Before a national TV audience the President said, "I am reluctant to accept this unprecedented responsibility because it means that some freedoms Americans have taken for granted will have to be suspended, but unless our people recognize their common interest in solving the energy problem, we will not survive as a nation. I cannot allow strikes against essential industries at a time when the entire economy is threatened. I cannot allow thousands of private businesses essential to our welfare to go bankrupt. I cannot allow endless litigation to block the necessary allocation of scarce fuel supplies. I cannot allow the banking system to collapse under the weight of uncollectable loans. I cannot allow special interest groups to gain preferred treatment at the expense of the nation as a whole. I cannot allow fuel or raw material scarcities to weaken our national defense or reduce food production. I cannot allow oil producers, coal producers, or any other producers of essential goods to reduce current output in expectation of higher prices and bigger profits later. I cannot allow environmental concerns to interfere with the rapid development of alternative fuel and energy sources. I need emergency powers to deal with these and many other aspects of this unprecedented crisis. Only with emergency powers can I cut through the obstacles that stand in the way of dealing with these questions quickly and effectively in the interests of the nation as a whole. I ask the cooperation and prayers of all Americans as we work together to preserve our nation."

Comment: Resounding but essentially empty talk — except that individual liberty is definitely being eroded.

San Francisco, California January 5, 1984

FUEL ALLOCATIONS CREATE UPROAR

Shouts and fist shaking disrupted a public meeting of the California Fuel Rationing Board as Charles Abernathy, Chief of the Federal Fuel Allocation Agency, tried to explain in the recent new allocation rules set up under the President's Emergency Program. "We have tried to take into consideration every legitimate need," said Mr. Abernathy, but he got no further. Shouts of "What about us?" drowned out further words. Los Angeles commuters are fuming because their greater travel distances are not sufficiently allowed for in the commuter's gasoline ration. "You must organize car pools," responded Mr. Abernathy. "There's no other solution." But the uproar continued. Farmers are angry because they feel they are not allowed enough fuel to operate all their farm machinery. Truckers do not receive enough fuel for their longer hauls. Homeowners in the northern part of the state are running out of fuel oil. Motel and restaurant owners are desperate because of the sharp drop in automobile travel. Electric power companies predict power blackouts. Industries dependent on petroleum supplies are forced to go on part time and lay off workers. Taxi companies cannot get enough fuel to operate their fleets. Warning that the nation must cut its overall fuel use 50% brings the reply, "For us, that's impossible; we can't stay in business." Mr. Abernathy responds, "We're all in the same boat. All I can say to you is: find a way to do it. It's up to you. Everybody else has to do it, too."

Washington, D. C. February 14, 1984

LOBBYISTS EVERYWHERE!

The President's Emergency Proclamation was intended to centralize authority so that the President could make necessary decisions on fuel allocation without discriminating in favor of special interests. But it hasn't worked that way. Lobbying has grown tenfold since the proclamation, as every corporation, industry association, and labor union has sent a swarm of lobbyists to "educate" the Allocation Agency on its particular fuel and energy needs. Any lobbyist worth his salt can give twenty good reasons why the fuel allocation for his particular industry or group should be increased. "Somebody is going to get hurt," said Samuel Atkinson of the Committee for Preserving People's Rights, who has been keeping tabs on lobbying activities for the past ten years. "It's ordinary Joe Citizen who'll be hurt most in the end. He hasn't a lobby to represent him."

New York City April 2, 1984

GIANT CORPORATIONS IN FINANCIAL CRISIS

Some of the biggest corporations in the United States, including such giants as General Motors, General Electric, and Dupont are in dire financial straits because of a catastrophic drop in sales. "Car sales since the oil embargo have dropped to less than one-tenth of normal," said Floyd Aberdeen, Chairman of General Motors at the Annual Stockholder's Meeting. "If this continues, we can't survive. Neither can any other automobile company. We've already laid off two-thirds of our workers and will soon lay off more. The depression of the 1930s was a minor ripple compared to this!" "Can you expect any help from Congress?" he was asked. "We are hoping for help," he replied. "It's our last chance. Congress is considering loan aid for us and for other hard-hit industries such as the recreation, hotel, restaurant, and construction industries. Without such help, our country's entire automobile-oriented economy could come crashing down."

Washington, D. C. June 30, 1984

EMERGENCY LEGISLATION TO AID
FAILING BUSINESSES

A complex aid bill to fend off massive bankruptcies of major corporations and banks in the United States was passed by a narrow majority of both Houses last night over opposition from consumer groups, liberals, and right-wing conservatives. The bill is intended to head off a financial disaster threatened by the difficulties of the automobile and its satellite industries, which in turn threaten the solvency of the banking system. Opposing it were consumer advocates and liberals who strenuously object to putting assistance to big corporations ahead of assistance to smaller businesses and consumers. It was opposed also by conservatives who fear such aid is a step toward governmental control of industry and might be used ultimately as a lever for socialization of the entire free enterprise system. The legislation provides for long-term, low-interest federal loans to the ailing companies after independent analysis of their books establishes that bankruptcy would otherwise be inevitable. A question haunting Wall Street tonight was whether these analyses could be made quickly enough to save the tottering economy. "You know who will be doing the analysis," commented a broker who declined to be quoted. "The accounting firms will be overloaded, of course, and there isn't time to be professional about this. So the biggest clients will get the quickest — and most favorable — treatment, as usual. But now it's a matter of life and death for most companies."

Comment: Congress stepped in to bail out Lockheed and Penn-Central. The precedents are now established.

Princeton, New Jersey July 7, 1984

RECYCLING URGED

A major effort to recycle waste materials would go far toward relieving the fuel crisis, according to Professor Gerard Appelbaum of the Institute for Energy Studies. "Recycling aluminum," he said, "uses only one-tenth as much energy as producing new aluminum from bauxite ore, and we've barely begun to take advantage of this differential. The recycling of glass bottles, paper, and other waste could save huge amounts of energy. Dumping trash in landfills, as most communities still do, is inexcusably wasteful. Here we are throwing away millions of BTU of recoverable fuel every day while we stagger under the blows of a worsening fuel shortage. Federal and state laws and regulations that give new materials an advantage over recycled ones must be repealed promptly and federal money channeled to help municipalities build modern recycling plants."

United Nations, New York October 3, 1984

UN ASSEMBLY CONDEMNS UNITED STATES

A stormy meeting of the United Nations Assembly last night passed a resolution condemning the United States for "extravagant and unjustified consumption of scarce world resources." "Despite the OPEC embargo on shipments of oil to the United States, that country still consumes three times as much oil per capita as the world average. Its voracious appetite for oil is impoverishing the rest of the world and hastening the exhaustion of resources without regard to the needs of future generations. Because of its indifference to the world's needs, the United States stands condemned of economic aggression and moral bankruptcy."

New York, New York November 4, 1984

DUITT WINS

Alex Duitt, the former wildcat oil driller, has been elected President of the United States after a campaign of attacking the present administration for its failure to solve the fuel and energy crisis. His election by a two to one popular majority opens the way for radical new policies. "Now we'll have action," he promised in a midnight press conference. "President Garrison had emergency powers but couldn't figure out what to do with them. I will use those powers to turn the country permanently away from excessive dependence on the automobile. A vastly expanded network of public transportation will be the first order of business. Following that will be an immense expansion of research and the most rapid possible development of coal and other new energy sources. The days of makeshift solutions are over."

Washington, D.C. March 17, 1985

ENERGY PROCLAMATION JARS NATION

In a nationwide TV address, President Duitt proclaimed an "energy revolution" for the United States. "These measures are tough," he announced, "but without tough measures we cannot hope to overcome our country's problems. For this nation to be at the mercy of a small group of oil-exporting countries is intolerable. Even if the embargo had not been imposed, such a crisis would have struck eventually because long-term world demand for fuel has been expanding so fast that no conceivable increase in the exploitation of oil reserves could have kept up with it. So, in fact, we are lucky the crisis hits *now* rather than ten years from now."

Comment: The last statement would also have been valid ten years ago or this year. It is still true.

"As of today, the conservation of fuel and electrical energy are established as the top priority of our society, and all laws, regulations, contracts, union rules, rate structures, social practices, and other restrictions of any kind that interfere with conservation measures established by the government or by state and local governments are hereby eliminated."

Major elements of the Duitt program are:

1. National standards on construction and insulation and on heating and air conditioning equipment will be established in ninety days, to be applicable to all new construction, public or private. Electric resistance heating and compression-type air conditioning are banned for all new buildings. Standards applicable to older structures will be developed and phased in over a seven-year period. Any local building codes or other regulations in conflict with these standards are abolished. Low-interest loans will be available through existing agencies (Federal Housing Administration, Department of Agriculture, Economic Development Administration).

2. National standards on heating and air conditioning for public and commercial buildings will be published in ninety days. Thermostats must not be set to activate air conditioning equipment at temperatures below 78°F nor heating equipment at temperatures above 68°F.

3. The use of gas or oil as a boiler fuel is prohibited in new construction and is to be phased out over a three-year period for large industrial and commercial users and electric utilities, and over a seven-year period for residential housing. Low-interest loans will also be made available to finance conversions to coal (in large installations only) or electric heat pumps.

4. The production of domestic hydrocarbon fuels is to be expedited by all possible means. A federal severance tax of $1 per ton will be levied on every ton of coal produced to finance a trust fund dedicated to restoration of former mines to parks, timber, or grazing land. The Army Corps of Engineers is

assigned full responsibility for supervision and implementation of this task. Offshore oil and gas are also taxed at a comparable rate, with the funds to be set aside for restoration of damages from spills, etc. Any law suits or injunctions based on Federal Law that are currently delaying the opening of new mines or wells will be vacated and superseded forthwith.

5. Federal Air Quality Standards will be revised to permit the use of coal as a boiler fuel for utilities and large industrial and commercial installations. Electrostatic precipitators will be mandatory for all coal-fired boilers. Sulfur dioxide scrubbers will also be mandatory for utilities. Any lawsuits or injunctions that are currently delaying the use of such scrubbers will be vacated and superseded forthwith.

6. Mandatory National Standards on fuel economy for new automobiles are to be tightened year by year for the next decade.

7. Private automobiles are prohibited from using class I federal or state highways during "rush" hours unless there are at least three occupants per vehicle. Car pools will be encouraged by all possible means. On-street parking will be prohibited along any street where there is a public bus route. Curb lanes are permanently reserved for buses and taxis, except at night, when trucks may load and unload. A bus-only lane will be reserved on all arterial roads, tunnels, and bridges during rush hours. Free or subsidized parking privileges must not be offered to employees, either in public or private sectors, where public transportation is available.

8. Gasoline rationing is imposed under an "entitlement" scheme whereby each licensed driver (up to a limit of two per household) receives coupons issued through designated banks entitling him/her to purchase 5 gallons per week free of federal tax and a further 4 gallons per week taxed at the rate of 50¢ per gallon. Purchases above this amount are taxed at $1 per gallon. Unused entitlements can be "cashed" at the issuing bank at market value in amounts less than $25 per transaction.

9. Local energy review boards will be set up in each district to monitor the application of these regulations. These boards will have discretionary authority to deal with special situations and hardship cases. The members of the boards will be appointed by the President. Each board will include ex officio representatives of public safety and public health services, public transit operators, local utilities, Chamber of Commerce, consumer's groups, and organized labor.

Comment: The Duitt program of 1985 is obviously similar in many respects to the Carter proposals of 1977, except that it is much more radical. To rally support, Carter called for "the moral equivalent of war," but although his program was actually a mild one, it was largely rejected by the Senate. The Duitt program, of course, is imposed by decree under the President's emergency powers. It works precisely because the usual political and legal obstacles are shortcircuited, for once, and Americans are forced to face up to the painful realities. Under the lash, as it were, the United States is able to increase coal production by 30%, reduce petroleum consumption by 60%, and reduce overall energy consumption by 25% from 1985 to 1990.

As the Crisis Deepens

Thus begins a radical transformation of the lifestyles and geographical distribution of the American people and people in many other countries as well. The "American Way of Life" that revolved around the single-family home in the leafy suburbs, served by the automobile, is in decline. Vast highway systems are used increasingly by heavy trucks and less by private cars. The railroads are gradually rehabilitated. Nearly all long-distance passenger transportation is by common carrier. Bus and railway services have to be greatly expanded, but it is difficult to keep up with the demand. For a number of years, public transportation is uncomfortable, crowded, and subject to delays.

Suburban life loses much of its attractiveness, which had previously been based on the ubiquitous private automobile. Property values stagnate or decline in the outer suburbs, as people in growing numbers return to the greater accessibility of central cities. This population shift, reversing the trend of previous decades, revives the core cities, which had been in decline. Now it is the suburbs' turn to deteriorate. Once-prosperous suburban shopping malls are abandoned, and out-of-town restaurants and stores begin to have trouble attracting customers. Meanwhile, downtown city dwellings are remodeled and refurbished. People become accustomed to living and working in much more compact quarters than formerly. The cost of new construction continues to rise, accelerated by the strict regulations imposed to prevent energy waste and to utilize the Sun's heat.

The automobile age fades into history, and the economy gradually adjusts to a lifestyle of much reduced — and more expensive — personal travel. The shock to the once great automobile industry and its satellite industries (motels, drive-in fast-food restaurants, shopping malls, and so on) causes economic distress in some manufacturing centers for many years. On the other hand, it is a boom period for the coal industry and for a number of industries that will profit from a massive "retrofit" of the United States insofar as insulation, heating, and air conditioning equipment and related hardware are concerned.

Other wasteful practices are also changed. Throwaway bottles and other containers are banned; more things are recycled. Unnecessary packaging is eliminated. People begin once again to buy many foods and beverages in bulk and supply their own containers.

Eventually (in this scenario) the fuel shortage is eased as the embargo is lifted after a negotiated settlement of the Palestinian problem with Israel. By 1988 the embargo ends, and oil begins to flow again, but oil never regains its former position as the *sine qua non* of industrial civilization.

Meanwhile, the 1983-1988 embargo leaves permanent alterations in the legal, political, and economic structures of all fuel-importing nations. Governmental institutions and agencies in most democracies were not equipped to deal with anything as disruptive of the internal workings of a nation, short of a war crisis. The usual leisurely deliberations of legislative bodies, extended public hearings, the investigative studies and commissions, are far too slow to meet a galloping emergency. The United States is composed of fifty states, each with executive, legislative, and judicial branches, each with separate governmental machinery. Energy matters are scattered among hundreds of different government offices and agencies at both federal and state levels. Again, the coordination of these branches, levels, and agencies is, by itself, a monumental task. It is not surprising that during the first two years after the embargo of 1983 the country floundered in confusion and disorganization. Only by giving the President temporary powers to rule by decree was the crisis surmounted. Luckily, the EEC countries were not directly affected, or the strain on the thin fabric of European supranational authority might have been too much.

The *legal systems* of the democracies, like their political structures, were not designed to withstand pressures of the kind brought on by an extreme energy shortage. They were constructed to protect civil rights and private property and to enforce laws and contracts. Meeting the challenge of the energy crisis required overriding many of these rights. Otherwise lawsuits and constitutional challenges would have tied up the proposed regulations and courts for years and thus, in effect, nullified them.

The device used to solve problems which were apparently insoluble under normal political/legal procedures was to suspend the operation of these procedures during a time of obvious national emergency. The

use of such a device in the United States is, of course, a major political/
legal innovation in itself. There are obvious historical precedents in
other countries, of course. The closest anology was the actions of 1958
DeGaulle government of France to resolve the otherwise insoluble
problem of the Algerian war. The parallel is not exact, however, since
DeGaulle revamped the French constitution itself, whereas Duitt simply used powers granted by the United States Congress under the
Constitution. When Congress declared the emergency to be "ended" in
1988 (before the election of that year), the normal system of government was restored.*

The long-term effect of the energy crisis, particularly in the United
States, is to accelerate the long transition from a *laissez faire* capitalist society to a planned economy in which government participates in
decisions at every level. Despite the lack of enthusiasm for explicit
"socialism" by a sizeable majority of the United States population, free
enterprise survives more as a slogan than a reality. Large industries
are increasingly government controlled and, in some cases, government owned. Under stress, many of the freedoms once valued by Americans erode, and the government becomes increasingly paternal and
omnipotent. (This evolution is not confined to the United States — indeed, the countries of Western Europe are already further along the
same road.)

The environmental movement is set back by the events of 1983
because a sizeable segment of the public blames environmentalism for
having retarded energy development. Projects such as offshore oil
drilling, which had long been opposed by a public concerned with ocean
pollution and the destruction of beaches, are now pushed ahead under
the Duitt program. Despite strong safeguards against "spills," some do
occur. There is serious damage to many beaches and to commercial
fishing, but there is also a fund available for financing restoration of
damage. Strip mining regulations are somewhat relaxed to stimulate
coal production. Sulfur dioxide and particulate levels in the air rise
noticeably — for a while. On the other hand, the reduced use of the
automobile results in some compensating reductions in the other major source of air pollution. Environmental concerns eventually regain
popularity.

Because of the disparity of energy resources among the various
nations, the relations between the United States and Japan and be-

*Incidentally, Duitt was defeated for reelection by an opponent who promised to rectify
all the "injustices" of the Duitt program. As it turned out, most of the program was
retained, and the modifications were largely cosmetic.

tween the members of the EEC and the NATO Alliance come under severe strain. Tensions arise partly because the United States is singled out as the subject of the embargo, which gives the countries of Europe and Japan a major economic advantage. Another cause of strain is the fact the United Kingdom, because of the North Sea oil fields, has (by the mid-1980s) become an oil exporter, whereas the other EEC countries must import oil. The nations most dependent on oil imports tend to seek special deals with the Arabs and other oil exporters to ensure uninterrupted supplies. This scrambling for short-term advantages undermines international cooperation for long-term solutions.

Long-term Consequences of the Energy Crisis

Over the longer term, oil- and gas-fired boilers or heaters and internal combustion engines pass away into the limbo of museums and history books. Petroleum and natural gas are far too valuable to be *burned;* they are used industrially for purposes such as the manufacture of fertilizer, plastics, synthetic fibers, and many other petrochemical products. Paper becomes too scarce for throwaway uses such as newspapers, packaging, paper toweling, and the like. Newspapers are largely replaced by electronic transmission and display using such facilities as TV screens. Computer operations replace most business forms. Aluminum is widely used in place of iron and steel because it is lighter and easier to recycle. There is increased use of magnesium for the same reason.

Superconducting transmission lines come into use after 2000, greatly reducing losses of electricity in transmissions. Electric power generation becomes more decentralized, and the by-product heat produced in small generating plants is utilized locally for space heating and water heating for schools, hospitals, office buildings, and apartment buildings. Most residential heating and air conditioning is accomplished via the electric heat pump—by itself in older structures, but solar assisted in newer ones.

Some long-distance business trips are replaced by visual-audial electronic communications, which use much less energy than travel. Electronic communication greatly extends its scope. The world, which has been growing effectively smaller at a very rapid rate during most of the twentieth century, continues to shrink.

High fuel and fertilizer costs make mechanized agriculture impractical in many parts of the world. There is a return to more labor-intensive agriculture, although not to the extent typical of less developed countries. Large-scale monoculture, such as the type of wheat farming now practiced in semi-arid areas, becomes less profitable because of fuel costs. Industrial processes for producing animal feed (cultivation of single-cell organisms and similar developments) gradually replace soya beans and corn as animal feeds. There is increased growing of food locally in controlled environments, using solar energy, recycling of water, and recycling of sewage wastes (by composting or other means.)

Thirty years after the crisis (about 2015) a new automotive industry begins to arise, based on more efficient power systems and electronic traffic controls. However, the new electronic-oriented automotive age does not bring back the massive dependence on private transport that characterized the old automobile age. It is still possible for people to travel long distances by private vehicle, but the costs are so much greater than those of public transportation that relatively few people do it. The automobile industry never regains its former preeminence in the economy.

SCENARIO 2 — WORLD FOOD CRISIS

This scenario sketches a disaster that could occur in the next decade or two if world population growth continues to outstrip food production. Regional food crises are nothing new. Historically, deaths from food shortages and other causes have comprised a natural mechanism by which population growth has been held in check. The present runaway population growth rates are largely a result of the reduction in death rates. Extrapolating these trends suggests that a crisis may be near: a catastrophic global food shortage resulting from a worldwide failure to keep population growth and resource availability in a sustainable balance. Food and other resources are now being used up much faster than the Earth can supply them under the prevailing conditions of human organization and existing technology. The consequences, as seen in this scenario, can hardly be less than starvation and epidemic on a mass scale.

Background of the Crisis

Malthus foresaw the crisis described here 180 years ago in his famous essay, *An Essay on the Principle of Population,* first published in 1798.[1] He was wrong about many things. He particularly failed to foresee the explosion of technology based on exploitation of fossil fuels and the colonization of undeveloped fertile lands in North America that were to postpone the crisis for nearly 200 years. Nor did he anticipate that a great rise in the material standard of living of the industrial societies would reduce the birth rate in those societies. He expected the opposite. But he put his finger precisely on the key relationship, namely, that population, if unchecked, grows at a geometric rate (like compound interest) whereas food production, being limited by the amount of arable land, tends to grow at an arithmetic rate at best. Technology can and has postponed the crisis for centuries, but in the end, the basic relationships must prevail. The number of people who are inadequately nourished cannot be counted. It goes almost without saying that such people normally live outside the realms where there are census takers and social workers. They live in shantytowns or barrios, or literally on the streets or on the railway platforms of Asian cities, or they work as share croppers or day laborers in rural squalor.

Numbers from 400 to 800 million are cited freely, if rather carelessly, by international officials.[2-4] It is clear that such figures must be arrived at by guesswork, not statistical analysis. Nevertheless, there is little doubt that very large numbers of people are malnourished, particularly in terms of protein. More ominously, nearly all these people live in countries which were once able to grow enough food to feed themselves but are no longer able to do so. Many countries have become dependent on imported food to make up their domestic deficits. In practice, the only surplus producer left in the world is North America. The margin of leeway is now getting very small.

According to this scenario, catastrophe occurs when imported food is no longer available to the hungry nations because of a combination of possible circumstances, including periodic drought conditions in the North American plains. Because the relevant topics are not systematically discussed together anywhere else in this book, I request the reader's indulgence for presenting a few pages of statistical material before leaping into the unknown.

Among the key factors contributing to the crisis is a decline in the recent rapid rate of increase in farm outputs, which has enabled food production to keep up with — even outpace — population growth for the past few decades. However, these increases in production have been purchased at the cost of accelerated soil erosion and approaching soil exhaustion. Recurring and ever more serious floods are attributable to the dire effects of upstream deforestation in the headwaters of major river systems. Soil experts have noted that topsoil layers in many parts of the world, including portions of the United States, are getting dangerously thin and infertile. Enormous quantities of topsoil have been eroded from plowed fields and semi-arid lands by water and wind. One estimate of loss, for the United States alone, is 5 billion tons a year. At this rate, "we lose 10 pounds of soil for every pound of grain we produce."[5] Needless to say, this cannot continue for very long before a reckoning.

Until the 1970s, such warnings made little impression in the United States, which had become the world's principal food exporter. The idea of possible food shortage in the foreseeable future seemed ridiculous to Americans in the 1950s and 1960s. The apparent problem was the opposite: There were persistent food surpluses which constantly threatened United States farmers with ruinous price drops. Farm productivity had increased by incredible leaps. In the twenty years from 1955 to 1975, American farmers more than tripled their productivity per man-hours of farm labor. Whereas in 1955 the highly productive American farmer produced enough food to feed himself and fifteen other people, by 1975 he could feed fifty-two people!

By a system of government payments to encourage farmers *not* to produce, some 50 million acres out of a total United States cropland base of 350 million acres were held out of production during the 1950s and early 1970s. Even so, there were annual grain surpluses throughout this period. There was also a fast-growing world demand for food as population climbed inexorably and people in the industrialized countries became more affluent and sharply increased their consumption of meat and other animal protein (see Chapter 5). Writes Lester R. Brown, President of Worldwatch Institute[6]:

> Grain exports from North America, a measure of growing worldwide food deficits, have doubled during the 1970's, expanding from 56 million tons in 1970 to nearly 100 million tons during the current fiscal year [1975]. Of the 115 countries for which data are available, all but a few now import grain. Of the countries that remain significant exporters, two dominate: the United states and Canada.* During the current fiscal year [1975], the two together will export enough grain to feed the 600 million people of India.

The grain surpluses of the United States diverted attention from the deeper problem of the world's capacity to feed itself. There resulted a false sense of security not only in the industrialized nations but in the less developed ones as well. The vast shipments of surplus grain to nations like India under Point Four (which ended up as gifts because

*The other is Australia.

India's debt for grain purchases was cancelled in December 1973) reduced some of the incentive of the recipient countries to take effective steps toward reducing population growth and increasing the productivity of domestic agriculture.

The phenomenal productivity of American agriculture has rested very heavily on mechnization, low cost fuel, a deep layer of alluvial topsoil, comparatively cheap fertilizer and pesticides, plenty of available water (ground water or rainfall), and advanced techniques of plant and animal breeding. The system demanded large capital investment, abundant energy, an effective method of propagating, technological developments among farmers, backed by well-funded research programs, and a high level of education on the part of farmers themselves. It is therefore not easily transferable to peasants or small farmers in developing countries unless they are given access to low-cost credit to finance equipment purchases, can get cheap fuel, and can be taught to accept advanced farming methods.

Thus the Great Plains of North America have become the breadbasket of the world. According to Montague Yudelman, director of agriculture and rural research for the World Bank[7]:

Iowa alone produces more corn than the world's second largest producer—mainland China. Kansas and North Dakota produce more wheat than Canada and Australia combined.

Dr. Yudelman quickly points out, however, the precarious nature of this unbalanced dependence on food production in a single region. ". . . Those three states—Iowa, Kansas and North Dakota—depend on rainfall to grow their crops." It takes no great leap of imagination to see what would happen if there were a prolonged drought in the upper Midwest.

The increasing dependence of modern agriculture on chemical fertilizers and pesticides, on abundant water and fuel supplies, and on a thin, eroding topsoil layer has long been a source of worry to scientists familiar with the problem. Chemical fertilizers do not enrich the soil in the long run, but are quickly leached out, leaving the soil increasingly susceptible to erosion and loss of fertility. Soil requires organic matter or its equivalent to preserve its moisture and nutrients. Years ago farmers enriched their soil with manure from their livestock, but modern systems of monoculture rule that out. (There are few livestock on big wheat farms.) Chemical fertilizer does not provide this organic, texturizing ingredient; hence soils fed only with chemical fertilizer become increasingly powdery and vulnerable to drought and wind erosion.

Evidence has been accumulating for decades about adverse side effects of the large-scale use of synthetic chemical pesticides. Early in the 1950s, when bumper crops were a problem to farmers in the United States, disquieting reports were coming in from many parts of the world on the rapidly diminishing effectiveness of "wonder" pesticides like DDT and the ecologically destructive results of its use. Pests were quickly developing immunity to the synthetic pesticides, so that heavier and more frequent applications were necessary. Soon more toxic chemicals like Dieldrin and Chlordane had to be used to achieve the same results, and pests rapidly built immunity to these, too. On the other hand, the birds and other natural predators that had formerly kept the pests under control—being higher on the evolutionary scale—did not develop immunity. When the insectivores ingested the poison-saturated bugs, they sickened and died. Furthermore, the poisons were getting into the human food chain. Traces of DDT are regularly found in fish and other foods, even in remote parts of the globe such as the Antarctic. Increasingly, pesticides are destroying fish, birds, and other wildlife and threatening human health.

These reports and their implications impelled Rachel Carson to write *Silent Spring* (published in 1962)—a book that had a major influence in beefing up the environmental movement. The book also challenged one of the basic assumptions of prevailing agricultural techniques: that the most effective—and, indeed, the only practicable—way to get rid of pests is to zap them with chemicals. In Rachel Carson's words[8]:

> ... intensive spraying with powerful chemicals only makes worse the problem it is designed to solve. After a few (insect) generations, instead of a mixed population of strong and weak insects, there results a population consisting entirely of tough, resistant strains.

This immunity does not develop slowly over many years, as many people had assumed, but happens with frightening rapidity:

> Ordinarily resistance takes two or three years to develop, although occasionally it will do so in only *one season,** or even less. At the other extreme, it may take as long as six years. ... What today may be the most promising of insecticidal chemicals may be the dismal failure of tomorrow.

The pollution of rivers, lakes, and oceans by pesticides had become

*Italics are mine.

so menacing by the 1960s that Rachel Carson referred to chemicals such as DDT as "elixirs of death." However, farmers dependent on these pesticides were caught in a trap from which they could not easily extricate themselves. If they stopped using pesticides under the prevailing system of mechanized monoculture, their crops were promptly eaten by pests, which are capable of multiplying far faster than natural biological controls. If they returned to crop rotation and diversification, which helped keep pests down in the past, they would have to give up some of the advantages of large-scale operations, low labor intensivity, and mechanization. More sophisticated biological controls, which selectively attack particular species of pests by the use of parasites, bacterial infections, viruses, synthetic sex attractants, and similar devices, offer a possible long-term solution. But much research on such controls remains to be done.

Another major uncertainty in regard to the prospects for future agricultural production arises from the variability of climate. The exceptionally high productivity of United States agriculture in the 1940s, 1950s, and 1960s was made possible by an unprecedented stretch of nearly thirty years of good growing weather. As Isaac Asimov pointed out in 1974: "This is very unusual; in fact, no such extended period of good weather has been seen on our planet for a thousand years."[9] Of great interest in this regard is a continuous record of mean temperatures in Iceland extending over 1100 years, which shows that *the past 30 years (1945–1974) have been the warmest in the entire millenium,* enabling bumper crops to be grown in areas such as Canada and Northern Russia where, prior to 1930, the growing season was generally too short for practical agriculture. No one knows the cause of this exceptional period of warm weather, and no one knows whether it will continue.[10] (Indeed, the period of good weather ended dramatically in 1976 with a harsh drought in Western Europe, northern California, and parts of the upper Midwest, followed by the coldest winter of a century in the United States.)

Still another food production worry is an already diminishing supply of water in the growing areas. Ground water tables are falling in many parts of the world. According to a study prepared by the ECE Secretariat in Geneva,[11] five areas of Europe (Cyprus, East Germany, Hungary, Malta, and the Ukraine) are already short of ground water, and seven more areas are expected to run short by the end of the century. The latter include Belgium, Bulgaria, Luxemburg, Poland, Portugal, Rumania, and Turkey. The United States Department of Agriculture warns of diminishing underground water throughout many of the food-producing regions of the West. In Texas, for example, the USDA estimates that as much as 60% of the farms now irrigating in that state—mainly in the Panhandle—will run out of underground water by the year 2000. The situation is similar in Nebraska and other Midwestern states. There are many reasons for the growing water shortage: increased urban populations, increased industrial usage, increased water usage in energy production, and increased recreational uses of water. The fact remains that much of the water now used for agricultural purposes in the United States is—like the soil—approaching the point of exhaustion.

These unfavorable long-term factors may even now be having an effect on the amount of food produced per hectare of farmland. A number of other factors are also involved, but studies suggest that, starting in 1973, the long-term upward trend of farm productivity has reversed itself. As Lester Brown points out in the article previously quoted, farm productivity, having risen for many years, now appears to have turned downward. If this is so, the world is in very deep trouble. Dr. Brown comments:

> One of the most disturbing trends in the world food economy during the 1970s has been the downturn in grain output per hectare. This new trend shows in recent U.S. Department of Agriculture data on all grains except rice, for which reliable yield data are not yet available. If the average world grain yield during the period from 1960 to 1975 is plotted as a three-year sliding average in order to smooth out the fluctuations associated with weather, a disturbing trend emerges. From 1960 until 1972 this three-year average increased each year, but then in 1973 it turned downward, dropping further in 1974 and still further in 1975. At its peak in 1972, the average grain yield per hectare was 1.91 metric tons, but over the next three years it dropped to 1.84 metric tons, a decline of 4 percent.

Dr. Brown then presents the following graph, which speaks eloquently for itself.

Finally, if these threats to the world food supply were not enough, the oceans are beginning to yield diminishing supplies of fish. In the twenty years from 1950 to 1970, the world fish catch doubled as a result of vast improvements in the efficiency of fishing equipment and techniques. However, after 1970 the fish catch started to decline, and for a number of important species the drop has been so precipitous that the survival of the species is in question. Catches of herring, according to Dr. Brown, have declined 40% in the Northwest Atlantic fishery area since 1970; the halibut catch has declined 90%, and the haddock

Figure 9.1 World grain yield per hectare, 1960 to 1976 (2) (excludes rice; plotted as three-year sliding averages).

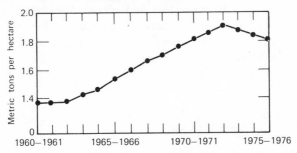

catch has fallen from 249,000 tons per year to 23,000 tons while prices have quadrupled.* Dams and river pollution have damaged the spawning areas of such fish as salmon and tuna. Eutrification of streams, ponds, lakes, and bays due to run off of chemical fertilizers and other substances has further reduced fish supplies. Oil spills, industrial pollution, and dumped sludge have also caused great damage to life processes in the oceans.

Although research is going forward on ways to expand food production and on "new" sources of food (such as harvesting krill from the Antarctic for conversion into protein concentrates), the capacity of the Earth to feed its burgeoning population cannot be taken for granted, even in the United States. Some writers, like Paul Ehrlich, flatly assert that the world has lost the food battle, it is too late now, and mass starvation is inevitable. Other experts are less pessimistic. John Hannah, Deputy Secretary-General of the World Food Conference, said,[12] "I am satisfied the world can feed whatever number of people there are going to be for the balance of this century. It isn't going to be easy, but it can be done." He admitted, however, that this is possible only if the less developed countries, such as those of South Asia and Africa, are able to increase their own food production by large increments. The job cannot be done by North America alone.

Meanwhile world population continues its dizzying rise. It is estimated by the United Nations (see Chapter 4) to have reached 4 billion early in 1976, having grown by 1 billion in only fifteen years. Yet it took thirty-one years for the third billion to be reached in 1961, eighty

*Now that most maritime nations have adopted the 200-mile "economic zone," the problem of overfishing may be somewhat reduced. Even so, it would take decades of careful management for fish populations to return to earlier levels.

years for the second billion in 1930, and the entire history of mankind to reach the first billion (1850). The annual growth in the world's population is variously estimated as between 70 and 90 million persons. This means that every three years the world's population *increases* by a number greater than the present population of the United States. Whether food production can keep up with this rate of increase and for how long is one of the most urgent questions mankind faces.

Assumptions Regarding the Genesis of the Crisis

It is assumed, to begin with, that weather is more variable during the late 1970s and early 1980s than had been the case in the previous three decades. This is a return to a pattern that had prevailed throughout most of recorded history and is expected by most climatologists. In consequence, temperatures fluctuate more widely, rainfall is less dependable—sometimes too much, sometimes too little—and crop damage is more frequent. Soil erosion increases substantially in the 1980s, as parched lands blow away as dust and recurrent floods scour the river valleys.

World population continues to grow at an average rate of 1.7% per year (one of the more modest estimates of the current increase rate), resulting in a population by 1985 some 655 million larger than the population in 1976. (Most of these additional people are (obviously) children. They live in the poorest countries in the world, especially in South Asia.)

Farmers in countries in which farm productivity is high continue to rely mainly on chemical fertilizers and pesticides, and the residues of those substances continue to pollute streams, lakes, and seas, with unfortunate effects on sea life and ultimately on human health. Industrial pollution, although not increasing at its former pace due to increasingly stringent controls, remains severe.

With the virtual disappearance of stored food reserves, the world has become excessively vulnerable to fluctuations in food production. In Lester Brown's words,

> Within a span of a few years the world's surplus stocks and excess production capability have largely disappeared. Today the entire world is living hand to mouth, trying to make it from one harvest to the next.

This scenario assumes that governments in most countries take very few practical steps during the late 1970s and early 1980s to alter the conditions that are bringing on a food crisis, or the measures came too late and are half-hearted. Among the steps governments have *not* taken are

1. With the exception of China, governments have not undertaken *effective* campaigns to reduce birth rates. Symbolic birth control programs do exist in a number of countries, but this activity is not given really strong backing or high priority.*

2. Governments in countries in which farm productivity is low have done very little to restructure the backward, inefficient rural economies of their countries or to modify their social patterns and agricultural practices. Cows are still allowed to wander at large in India, denuding the land of vegetation. Governments generally put much higher priority on industrial development than rural development. Thus little is accomplished to remedy the inefficient methods, mismanagement of the land, poor equipment, inadequate stock breeding, lack of fertilizer, and absentee land ownership that combined to keep farm productivity low.

3. Destructive practices such as overgrazing, deforestation, "mining" of ground water, and burning of dung for fuel have been allowed to continue. In North Africa, for example, 250,000 acres of land continue to be lost to desert each year.[13]

4. Governments in low productivity countries have not provided adequate incentives for farmers in their countries to produce. A number of countries with socialist-oriented governments maintain price controls on food, with the result that farmers do not invest. In some cases they discontinue farming in marginal areas. Erratic farm performance continues in the USSR, partly because of irrational pricing,[†] generally insensitive centralized bureaucratic mismanagement, and partly because of heavy dependence on marginal land. The accumulation of food reserves is actively discouraged in some of these countries. The storage of large quantities of grain, for example, is considered "hoarding" in India, where brokers and middlemen are regarded by much of the public as profiteers with no socially valuable function. Hence incentives to provide a cushion against future shortages is actually reduced.

5. The United States and other industrialized countries have not increased development aid in the late 1970s and 1980s to help the

---

*A hasty and badly administered program of sterilization in India recently backfired badly on Mrs. Gandhi's government, contributing to her resounding defeat in the 1977 election.
† Which makes it worthwhile, for instance, to feed (heavily subsidized) bread to chickens and pigs!

Third World nations to strengthen their economies, expand agricultural production, and upgrade the living standards of their people.
6. In the United States, policy decisions on allocation of water resources tend to favor urban needs and energy development (such as coal mining) at the expense of water supplies for agriculture. This reduces the amount of surface runoff water available for irrigation in some regions.
7. The United States government fails to set up a policy or program to stop the loss of productive farm and grazing lands to urban development, new highway construction, power lines, and so on. (In the twenty years from 1955 to 1975, the loss of croplands, pastures, and forests because of these encroachments totaled an area larger than Ohio.[14]) Soil conservation work, although carried on for many years, has not stopped the continuing soil erosion that threatens the very basis of food production in the United States.

The Global Crisis

There has always been a food crisis somewhere in the world. In some of these regional crises, such as the recurring famines in China in the past centuries and the Irish potato famine in the nineteenth century, millions died. But never before in history (as far as we know) has there been a global food crisis — one substantially affecting the lives of every human being on Earth.

It is assumed in this scenario that such a crisis strikes in the mid-1980s, although it might very well occur earlier. The crisis is global because no large region of the world except North America is self-sufficient in food. All depend heavily on being able to import food from the United States and Canada. By 1985 the skyrocketing world demand for food far exceeds the capacity of these two countries alone to supply it. Food shortages everywhere turn to acute famine when a combination of circumstances reduces the exportable food surplus in the North American continent while diminishing crops in the Soviet Union, South Asia, and Africa.

Here is a series of imaginary quasi-journalistic accounts portraying some aspects of the unfolding of the crisis.

Des Moines, Iowa July 9, 1985

DROUGHT DEVASTATES IOWA CROPS

The sun shines endlessly on the parched farmlands of Iowa. "Corn?" says Leslie Norris, Shelby County farmer, waving at his fields of shrivelled plants. "There is no corn. My crop is totally ruined. I still can't believe it. We've always had *some* rain here. This is the first season in my memory we haven't had a drop. I tried pump irrigation, but the water table is so low the wells went dry." He shrugged and looked despairingly at his fields of dry stubble. "Why do I farm? I don't know."

Kansas City, Kansas August 12, 1985

EMPTY GRAIN ELEVATORS SPELL CATASTROPHE

Driving through central Kansas is like participating in a funeral procession. Mile after mile of withered wheat fields extend to the horizon in all directions. Those massive grain elevators, full to bursting a few years ago, are empty and look abandoned. Once busy farm owners and operators sit in dejection contemplating, in many cases, the collapse of their livelihoods and possible loss of their land. "If the government doesn't give us some help, a lot of us are finished," says Raymond Rawson, until this year a typical prosperous Kansas wheat grower. His equipment is modern and sophisticated; he has hundreds of thousands of dollars tied up in machines now standing idle for lack of crops to harvest. "Like all businesses, we have overhead costs and debts. But what happens if we have no income? We face loss of our farms. Not that foreclosure would do the banks much good, unless they know where to get some water."

Rome, Italy September 9, 1985

STARVATION LOOMS FOR THIRD WORLD

A gloomy report of the UN Food and Agriculture Organization offers little hope of avoiding an enormous food deficit in many parts of the world. "The North American drought dooms millions," the report says, "for world grain reserves on a per capita basis are at the lowest point recorded in modern times." Where will the food come from to keep people alive? North America cannot supply it now; United States corn and wheat production for 1985–1986 is estimated to be half of normal. For regions like Africa and Southern Asia, the outlook is for a food shortage of unprecedented severity." There is a strong likelihood of social and political disruptions in conseqnence." The report calls for an emergency world food conference in mid-October to seek international agreement on the allocation of available food resources.

Geneva, Switzerland October 21, 1985

THIRD WORLD DEMANDS FOOD
RATIONING ON WORLD BASIS

On the opening day of the Emergency World Food Congress, Pakistani Delegate, Bakutar Mufti, presented a resolution, already signed by representatives of eighty Third World Nations, calling for imposition of food rationing by all nations under United Nations supervision and "fair allocation" of world food resources among the world's peoples. In a fiery speech, he proclaimed, "The starving billions of this planet are not going to permit comfortable Europeans and Americans to consume the food which by right belongs to all mankind. The rich have gorged themselves for generations at our expense — but no more! Let them taste scarcity for a change — we have tasted it for generations. Let them tighten their belts and awaken hungry in the morning as our people regularly do. Let them see the ribs of their own children and feel what it means to have little to eat." A reporter asked Mr. Mufti (who did not look at all like a starving man) what he had for dinner the night before. He gave no answer.

Comment: As the reader can see, I am a trifle cynical of the sort of posturing that has regularly been associated with the General Assembly of the United Nations.

Geneva, Switzerland October 22, 1985

UNITED STATES REJECTS THIRD WORLD
FOOD RESOLUTION

Amidst a storm of protest, Donald Davis of the United States condemned the "fair food allocation" resolution as theatrics. "Do the countries associated with this resolution want solutions or confrontations?" he inquired. "The people of the Western World are not prepared to submit to a totalitarian form of government — which is what the Fair Food Allocation scheme would imply — to rescue the Third World from a situation entirely of its own making. We have warned these same countries for decades that they must alter policies and practices that discourage food production while permitting population to grow unabated. They haven't chosen to do so. Now the consequences of folly are apparent. We will help to the extent we can, on humanitarian grounds, but we will not be bullied. The Third World is going to have to show much more determination to solve its own problems. When we see some constructive action on their part, we'll consider what kind of help —and how much—to give out of our very limited food stocks this year. We are more interested in long-term solutions: help in the form of capital and technology to enable farmers in African and Asian nations to increase their productivity."

Geneva, Switzerland October 30, 1985

FOOD CONFERENCE CLOSING IN BITTERNESS AND FAILURE

"We're worse off than when the conference began," said a Third World delegate who declined to have his name printed. "The world had a chance to pull together here to help build a new economic order, but the rich countries just want to hold on to what they have. What's coming now is world revolution." More impartial observers, although agreeing that the conference has failed, attribute the failure to the confrontation tactics adopted by the Third World nations and their immoderate demands for measures the Western democracies could not be expected to adopt. "They are naive," said Mexico's Fernando Ramirez, refer- ring to the sponsors of "fair food allocation." "They have an idea that denunciations and threats will gain sympathy among "rev- olutionary elements" in the West. No one who understands the West could make such an assumption, but these people don't un- derstand democracy at all. Virtually all the sponsors of the "fair food allocation" are dictatorships. They have had little or no expe- rience in cooperation, group action, or negotiation; their rulers mostly come to power by means of *Coups de'Etat*. That's their style. Can America understand this and look beyond the political charade to the real agony of the silent millions for whom no one really speaks?"

Comment: Mexico is a one-party country with some police-state tendencies, although it also has a free press and a free judiciary. The Echevarria Administration of Mexico (1971–1976) might have sided with the Third World on this volatile issue, but the disasters brought by foolish Echevarria's extravagance will prob- ably teach caution to his immediate successors.

Calcutta, India November 7, 1985

CALCUTTA IN GRIP OF FOOD RIOTERS

The ragged, underfed millions who inhabit the streets and shanties of this vast ungovernable city have apparently gone berserk. A new brand of radical leader has aroused the normally passive poor to frenzy. Mobs have sacked the warehouses and food stores and swarmed through the more affluent sections of the city, dragging some homeowners from their houses and hacking them to death with knives and clubs. Troops have been rushed to the city to restore order. No food is reaching the slum areas now. There is little water. Fires are raging unchecked. Electric power is cut off in many sections of Calcutta. "How long," asked Samooy Chandrasekhar, Chief Minister of Bengal, "until riots like this will sweep all South Asian cities? We cannot grow enough food. Will America send help soon?"

Teheran, Iran November 21, 1985

INDIA DECLARES NATIONAL EMERGENCY

India today suspended civil rights and put the entire nation under military law as food riots spread to a dozen cities. The streets of Calcutta are patrolled by armed guards who shoot looters on sight. Major sections of the city have been sealed off by barbed wire, allegedly to prevent the spread of disease. Dead bodies are simply thrown by the thousands into the Hooghli; the problem of disposing of corpses has overwhelmed the authorities. Internal communications have broken down. Few doctors remain in the city. Parts of Calcutta lie in ruins from fires, and many square miles are still burning. There is little food, and no facilities exist for distributing what food supplies do reach the city. Attempts by the International Red Cross to organize distribution of emergency rations have been rebuffed by New Delhi, perhaps because of unwillingness to reveal to the world the extent of the disaster and the government's helplessness to deal with it. (This dispatch had to be smuggled out of India by a departing correspondent to avoid rigid government censorship on all news.)

New Delhi, India November 23, 1985

INDIAN REGIME DENIES REPORTS OF FOOD RIOTS

The government today issued a blanket denial of earlier news reports about food riots in Calcutta and other cities. "These reports are irresponsible and totally erroneous," a government spokesman said. "There were a few minor demonstrations by a small group of malcontents. We dealt with them in the normal way." "Why, then, was martial law proclaimed? Why is no one permitted to enter or leave the city?" a reporter asked. "Merely to prevent the problem from spreading to other towns," the spokesman answered. "There are a few troublemakers there and we want to eliminate them quickly."

Comment: The policy of the Indian government of 1985–1988 — never publicly stated — was a form of "triage." Being unable to employ or feed the millions of slum dwellers, the urban slums were gradually converted into vast concentration camps and literally sealed off. During this period the ancient profession of begging finally disappeared from India, since all beggars and indigents were systematically rounded up and herded into the enclosures, where they died by the tens of millions. Western journalists were kept out of India from 1985 to 1993, and the full story will never be known. However the population of India apparently declined by over 50 million in a decade.

The experience of India is repeated, more or less, in a number of other countries from 1985 to 1990 or so. The drought in the United States Midwest continued through 1986 and 1987. Food shortages appear not only in the Third World countries but also in parts of Europe. Soaring food prices bring protests, strikes, and boycotts in many Western countries, including the United States. People all over the world are forced to modify long-established eating habits — to eat much less meat, for example, because meat has become too expensive for all but the well-off to buy. Because many Europeans and North Americans had grown accustomed to a diet based largely on animal proteins plus a variety of prepared convenience foods, many lack practical knowledge of how to obtain adequate protein from a more vegetarian diet. As a result, some less affluent city dwellers in the United States and Western Europe suffer from protein deficiency. On the other hand, obesity declines, and this brings significant health benefits. As people generally learn to adapt to reduced meat consumption and obtain adequate protein in other ways, the wealthier nations eventually experience net health gains. It is otherwise in the poor countries of South Asia, South America, Africa, and many Pacific islands, where food shortages lead to sickness, epidemics, bloodshed, and political repression.

Rome, Italy   August 10, 1987

CATASTROPHIC DROP IN THIRD WORLD
FOOD PRODUCTION

A report of the Food and Agriculture Organization reveals an alarming drop in food production in precisely those parts of the world where shortages are greatest: South Asia, Africa, and Indonesia. The causes are varied and include floods, drought, dust storms, insect infestation, desert encroachment, and the inability of farmers to buy fertilizer at current prices. The biggest factors in most regions are social breakdown, political oppression, and short-sighted economic policies. Family and village life, which had changed little for centuries, has become uprooted, impoverished, and unstable. Mr. Ram Singh, Secretary General of the Organization, issued a statement with the report calling on the food exporting countries to agree soon on a vastly increased food assistance program to help the suffering. Asked for his comments, former FAO Secretary-General Marco Nicoletti, remarked, "The food emergency is so vast, and the resources for meeting it are so inadequate, that government officials simply don't know what to do. They have made incredible blunders — such as sending troops into the countryside to requisition food for the cities, leaving peasant families to starve. Many peasants, as might be expected, abandoned their farms and flocked to the cities where, after a few months, everybody was starving. It never seems to cross the minds of some of these government officials that efficient food production comes about only when you give farmers incentives to work their lands and provide for the future."

Comment: Faced with an urban food crisis as a result of the Civil Wars in Russia in 1919–1921, Stalin devastated the Ukraine, seizing crops, seeds and animals indiscriminately, slaughtering millions of independent peasant farmers (Kulaks), and setting back agriculture two decades, at least, in productivity.

Rome, Italy September 10, 1988

WORLD FOOD SITUATION DESPERATE

The Food and Agriculture Organization has issued a report warning that the food situation in the Third World has passed the
point of "alarming" and can only be described as "catastrophic."
"Although food production is rising once more in the drought-
stricken fields of the North American midwest," says the report,
"the situation in the less developed countries continues to deteriorate. Now that some surplus is finally available to relieve some of
the hunger in the food-short countries, there is doubt that these
surpluses can be distributed where they are most needed. Food
storage and transportation facilities are lacking or in disrepair,
political instability is an obstacle, and there is doubt that food
would ever get past the point where it is unloaded. Several small-
scale attempts to ship food to India, Bangladesh, and North Africa recently were unsuccessful. In each case, hungry mobs overwhelmed the police and seized the food shipments before orderly
distribution could be made. Until local authorities in the food-
short countries manage to restore some kind of order, it is doubtful whether the agricultural recovery of the United States and
Canada will help the poor nations much. Those nations are suffering the consequences of years of neglect of their own agricultural economies. The problem is complicated by the spread of a
radical political movement opposing the acceptance of any kind of
help from the wealthier nations."
Commented one anonymous American official, "The irony is that
the people who are really dying are the helpless poor. The noisy
radical fringe who say 'We'd rather die!' aren't starving personally—you can bet on it! They're screaming themselves hoarse to
cover up their failure to implement adequate long-range agricultural development policies and population planning in their own
countries."

Denver, Colorado November 1, 1988

WATER DIVERSION CHALLENGED

Ten Midwestern cities have brought suit in Federal Court to
block a decision of the Federal Water Authority to divert 5 million gallons of water daily from these cities to irrigate drought-
stricken farmlands in Colorado, Wyoming, Nebraska, and Kansas. "This diversion of water is an intolerable infringement on

the rights of city dwellers," said Frank Wellerby, Denver City Attorney, in announcing the suit. "It is clearly unconstitutional, and we intend to fight it all the way. There's no conceivable justification for a few farmers to be supplied with water at the expense of hundreds of thousands of city dwellers." Raymond Terry, Colorado Director of the Federal Water Authority, had a contrary view: "This water diversion is essential to the recovery of agriculture in this four-state region after the disastrous drought," he said. "The decision has already come three years later than it should because of disputes between states regarding their water quotas. Now that the states have reached agreement, the cities are giving us trouble. Sure, some city people will be inconvenienced, but they can wash their cars and take showers less often. Food growing has to take precedence."

Comment: Lawsuits of this kind are rife. They are almost unavoidable, since the attorneys representing any party at issue (whether a municipality, a corporation, or a citizen's group) consider it their duty to pursue each legal avenue as far as it will go.

Washington, D. C. September 9, 1989

ANTI-WHITE RIOTS BLOCK FOOD AID

Anti-white sentiment in a number of Third World countries is hamstringing long-term food aid. The World Bank, in cooperation with the UN Development Program (UNDP), has been attempting to provide technological aid for developing nations to increase their food production. A number of these projects in recent months have had to be abandoned because of growing antagonism to any help from "white peoples." Agricultural specialists in countries like India, Indonesia, and several African nations have been attacked by local residents and driven out or murdered. Offices of multinational corporations in a number of cities have been invaded and wrecked and their employees forced to flee for their lives. International Harvester, for example, has had to withdraw all its representatives from Central and North Africa. Even trading firms in nations dependent on exports for their livelihood have had to close their doors because police cannot control hostile mobs. "The international economic order on which all nations depend is falling to pieces," says Darrell Flynn, President of the World Bank. "The Western world and the developing nations seem to have lost the will to sit down together and try to work out their problems. They have reached the name-calling stage. In that climate, nothing constructive can be accomplished."

Kinshasa, Zaire November 4, 1990

NEW REVOLUTIONARY MOVEMENT FORMED

In a little-noticed conference held here in mid-October, representatives of forty-three Third World countries agreed to set up a
movement to overthrow the economic dominance of the Western
world. "The Western nations," declared Anand Mbeka, Foreign
Minister of Zaire, "depend totally on the Third World to supply
their industries with the raw materials they need. Zaire, for example, supplies 7% of the world's copper, two-thirds of its cobalt,
and one-third of its industrial diamonds. Ghana supplies nearly
one-third of the world's cocoa, and Zambia 10% of the world's
copper. The Third World as a group has enormous economic leverage which it has not up to now learned how to use. But we are
going to use it, this power. We intend to bring western industry to
its knees if they don't give us fair treatment. Fair treatment
means much higher prices than we've been getting for our exports — several times higher. Maybe ten times higher." The name
of the new movement is Union for Economic Liberty
(ECONOLIB).

*Comment: Why Zaire? Why not? It could be anyone. ECONOLIB
is the "new economic order," with strong-arm tactics added.*

Dacca, Bangladesh July 9, 1991

ECONOLIB THREATENS WEST

Open threats to bring the world's economy to a halt marked a
meeting of the executive council of Econolib — an organization of
Third World states. This organization, which came to light in
Zaire only eight months ago, has grown with astonishing rapidity, offering Third World countries for the first time what is said
to be a chance to exert economic leverage to improve their lot. But
so bitter is the anti-West hostility exhibited by the organizers of
this group that real economic cooperation seems more unlikely
than ever. "Western agencies and corporations have already been
barred from many of the countries involved, and there is a go-it-
alone fervor that is quite incompatible with economic realities,"
points out Raphael Ginslow of AID. "None of the Econolib people
seem to understand that technology is a product of training, education, and human effort, not something you bargain for and buy
like a carload of coal. They are trying to solve their problems by
pressure and threats. At the same time, some of these countries

are making it impossible to transfer technology. Where do we go from here? Frankly, I don't know."

Tripoli, Libya June 8, 1992

NEW POLITICAL PARTY TO FOMENT WORLD
REVOLUTION

Econolib, the organization of Third World states formed by the Kinshasa Declaration eighteen months ago has established an international revolutionary party to overthrow the capitalist governments of the West. "There cannot be international justice until the power of the West is broken," states the proclamation of the new party. "We are a Marxist party, but we repudiate all connection with the socialist states and communist parties that are controlled by Moscow or Peking. All of them are opportunistic. Most of them have gone soft, seeking accommodation with the capitalist world. We want no accommodation of any kind. We seek the overthrow and downfall of the capitalist West, which is solely responsible for the death by starvation of millions throughout the world. We will organize in all countries and strike blows that cannot be resisted until the imperialists are defeated. Only when this objective is finally achieved will our people be able to lift up their heads at last."

Attempts by Third World countries to change the economic structure of world trade to their advantage make little and slow progress because they require people to act in ways contrary to their economic interest. The number of individuals and nations willing to sacrifice for humanity's sake is not large enough to reallocate the world's food resources substantially. Hence the bulk of exported food goes, not to the starving peoples, but to the more affluent ones (already comparatively well fed) who can afford to pay for luxuries. This fact creates terrible resentment and fury in the countries at the bottom of the economic pyramid.

Meanwhile, exploitation of available croplands, throughout the Third World, is pushed to the limit. Sound practices such as crop rotation, diversification of crops, and the addition of organic materials to the soil are abandoned in favor of reaping quick harvests at the expense of future productivity. Overgrazing, instead of being prohibited, becomes increasingly prevalent, and the loss of farmlands to desert increases. Ground water is drawn on to its utmost limits, and, in more areas, wells run completely dry. Thus, in a few years world food production, instead of expanding to keep up with population growth, shrinks further, and the rate of deaths by starvation rises even higher. The crisis broadens and deepens.

These developments cause a disastrous deterioration of the *international order*. Instead of drawing together to seek reasonable solutions to their common problems, the nations contend with each other for short-term advantages. All nations feel increasingly insecure. This scenario presupposed that no world conflict breaks out and that the great powers—the United States, the USSR, Western Europe, and China—maintain some sort of effective detente. However, tensions are extremely high and rising.

Countries which had previously depended for their defense on a military alliance with the United States begin to develop their own military strength. Japan, for example, which had not been a major military power after its defeat in World War II, starts to rearm, and there are rumors that it is building nuclear weapons. This alarms China, which increases its own military preparations.

The USSR, on the other hand, is forced to reduce armaments expenditures. The Soviet regime had for years poured a disproportionate share of its growing industrial power into armaments and had kept promising its people that at some future time they would enjoy a greater availability of consumer goods. When food shortages hit and the Soviet government is unable to make up the deficit by huge grain purchases from the United States and Canada, the regime feels it necessary to appease its people by increasing the production of nonfood consumer items. To produce these, some of the industrial capacity formerly devoted to armament production must be shifted away from it, with the result that weapons production is slowed. This reduces the pressure on the United States to build armaments in competition with the USSR, and the United States arms expenditures also drop. Furthermore, the Soviet Union reduces its political pressures against the United States to secure more favorable terms for its necessary purchases of food.

The world that evolves is one in which nations able to purchase North American food vie with one another to secure preferred treatment, and those shut out become sworn enemies of the West.

As the crisis deepens, the social structure of many developing countries begins to unravel. Huge crowds of poor jobless people inundate the cities. To contain them, governments rely more and more on armed forces, recruited from the peasantry or urban lower middle class. Health services almost vanish. The governments are too poor to provide welfare. A series of military *coups d'etat* shuffle the leadership. but fundamental conditions do not change for a long time and cannot change because there are far too many people in these regions for the resources available. The situation seems beyond remedy. Malnutrition is nearly universal. Epidemics sweep Africa and Asia. Many of the people who survive are weakened by protein deficiency and are unable to work efficiently or think clearly. Of the less developed nations, only China is able to deal successfully with the situation because of its tightly controlled organization of human effort and its ability to divide equitably what food it has.

Slowly, after enormous suffering and travail, the stronger of the Third World countries, including India and Brazil, are able to bring population levels and resources into balance. Civil order takes decades to restore. By the second decade of the twenty-first century, the governments of these countries are able to make some progress in controlling birth rates, stimulating agricultural production, distributing food equitably, rebuilding cities, establishing modern transportation systems, and developing industrial strength. Toward the end of the thirty-five year period covered by this scenario, both India and Brazil are moving toward becoming great powers, and Brazil becomes an exporter of food.

Over the long term, all advanced countries find ways to recycle garbage, human waste, vegetable waste, and animal manure, recovering from them reusable materials and converting much of the waste into organic fertilizer, which more and more replaces or supplements chemical fertilizers and slowly rebuilds partly exhausted soils and reduces their rate of loss by erosion. Water, too, is recycled by purifying systems and then reused. Because of these recycling operations, required in all urban areas, water pollution is gradually reduced, and the oceans, lakes, and rivers can again produce fish. Fishing is carefully managed worldwide so it can be kept on a self-sustaining basis. New varieties and sources of food are discovered and exploited. New food industries, such as mariculture, are developed. Greenhouses and backyard gardens appear everywhere. People learn to grow food for themselves in odd places, such as on rooftops in cities.

There is less personal and political freedom in the world of the twenty-first century than in that of the twentieth. Some kinds of freedom have been found too great a luxury in a world with one-third or one-half its population undernourished or starving due to unnecessary food shortages. People can no longer be allowed to have all the children they want, to damage the environment in any way they choose, or to use ecologically unsound farming practices. The world gradually learns, at enormous cost in human life and suffering.

SCENARIO 3—UNITED STATES ISOLATION, NUCLEAR PROLIFERATION, AND CRISIS IN THE USSR

This scenario focuses on world political development evolving out of the growth of isolationist sentiment in the United States and the unrestrained commercial exploitation of nuclear technology. It envisions the poliferation of nuclear weapons throughout the world, as nation after nation loses confidence in multilateral security arrangements or the will and ability of the United States to provide an "umbrella" of protection. A growing nuclear industry, especially in France and West Germany, seeks wider and more lucrative outlets for its products.

Nuclear materials are eventually acquired by ambitious dictators of developing countries—like Qaddafi—who use them recklessly and ignore proper safeguards. They fall into the hands of terrorist groups that attempt to blackmail the industrialized world. Western nations sharply restrict travel and commerce across their boundaries to intercept terrorists and prevent the smuggling of nuclear weapons. Small nuclear wars break out in various parts of the world, although no world nuclear Armageddon occurs. In reaction to the threat of nuclear violence, especially following the first actual use of a nuclear bomb for political/military purposes since Nagasaki, international commerce and tourism are sharply restricted, and many civil liberties in the democratic countries are eroded in the name of security.

This scenario is derived by a logical extension of the following trends that are already clearly evident in the world:

- In the United States, there is a popular and deep-seated aversion to political and military entanglement abroad—a consequence of the Vietnam debacle. (One recent indication was the refusal of the United States to supply direct aid to forces in Angola opposing the faction supported by the USSR and Cuba.)
- Construction of nuclear power plants in many energy-poor parts of the world to provide energy from nonpetroleum sources.
- Particular emphasis on breeder reactor technology because it produces more fuel than it uses. (The major fuel byproduct is plutonium, an ingredient of nuclear weapons.)

- "Business as usual" in the promotion and sale of nuclear power plants and eventual reprocessing facilities to many less developed countries.
- Increased use of indiscriminate terror tactics by extremist groups and the growing sophistication of their methods and organization with the encouragement and cooperation of certain small African states (e.g., Libya, Uganda, and Angola.)
- Continued failure of the existing nuclear "club" to implement an effective system of safeguards.

This scenario, like the other two, is portrayed by a series of vignettes in the form of imaginary newspaper accounts.

Brussels December 20, 1982

WARNS EUROPE: ARM OR DIE

Chancellor Willi Weinreich of West Germany at a meeting of NATO warned that Europe is living on illusions. "For three decades we have accepted the comfortable idea — perhaps illusion — that, in case of Soviet military aggression in Western Europe, the United States would automatically come to our defense," he said. "But what basis have we for continuing to assume this? The Soviet Union has built overwhelming strength on our Eastern borders, while the United States has reduced its defense expenditures and its commitment to Europe. Would the United States still risk nuclear holocaust to defend us? We can no longer base our security on this alliance of dreams and shadows. We have to prepare to defend ourselves."

Comment: President Charles DeGaulle said almost the same thing many times, as far back as 1958–1960. DeGaulle subsequently took France out of the NATO command structure and proceeded with an independent French nuclear deterrent or "Force de Frappe." West Germany has not yet rocked the NATO boat.

Paris May 30, 1983

FRANCE LEADS IN NUCLEAR TECHNOLOGY WITH SUPER-PHENIX BREEDER REACTOR

President Albert Hombert formally announced successful completion of the third successful year of safe operation of the "Super-Phenix" breeder reactor. "It has exceeded original specifications," said the French President, "and we have begun construction of three more Phenix complexes within French territory to be completed within the next four years. We also are engaged in talks with a number of governments interested in this process." Asked if he feared that nuclear proliferation might get out of hand, he replied, "As a condition of sale of this technology, we will require strict accounting and safeguards to prevent misuse of the processed fuel. Furthermore, you must bear in mind that others are willing to fill the demand if we do not."

Comment: The Phenix breeder is already quite advanced. Scaling up to economic dimensions should not introduce any insurmountable technical problems.

Ankara August 11, 1983

TURKEY TO PURCHASE BREEDER REACTOR FROM FRANCE

A Turkish government spokesman who declines to be identified by name told this reporter that his government is negotiating to purchase a Super-Phenix breeder reactor power plant as soon as details can be arranged. "We need the clean energy," he said, "and we are convinced that the breeder is the energy producer of the future. As you know, Ankara suffers greatly from air pollution due to burning so much coal. It is one of the most polluted cities in the world."

Athens December 12, 1983

GREECE INTERESTED IN THE BREEDER REACTOR

The Greek government has initiated talks with France on obtaining a Super-Phenix breeder reactor, according to a spokesman in the Central Electricity Authority. Asked if Greece's interest in the reactor is in response to the news of Turkey's intention to purchase one, he answered, "Certainly not! There is no connection at all. Greece must depend on nuclear power because we have no oil or gas."

Peking May 21, 1985

CHINESE ACCUSE JAPAN OF EXPLODING NUCLEAR DEVICE

Prime Minister Chung announced today that an analysis of seismic recordings shows that on November 30 an underground nuclear explosion took place in the Ryukyu Islands, which are administered by Japan. "Clearly," he said, "Japan is testing nuclear weapons. The Japanese militarists have finally emerged from their long hibernation. The world should take note."

Honolulu May 23, 1985

AMERICAN SCIENTISTS VERIFY NUCLEAR DETONATION IN PACIFIC

Dr. Theodore Sanford, seismologist of the University of Hawaii, verified Peking's report of a nuclear explosion in the Pacific. "They pinpointed it exactly," he said. "It was in the area of the Ryukyu Islands and it was not a natural earthquake." "Does this mean that Japan is testing nuclear weapons?" he was asked. "It could mean that," was his reply.

Washington, D.C. July 8, 1986

U.S. NAVY SEIZES OUTLAW BOMB FACTORY IN PACIFIC

In a surprise maneuver, the United States Navy last night dropped troops by helicopter on the deck of an outlaw ship said to be assembling nuclear bombs for the international arms trade. The ship was anchored in the harbor of Nauru, an island nation in the Pacific, and the United States action was technically an act of war against Nauru. "We have no quarrel with Nauru," said Admiral Seth Osborne, who commanded the operation, "but we couldn't let this activity continue. This operation was assembling plutonium bombs from parts made all over the world and selling them to anyone willing to pay the price." According to Osborne, the casings were manufactured in South Africa as "oil drilling equipment," the timing mechanisms in Switzerland, electronic parts in Japan and West Germany, the triggering device in Italy, and so on. The plutonium appears to have been smuggled out of several countries, including the United States, the United Kingdom, and France. It is obviously a very well-financed operation, and its profits are hidden away in tax havens like Liechtenstein and the Bahamas. CIA and Interpol agents have been trying to find out who is behind the operation — we don't know that yet. But we couldn't wait any longer.

Comment: Obviously speculation. But why not? There are many recent cases of businesses that have been operated from ships in "international waters" to escape taxation. Nauru is a reasonable choice of location because it is a major phosphate producer, although a very tiny country. Its harbor is normally busy due to phosphate shipping.

New York, New York   July 9, 1986

U.S. NAVAL ACTION AROUSES STORM OF CONTROVERSY

Praise and protest poured on the United States today in response to its action yesterday in seizing the "bomb factory" ship in Nauru. Libya, Angola, Pakistan, Zaire, and several other Third World nations expressed outrage at the violation of Nauru's sovereignty and urged the UN Security Council to take action. Most European governments except France approved the action. France labeled the action "piracy." Japan, on the other hand, sent a congratulatory telegram to the President of the United States. A Swiss legal firm representing the Greek owners of the ship filed suit, demanding reparations and the return of the ship. Nothing has been heard from the owners of the bomb-making operation or the disappointed customers.

Washington, D.C.   August 30, 1986

WHO ORGANIZED FLOATING BOMB FACTORY?

All attempts to discover who financed and directed the bomb-building operations in the ship seized at Nauru have run into a blank wall. Key technical operations on the ship were run by a computer. It is known, however, that the ship itself was leased from its Greek owners by a firm called "Nemo, S.A." with headquarters in Buenos Aires. Actual owners and directors of "Nemo" are hidden behind a maze of anonymous interlocking corporate groupings registered in a half-dozen countries, including Paraguay, Liechtenstein, Switzerland, Hong Kong, Bahrein, Taiwan, and South Korea. Investigators believe that the real owners are a group of men prominent in the more shadowy business of the international arms trade. The Mafia has not been ruled out. But the more crucial question is, where did the assembled bombs go, and how many were sold?

Vienna, Austria June 10, 1987

PLUTONIUM PRODUCTION OUT OF CONTROL

Gerhard Schwartz, Director-General of the International Atomic Energy Agency in Vienna, admitted yesterday that his organization cannot keep track of reprocessed nuclear fuels, including plutonium. "We are understaffed and underfinanced," he said. "We are expected to keep track of the reprocessed fuels from nuclear plants in twenty-five countries, many of which give us little cooperation. We couldn't do it with a staff ten times larger than we have. In a lot of cases all we can do is accept the reports governments send us. Yes, we send our inspectors to check, at intervals, but what can they do? It's a charade."

Tel Aviv, Israel March 19, 1988

HIDDEN NUCLEAR BOMB FOUND IN TEL AVIV

Brigadier General David Rothstein of the Israel Defense Ministry revealed today that a live nuclear bomb lay hidden for a week in downtown Tel Aviv while the government engaged in frantic behind-the-scenes maneuvers to deter the "Avengers for Allah" terrorist organization, based in Libya, from setting it off. "We received a threat on March 12 that a bomb was here and would be detonated if we did not release all 347 Arab terrorists now in our prisons," said General Rothstein. "This is routine—we get several such threats every year. But this time we learned through our own agents in Libya that the bomb was real. We did two things: We moved all the prisoners to downtown Tel Aviv where they would be in the path of any blast. We informed Avengers for Allah that if they blew up Tel Aviv we would drop a nuclear bomb on Tripoli and every community containing a PLO refugee encampment. That made them think twice. Meanwhile, we launched an intensive secret search for the bomb, and today we found and disarmed it." Asked why the public had not been warned, he said, "That would probably have caused terrorists to set off the bomb as well as caused a panic. We felt pretty sure they wouldn't set off the bomb if they understood the consequences."

Comment: Avengers for Allah is fictional (as far as I know), but there are plenty of real counterparts. Terrorists' willingness to sacrifice the lives of innocent hostages need not be further documented. The fact that the Israeli authorities choose not to inform the citizens of their danger is well within the tradition of government secrecy.

Islamabad, Pakistan December 11, 1988

PAKISTAN ABROGATES NONPROLIFERATION TREATY

The Foreign Office announced today that Pakistan no longer regards itself as bound by the Nuclear Nonproliferation Treaty. "The treaty is one-sided," said the brief statement. "It binds some nations while leaving others free not to accept such a limitation." Pakistan's action undoubtedly is a response to intelligence reports that India — a nonsignatory — has been building a stockpile of nuclear bombs and missiles.

Tel Aviv, Israel March 7, 1989

ISRAEL WARNS LIBYA

The Israeli government warned Libya today that any nuclear strike at Israel would bring tenfold retaliation. Israel has finally taken seriously President Addoubi's boast that he has nuclear bombs and will "wipe Israel off the map." "We have them, too," said Israel's Prime Minister. "For every bomb Libya can deliver, we can deliver ten."

Tripoli, Libya June 6, 1989

REPORT FORMATION OF WORLD TERRORIST CARTEL

Foreign observers report a secret meeting here of terrorists from a number of countries — apparently a kind of terrorists' convention. Known leaders of several Arab terrorist groups including

Avengers For Allah, have been meeting here with the West German Baader-Meinhof gang, the Japanese Red Army, the provisional wing of the Irish Republican Army, and Montanero Guer-
rillas from Uruguay, Venezuela, and Chile. Apparently there are
also representatives from Zaire, Ethiopia, Uganda, India, and
several other Asian and African nations. There are persistent
rumors that the terrorists have acquired nuclear weapons and are
planning strategy for their use.

Washington, D.C. July 26, 1989

UNITED STATES TIGHTENING COAST GUARD,
BORDER CONTROLS

In response to fears that international terrorist groups are plotting nuclear strategy, the United States is greatly tightening
border controls. Immigration and inspection teams are being en-
larged. All imported goods are much more closely scrutinized.
The government is reportedly considering further security measures, including routine searches of foreign vessels in United
States waters, identity cards for all citizens, and border patrols.

Summary of the years 1980-1998

The world is on edge. Nuclear blackmail has become an everyday affair. Some of the bombs go off, and hundreds of thousands of people are
killed in various parts of the world, particularly Africa, Latin America, and Asia. I do not attempt to specify the nations and localities
involved; they fit no particular pattern except that the more advanced
countries refrain from using bombs on each other. There is no world
nuclear war, but enough small, "dirty" bombs go off to produce a significant environmental hazard for some populations. Eventually, tighter
security precautions result in effective suppression of the terrorists,
already abandoned by their former sympathizers among the major
powers.

The arming of Japan with nuclear weapons drives China to seek
renewed accommodations with Soviet Russia. Outstanding border disputes in Western China and the Mongolian border are finally settled
by negotiation; thus China is no longer threatened on two fronts. This
also reduces pressure on the USSR. With the EEC countries concerned
with severe economic problems, China preoccupied by fear of the

Japanese, and the United States avoiding military entanglement, outside the Western Hemisphere the USSR is, for the first time in centuries, secure from serious military threat of any sort. As this fact is gradually perceived within the USSR, pressure grows on the Soviet regime from its own people to improve housing and produce more and better-quality consumer goods. The Soviet military establishment no longer has the strong internal support it once had to justify diverting a large proportion of the nation's production into military hardware.

There now begins a series of crises in the USSR:

Helsinki, Finland April 17, 1998

POPULAR UNREST IN SOVIET UNION

Even though tight Soviet censorship, observers in nearby countries see increasing evidence of rising popular discontent. Food is scarcer than it has been since the time of Khruschev. The collective farms, which were never very efficient, are showing signs of rapidly falling productivity, aggravated by unusually cold weather in the north and drought in the south. Attempts to force increased productivity by arresting and punishing poorly performing agricultural workers have been counterproductive. The military, which still absorbs the bulk of the country's productive effort, is becoming unpopular, and many letters are appearing in Pravda and Izvestia demanding that the armed forces be cut back. Soviet citizens are demanding some of the comforts and luxiries that are commonly enjoyed in Western countries. Such previously unheard of behavior as popular demonstrations *against* government policies have been observed in Moscow, Kiev, Leningrad, and other cities. The demonstrations are still on a small scale and are quickly suppressed by police, but they indicate a shift in public attitudes that clearly disturbs the authorities. Something seems to be boiling beneath the surface here. It will be interesting to see what emerges.

Moscow, USSR October 27, 1998

FOOD RIOTS IN USSR

Severe food shortages due to a poor crop year touched off an explosion of popular resentment today. A crowd in the principal market area got out of hand, stoned the police, and had to be quelled by troops firing into the crowd. Such disturbances have been occurring with increasing frequency this year in various parts of the USSR.

Hamburg, W. Germany January 20, 1999

MILITARY COUP IN USSR

An interrupted telephone call from the Moscow correspondent of *Die Welt* in Hamburg reports some kind of military coup in the USSR. All communication between Moscow and the outside world has now been interrupted, but enough of the telephone conversation got through to indicate that a major upheaval has taken place. No details are available.

Summary of the years 1999–2012

The *Coup* turns out to have been a seizure of power by a military junta in opposition to Communist Party policy calling for a production shift from military hardware to consumer goods. This is a very tense period in East-West relations. The generals, however, find themselves unable to manage the top-heavy, centralized, bureaucratic economy. The bureaucracy has become too cumbersome and rigid to adapt to new conditions. Economic chaos from "bull-in-china-shop" central management and popular rebellion against misplaced priorities ultimately reached the boiling point. In the year 2008 the military regime collapses of its own inefficiency, and the USSR returns to civilian rule: Communism remains, but in a more decentralized form, similar to the Yugoslav model. The new regime allows greater freedom of expression and freedom of movement than the old. Meanwhile, the East European satellite countries take advantage of the Soviets' internal problems to increase their ties to the West and liberalize their repressive regimes. The communist world after 2008 becomes less "closed" and more willing to cooperate with the rest of the world. A renewed effort at detente becomes possible.

OTHER POSSIBLE SCENARIOS

There is no limit to the number of scenarios that could be constructed to explore various interesting themes. The three given here are merely representative. When I first planned this book I envisioned adding other scenarios. One group might extrapolate the recent trends in Western societies toward increased emphasis on public sector activities at the expense of the private sector and the growth of egalitarianism in all spheres. Declining growth in productivity—even static or declining productivity *per se*—uncontrollable inflation, and a burgeoning bureaucratic apparatus for regulating every aspect of life appear to be the probable consequences.

Financial collapse of some weaker countries (e.g., Italy, France, or the United Kingdom) is another not unlikely consequence. Of course, in the event of such a collapse, left-wing, socialist, or even communist governments would probably follow. This could easily lead to the effective dismantling of NATO and/or the EEC. That, in turn, might open the door for open Soviet hegemony over Western Europe, leaving the United States isolated.

Another theme that could be explored arises from an extrapolation of the continued growth of Soviet military power *vis-à-vis* NATO forces. If current trends continue, more and more countries in Africa and the Middle East will permit the USSR to establish a permanent military presence (i.e., bases) on their territory. As United States bases around the world "contained" the USSR in the 1950s and 1960s, a growing number of Soviet bases might conceivably outflank the United States by 1990. In particular, the United States could find itself militarily impotent in the western Indian Ocean and region of the Persian Gulf, which is the most critical spot on Earth (at least until the end of the age of oil).

I have not fully developed these scenarios, in part out of sheer laziness, and in part because there is probably enough emphasis on gloomy possibilities. I will certainly be criticized by some (Herman Kahn, for one) for failing to give equal time to the more cheerful outcomes. Frankly, however, I think Mr. Kahn has already made as good a case as can be made for high optimism.[15]

However, it is not at all a question of who is "right." Any reader or reviewer who tries to debate with me as to whether I have been too gloomy or not gloomy enough is certainly missing the point. As I have tried to say in many places in this book, nobody can *know* the future before it happens. Our chief task for the next fifty years is to *make* the future, as best we can, for ourselves and our children. The purpose of looking at a number of projections and scenarios is simply to examine the most likely consequences of certain existing facts and policies and plausible future actions. Hopefully, these possible chains of consequences will be taken into account in the formulation of future decisions and policies. In short, the whole purpose of this book is to provide advice and guidance to the movers and shakers of this world — which includes all the citizens of this beleagured democracy. Whether the analysis is convincing and the advice is worth considering is, of course, one of the decisions they will have to make.

REFERENCES

1. Thomas Malthus, "An Essay on the Principle of Population," (1798), in *Masterworks of Economics* (Leonard Dalton Abbott, Ed.), Doubleday & Company, Inc., Garden City, New York, 1946.
2. John Hannah, Deputy Secretary General, World Food Conference, October 31, 1974.
3. Robert S. McNamara, Preface to *The Assault on World Poverty*, International Bank for Reconstruction and Development, Washington, D.C., 1975.
4. Kurt Waldheim, Secretary General of the United Nations Organization, quoted in *Christian Science Monitor*, June 11, 1976.
5. Wesley F. Buchele, Professor of Agriculture Engineering, Iowa State University, quoted in *Christian Science Minitor*, March 12, 1976.
6. Lester R. Brown, "The World Food Prospect," *Science*, December 12, 1975, p. 1053.
7. Montague Yudelman, World Bank, quoted in *Christian Science Monitor*, May 10, 1976.
8. Rachel Carson, *Silent Spring*, Chapter 16, Fawcett World Library, New York, 1973
9. Isaac Asimov in *TV Guide*, November 9, 1974, commenting on an NBC News White Paper, "And Who Shall Feed This World?"
10. Study by a group of meteorologists under the direction of Reid A. Bryson, University of Wisconsin, released by the CIA in May 1976, forecasts increasing variability of weather with disastrous effects on crops.
11. Economic Commission for Europe.
12. John Hannah, quoted in *Christian Science Monitor*, December 4, 1974.
13. United Nations Food and Agriculture Organization.
14. David Pimental, William Dritschilo, John Krummel, and John Kutzman, "Energy and Land Constraints in Food Protein Production," *Science*, Vol. 190, p. 760.
15. Herman Kahn et al., *The Next 200 Years*, William Morrow and Company, New York, 1976.

CHAPTER TEN

EPILOGUE

In this brief concluding chapter it is my task to gather up the dangling strands of many partial arguments that have been taken up, set aside earlier in this book, and weave, if possible, some sort of coherent tapestry. The persistent reader who has followed me this far may well agree with the sage who said, "The future is not what it once was." Perhaps it never was. Yet, many golden visions have turned to grey. Feelings of optimism, which used to be widespread, are becoming scarcer in the Western world. And this phenomenon seems to be more than a momentary discouragement associated, for instance, with a temporary economic slowdown. Surely there will be renewed spurts of economic expansion, and the Dow Jones average will eventually rise again to a new high. Even so, I have the strong feeling that something rather fundamental in Western civilization has changed, and that the change is one with which people of my generation, at least, will not be happy.

Probably a good many readers even more pessimistic than I will have no difficulty with this sort of conclusion. Certainly, any who believe nuclear war to be inevitable, sooner or later, may feel I have unconscionably ignored the paramount threat to civilization. There is another group, of unknown size, that seems to feel that Western civilization is totally corrupt and *deserves* to crumble. Presumably these characters rejoice at just those signs of senescence that worry me. Yet they themselves — their existence — is not necessarily symptomatic of a declining civilization. Extremist terrorist organizations such as the Baader-Meinhof gang or the Japanese Red Army seem to be recruited from a tiny fringe of disillusioned, middle-class intellectuals. The typical terrorist of the 1970's is hardly distinguishable from his anarchist or nihilist counterpart of the late nineteenth century, except possibly in terms of technological capabilities. Civilization has always had its discontents.

One of the commonest (and most hotly disputed) themes of doomsday forecasting in recent years has been the New Malthusianism. That finite reserves of essential natural resources must be exhausted by exponentially growing population seems logically inescapable (and inevitably catastrophic) to certain — I have called them alpha — mentalities. However, there are actually some major loopholes in the Malthusian thesis (as I and others have argued elsewhere), and the truth is nowhere near as simple. The neo-Malthusians are probably not much more wrong-headed than some of the most ardent Cornucopians, but, in my opinion, exhaustion of natural resources is not a major threat to Western civilization in the next fifty years.

There are many, apart from the neo-Malthusians, who think economic growth — at least, if it is to be achieved by harnessing technology — is somewhere between a doubtful benefit and an absolute vice. Many of the critics of technology cited in Chapter 6 belong to this group. Apart from its distaste for change in general and its professed dislike for the manipulative aspects of our mass-production, mass-consumption economy, this school has adopted an egalitarian stance. Growth is criticized for its failure to alleviate the phenomenon of poverty. It is asserted that "consumption foregone in a consumer society such as ours is meaningless."[1]

There is much more to be said on both sides of the pro-growth/anti-growth debate. Skipping over the details of the arguments should not be taken as an indication that I do not consider some of the criticisms of "growth," at least, to be well taken. However, it seems to me quite absurd to criticize a policy of encouraging economic growth for failing to eliminate (relative) poverty without offering some plausible reason to think that any society would be more likely to redistribute a fixed pot of wealth than an increasing one.

On the other end of the spectrum of viewpoints, there has been an excess of essentially foolish optimism — mostly exhibited by technologists — the abatement of which is no loss to civilization. Quite the contrary, the deglamorization of nuclear physicists and aerospace engineers was inevitable, and the creation of some political barriers to society's adoption of, and dependence on, too much hard technology is really overdue. To the extent these barriers also tend to stand in the way of the adoption of other more benign technological innovation, the recent denigration of technologists is mildly regrettable, but not a cause for discouragement over the long-term prospects for mankind.

If there is a real cause for alarm and despondency about the future — as I believe — the signs are more subtle, and the causes are deeper. I do not think the "problem" is the proliferation of nuclear (and other) weapons, or rampant international terrorism, or the exhaustion of natural resources. What is it that is really wrong? Why is the "motor" of Western civilization showing signs of slowing down, even, perhaps, burning out? I am talking about undifferentiated economic growth, to be sure, but not only growth *per se*. Where the impulse to change dies or is smothered, much more than consumer aspirations are at stake.

This is a difficult question with which to grapple, especially since there is no general agreement on what exactly motivates a civilization in the first place. Still, it may be worthwhile to make the attempt.

I believe, in brief, that the motive power of civilization, at least in recent centuries, is derived largely from the resolution of conflicts between societal goals, which mold and are molded by the personal values of individuals. It is not simply a question of conflict between forces for "good and "evil" in the world, although some recent conflicts have superficially seemed almost that simple. The evolution of civilization seems to me to be driven primarily by conflict between incompatible but competing "goods." In Chapter 2 I pointed out at some length the pervasiveness of such conflicts.

The next fifty years will, I fear, be the declining decades of the age of democracy as we know it, because of its inability to cope with the imperatives of human survival in a world in which there are no longer any easy solutions where "everybody can win." More and more often, *somebody has to lose*. Democratic institutions, never deeply rooted in most countries, have already proved to be pretty much incapable of grappling with problems for which all the solutions are painful. In particular, libertarian social-democratic governments in Germany failed to come to grips with serious world economic adjustment problems in the decade after World War I. As a consequence, such regimes were replaced by Fascists* in Italy, Germany, Spain, and Portugal. A short-lived moderate Menshevik government in Russia was unable to cope with chaos and was quickly replaced by the extremist Bolsheviks. In Japan, the traditional governing oligarchy of paternalistic aristocrats was supplanted by a faction of extreme nationalist militarists.

When the first "crunch" came in Europe in 1938, libertarian social-democratic Czechoslovakia yielded to Nazi Germany with hardly a whimper. France and the low countries collapsed a year later in barely more than the time it would have taken the German army to walk to Paris unopposed. England was barely saved by the Channel, a few brave Spitfire and Hurricane pilots, and Hitler's indecision over when and how to mount a cross-channel invasion.

---

*The term Fascist is often loosely used, but a good enough definition is one-party totalitarian regimes devoted to extreme nationalist goals. All these regimes were violently anti-Communist, but their ideologies were not really very different from those of communism, except as regards the question of private ownership of large industrial enterprises. (In Italy, many were actually nationalized.)

416   Epilogue

By 1940 virtually the only viable democratic regimes remaining were the English-speaking countries: Britain, the United States, and the British Dominions (Canada, Australia, New Zealand).

To successfully prosecute a two-ocean war against Germany and Japan—even with the help of Soviet Russia—these democratic regimes were forced to adopt a number of "emergency" measures that were and are fundamentally incompatible with their own ideals. These included universal conscription of men up to forty or forty-five years old, nearly total government control over the civilian economy, including rationing of most things, forced evacuation of civilians from "critical" areas and forced rebilleting,* confiscation of private property for government purposes with nominal or no compensation, and of course creation of secret intelligence agencies for espionage and counterespionage purposes. It need hardly be added that some of these innovations were discontinued or cut back at the war's end. But others were continued or even (as in the case of peacetime military and secret intelligence activities) expanded.

Democratic self-government has made a significant comeback in the years since World War II, especially in Germany and Japan. It must be noted, however, that the first trial postwar years of newly minted social-democratic regimes were guided, protected, and heavily subsidized by the United States of America. In the 1980s and beyond, a different world with different problems is coming of age. The ability of libertarian democracy to cope with threats, especially of a nonmilitary nature, remains unproven and seriously in question.

Despite the apparent economic strength of democratic countries today—if one counts by "units of GNP"—the libertarian democratic societies of the West have proven to be, at best, semicompetent (or semi-incompetent) economic managers. Only the easy half of the Keynesian prescription is used. Politicians in a democracy are willing and able to provide economic stimulation—in the form of government spending—to increase demand for underutilized resources of labor or capital. The other part of the Keynes economic prescription, which calls for high interest rates, austerity, tax increases, and budget *surpluses* in times of inflation, is persistently unheeded.† The need to restrain wage increases at or below the level of productivity growth

*In California, Japanese Americans were rounded up and put into concentration camps for the duration of the war. In England, many Londoners were evacuated to rural areas and imposed on the local residents.

†In all fairness, Germany and Japan have done much better in this regard than the English-speaking countries. But for how much longer?

has also been widely ignored in public (as well as private) sectors, to the great cost of the public. Demand for public services, paid for out of tax dollars, grows unchecked—along with the idea that a beneficent government should protect the individual from every hazard or vicissitude of life. The fact that government literally cannot take on every burden—indeed, is already overburdened—has yet to penetrate the consciousness of either public or politician.[†]

The inability of the United States—still by far the richest and most powerful country on Earth—to prevent itself from becoming economically and politically dependent on a group of medieval Arab sheikdoms and emirates is one more symptom of political incompetence. Not that the Arabs who now own the petroleum reserves are evil men. Some of them appear to be wiser and more farseeing than our own legislators. Nor is economic interdependency necessarily bad *per se*. However, in this particular case, the United States is forced by its extreme economic dependency into a very dangerous and compromising position. To protect its vulnerable petroleum lifeline (and also to pay for the imported energy), the United States must sell large quantities of modern arms to all its "friends" in the Middle East, any of which could be subject to a change of government by a *Coup d'Etat* at almost any time. In the event of disagreements with third countries, this inevitably makes the United States a sort of automatic silent partner of, and possible co-conspirator with, governments that are undemocratic, to say the least, and might be extremely antithetical to American values.

The sad thing is that it is quite unnecessary. If the United States were merely as conservationist as Sweden or Germany, oil imports would be a bare trickle, and the dollar would be as strong as the Swiss Franc—or stronger. The policies necessary to achieve such a level of conservationist practice are fairly obvious (see the Duitt program). However, the people of the United States and our representatives in Congress, who "lead" us from the safety of the rear echelon—after reading the latest public opinion polls—will not, apparently, swallow the bitter pill. Americans have always been able to have their cake, while still eating it, and they see no compelling reason to stop. Americans seem to vote for leaders who promise gratification without pain; what they will probably get in consequence is a much bigger stomach ache than was necessary.

The population/food crisis is still another case in point. Here it is the politicians of the less developed countries who are chiefly at fault.

[†]In fairness, I should also acknowledge that the furore over "Proposition 13" might be the first indication of a shift in perceptions.

The portents have been visible for decades. Without effective measures to limit population *there will be* famines, epidemics, and political upheaval. Technology, everyone's favorite *Deus ex machina,* cannot continue to multiply the proverbial loaves and fishes without limit. Nor can the overcultivated, rapidly eroding grainbelt of North America make up the deficits indefinitely. We are fresh out of "green" miracles. The questions are merely, how soon and how bad will the coming catastrophe be?

Again, the policies that could have prevented the debacle or ameliorated it are clear enough. They are not and could never be popular. No libertarian social democracy — such as India purports to be — can afford to flaunt the religious prejudices, however irrational, of the vast majority of its citizens. Yet nothing short will serve: A thousand million humans and 200 million sacred cattle wandering at will cannot hope to share that parched subcontinent. The people of South Asia must choose — implicitly or explicitly — between upholding religious taboos and their own, or their children's, lives. I fear the harshness of the choice will not be recognized while there is still some possibility of softening the crunch, and the decision of the politicians will be — as usual — to defer any action until events are completely out of control and all decisions are trumped by inexorable circumstances. The game of politics in a libertarian democracy is not to solve problems but to avoid being blamed for failure to solve them — which is a very different matter.

Is there yet hope for the survival of government "of the people, by the people and for the people" in a viable form? Obviously, there is hope, although the prospects are not bright. I am only sure that, to survive, we will have to discover a new and unexpected lode of enlightened, fareseeing political leader or a new form of government. If democracy is to last out the twentieth century, individual citizens will have to bear much greater — rather than lesser — burdens of personal responsibility. It has never been said better than by President Kennedy in his inaugural address:

Ask not what your country can do for you,
Ask what you can do for your country, . . .

He might have added:

for our common-property world,
and for all the generations yet unborn.

REFERENCES

1. Robert L. Stivers, *The Sustainable Society: Ethics and Economic Growth,* Westminster, Philadelphia, 1976, p. 97.

GLOSSARY OF ABBREVIATIONS

ABM	Anti Ballistic Missile
AC	Alternating current
AEC	Atomic Energy Commission (now absorbed in the U.S. Department of Energy)
AID	Agency for International Development, in the U.S. State Department
AT&T	American Telephone and Telegraph Co. (Bell System)
bbl	Barrels (of oil)
BMW	Bavaria Motor Werke
Btu	British thermal unit (measure of heat content)
CIA	Central Intelligence Agency (U.S. Government)
CO_2	Carbon dioxide
COMRATE	Committee On Mineral Resources And The Environment of U.S. National Academy of Sciences
3-D	3-dimensional
DC	Direct current
DDT	Dichlorodiphenyltrichloroethane, insecticide
DNA	Deoxyribo nucleic acid (basic genetic material)
EEC	European Economic Community ("Common Market")
EM	Electro magnetic
EPA	Environmental Protection Agency (U.S. Government)
ERDA	Energy Research and Development Agency (successor of AEC, now merged into U.S. Department of Energy)
ESP	Extra sensory perception
FAO	Food and Agriculture Organization, agency of U.N.
FDA	Food and Drug Administration (part of Department of Health, Education and Welfare, U.S. Government)
GDP	Gross Domestic Product
GE	General Electric (Co.)
GEM	Ground effect machine
GM	General Motors (Corp.)
GNP	Gross National Product
GP	General practitioner (of medicine)
GWP	Gross World Product

HEW	Health, Education and Welfare, Department of (U.S. Government)
ICBM	Inter Continental Ballistic Missile
IR	Infra red (part of electromagnetic spectrum)
IRA	Irish Republican Army
kwh(e)	kilowatt-hours (electric)
LDC	Less developed country
LSD	Lysergic acid diethylamide
MHz	Mega Hertz (measure of frequency)
MIRV	Multiple Independent Reentry Vehicle
MIT	Massachusetts Institute of Technology
mpg	Miles per gallon (of gasoline or motor fuel)
MTCE	Metric tons coal equivalent (measure of energy content)
NATO	North Atlantic Treaty Organization
NIH	National Institutes of Health (part of Department of HEW)
OECD	Organization for Economic Cooperation and Development
OPEC	Organization of Petroleum Exporting Countries
PCE	Personal Consumption Expenditure
PLO	Palestine Liberation Organization
PMT	Passenger miles travelled
PVC	Polyvinylchloride (plastic)
SAT	Standard Achievement Test
SRI	Stanford Research Institute
STOL	Short Take Off and Landing (aircraft)
TOSCA	Toxic Substances Control Act
TNT	Trinitrotoluene (explosive)
TRIS	(chemical used as fire retardant)
TV	Television
TVA	Tennessee Valley Authority
TWX	Telephone Wire eXchange (telegraph using phone lines)
UN	United Nations
UNCTAD	U.N. Commission on Trade and Development
UNDP	U.N. Development Organization
US	United States (of America)
USDA	U.S. Department of Agriculture
USSR	Union of Soviet Socialist Republics
VTOL	Vertical Take Off and Landing (aircraft)
VW	Volks Wagen

INDEX